The Embryo: Scientific Discovery and Medical Ethics

The Embryo: Scientific Discovery and Medical Ethics

Editors

Shraga Blazer Haifa

Etan Z. Zimmer Haifa

63 figures, 21 in color, and 21 tables, 2005

KARGER Basel · Freiburg · Paris · London · New York · Bangalore · Bangkok · Singapore · Tokyo · Sydney

Shraga Blazer, MD

Clinical Senior Lecturer
The Bruce Rappaport Faculty of Medicine
Technion – Israel Institute of Technology;
Director, Neonatal Unit
Meyer Children's Hospital of Haifa
Rambam Medical Center
Haifa, Israel

Etan Z. Zimmer, MD

Clinical Associate Professor
The Bruce Rappaport Faculty of Medicine
Technion – Israel Institute of Technology;
Director, Obstetrics Unit
Rambam Medical Center
Haifa, Israel

Library of Congress Cataloging-in-Publication Data

The embryo: scientific discovery and medical ethics
/ editors, Shraga Blazer, Etan Z. Zimmer.
p. ; cm.
Includes bibliographical references and index.
ISBN 3-8055-7802-4 (hard cover : alk. paper)
1. Human reproductive technology – Moral and ethical aspects. 2. Human reproductive technology – Religious aspects. 3. Medical genetics – Moral and ethical aspects. 4. Medical genetics – Religious aspects. 5. Embryology, Human – Moral and ethical aspects. 6. Embryology, Human – Religious aspects.
[DNLM: 1. Embryo Research – ethics. 2. Embryo Research – legislation & jurisprudence. 3. Beginning of Human Life – ethics. 4. Cloning, Organism – ethics. 5. Fetal Research – ethics. 6. Gene Therapy – ethics. 7. Religion and Medicine. QS 620 E535 2005] I. Blazer, Shraga. II. Zimmer, Etan Z.
RG133.5.E45 2005
176–dc22

2004013092

All opinions and conclusions are those of the authors, and do not necessarily reflect the views of the publisher.

Bibliographic Indices. This publication is listed in bibliographic services.

Drug Dosage. The authors and the publisher have exerted every effort to ensure that drug selection and dosage set forth in this text are in accord with current recommendations and practice at the time of publication. However, in view of ongoing research, changes in government regulations, and the constant flow of information relating to drug therapy and drug reactions, the reader is urged to check the package insert for each drug for any change in indications and dosage and for added warnings and precautions. This is particularly important when the recommended agent is a new and/or infrequently employed drug.

www.karger.com
Printed in Switzerland on acid-free paper by Reinhardt Druck, Basel

ISBN 3–8055–7802–4

In memory of my beloved parents Yitzhak and Sarah Blazer,
and with love to Tova, Tamar and Yitzhak

Shraga Blazer

In memory of my dear parents Cilli and Dr. Josef Zimmer,
and with love to Lihi, Yoni and Esther

Etan Z. Zimmer

Contents

Contributors

Michal Amit PhD ..... p. 74

Research Scientist, The Bruce Rappaport Faculty of Medicine, Technion – Israel Institute of Technology; Department of Obstetrics and Gynecology, Rambam Medical Center, Haifa, Israel.

Baha'eddin Bakri LLM ..... p. 53

Washington College of Law, American University, Washington, D.C., USA; Researcher of Islamic Law, Noon Center for Quranic Researches and Studies, Ramallah, Israel.

Shay Ben Shachar MD ..... p. 236

Faculty Member, Prenatal Diagnosis Unit, Genetic Institute, Tel-Aviv Sourasky Medical Center, Israel.

Shraga Blazer MD ..... p. 202

Clinical Senior Lecturer, The Bruce Rappaport Faculty of Medicine, Technion – Israel Institute of Technology; Director, Neonatal Unit, Meyer Children's Hospital of Haifa, Rambam Medical Center, Haifa, Israel; Chair, National Statutory Committee for the Status of the Embryo and Fetus in the Medical Sciences.

Moshe Bronshtein MD ..... p. 202

Director, Alkol Institute of Ultrasound in Obstetrics and Gynecology; Senior Physician, Department of Obstetrics and Gynecology, Rambam Medical Center, Haifa, Israel.

Rivka Carmi MD ..... p. 223

Professor of Pediatrics, Dean, Faculty of Health Sciences, Ben-Gurion University of the Negev; Former Director, Genetics Institute, Soroka University Medical Center, Beer Sheva, Israel.

Rev. Roberto Colombo PhD ..... p. 40, 120

Professor of Neurobiology and Genetics, Laboratory of Human Molecular Biology and Genetics, Catholic University of Sacro Cuore, Milan; Member, Pontifical Academy Pro Life, Vatican; Member, Bioethics Committee, National Institute of Health, Ministry of Health, Rome, Italy.

Michael Y. Divon MD ..... p. 291

Professor of Obstetrics and Gynecology, The Albert Einstein College of Medicine, Bronx, New York, N.Y.; Chairman, Department of Obstetrics and Gynecology, Lenox-Hill Hospital, New York, N.Y., USA.

Jeffrey M. Drazen MD ..... p. 120

Professor of Medicine, Harvard Medical School, Boston; Editor-in-Chief, New England Journal of Medicine, Boston, Mass., USA.

Arthur I. Eidelman MD ..... p. 351

Professor of Pediatrics, Faculty of Health Sciences, Ben-Gurion University of the Negev, Hebrew University School of Medicine; Chairman, Department of Pediatrics, Shaare Zedek Medical Center, Jerusalem, Israel; International Neonatology Editor, Journal of Perinatology.

Mark I. Evans MD ..... p. 236, 259

Professor of Obstetrics and Gynecology, Columbia University, New York, N.Y.; Director, Institute for Genetics and Fetal Medicine, St. Luke's Roosevelt Hospital Center, Columbia University, New York, N.Y., USA; President, International Fetal Medicine and Surgery Society Foundation; President, Fetal Medicine Foundation of America.

Michael R. Harrison MD . . . . p. 259

Professor of Surgery, Pediatrics, Obstetrics, Gynecology and Reproductive Sciences; Director, Fetal Treatment Center, Chief, Division of Pediatric Surgery, Department of Surgery, University of California, San Francisco, Calif., USA.

Joseph Itskovitz-Eldor

MD, DSc . . . . p. 74

Professor, The Bruce Rappaport Faculty of Medicine, Technion – Israel Institute of Technology; Director, Department of Obstetrics and Gynecology, Rambam Medical Center, Haifa, Israel.

Asa Kasher MSc, PhD . . . . p. 371

Laura Schwarz-Kipp Professor of Professional Ethics and Philosophy of Practice, and Professor of Philosophy, Tel-Aviv University, Tel Aviv; Editor, Philosophia; Israel Prize Laureate.

Gideon Koren MD, FRCPC . . . p. 284

Professor and Senior Scientist, University of Toronto; Director, MotherRisk Program, Division of Clinical Pharmacology, The Hospital for Sick Children, Toronto, Ont.; The Ivey Chair in Molecular Toxicology, The University of Western Ontario, London, Ont., Canada.

Neri Laufer MD . . . . p. 166

Professor of Obstetrics and Gynecology, The Hebrew University, Jerusalem; Chairman of the Department of Obstetrics and Gynecology, Hadassah Hebrew University Medical Center, Jerusalem, Israel.

Qadi Ahmad Natour

MA, LLM . . . . p. 53, 120

President of Moslem High Court of Appeals, Jerusalem, Israel; Lecturer, Faculty of Law, Tel-Aviv University, Tel Aviv; Natanya Academy College Law School, Interdisciplinary Institute, Herzliya, Israel.

Michel Revel

MD, PhD . . . . p. 107, 120, 143

Professor of Molecular Genetics, Department of Molecular Genetics, Weizmann Institute of Science, Rehovot; Chairman, Bioethics Committee, Israel Academy of Sciences and Humanities, Jerusalem, Israel; Member, UNESCO's International Bioethics Committee; Israel Prize Laureate.

Vardit Rispler-Chaim PhD . . . . p. 53

Senior Lecturer, Department of Arabic Language and Literature, University of Haifa, Haifa, Israel; Author of 'Islamic Medical Ethics in the Twentieth Century', Leiden, Brill, 1993.

Guy Rosner MD . . . . p. 236

Faculty Member, Prenatal Diagnosis Unit Genetic Institute, Tel-Aviv Sourasky Medical Center, Israel.

Amos Shapira

MJur, MCL, JSD . . . . p. 340

Professor of Law; Incumbent of the K. Lubowski Chair of Law and Biomedical Ethics, Faculty of Law, Tel-Aviv University; Former Director, Cegla Institute for Comparative and Private International Law, Tel-Aviv University; Former Dean, Faculty of Law, Tel-Aviv University, Tel Aviv, Israel.

Yoel Shufaro MD . . . . p. 166

IVF Unit, Department of Obstetrics and Gynecology, Hadassah Hebrew University Medical Center, Jerusalem, Israel.

Alex Simon MD . . . . p. 166

Associate Professor of Obstetrics and Gynecology, The Hebrew University, Jerusalem; Director, IVF Unit, Department of Obstetrics and Gynecology, Hadassah Hebrew University Medical Center, Jerusalem, Israel.

Karl L. Skorecki
MD, FRCP .... p. XV, 120

Annie Chutick Professor and Chair in Medicine, The Bruce Rappaport Faculty of Medicine, and Director, Rappaport Research Institute, Technion – Israel Institute of Technology; Director, Department of Nephrology and Molecular Medicine, Rambam Medical Center, Haifa, Israel.

Shimon Slavin MD .... p. 91

Professor and Chairman, Department of Bone Marrow Transplantation and Cancer Immunotherapy; Director, Cell Therapy and Transplantation Research Center, Hadassah-Hebrew University Hospital, Jerusalem, Israel.

Ido Solt MD .... p. 291

Senior Physician, Department of Obstetrics and Gynecology, Rambam Medical Center, Haifa, Israel.

Avraham Steinberg
MD .... p. 21, 120

Clinical Associate Professor of Medical Ethics; Director, Center for Medical Ethics, The Hebrew University-Hadassah Medical School; Director, Medical Ethics Unit, and Senior Pediatric Neurologist, Neurological Institute, Shaare Zedek Medical Center, Jerusalem, Israel; Israel Prize Laureate.

Justice Tova Strasberg-Cohen .... p. 329

Supreme Court Justice, Jerusalem, Israel.

Alan R. Templeton
PhD .... p. 1, 120

Charles Rebstock Professor of Biology, Professor of Genetics and Biomedical Engineering; Department of Biology, Washington University, St. Louis, Mo., USA.

Ilan E. Timor-Tritsch
MD .... p. 309

Professor of Obstetrics and Gynecology; Director, Division of Obstetrical and Gynecological Ultrasound, Department of Obstetrics and Gynecology, New York University School of Medicine, New York, N.Y., USA.

Avi Tsafrir MD .... p. 166

IVF Unit, Department of Obstetrics and Gynecology, Hadassah Hebrew University Medical Center, Jerusalem, Israel.

Yuval Yaron MD .... p. 236

Senior Lecturer, Department of Obstetrics and Gynecology, Tel-Aviv University, Israel; Director, Prenatal Diagnosis Unit, Genetic Institute, Tel-Aviv Sourasky Medical Center, Israel.

Etan Z. Zimmer MD .... p. 202

Clinical Associate Professor, The Bruce Rappaport Faculty of Medicine, Technion – Israel Institute of Technology; Director, Obstetrics Unit, Department of Obstetrics and Gynecology, Rambam Medical Center, Haifa, Israel.

Preface

In November 2002, a historic scientific conference took place. With the benefit of the 'retrospectoscope', the historic nature of this conference is now crystal clear. Today, virtually every issue of the world's leading scientific, medicolegal and medical ethics periodicals and monographs devote numerous pages to questions in their cognate disciplines dealing with controversial aspects of research pertaining to the embryo and fetus. This explosion of interest is the result of breakthroughs in areas such as fetal ultrasonography, prenatal genetic diagnosis, human embryonic stem cell research, therapeutic cloning and reproductive cloning. The breathtaking pace of progress and development at the scientific level has outstripped the pace of intelligent civil discourse and thoughtful scholarly work in the legal and ethical domains. Therefore, we can be truly amazed by the prescience shown already at the beginning of year 2000 by Drs. Shraga Blazer and Etan Zimmer and their colleagues in conceiving, planning and finally implementing the conference entitled: 'The Unborn Child: Scientific Discovery, Medical and Ethical Dilemmas'. The current publication represents a complementary monograph which reflects the high quality of scholarly input from the speakers, as well as the audience participants.

Organization of the conference, as reflected in this monograph, represented a masterful orchestration of input from a wide panoply of disciplines. Approximately 17 speakers and 1,000 members of the audience were literally riveted to their seats throughout the 2-day conference, and were deeply engaged in the high level of scholarly dynamic interaction. One would have thought that with such an eclectic mix of topics, speakers and audience, it would be difficult to find common ground for multidisciplinary dialogue. In fact, the opposite occurred. Highly thoughtful individuals from the audience and from among speakers with varying backgrounds and quite different opinions exchanged ideas with the highest level of mutual respect. Theologians representing viewpoints of the Holy See exchanged their views with evolutionary biologists regarding such cosmic questions as 'the beginning of life', and 'the sanctity of life'. Legal authorities and molecular geneticists exchanged views regarding the tension between scientific imperative on the one hand, and social responsibility and genetic privacy on the other hand. Numerous other examples can be cited and are reflected in the elegantly worded chapters and overall organization of this book. It is clear, that this book will become a 'standard', against which all future professional and scholarly literature dealing with this important area, will be measured.

Perhaps the importance of the conference, and the book describing many of the topics covered at the conference, can be best understood by relating one of the most frequently heard comments regarding the conference itself. Despite the difficult security situation which prevailed in the State of Israel at the time of the conference, there were numerous participants from other countries. Among these participants there was the uniform feeling that, given the emotionally and politically charged content of many of the topics, a conference such as this could not have been held in most other constituencies around the world. The title of the conference, and certainly its content, would have drawn protest and bias from interest groups that would likely have disrupted what is most needed, namely 'civil discourse'. It is perhaps paradoxical that of all places in the world, it is in Israel that a sanctuary was found wherein representatives of the three dominant religions, jurists, ethicists, scientists, politicians, members of the press, health professionals, and the public found a comfortable and secure environment to sit together and conduct a high-level productive discussion pertaining to pressing issues which are becoming a more acute and important part of the public health research agenda throughout the world.

It is our hope that future international conferences on this topic will also yield further progress that will shape and guide human progress in the light of scientific and medical discovery.

Karl L. Skorecki, MD, FRCP

Blazer S, Zimmer EZ (eds):
The Embryo: Scientific Discovery and Medical Ethics.
Basel, Karger, 2005, pp 1–20

When Does Life Begin?

An Evolutionary Genetic Answer to a Central Ethical Question

Alan R. Templeton

Department of Biology, Washington University, St. Louis, Mo., USA

When does life begin? This is the central ethical question in many of the debates concerning the passage from conception to birth. This question has been answered in many ways, and depending upon the answer certain ethical problems arise or disappear. Of the many scientific perspectives people have used to answer this question in these ethical debates, one has been notably absent, i.e. the perspective of an evolutionary biologist. Given that evolution is the central theory of all modern biology, this absence is unfortunate. The purpose of this chapter is to provide an evolutionary genetic answer to this question, but the resulting answer raises further questions that will also be explored.

The question of when life begins is an easy one to answer for an evolutionary biologist: Life began over 3.5 billion years ago and has existed continuously ever since. Figure 1 presents an evolutionary tree of the major groups of life on this planet. All beings alive today are linked to the root of this tree by an unbroken chain of life that extends billions of years into the past. This evolutionary tree that unites all life on this planet has many ethical and philosophical implications. It is therefore not surprising that many evolutionary biologists have felt a sense of awe at this evolutionary

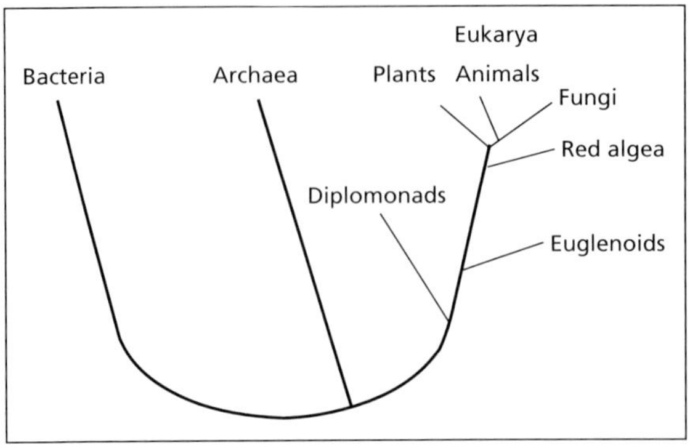

Fig. 1.
The evolutionary tree of life. Modern molecular evidence indicates there are three major branches to the tree of life: bacteria, archea (another group of bacterial-like organisms), and eukarya. Several groups of eukarya are shown, including animals, the group containing humans (see Tourasse and Gouy [11], for more details).

insight. For example, the well-known evolutionary biologist, Stephen J. Gould wrote in one of his last publications before his untimely death [1]:

'... I would nominate as most worthy of pure awe – a metaphorical miracle, if you will – an aspect of life that most people have never considered, but that strikes me as equal in majesty to our most spiritual projections of infinity and eternity, while falling entirely within the domain of our conceptual understanding and empirical grasp: the continuity of *etz chayim*, the tree of earthly life, for at least 3.5 billion years, without a single microsecond of disruption.'

Gould calls this continuity of life a 'miracle', and indeed it is in the sense that Maimonides wrote about centuries ago in his *Guide of the Perplexed* [2]: 'For a miracle cannot prove that which is impossible, it is useful only as a confirmation of that which is possible.' As miraculous as it sounds, the life contained in each and every one of us and all other organisms on this planet began over 3.5 billion years ago.

The miracle of the unbroken continuity of life undermines the very relevancy of the question 'When does life begin?' to the ethical issues pertaining to the passage from conception to birth. Indeed, the evolutionary answer indicates that the question must be fundamentally reformulated.

Because many of the non-evolutionary answers to the question of when life begins center around the biological phenomenon of fertilization, the evolutionary significance and meaning of fertilization must first be examined before a proper question can be framed. The significance of fertilization will also be examined from an evolutionary perspective, one that is quite compatible with Maimonides' idea of using miracles as a confirmation of that which is possible. There are many ways of doing science besides the controlled experiment. One alternative in evolutionary biology is the comparative method. The comparative method uses the variation found across living forms in the context of their evolutionary unity to study and understand a biological phenomenon. By utilizing the realized miracle of the diversity of life on this planet, evolutionary biologists can achieve a much deeper and broader context for understanding how a biological phenomenon should be interpreted in any particular individual species, including humans.

The Significance of Fertilization: A Comparative Approach

The evolutionary answer to the question of when life begins tells us that fertilization is *not* the beginning of life. Before performing a comparative analysis to gain insight into the true role of fertilization, some definitions are first required.

The genetic material of all eukaryotic species (fig. 1) is contained in one or more molecules of DNA called chromosomes. A genome is a complete set of a species' chromosomes. For example, figure 2 shows a diagrammatic representation of the human genome. The human genome consists of 23 chromosomes, each with its own separate DNA molecule and set of genes. There are 24 chromosomes shown in figure 2 because humans have two types of sex-determining chromosomes, the X and the Y. A human genome has one set of each of the 22 chromosomes (numbered one through 22 in figure 2) plus either an X chromosome or a Y chromosome, bringing the full genome set up to 23 chromosomes. Eukaryotic organisms are made up of basic units known as cells. In some species, the entire organism is just a single cell, in other species an individual organism consists of many cells. Eukaryotic cells come in two basic types (there are other types, but they will not be considered in this chapter). One type is a haploid cell that contains a single genome. The other type is a diploid cell that contains a matched pair of genomes. Figure 3 shows the chromosomes found in a single cell of an

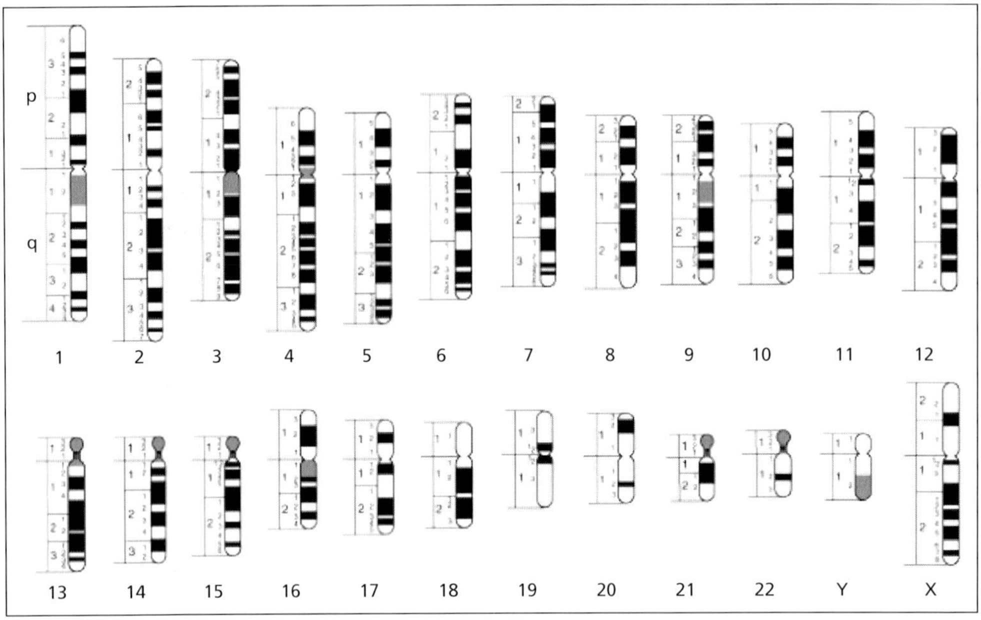

Fig. 2.
The human genome.

adult male human. This diploid cell contains 46 chromosomes (twice the haploid number of 23, shown in figure 2). As can be seen from figure 3, these 46 chromosomes can be placed into pairs, with the exception of the unpaired X and Y chromosomes in this male cell (females have a pair of X chromosomes).

There are three basic ways in which cells can reproduce. The first is mitosis in which a single cell, either haploid or diploid, produces two genetically identical daughter cells (fig. 4). The daughter cells have the same level of ploidy (haploid or diploid) as the parental cell. The second type of cellular reproduction is meiosis in which a single diploid cell produces four genetically diverse haploid cells (fig. 5). The third type of cellular reproduction is fertilization in which two haploid cells fuse to become a single diploid cell (fig. 6). These three types of cellular reproduction can be combined in various ways to define a life cycle, the journey of life from a particular stage at one generation to the comparable stage at the next. Life

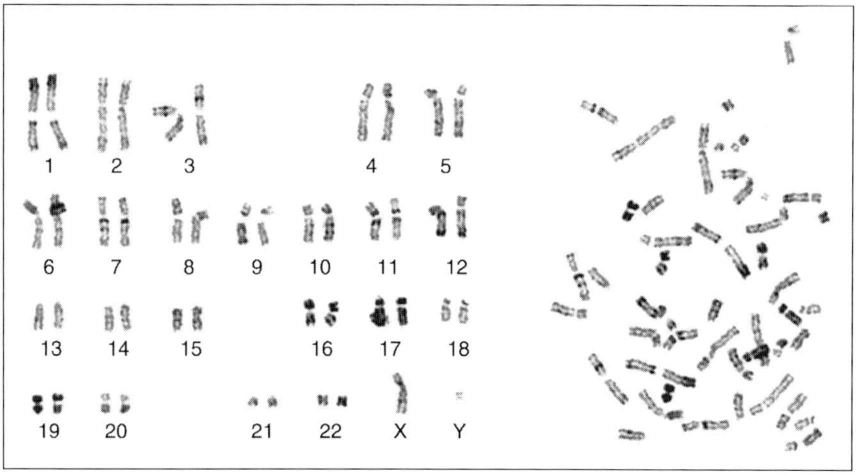

Fig. 3.
The chromosomes found in a human male diploid cell.

cycles are generally presented as a circle of life to emphasize the fact that life is continuous throughout the cycle.

Note that meiosis and fertilization are complimentary to each other on their impact on ploidy level. Meiosis reduces a diploid parental cell to haploid daughter cells. Fertilization takes two haploid cells to produce a single diploid cell. Without meiosis to restore the haploid state, fertilization would keep increasing the number of genomes per cell beyond the diploid level (indeed, this can occur, resulting in 'polyploidy', but polyploidy will be ignored in this chapter because it is not relevant to the human life cycle). Similarly, reducing the number of chromosomes in a haploid cell would result in the daughter cells losing some of the genetic information of the species. Stable life cycles must therefore have exactly one meiotic event that halves the number of chromosomes counterbalanced by exactly one fertilization event that doubles the number of chromosomes. Because mitosis maintains the same level of ploidy, there is no such constraint on the number and placement of mitotic events in the life cycle.

The comparative approach of evolutionary biology reveals a tremendous diversity in the life cycles of the world's organisms, with three of the more common types being shown in figure 7. As expected, all these life cycles

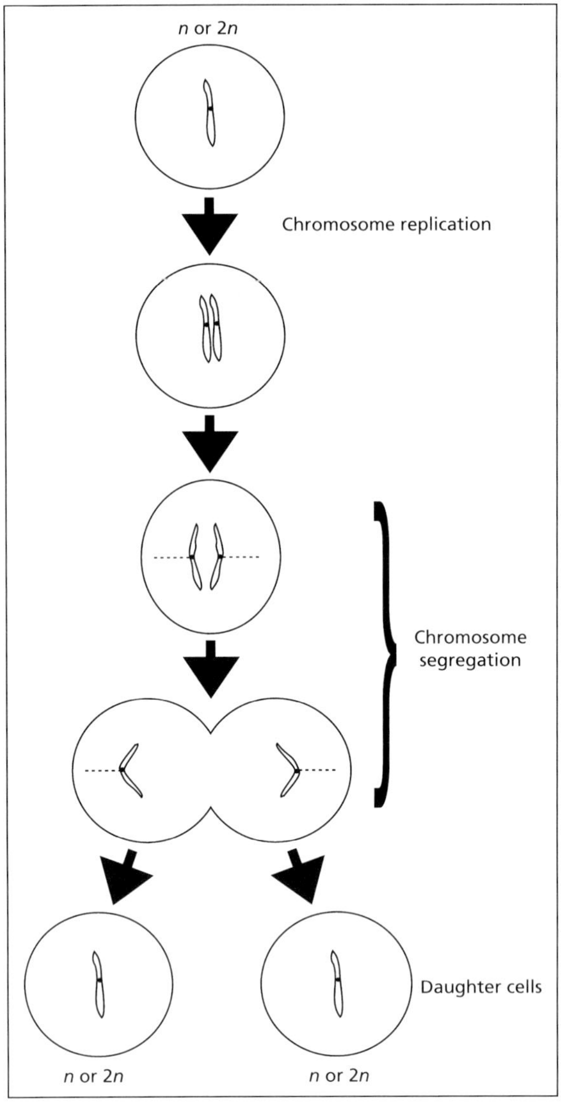

Fig. 4.

Mitosis. The fate of a single chromosome is shown, although other chromosomes may be present in the cell.

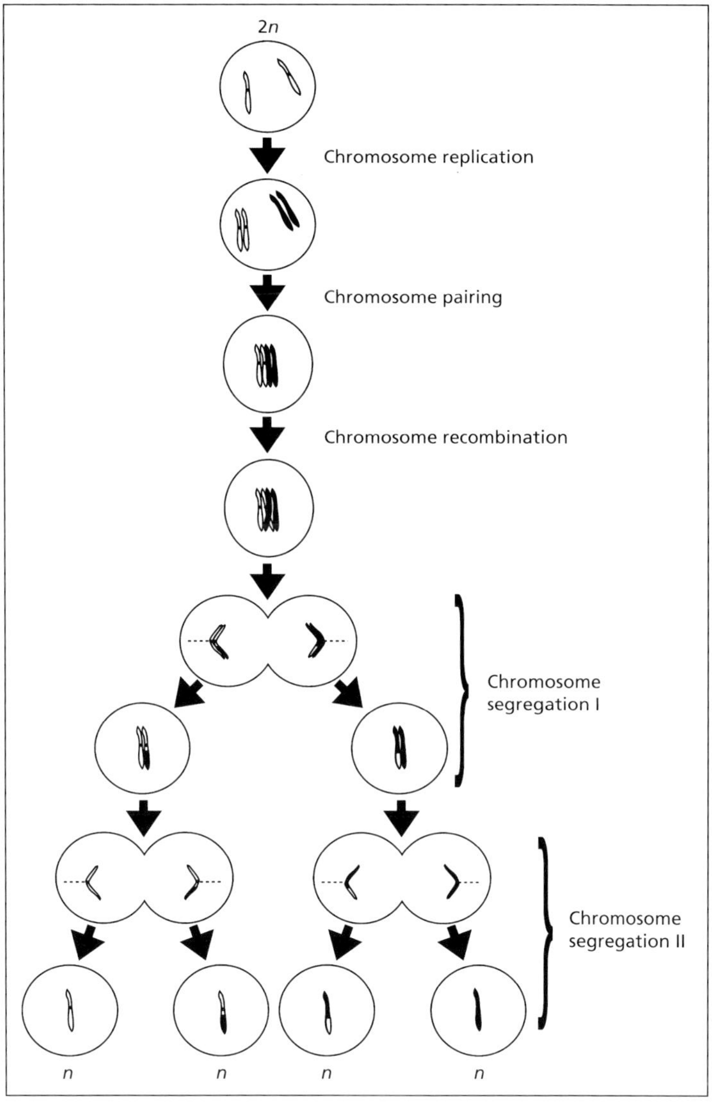

Fig. 5.

Meiosis. The fate of a single pair of matched chromosomes is shown. The chromosome from the maternal genome of the initial diploid cell is shown in white, and the homologous chromosome from the paternal genome is shown in black.

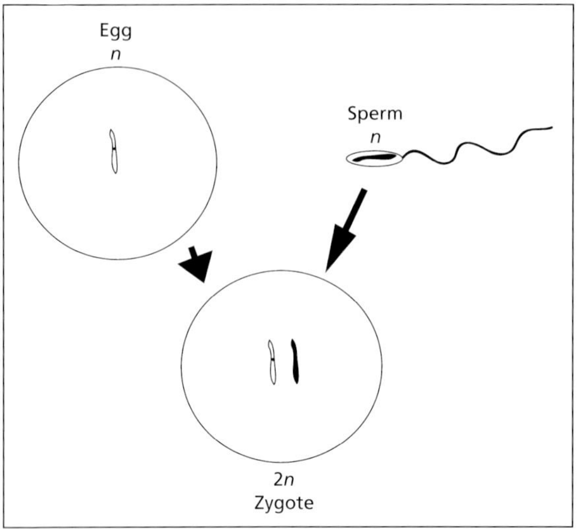

Fig. 6.
Fertilization.

have one meiosis and one fertilization, but there is evolutionary diversity in the number and placement of mitotic events. Figure 7a shows the human life cycle. As there is no true starting point in this circle of life, we are free to choose an arbitrary starting point. Starting with meiosis, figure 7a shows that meiosis produces two types of haploid gamete cells called sperm and egg. To continue the life cycle, the sperm and egg must immediately undergo fertilization to produce a diploid zygote, which in turn undergoes many rounds of mitosis to form multicellular, diploid adult humans. Meiosis then occurs in specialized tissues in these diploid adults to produce sperm and eggs, thus completing the life cycle.

In contrast to the human life cycle, consider now the life cycle of the bread mold, *Penicillium*, shown in figure 7b. In this case, a haploid cell produced by meiosis undergoes several rounds of mitosis to produce a multicellular, haploid adult. Certain cells in these haploid adults then produce haploid gamete cells by mitosis. These haploid gametes then undergo fertilization to form a diploid cell, which immediately undergoes meiosis to complete the life cycle.

The sea lettuce *Ulva* (fig. 7c) has a more complicated life cycle than either humans or *Penicillium*. As with the bread mold, the haploid cells

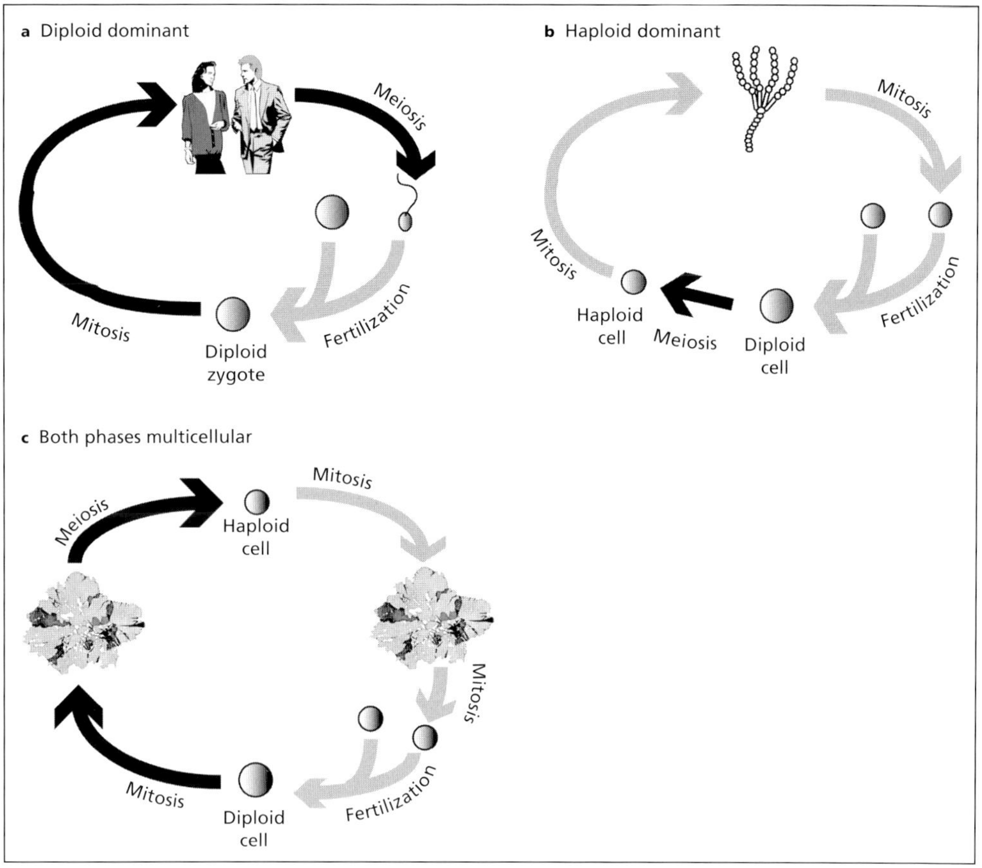

Fig. 7.

Three common types of life cycles. **a** Humans. **b** The bread mold *Penicillum*. **c** The sea lettuce *Ulva*. The diploid phases are shown by black arrows, and the haploid phases are shown by gray arrows.

produced by meiosis in the sea lettuce undergo many rounds of mitosis to produce a multicellular, haploid adult. Certain cells in these haploid adults then produce haploid gamete cells by mitosis. These haploid gametes then undergo fertilization to form a diploid cell. Then, as with humans, the resulting diploid cell undergoes many rounds of mitosis to produce a multicellular, diploid adult sea lettuce.

Most human societies and cultures place greater ethical value upon the diploid phase of human life than upon the much more transitory and single-celled haploid phase. However, the comparative approach reveals that the haploid phase of life need not be transitory. In many species, the haploid stage develops into a multicellular adult, and no biologist of any sort would ever regard these haploid adults as not being fully alive. Moreover, in some species the diploid phase is transitory and single-celled (fig. 7b), but that would not justify dismissing the diploid phase as not being fully alive. The diversity of life cycles that is partially illustrated in figure 7 makes it clear that all stages of life, both haploid and diploid, are fully alive and either one or both can become the dominant phase of life in a particular species. Thus, there are four kinds of humans, two types of diploid humans called men and women, and two types of haploid humans called sperm and eggs. All four kinds of humans are equally alive. Life does not begin at fertilization because the sperm and egg are alive before fertilization and the zygote is alive after fertilization. Life is continuous throughout the entire process of fertilization.

The life cycles shown in figure 7 reveal that the biological significance of fertilization is that it marks the *transition* from the haploid stage of life to the diploid stage of life. It does not mark the *beginning* of life. However, fertilization does mark the beginning of a genetically unique diploid individual in the sense of bringing together a specific pair of genomes. This observation raises another question: Does the determination of a unique genetic identity confer special ethical value upon fertilization? The comparative approach reveals that the answer to this question is 'no'. The reason is that meiosis also produces unique genetic identities for the haploid phase of life. Going back to figure 5, we see that meiosis can produce chromosomes that are partially maternal in origin and partially paternal through the process known as recombination. Moreover, the meiotic segregation of the paired diploid chromosomes to the unpaired haploid state occurs independently for all chromosomal pairs, a phenomenon known as independent assortment. Recombination and independent assortment together create unique gene combinations from those genes at which the original maternal and paternal genomes differed. Modern molecular genetic studies have revealed that there are alternative variants of a basepair (the fundamental unit of DNA, our genetic material) in at least every 100–250 basepairs examined [3]. Given that the total human genome contains about 3 billion basepairs, this means that there is variation at between 12–30 million basepairs. This variation is contained in the human species in toto and not necessarily as variation between the specific pair of genomes that came together to form a diploid human. However, these figures suggest that the average pair of genomes found in a single diploid adult differs by at least one million sites. Meiosis can then scramble the genetic variation at these million sites into $10^{301,000}$ genetically distinct haploid gametes. To put this number into perspective, cosmologists have estimated that there are about 10^{80} electrons in the universe: a number far, far smaller than the number of genetically distinct haploid gametes that an average diploid human can produce through meiosis. Therefore, all phases of human life consist of genetically unique individuals. If genetic identity and uniqueness confers special ethical value, then meiosis and fertilization should be equally valued, and haploid humans should be as valued as diploid humans. However, most human cultures and societies do not place equal ethical value upon the products of fertilization and meiosis, so genetic identity and uniqueness per se are not what confer special ethical status in most human cultures.

Thus, we have a dilemma. Both fertilization and meiosis mark transitions in ploidy level in our life cycle, and both fertilization and meiosis create genetically unique individuals. Yet, fertilization is given far more ethical examination than meiosis. The probable reason is that the diploid phase is dominant in our species (fig. 7a). We value our diploid phase more than our haploid phase because it is our diploid phase that can develop into a complex, multicellular individual whereas the haploid phase is unicellular and transitory. For species with a haploid-dominant life cycle, it is the haploid phase that we value and not the diploid phase. For example, we place great value and attention on the haploid phase of the bread mold *Penicillium* (fig. 7b) because it is the haploid phase that is the source of the antibiotic penicillin and it is the haploid phase that can spoil our bread. Most people are not even aware of the transitory diploid phase of this medically important species. It is patent that we place greater value on the phase (or phases) of life that becomes a multicellular individual.

The comparative approach to life cycles (fig. 7) makes it clear that it is *mitosis* after a transition in ploidy level that marks the phase of life to which we ascribe greater ethical value. It is *mitosis* that creates a multicellular individual from an initial single cell, regardless of whether or not that initial cell is haploid or diploid. Thus, the ethical focus upon fertilization has been misdirected; rather, we need to focus upon *mitosis* because it is the position of mitosis in the life cycle that determines where we place our ethical value and *not* fertilization or meiosis.

Mitosis following a ploidy change is not one event but instead is typically many mitotic events that effectively form a continuum throughout the individual's entire lifespan. Hence, our focus upon mitosis as the determiner of ethical value raises yet another question: At what point in this mitotic continuum does the individuality of a diploid human begin? To answer this question, we leave the realm of evolutionary biology and enter that of developmental genetics.

Lessons from Developmental Genetics

The diploid human zygote is initially called a pre-embryo because many, if not most, of the cells are destined to become part of the placenta, not the embryo [4]. After fertilization in the upper part of the fallopian tube, the pre-embryo moves down the fallopian tube while a series of mitotic events occur to yield a ball of about 32 cells called the morula (fig. 8). The morula is swept into the uterus, usually around the fourth day after fertilization. Implantation occurs during days 7–14 after fertilization. It is only after implantation and the differentiation between placental and embryonic tissues that we can properly speak of an embryo. Much of the research on human 'embryos' does not actually involve human embryos at all, but rather pre-embryos.

Modern genetics has revealed that fertilization is *not* the time at which a pre-embryo's genetic identity begins to influence development nor is it even the time at which a zygote's functional genetic identity is determined [5]. The genomes borne by the sperm and the egg are chemically inactivated both before and immediately after fertilization. This inactivation is accomplished by adding methyl groups (a common organic molecule) to cytosine, one of the basic components of DNA. When the DNA that codes for a gene is methylated, the gene is 'silenced' and the cell cannot use the information contained in the gene. This means that the initial zygotic genes cannot be expressed and therefore have no influence on development. Instead, development and growth after fertilization and during the initial rounds of mitosis is determined by information encoded in the structure of the egg and in gene products made by the mother. The pre-embyro's new and unique diploid genotype is irrelevant during early development. Silenced genes can be activated by removing the methyl groups, a process known as demethylation.

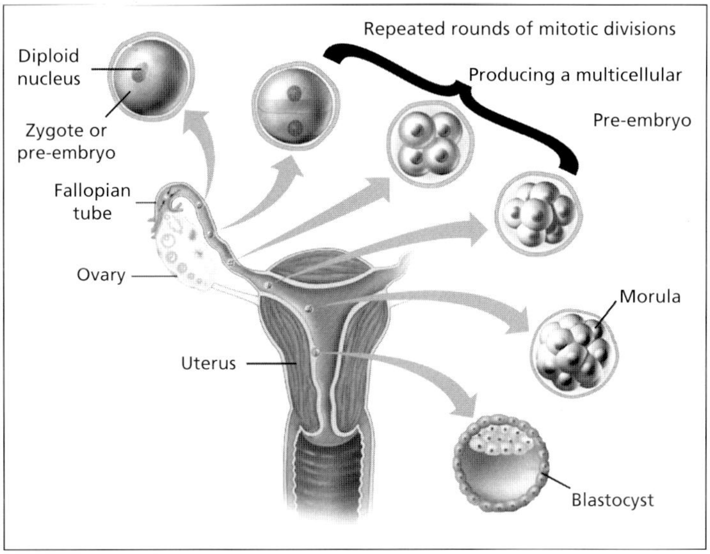

Fig. 8.
The early events in human zygotic development from fertilization to the initiation of implantation in the uterus.

The demethylation of the pre-embyro's genomes takes place gradually during the initial rounds of mitosis up to the morula. Hence, it is at the morula stage, some 4–7 days after fertilization, when the new diploid genotype begins to influence development and when diploid individuality begins.

An individual's *functional* genotype (the subset of genes that actually influences an individual's development) is not determined even at the morula stage. After the global demethylation of the pre-embryo's genomes at the morula stage, de novo methylation is reestablished at the blastocyst stage (fig. 8) [5]. This de novo methylation is not a single event, but rather an ongoing process. In some cases the paternal gene copy is silenced while the maternal copy is active or vice versa [5]. Thus, the functional genotype of the diploid individual begins to be determined at the blastocyst stage and is a gradual process thereafter.

The de novo methylation that starts at the balstocyst stage is influenced by many factors, including both chance and environment. As an example of a random factor, consider X inactivation in human females. Normal development usually requires a precise balance of the dosage of genes across the different chromosomes. In those species in which sex is determined by X and Y chromosomes (with XX being female and XY being male), there is a serious problem of gene dosage. The Y chromosome contains very few genes compared to the X chromosome, so those genes that are uniquely found on the X chromosome exist as a double dose in females but as a single dose in males. Different species with X and Y chromosomes have evolved diverse strategies for dealing with this problem of dosage compensation, but most mammals achieve their dosage compensation via the methylated inactivation of one of the X chromosomes in each cell of a developing female individual. Thus, at the cellular level, both males and females effectively have only a single dose of X-linked genes, thereby eliminating the potential dosage imbalance between the sexes. X chromosome inactivation occurs only after many rounds of mitosis, and remarkably the particular X chromosome inactivated occurs at random and independently in each cell. Once inactivated, the inactive X chromosome stays inactivated in subsequent rounds of mitosis, yielding patches of cells with the same functional genotype. Because inactivation is random, different cell patches have different active X chromosomes, making adult mammalian females a functional genetic mosaic.

This pattern of random inactivation can be clearly seen in calico cats (fig. 9). One of the genes influencing coat color in cats is found on the X chromosome and comes in two forms, one resulting in black hair and one in orange hair (the white hair on calico cats is determined by an independent gene that is not on the X chromosome and is therefore not influenced by random X inactivation). If a female cat inherited an X from her father with one type of coat color gene and an X from her mother with the alternative coat color gene, the result of random X inactivation at a multicellular stage is an adult female that is a mosaic of orange and black patches (fig. 9). Because of the random nature of X inactivation, no two calico cats have exactly identical patterns despite a shared genotype for this X-linked gene.

The random nature of mammalian X inactivation has profound implications in human genetics. For example, the fragile X syndrome is one of the more common forms of inherited mental retardation in humans. As its name implies, this genetic disease is associated with a gene on the X chromosome. Because males have only one X chromosome, all males with a fragile X chromosome are mentally retarded. 60% of females with one fragile X and one normal X are mentally retarded, and the others are normal. This

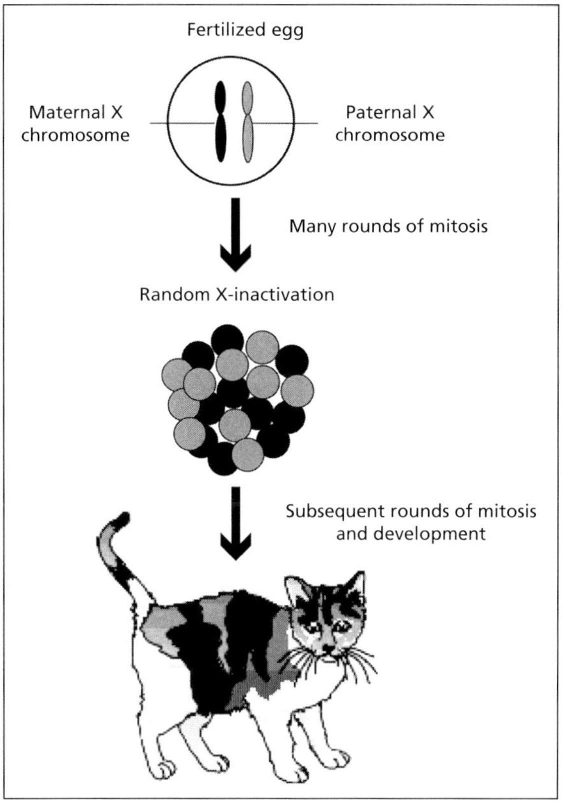

Fig. 9.

Calico cat. The initial diploid zygote has one X chromosome from the mother with a gene coding for a black hair (shown in black) and one X chromosome from the father with a gene coding for orange hair (shown in gray). After several rounds of mitosis, each cell randomly inactivates one X, with black cells indicating an inactivation of the paternal X and gray cells indicating an inactivation of the maternal X. Subsequent rounds of mitosis preserve these inactivation patterns, resulting in an adult female cat that is a mosaic of hair colors.

raises an intriguing question; all of these females have the same genotype for fragile X, so why are some afflicted by the genetic disease while others are not? The answer to this question is that females who are not retarded are those who by chance primarily inactivated the fragile X chromosome.

A dramatic example of this is given by a pair of monozygotic, 'identical' female twins who inherited one normal and one fragile X [6]. Despite sharing a common fertilization event, one twin developed into a mentally retarded child while the other did not. This tremendous difference in developmental outcome of a common fertilization event was due to the randomness of X inactivation well after fertilization; the fragile X was primarily inactivated in one twin, whereas the normal X was primarily inactivated in the other. Obviously, the functional genotype that influences human individuality is determined well after fertilization and well after many rounds of mitosis in this case.

The inactivation of an entire chromosome is a dramatic event that has long been observable and studied. Recently, modern molecular genetics has provided powerful tools for monitoring gene expression and inactivation at the level of single genes. These studies have revealed that phenomena similar to X inactivation are occurring throughout the genome on a smaller scale [5]. In a recent review of studies on monozygotic (MZ) twins that share a common fertilization event, Singh et al. [7] concluded that '... no MZ twins could be considered genetically/epigenetically "identical".' These studies using new technologies undercut the old idea that an individual's genotype is determined at the moment of fertilization. An *individual*'s genotype is meaningfully defined only by those genes that are active in that *individual.* The individual's functional genotype gradually unfolds in the mitotic continuum that begins at the blastocyst stage and continues throughout the remainder of diploid life.

In addition to the notion that fertilization determines an individual's genetic identity, there is also the notion that an individual's genotype determines the traits and attributes that the individual will develop. The combination of these two notions has provided a compelling argument for the ethical importance of fertilization. However, the first notion is now outmoded by the modern genetic studies mentioned above and no longer has scientific validity [7]. The second notion is based upon a naïve genetic determinism that has long been known to be false. Genotypes, even functional genotypes, do not determine an individual's traits or attributes; rather, an individual's traits emerge from the interaction of genes with environment.

Consider, for example, the trait of coronary artery disease (CAD), the leading cause of death in the developed world. There is a strong genetic component for CAD risk. However, no gene or genotype has been discovered

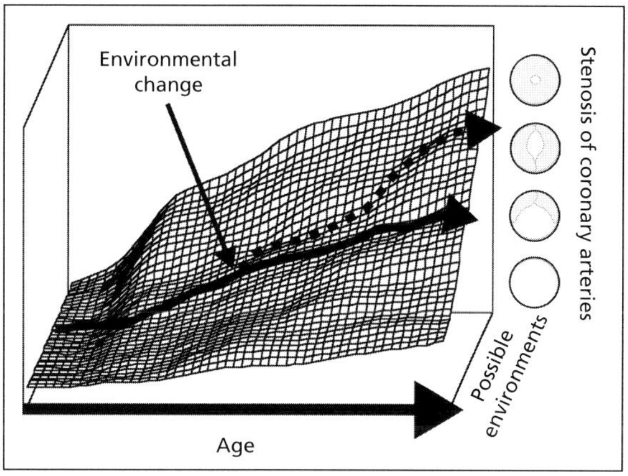

Fig. 10.

A model for the interaction of genotype, environments, and aging in producing the trait of degree of stenosis (blockage) in a coronary artery. The genotype defines a potential reaction surface, with higher positions on this surface corresponding to greater degrees of stenosis. This surface varies as a function of the environments in which the individual is living and of the age of the individual. The dashed line shows an alternative trajectory for an individual who experiences an environmental change at the age indicated in the figure.

that is either necessary or sufficient for CAD, and the same is true for all the many environmental factors that also influence the risk for CAD. Like most traits, the risk for CAD arises from the interaction of genetic and environmental factors [8, 9]. As a consequence, there is no such thing as the 'best' or 'worst' genotype; any given genotype can generally yield a wide variety of clinical endpoints depending upon the environmental context in which that genotype is embedded [10]. These studies suggest a model for CAD that is illustrated in figure 10. In this model, a particular genotype does not determine a trait such as stenosis of the coronary arteries (the physical prelude to CAD), but rather the genotype defines a surface of potential outcomes that vary as a function of the environment. Moreover, stenosis of the arteries develops over time as we age, and similarly, our environments can change as we age, including those aspects of the environment upon which we can exercise some degree of choice and that are known to interact with the genotype (e.g. diet, exercise, smoking habits, alcohol consumption). Therefore, what determines the clinical outcome for an individual is the environmental trajectory as one ages over this genetic reaction surface. At any point in this aging process, an individual can experience a new set of environments and thereby alter the trait outcome (fig. 10).

The model shown in figure 10 is applicable not only to CAD, but is a general model for most traits. Human individuality is determined by the traits and attributes that the individual actually has, and this individuality is influenced but not determined by the functional genotype. Under the model shown in figure 10, our individuality is continually redefined throughout our entire life span as our functional genotypes respond to the ever-changing environments that we experience as we age. Our individuality is not determined at fertilization nor is it determined by our genes. Individuality is a process that begins a few days after fertilization in the morula stage and continues throughout our lives.

In the Jewish prayer book, God is thanked for many reasons, including that '...in His Goodness, He renews daily, continually, the work of creation.' This phrase applies to each and every one of us, as all of us are part of creation. And as part of creation, our individuality is renewed daily, continually.

The Central Ethical Question

This chapter began with the central ethical question of 'when does life begin?' The evolutionary answer to this question makes it devoid of ethical implications concerning the sojourn from conception to birth (although it has other, profound ethical implications). Instead, the evolutionary and genetic arguments presented in this chapter indicate that a more meaningful ethical question is:

Where do we place ethical thresholds in the continual process of human individuality?

Biology provides no clear defining event to answer this question because diploid human individuality arises gradually during the mitotic phase of our life cycle and *not* at fertilization. Perhaps there is no single ethical threshold in dealing with the mitotic continuum and the attendant gradual emergence of functional genotypes and individual traits. Although modern biology does not provide an answer to the above question, knowing what the question should be and what it should not be is the critical first step in any debate. Thus, modern biology, and particularly evolutionary biology and genetics, can play an important role in the ethical debates concerning the passage from conception to birth.

Acknowledgements

I would like to thank Dr. Blazer and Dr. Karl Skorecki for their comments on an earlier draft of this chapter. I would also like to thank my wife, Bonnie Templeton, for being a critical sounding board for the ideas presented in this chapter. Finally, I would like to thank the Burroughs Wellcome Fund for financial support through an 'Innovation Award in Functional Genomics.' The issues raised by my research in applying evolutionary theory to functional genomics had a strong impact on the ideas presented in this chapter.

References

1 Gould SJ: I Have Landed: The End of a Beginning in Natural History. New York, Harmony Books, 2002, p 14.
2 Maimonides: The Guide of the Perplexed. Chicago, University of Chicago Press, 1963.
3 Nebert DW: Proposal for an allele nomenclature system based on the evolutionary divergence of haplotypes. Hum Mutation 2002;20:463–472.
4 Johnson MD: Human Biology: Concepts and Current Issues, ed 2. San Francisco, Benjamin Cummings, 2002.
5 Kierszenbaum AL: Genomic imprinting and epigenetic reprogramming: Unearthing the garden of forking paths. Mol Reprod Dev 2002;63:269–272.
6 Willemsen R, Olmer R, De Diego Otero Y, Oostra BA: Twin sisters, monozygotic with the fragile X mutation, but with a different phenotype. J Med Genet 2000;37:603–604.
7 Singh SM, Murphy B, O'Reilly R: Epigenetic contributors to the discordance of monozygotic twins. Clin Genet 2002;62:97–103.
8 Kardia SLR, Stengård J, Templeton AR: An evolutionary perspective on the genetic architecture of susceptibility to cardiovascular disease; in Stearns SC (ed): Evolution in Health and Disease. Oxford, Oxford University Press, 1999, pp 231–245.
9 Sing CF, Zerba KE, Reilly SL: Traversing the biological complexity in the hierarchy between genome and CAD endpoints in the population at large. Clin Genet 1994;46:6–14.
10 Templeton AR: The complexity of the genotype-phenotype relationship and the limitations of using genetic 'markers' at the individual level. Sci Context 1998;11:373–389.

11 Tourasse NJ, Gouy M: Accounting for evolutionary rate variation among sequence sites consistently changes universal phylogenies deduced from rRNA and protein-coding genes. Mol Phylogenet Evol 1999;13: 159–168.

Alan R. Templeton, PhD

Department of Biology, Washington University,
St. Louis, MO 63130–4899 (USA)
Tel. +1 314 935 6868, Fax +1 314 935 4432, E-Mail Temple_a@biology.wustl.edu

Blazer S, Zimmer EZ (eds):
The Embryo: Scientific Discovery and Medical Ethics.
Basel, Karger, 2005, pp 21–39

Jewish Perspectives

Avraham Steinberg

Center for Medical Ethics, The Hebrew University-Hadassah Medical School, and Medical Ethics Unit and Neurological Institute, Shaare Zedek Medical Center, Jerusalem, Israel

First Perspective

Introduction

This article presents the Jewish approach toward the beginning of life based upon Jewish sources from the Bible to current responsa literature. It is, therefore, pertinent to summarize the fundamentals and the structure of Jewish Law:

Halakhah is the generic term for the whole legal system of Judaism, embracing all the laws, practices and observances. Orthodox Jews consider the *Halakhah*, in its traditional form, to be absolutely binding.

The source of *Halakhah* is Divine revelation. To the basic corpus of biblical law were added rabbinic enactments and decrees. The sources of authority in *Halakhah* are composed of two fundamental parts: (1) the Written Law, a composition of 613 positive and negative commandments of Sinaitic origin, which are included in the five books of the Pentateuch; (2) the Oral Law, which includes the interpretation of the written law transmitted in its entirety with its details and minutiae at Sinai, as well as logical deductions, rabbinical decrees, customs, and positive and negative enactments.

The development of *Halakhah* may be divided into six periods:

- The earliest and most important source is the **Bible**.
- The ***Tannaitic*** period (1–220 CE): The major work of this period is the *Mishnah*, edited by Rabbi Judah *Ha'Nasi* ('the Prince') at the end of the 2nd century, in which were summarized all the legal debates and decisions of the Jewish leading scholars up to that era. The *Mishnah* includes early traditional understandings of the written law, original interpretations of the written law, ancient customs and regulations which are not mentioned in the Bible, and post-biblical decrees, customs and regulations. The *Mishnah* is composed of six major sections ('orders'), which cover all aspects of human life. Each order is subdivided into tractates, which are devoted to specific issues. There are about 60 tractates. This work became a sacred text second only to the Bible.
- The ***Amoraic*** period (220–470 CE): the *amoraim* were the interpreters of the *Mishnah*, and their work is termed *Gemara*, in which discussions and comments on the *Mishnah* constitute the major part; but also included are numerous new issues of legal importance, as well as folklore, history, astronomy, geography, botany, zoology, and medicine. The combination of *Mishnah* and *Gemara* is termed *Talmud*. With the closing of the *Talmud*, this work virtually became the infallible source of the *Halakhah*, and the history of post-Talmudic *Halakhah* is founded on recourse to the *Talmud* as the final and overriding authority. Rules for determining the actual decision in law from the labyrinth of legal debate in the *Talmud* have been formulated.
- The ***Gaonic*** period (7th century to mid-11th century): This period is marked by a significant expansion of the *Talmud* among Jews of the world, further analysis and deeper comprehension of the *Talmud*, and the beginning of formal codification.
- The period of the ***Rishonim*** (mid-11th century to 16th century): The early rabbinic authorities (*Rishonim*) were divided into commentators, whose major activity consisted of exposition of the classical texts of the *Talmud* and other early rabbinical works, and decisors, whose major activity was to formulate and finalize legal conduct. The works of the decisors are divided into *responsa* and codification. The greatest interpreter of the Bible and the *Talmud* was Shlomo Yitzchaki [*Rashi*] (1040–1105). The greatest Jewish codifier was Moses Maimonides [*Rambam*] (1138–1205) who compiled his gigantic code, the *Mishneh Torah* (called after his death the *Yad Ha'chazakah*), in which he

presented the final decisions in all matters of *Halakhah*, including those laws which were no longer applicable in his (and our) days. This magnum opus is composed of 14 books, which are subdivided into specific laws (*halakhot*). Each collection of laws is further subdivided into chapters and paragraphs. The other major work of codification of the Jewish law was done by Yoseph Karo (1488–1575) in his *Shulchan Aruch*. This work is divided into four major parts. The *Shulchan Aruch* marked a turning point in the history of *Halakhah*. Adherence to the *Shulchan Aruch* became the test of Jewish *Halakhic* fidelity. *Responsa* is a rabbinic term denoting an exchange of letters of queries and replies in which one party consults another on a *halakhic* matter. The beginning of *responsa* literature as a literary and historical form of important dimensions took place in the middle of the *Gaonic* period, and has continued to this day. Since the publication of the *Shulchan Aruch*, most responsa are organized in accordance with the four subdivisions of the *Shulchan Aruch*. This form of *Halakhic* discourse has served as the major opus of normative Jewish legal formulation. It is estimated that there are about 400,000 *responsa* collected in over 3,000 books of *responsa*.

- The period of the ***Acharonim*** (16th century to present time): The later rabbinic authorities (*Acharonim*) are similarly subdivided between commentators, codifiers and responders. Most rulings of modern times are based upon these authorities.

The Torah and its precepts are continually interpreted and expanded by the rabbinic Sages of each generation who rule on matters as they come up, add protective rules and regulations and provide legal, ethical and personal guidance to the Jewish people.

General Jewish Ethical Approaches

A fundamental difference exists between Judaism and secular philosophical ethics in many facets of life. The basis, validity and source of Jewish ethics is rooted in the belief in God and His Torah, whereas the basis of secular ethics is primarily humanism and rational intellect.

Jewish ethics and law are derived from the written and oral law, described above, which were Divinely given to Moses on Mount Sinai. The Jewish rules of law and principles of ethics include commandments governing the relationship between man and God, as well as precepts governing man's relationship to his fellowman.

The following are some basic principles of Jewish ethics as viewed by Orthodox Judaism:

- In Judaism, there is no basic difference between laws and regulations and morals and ethics because both are integral parts of the Torah and their validity flows from the power of the Torah and the Divine revelation. Therefore, basic principles, discussions and debates on Jewish ethical issues do not differ from those of Jewish legal issues. This view is contrary to the social and secular systems of law and ethics.
- Jewish ethics includes the guidelines for proper conduct for man in relation to his fellow man as well as in man's relation to God. Therefore, there is no difference in the binding nature of the law between the laws prohibiting stealing, killing, falsehood, revenge, carrying a grudge and the like, and the laws prohibiting idol worship, Sabbath desecration, eating on the Day of Atonement, and the like. So, too, there is no difference between the obligations of giving charity, visiting the sick, burying the dead, caring for orphans and widows and their like, and the observance of dietary laws, eating unleavened bread (*matzah*) on Passover, and the like. This view is contrary to the humanistic approach in which only relations among human beings are dealt with.
- According to the Torah and Jewish law, one is obligated not only to refrain from doing bad but one must do good by being compassionate and charitable with one's fellow human beings as it is written, *turn from evil and do good* [Psalms 34:15]. These are two equal parts of the Jewish ethical obligation. Therefore, not only are harmful acts such as stealing, wounding and killing prohibited but there exist positive commandments: to give charity, to visit the sick, to be hospitable, to return lost objects, and the like. This view is contrary to the legal approach which is primarily concerned with the avoidance of harm to others but does not require doing good to others.
- The Jewish principles require not only proper acts but also proper thoughts and intentions. The Torah forbids hatred, covetousness, revenge, carrying a grudge, and the like, and requires one to love God, to love one's fellow man, to love one's parents, to love a stranger, and the like, in spite of the obvious difficulties in controlling one's thoughts.
- One of the important Jewish ethical principles is to sanctify the profane and to raise every day human endeavor to a level of holiness. Some ethical

and religious systems praise those who abstain from normal life's activities, who are celibate, and who practice asceticism in various ways. This is not the normative Jewish view. Judaism does not demand the uprooting of one's natural inclinations but an even more difficult task, i.e. the conquering and appropriate channeling of one's natural instincts. To fight one's evil inclination does not mean to withdraw from the world but to overcome the inclination while living in the world. This requirement is more difficult because it compels one to conduct oneself ethically during daily living which is full of ethical traps and obstacles. The Bible and Talmud are replete with references to proper conduct, both between man and man, and man and God. These references and teachings are especially numerous in the books of the early and late prophets, Ecclesiastes, Proverbs, Ethics of the Fathers, and the *Aggadic* portions of the Talmud.

The Torah itself presents two types of teachings in regard to ethical conduct:

- The precepts and laws including specific obligations.
- The stories about the ethical conduct of the Patriarchs and Matriarchs which should be emulated.

The Book of Genesis, for instance, only includes 3 of the 613 commandments but is full of stories illustrating the ethical characteristics of the Patriarchs and the Matriarchs.

According to the rabbinic Sages, the attributes and 'conduct' of God should also be emulated by man, in the performance of what is good and just.

Jewish ethical teaching involves general concepts and principles on the one hand, and specific rules and regulations on the other. The Bible cites a number of basic principles about the proper relationship between man and man, such as:

- *Love your fellow man as yourself* [Leviticus 19:18] – 'this is a major principle in the Torah' [1]; 'what is hateful to you, do not do to your neighbor, that is the whole Torah, while the rest is commentary, go and learn it' [2].
- *Do not profane the name of your God* [Leviticus 18:21], namely do not conduct yourself in a way that profanes the name of God [3].
- *You shall do what is righteous and good in the eyes of the Lord* [Deuteronomy 6:18].
- *Observe justice and perform righteousness* [Isaiah 56:1].
- *Despise evil and love good, and establish justice by the gate* [Amos 5:15].
- *Do justice, love kindness, and walk humbly with your God* [Micah 6:8].

- *The righteous lives through his faith* [Habakkuk 2:4].
- *That you may walk in the way of the good, and keep the paths of the righteous* [Proverbs 2:20].
- *Its ways are ways of pleasantness, and all its pathways are peace* [Proverbs 3:17], etc.

However, the Jewish ethical system, like the *halakhic* system, is not satisfied with general theoretical rules alone but is filled with practical and individual guidelines. The Torah requires every human being to strive for perfection in one's conduct *vis-à-vis* another person, in actions, in speech and in thought, and not just abstract general good behavior.

In addition to the aforedescribed biblical ethical system, the rabbinic sages in the Talmud and thereafter also decreed and implemented ethical guidelines for moral conduct, both on a societal and on an individual level. Many ethical discussions are scattered throughout rabbinic literature including the Talmud and *Midrashim*. These discussions provide the foundation for the organized ethical theories and views in the Middle Ages and in more recent times.

Jewish Medical Ethics

Discussions of medical ethical dilemmas from a Jewish-*halakhic* viewpoint go back to antiquity. The basic principles are already enunciated in the Bible and the Talmud and the rabbinic literature of all eras.

In recent years, many discussions of medical ethics and Jewish law have been published.

Jewish medical ethics, in terms of the application of *halakhic* and Jewish ethical principles to the solution of problems, differs from secular medical ethics on four planes:

- The range of discussions and attitudes.
- The methods of analysis and discussion.
- The final conclusions.
- The basic principles [4–6].

The Range of Discussions and Attitudes

Halakhah addresses all the medical ethical questions which secular medical ethics raises, whether old or new. *Halakhah* also addresses specific medical issues that affect only Jews who observe the precepts of the Torah. The basic Jewish approach is the same for questions relating to the terminally ill, abortion, organ transplantation and questions relating to the treatment of patients on the Sabbath, the laws of seclusion or the laws of a menstruant woman.

Methods of Analysis and Discussion

Jewish medical ethics analyzes medical ethical questions with the same methods and *halakhic* principles used for any *halakhic* analysis using basic principles and sources enunciated in the Talmud, Codes of Jewish law, and the responsa literature of all generations. The scientific or medical data are presented and the relevant *halakhic* sources are then applied to the data. It is not always easy to arrive at a *halakhic* conclusion regarding a medical question. A far-reaching knowledge of *halakhah* as well as an expert and precise understanding of the relevant scientific facts is required in order to arrive at the proper *halakhic* conclusion.

Final Conclusions

Halakhah attempts to give final and operative decisions to questions posed to the rabbinic decisor. This is in contrast to secular medical ethics which views its function as defining the relevant ethical dilemma, sharpening the focus of the various views and not necessarily arriving at final and practical conclusions. Since time immemorial, however, Rabbis have differed in their opinions and not always is the final decision unanimous. This situation is no different than any other normative legal matter. Mechanisms exist in *halakhah* to decide among the various opinions. In this respect, there is no difference between a medical question and any other question in any area of Judaic practice or belief.

The *halakhic* construct in resolving a medical ethical question is a tripartite one involving the patient and/or family, the physician, and the rabbinic decisor. The patient is obligated to seek the best possible medical care. He has the autonomous right to choose his physician and his rabbinic decisor and has the right to make his personal wishes known. The physician is obligated to treat the patient and must use the best diagnostic and therapeutic interventions according to his knowledge and judgment. The rabbinic decisor is obligated to understand all the facts of the medical questions, to consider the views presented by the patient and the physician, and then to decide according to halakhic principles how to proceed in any given situation. His decision is binding on both patient and physician.

Basic Principles
The basic principles of Jewish medical ethics compared to secular medical ethics are the following:

Jewish ethics is based on duties, obligations, commandments, and reciprocal responsibility. The acceptance upon oneself of this yoke is the ultimate purpose of Jews on this world and provides spiritual fulfillment. The word 'right' in its modern sense meaning 'I am entitled to it' does not exist in biblical or talmudic literature. By contrast, **secular medical ethics** is based heavily on the concept of rights and autonomy. This is a minimalistic view and justifies human decisions which cannot be criticized as long as they do no harm to others. Judaism, however, requires self-fulfillment based on obligatory and binding moral requirements which are beyond the personal, temporal feeling of individuals but rather founded on values mutually beneficial to society.

Judaism in general prefers the casuistic approach to resolve *halakhic* questions. This means that one must examine each situation according to the individual circumstances and develop the response according to the specific details and characteristics of that situation using many of the basic *halakhic* rules and regulations and principles. This is the methodology of the rabbinic responsa literature and is ideally suited for medical questions where the circumstances differ from patient to patient. By contrast, the current approach of **Western secular medical ethics** uses a limited number of ethical principles and applies them to all situations involving medical ethical questions.

Judaism recognizes absolutism only with respect to the Divine source of authority of Jewish law, the supreme authority of the prophets who speak the words of God and the eternity of Torah. Judaism does not, in general, subscribe to a set of principles and values as absolute imperative categories but rather favors a middle of the road approach, the 'path of the golden mean', which is a proper balance between different values or laws in any specific case. The ethical imperative for the average person is to conduct oneself properly with the appropriate balance between opposing values and to avoid extreme positions. There are, however, unusual circumstances or for specific pious individuals where it might be justified or even desired to act 'over and above' what is required and with special holiness and sanctity. This is the exception, however, and not the rule. Hence, for Judaism there is no definitive value which is absolute so that it takes precedence in every case or situation. Various values have different moral weight and there is a system for ascribing priorities in specific situations where conflicting values exist. This view is based on the principle that 'the Torah was not given to ministering angels' [7] but to ordinary human beings who, by definition, are not perfect. Man's obligation is 'to be strong as a lion to arise in the morning to the service of one's Creator', namely one must seek and strive to reach Divine understanding and perfection in Torah. One's reward is the effort in striving for perfection although the latter is unattainable, as stated by King Solomon, *There is no righteous man on earth who only does good and does not sin* [Ecclesiastes 7:20].

The physician-patient relationship in **Judaism** is not a voluntary-contractual arrangement but a Divine commandment and obligation. The patient is commanded to seek healing from the physician and to prevent illness if possible. The physician is obligated to heal and is considered to be the messenger of God in the care of patients. The patient is not free to decide autonomously to refuse treatment which might be beneficial or save his life. He is prohibited from relying on miracles, but must do whatever is necessary to heal himself according to standard medical practice.

Second Perspective

The Sanctity of Life

In **Judaism**, the value of human life is supreme; therefore, to save a life, nearly all biblical laws are waived. This is certainly true concerning killing or hastening death. This approach is in contrast to the **secular ethical** view which considers human life to be one of many values and often gives greater weight to 'the quality of life'. However, even in **Judaism**, the value of human life is not absolute and in certain rare and well-defined circumstances other values may supercede it. Nonetheless, this does not in any way diminish the supreme value of human life in Judaism.

The obligation to save life is one of the cardinal principles of Judaism because he who destroys a life is as if he destroyed a whole world and he who saves a life is as if he saved a whole world [8]. Almost all biblical and rabbinic commandments (except three: idolatry, murder, and forbidden sexual relations) are suspended in order to save a life. Thus, a dangerously ill patient must desecrate the Sabbath or eat on the Day of Atonement or violate any other prohibition, if necessary, to save his life. Even if someone is coerced to violate biblical laws or be killed, he is obligated to violate them if one can do so in private, even if it means violating religious tenets.

One soul is dearer to God than the observance of all the Torah precepts, thus testifying to the extreme importance of saving a life. This is the meaning of the phrase '*and thou shalt live by them*' (i.e. the commandments) but not die by them. From this interpretation we learn that 'the laws of the Torah are not vengeful but merciful and compassionate to bring peace to the world'. About heretics who claim that it is prohibited to desecrate the Sabbath even to save a life it is written, '*Wherefore I gave them also statutes that were not good, and ordinances whereby they should not live*' [9].

The individual's permission is not required in order to save his life. Even if the person in danger cries out 'Do not save me', one disregards his wishes and saves him.

According to *halakhic* rulings, he who desecrates the Sabbath to save a life does not transgress; rather he fulfills a biblical commandment. Even if his rescue attempts are unsuccessful and even if someone else has already effected the rescue, he has still done the right thing and will be rewarded by God. Even if he erred and thought the person was in danger and acted accordingly, he is exempt from any spiritual liability.

Even only a doubtful or possible but not definite danger to life requires the waiving of all Torah precepts [10]. The rule of the majority is, therefore, not invoked when it comes to saving lives because the Torah says that '*you shall live by its* (precepts)'. This means that no one should die because of the observance of its precepts.

One may not sacrifice one life to save another life. Therefore, during the birth of a baby, if the head has emerged from the birth canal but the baby is endangering the mother's life, one may not destroy it to save the mother [11–13].

A number of sources form the basis of the obligation to save lives.

The main source is the negative precept '*Thou shalt not stand idly by the blood of thy fellow man*' [Leviticus 19:16]. If one sees one's fellowman drowning or being attacked by wild animals or by robbers, one is obligated to try to save him. The Torah warns against negligence in the saving of even a single life if one is able to do so.

One is obligated to save a life not only if the rescue is assured. Even if it is not sure that it will be successful one must attempt it, thereby fulfilling the biblical precept. One must attempt in any way possible, to prevent loss of a human being even if the chances of success are poor.

Additional principles regarding the saving of life are as follows:

- The commandment of returning a lost object [Deuteronomy 22:2] also includes the restoration of one's 'lost' health [14].
- The precepts '*and he shall live with thee*' [Leviticus 25:35] and '*that thy brother may live with thee*' [Leviticus 25:36] also include the saving of life.

Nonetheless, although Jewish law requires that Torah and rabbinic laws be set aside in the face of danger to life, there are a few exceptions:

- With regard to the three cardinal sins, idolatry, murder, and forbidden sexual relations, a person should rather be martyred and not transgress them [15].

The Rabbis also discuss situations other than the cardinal three precepts where Torah laws are not waived even for saving life:

- If the violation of any Torah law must be done in public and involves a desecration of God's name one should rather suffer death than transgress [16].
- During times of persecution, if a ruler decrees that the Jews must abandon their religion or nullify a Torah precept, they should suffer death rather than transgress [17].
- In times of war, the danger to each individual is not as important as the welfare of the entire population at war. Therefore, soldiers must obey commands to go to war in spite of personal danger and the principle of individual danger of life is waived.

The principle of autonomy which is dominant in **Western secular medical ethics** is modified in Judaism. **Judaism** asserts that man was created in the image of God [Genesis 9:6] and that all people are, therefore, considered special and equal. Thus, Judaism requires that people must respect and help one another. Judaism also accepts a degree of patient autonomy in the physician-patient relationship. However, in certain situations in which autonomy conflicts with other fundamental principles of Judaism, such as the obligations to preserve one's health and life, to avoid harming others and to do good for others, the *halakhah* may be in direct conflict with autonomy.

In **Judaism**, man is said to have free will and choice. This does not mean that he is permitted to choose to live immorally or to violate Torah laws. A person is commanded to live within *halakhah* and thus his autonomy and free choice are restricted. Decision-making in areas which do not involve *halakhah* can be totally autonomous. However, in every life situation in which there is a clear *halakhic* position any Jew, be he physician or patient, must always act within the parameters of *halakhah* and not on one's own inclinations and desires.

Third Perspective

The Moral Status of an Embryo

From time immemorial, scientists and philosophers have argued about when life begins. From a pure scientific viewpoint it is impossible to answer this query. In fact, it is impossible to define scientifically the very term 'life'. Indeed, the definition of life and of the beginning of life involves religious, ethical, legal and social considerations.

Similarly, from time immemorial scientists and philosophers have debated the status of the embryo/fetus. There has been, and continues to be, a great dispute as to whether or not an embryo has an independent claim for life and/or whether or not he possesses a status of an independent person.

(a) Some scholars have opined positively to this query but they differ as to the stage of the fetal development at which the fetus has its own rights and personhood:

- The moment of conception
- The time of implantation of the fertilized egg in the uterine wall
- The time that the fetal shape or human form is recognizable
- The time that the brain develops
- The time of fetal movement
- The time of viability of the fetus outside the uterus, which differs according to the scientific ability to sustain extrauterine life.

(b) Some scholars believe that the fetus is never considered as an independent human being, and has no independent claim for life.

(c) Yet other scholars opine that the fetus does not possess self and independent moral rights but it has a relative claim for life and for rights based upon its eventual personhood in that it is a potential human being while in utero. According to this view, the closer to birth the fetus is, the closer to personhood it can be considered and the greater justification it has to be accorded rights [summarized in 18].

Hence, three views pertain to fetal rights:

- The fetus has no independent rights and is merely an integral part of the mother.

- The fetus has full rights, identical to a born, fully formed and independent human being.
- The fetus has some rights but less than a person has after birth.

The philosophical argument about when 'personhood' endows someone with rights is, thus, an unresolvable issue. It varies according to one's religious, cultural and social beliefs [19–22].

Another moral issue pertains to the question whether or not there is a moral distinction between an embryo that is already implanted and developing in utero compared with a pre-embryo in a test tube after an in vitro fertilization is performed.

Yet another moral issue concerns the status of a fetus as a patient. The advancement of medical technology and knowledge has stimulated the notion that the fetus should be considered a separate patient with its own rights and needs for protection [23]. Hence, a variety of ethical questions pertain to the moral aspects of intrauterine treatment:

- The mother's right to autonomy and the need for her informed consent for any fetal treatment which requires invasion of her body, versus the right of the fetus to receive effective therapy and to be protected from harm.
- The uncertainty of the outcome of fetal therapy.
- The proper allocation of limited resources – is it proper to utilize enormous resources for an unborn fetus rather than for urgent care of living people?
- Can the parents and/or physician be sued by the newborn for malpractice for not treating an unborn fetus?
- Can the mother request abortion if the fetus is defective, at least during the first stage of pregnancy (in countries where abortion is legal), or is the fetus a separate entity from the mother? [concerning ethical issues in treating fetuses, see 24–29].

Jewish Perspectives

The fundamental Jewish position toward the status of an embryo/fetus is based upon the assumption of a **progressive acquisition of a human status**. The gametes, the zygote, the blastocyst, the early organogenesis, and the progressive physical development and viability of the pre-embryo/embryo/fetus all indicate and express a progressively growing potential for human life and existence. The biological progression of the fetal development also reflects a moral and legal progression of rights and dignity. Hence, these various stages of biological development merit a progressively growing respect, dignity and rights. The changing moral status of the developing embryo/fetus can be, and in fact should be, balanced and weighted against other moral values and rights. Full, complete and unrestricted rights as a human being are achieved only after childbirth.

Moreover, Judaism sharply distinguishes and differentiates between pre-implanted embryos and those who are already implanted in utero, as shall be discussed below.

Ensoulment

The Talmudic Sages, as well as some subsequent Jewish scholars, have debated the theological and meta-physical question whether or not a fetus acquires a soul, and if it does – at what stage of its development does this occur. The Talmud quotes the following dispute:

Antoninus said to Rabbi Judah the Prince: 'when is the soul placed in man, as soon as it is decreed that it shall be male or female or when the fetus is actually formed?' He replied: 'from the moment of formation'. He objected: 'can a piece of meat be unsalted for 3 days without becoming putrid? But it must be from the moment that God decrees its destiny'. Rabbi Judah the Prince said: 'This thing Antoninus taught me and the Scriptures supports him' [30].

Nonetheless, most Rabbis exclude a fetus from the Biblical term *nefesh*, meaning soul or person [31–34]. Other Rabbis call a fetus *a safek nefesh*, meaning a partial or a potential person [35]. Maimonides' position on this matter is questionable and debatable.

The theological question of the timing of ensoulment has not, and cannot be resolved by Jewish practical, legal mechanisms; this question is beyond human ability to solve.

The Talmudic Sages and subsequent authoritative Jewish scholars have been engaged in another interesting legal-moral debate concerning the status of a fetus. Some Rabbis consider the fetus to be an appendage of the mother, whereas others disagree [36, 37]. Such discussions are common in the Talmud, either directly or applied indirectly. This question may be dependent on the issue of when the soul enters the body. There is, however, a difference of opinion among Jewish scholars whether or not this statement has any legal ramifications.

Nonetheless, these theological and legal debates have an insignificant impact on the application of Jewish law concerning the rights appropriated to the different stages of fetal development. Whether or not ensoulment occurs at fertilization, conception or formation of the fetus, and whether or not the fetus is or is not an appendage of the mother is irrelevant to the issue of rights and claim for life for the following considerations:

On the one hand, the developing human being from the gamete to the newborn deserves respect and dignity and should not be emitted and/or destroyed for naught. On the other hand, in face of conflicting values and rights the decisions will shift for or against the rights of the fetus depending on the fetal stage of development and on the moral-legal weight of the opposing values and rights, as will be shown below.

Jewish-Legal Position Regarding Stages of Embryonic Development

Several stages of the human fetal development have particular significance in Jewish law and philosophy. These are: semen, pre-embryo (i.e. a pre-implanted fertilized ovum), embryo in utero up to 40 days, embryo/fetus in utero from 41 days on, and newborn.

Semen

Jewish theology attributes respect to semen as a human part and as a potential for future life, but does not regard it as life. The Jewish legal consequence of this position is a clear and unqualified prohibition of improper emission of semen, including masturbation.

Expending semen for naught is considered a very serious offense in Judaism [38, 39]. According to *Kabbalah*, it is the most stringent of all transgressions in the Torah. He who expends semen for naught is as if he shed blood by destroying a soul [40–42], because every drop is capable of producing human beings.

Since the prohibition of destroying semen is not explicitly stated in the Torah, there is disagreement among the rabbinic decisors as to the biblical source for this prohibition. Some Rabbis write that the source for this is the verse *thou shalt keep thee from every evil thing* [Deuteronomy 23:10] which is interpreted to mean that a man should not indulge in erotic thoughts by day that may lead him to uncleanness by night [43]. Some Rabbis state that the prohibition of destroying semen is derived from the law of wounding and destroying; just as it is prohibited to intentionally wound one's body, so too it is prohibited to destroy one's semen [44]. Some Rabbis derive the prohibition from the acts of Er and Onan [Genesis 38:7 and 10; 45].

Pre-Implantation Embryo

This entity deserves dignity and respect as a human part and as a potential for future life, but it is not considered as life. The potential for future life of this entity is still very low and very remote. It also requires further unnatural human intervention in order to continue its existence and to enable it to become a human being. Hence, this entity has no humanhood status.

One of the basic sources for the Jewish position designating an inherent different legal and moral status to a pre-implanted embryo as compared with an in utero embryo is the following:

The Bible states '*One who spills the blood of a human, in a human, his blood shall be spilled*' [Genesis 9:6]. This verse teaches us that the prohibition of murder applies exclusively to a human formed within another human, i.e. a fetus within its mother's womb [46]. Hence, a pre-implanted fertilized ovum does not have the status of a human being regarding the prohibition of murder.

Pre-implanted zygotes or blastocytes, as such, are entitled to full protection and dignity. However, when these rights come into conflict with other values one ought to weigh the relevant merits and rights and balance between them.

One of the consequences of such a balance is the permission to perform a pre-implantation genetic diagnosis and to discard defective pre-embryos. The potential damage of giving birth to a seriously defective child overrides the minimal dignity that the zygote deserves and the remote potential of life of a pre-implanted fertilized egg.

Another consequence of current importance is the permission to derive stem cells from superfluous frozen fertilized eggs in order to advance potential cures for many people with chronic, debilitating, fatal, degenerative disorders. The ethical dilemmas concerning stem cell research are currently intensely and passionately debated in all western countries, and it is beyond the scope of this article to discuss all its ramifications in depth from a Jewish point of view. Suffice it to say that the balance between the enormous potential benefit of life-saving derived from stem cells outweighs the responsibility of dignity towards the fertilized egg [47].

Embryo in utero – First 40 Days

According to the Talmud, until 40 days postconception, the fetus is 'mere fluid' [48]. Current obstetrical calculation of the gestational period starts from the first day of the last menstrual period. Since the Talmudic Sages calculated the gestational period from conception, this '40 day' stage is at the end of the seventh week of pregnancy according to current obstetrical terminology.

This stage per se does not yet constitute a status of a human being. Hence, all Rabbinic authorities agree that if a woman miscarried within 40 days of conception, the laws of uncleanness of childbirth do not apply to her, because the aborted embryo at that stage is not considered a human being [49–52].

However, since the embryo at this stage is already implanted in the womb its potential for becoming a human being is a natural process. Nonetheless, this is still a remote possibility. These two sides of the coin have generated a debate amongst the Rabbinic authorities concerning a deliberate cessation of the embryo's existence. Some Rabbis assert that up to 40 days one can be very lenient in regard to abortion and it is not forbidden to abort a fetus at that stage, or at least it is an additional reason to permit the abortion when other reasons exist [53–56]. Other Rabbis, however, state that it is biblically prohibited to abort any fetus, even prior to 40 days, just like it is prohibited after 40 days [57, 58].

Embryo in utero – After 40 Days

At this stage, the potential of becoming a full and complete human being is getting greater and closer. Hence, a negative attitude toward abortion is expressed unanimously among the rabbinic decisors and commentators. Nearly all agree that some type of prohibition is involved in the performance of an abortion. However, there are differing views as to the nature of the prohibition, its seriousness, the reason for the prohibition, and the conditions under which abortion may be considered. It is beyond the scope of this article to discuss in-depth all the aspects of abortion according to Jewish law.

Many of the current authoritative Rabbis consider abortion as a moral and theological form of murder, though all agree that the fetus still has no full claim for life at this stage. Hence, on the one hand, it is strictly forbidden to abort a fetus, but on the other hand, the life of the mother takes precedence over the life of the fetus, so that if the mother's life or health is seriously threatened by the continuation of the pregnancy than abortion is not only permissible but actually required. Also, no capital punishment is administered upon the transgressor, as would have been the case if one murders an existing human being out of the womb.

References

1 Jerushalmi Talmud, Tractate Nedarim 9:4. See further Maimonides' Mishneh Torah Deot 6:3.
2 Babylonian Talmud, Tractate Shabbat 31a.
3 Babylonian Talmud, Tractate Yoma 86a.
4 Steinberg A: A Jewish perspective on the four principles; in Gillon R (ed): Principles of Health Care Ethics. Chichester, Wiley, 1994, pp 65–73.
5 Steinberg A: Jewish medical ethics; in Brody BA, Lustig A (eds): Bioethics Yearbook. Amsterdam, Kluwer Academic Publishers, 1991, vol 1, pp 179–199.
6 Steinberg A: What is 'Jewish medical ethics?' Jewish Med Ethics 1988;1:2–3.
7 Babylonian Talmud, Tractate Berachot 25b.
8 Babylonian Talmud, Tractate Sanhedrin 37a.
9 Maimonides' Mishneh Torah, Shabbat 2:3.
10 Babylonian Talmud, Tractate Yoma 83a–84b.
11 Babylonian Talmud, Tractate Sanhedrin 72b.
12 Maimonides' *Mishneh Torah Rotzeach* 1:9.
13 Joseph Karo's *Shulchan Aruch, Choshen Mishpat* 425:2.
14 Babylonian Talmud, Tractate Sanhedrin 73a.
15 Babylonian Talmud, Tractate Yoma 82a.
16 Babylonian Talmud, Tractate Sanhedrin 74a–b.
17 Babylonian Talmud, Tractate Sanhedrin 74a.
18 Strong C, Anderson GD: An ethical framework for issues during pregnancy; in Gillon MR (ed): Principles of Health Care Ethics. Chichester, Wiley, 1994, pp 587–600.
19 Lockwood M: Warnock versus Powell (and Harradine): When does potentiality count? Bioethics 1988;2:187–213.
20 Hare RM: When does potentiality count? A comment on Lockwood. Bioethics 1988;2:214–226.
21 Buckle S: Arguing from potential. Bioethics 1988;2:226–53; Crosby JF: The personhood of the human embryo. J Med Philos 1993;18:399–417.
22 Engelhardt HT: Personhood, moral strangers, and the evil of abortion: The painful experience of post-modernity. J Med Philos 1993;18:419–421.
23 Harrison MR, Golbus MS, Gilly R, Filly RA (eds): The Unborn Patient: Prenatal Diagnosis and Treatment, ed 2. n. Philadelphia, Saunders, 1991.

24 Barclay WR, McCormick RA, Sidbury JB, Michejda M, Hodgen GD: The ethics of in utero surgery. JAMA 1981;246:1551–1552.
25 Robertson JA: The right to procreate and in utero fetal therapy. J Leg Med 1982;3:333–366.
26 Elias S , Annas GJ: Perspectives on fetal surgery. Am J Obstet Gynecol 1983;145:807–812.
27 Fletcher JC: Ethical considerations in and beyond experimental fetal therapy. Semin Perinatol 1985;9:130–135.
28 Johnsen DE: The creation of fetal rights: Conflicts with women's constitutional rights to liberty, privacy, and equal protection. Yale Law J 1986;95:599–625.
29 Sgreccia E: Ethical issues in prenatal diagnosis and fetal therapy: A Catholic perspective. Fetal Ther 1989;4(suppl 1):16–27.
30 Babylonian Talmud, Tractate Sanhedrin 91b.
31 Rashi's Commentary, Babylonian Talmud, Tractate Sanhedrin 72b, s.v. yatza.
32 Meiri and Ramah's commentaries, Babylonian Talmud, Tractate Sanhedrin 72b.
33 Novellae Ramban and Ritva, Babylonian Talmud, Tractate Niddah 44b.
34 Minchat Chinuch, precept #296.
35 *Rosh*, in *Shitah Mekubetzet*, Babylonian Talmud, Tractate Arachin 7a #5; *Aqudah*, Arachin #6.
36 Babylonian Talmud, Tractate Yebamot 78a–b; Tractate Nazir 51a; Tractate Gittin 23b; Tractate Baba Kamma 78b; Tractate Sanhedrin 80b; Tractate Chullin 58a; Tractate Temurah 10b, 11a, 19a, 25a and 31a.
37 Jerushalmi Talmud, Tractate Kiddushin 1:3.
38 Maimonides' Mishneh Torah, Issurei Biyah 21:18.
39 Joseph Karo's Shulchan Aruch, Even Haezer 23:2.
40 Babylonian Talmud, Tractate Niddah 13a.
41 Maimonides' Mishneh Torah, Issurei Biyah 21:18.
42 Joseph Karo's Shulchan Aruch, Even Haezer 23:3.
43 Babylonian Talmud, Tractate Ketubot 46a; Tractate Abodah Zarah 20b.
44 Responsa Binyan Tzion #137.
45 Babylonian Talmud, Tractate Yebamot 34b; Tractate Niddah 13a.
46 Babylonian Talmud, Tractate Sanhedrin 67b.
47 Testimony of Rabbi Tendler MD before the American National Bioethics Advisory Commission, vol 3, p H-1ff, 2000.
48 Babylonian Talmud, Tractate Yebamot 69b.
49 Maimonides, *Mishneh Torah*, *Terumot* 8:3 and *Issurei Biyah* 10:1.
50 Babylonian Talmud, Tractate Niddah 30a.
51 Maimonides' Mishneh Torah, Issurei Biyah 10:2.
52 Joseph Karo's Shulchan Aruch, Yoreh Deah 194:2.
53 Responsa Chavat Yair #31; Responsa Seridei Aish, part 3 #127; Responsa *Tzitz Eliezer*, part 7 #48:1:8.
54 *Achiezer*, part 3, end of #65.
55 Rabbi Auerbach SZ: Cited in Nishmat, Abraham part 5, Choshen Mishpat 425:2.
56 Rabbi Henkin YH: Assia #59–60, 5757, 1997, pp 133ff.
57 Rabbi Unterman IY: Noam, vol 6, 5723, 1963, pp 1–11.
58 Responsa Iggrot Moshe, Choshen Mishpat, part 2 #69.

Avraham Steinberg, MD

Neurological Institute, Shaare Zedek Medical Center,
PO Box 3235, IL–91031 Jerusalem (Israel)
Tel. +972 2 6555215, E-Mail steinberg@szmc.org.il

Blazer S, Zimmer EZ (eds):
The Embryo: Scientific Discovery and Medical Ethics.
Basel, Karger, 2005, pp 40–52

The Status and Rights of the Human Embryo and Fetus

A Catholic Perspective on the Unborn Child

Roberto Colombo

Laboratory of Human Molecular Biology and Genetics,
Catholic University of Sacro Cuore, Milan; Pontifical Academy Pro Life, Vatican;
Bioethics Committee, National Institute of Health, Ministry of Health, Rome, Italy

Let me begin by pointing out that the Catholic view on human prenatal life and the duty to respect the unborn child since its embryonic stage of development is neither an unreasonable statement based exclusively on Christian belief or tradition nor a question of morality pertaining to the Church only: it is a call for everyone's reason and freedom. As John Paul II recognized in his encyclical letter *The Gospel* of *Life*, 'the issue of life and its defense and promotion is not a concern of Christians alone. Although faith provides special light and strength, this question arises in every human conscience which seeks the truth and which cares about the future of humanity. Life certainly has a sacred and religious value, but in no way is that value a concern only of believers. The value at stake is one which every human being can grasp by the light of reason; thus it necessarily concerns everyone' [1].

Indeed, the unconditional respect for the right to life of every innocent person is not only a matter of rational evidence but constitutes one of the pillars on which civil societies stands. The defense of the fundamental rights of the person, especially of the weakest, is among the primary duties of a democratic State [2]. To raise the question of human life and its protection is to contribute to the renewal of society through the promotion of the common good. 'It is impossible to further the common good without acknowledging and defending the right to life, upon which all the other inalienable rights of individuals are founded and from which they develop. A society lacks solid foundations when, on the one hand, it asserts values such as the dignity of the person, justice and peace, but then, on the other hand, radically acts to the contrary by allowing or tolerating a variety of ways in which human life is devalued and violated, especially where it is weak or marginalized. Only respect for life can be the foundation and guarantee of the most precious and essential goods of society, such as democracy and peace' [1].

The Catholic Church rejoices in being able to share its commitment to recognize and defend the value of human life with so many others, and I am glad to share with you the great scientific, medical and ethical concern for the life of the unborn child.

(1) The duty to respect the embryo's life and integrity together with the need to safeguard it juridically relies on two assumptions: the embryo's total innocence, and its belonging to the category of beings possessing personal human life. Whereas the embryo's innocence is unanimously accepted nowadays, its human subjectivity is not always acknowledged. Some question the fact that an embryo might be defined – right from its one-cell stage (zygote) – as a human being with full rights or as a human person. The issue has been tackled by the Catholic Magisterium with 'two types of argument which are closely linked' [3]. The second, of a probabilistic nature, can be found in John Paul II's 'indisputable observation' [3] that 'the mere probability that a human person is involved would suffice to justify an absolutely clear prohibition of any intervention aimed at killing a human embryo' [4]. The first argument is based upon the anthropological assertion of the substantial unity of body and soul in the human being '*corpore et anima unus*' [5], '*una summa*' [6], and on the biological observation that 'from the time that the ovum is fertilized, a life is begun which is neither that of the father nor the mother; it is rather the life of a new human being with his own growth' [7, quoted in ref. 4]. Neither the anthropological assertion nor the biological observation are plain to Christians alone, for reason itself unveils this correctness, even if divine Revelation casts an extraordinary light on the road that seeks to find man's whole truth.

'Even if the presence of a spiritual soul cannot be ascertained by empirical data' – remarks the Pope – 'the results themselves of scientific research on the human embryo provide a valuable indication for discerning by use of reason a personal presence at the moment of the first appearance of human life' [7, 60: AAS 87, 78; quoted in ref. 4]. But what is this 'valuable indication' and on what results is it based? Does the continuous advancement of biological and clinical studies on the human embryo and fetus strengthen or weaken these results? Moreover, what concept of «personal presence» is corroborated by the results of scientific research?

(2) The Catholic Church 'is aware of the current debates concerning the beginning of human life, the individuality of the human being and the identity of the human person and has not expressly committed itself to an affirmation of a philosophical nature' [8] in order to define the human embryo, but does declare that 'the human being is to be respected and treated as a person from the moment of conception' [8, AAS 80, 79; quoted in ref. 4]. Nevertheless, the Magisterium and theology understand – both ontologically and axiologically as is fit for the human being – the concept of person as a substantial individual endowed with a rational nature [9], even if 'each of its capacities requires time – a rather lengthy time – to find its place and to be in a position to act' [7, 13: AAS 66, 738; quoted in ref. 4]. Man's rational nature, however, is not reducible to some or all of his/her abilities, activities and functions that remain hidden in the initial stages of the human body's development. Thus, identifying the person with the bundle of his/her faculties or currently functional operations, not only irretrievably jeopardizes the ontological unity and identity in the human person, but also legitimizes an unfair form of discrimination among human beings on the arbitrary basis of their attributes and abilities.

The full human nature of the embryo, right from its zygotic stage, is testified to by modern genetics, which 'has demonstrated that from the first instant there is established the programme of what this living being will be' [7, 13: AAS 66, 738; quoted in ref. 4]. Right from fertilization the embryo's karyotype is, in fact, composed of DNA molecules which contain specifically human polydeoxyribonucleotide sequences that are immediately yet gradually expressed in the embryonic cells.[1]

[1] In the light of several studies carried out by independent groups of researchers, the hypothesis of a complete early embryo's genome expressive inertia during a transcriptionally silent period exclusively controlled by maternally inherited components should be revised. For example, the SRY gene, whose locus is on the telomeric region of the

However, to this so far undisputed fact, some oppose the argument that the embryo in its initial stages of life – which according to some last up to the 7th–8th day, according to others, up to the 14th–15th day – does indeed have a genetic identity and individuality, but not a definite organismic individuality. Ontogenetically speaking, the embryo is not the same human individual that we will recognize in the implanted embryo, the fetus or the newborn child. Thus, by not possessing a substantial individuality, one of the two requisites characterizing the human person would be missing in the embryo. We are here referring to the well-known objections concerning the early embryo's cell totipotency, monozygotic twinning and chimeric aggregation, which are, nonetheless, surmountable if supported by a rational argument which takes into account all the factors that biologically make up a human being.[2] Such an argument can theoretically be based on the diachronic and individual unity of the organism's life cycle. This does not exclude, but rather implies the possibility of becoming in the form of generating ('to give rise to') and de-generating ('to cease to exist as'), and is empirically based on the interpretative models of the phenomena cited above which are logically not contradictory but are biologically compatible with current scientific data. Some of these models, such as the one that explains the formation of monochorionic monozygotic twins by the splitting of the blastocyst's inner cell mass, a process which is analogous to gemmation in the agamic reproduction of some multicellular organisms, has been confirmed through the direct microcinematographic observation of a

human Y chromosome's short arm, is expressed and is transcripted right from the very beginning of embryonic development, even during the pronuclear stage [10, 11].

2 At this point, it must be noted that when dealing with moral truths, which not only imply the description of reality, but also the meaning this reality holds for the life of every man and of humanity, it is not possible to reach reasonable certitude without involving one's freedom in the cognitive act. This corresponds to what the National Committee for Bioethics (Italy) admitted, on the influence of morality in the dynamics of knowledge, in its document on the human embryo: 'The ontological interpretation of biological data ends up being influenced by the subject's moral options, that is by his/her true feelings toward the embryo since fertilization. If the subject regards the embryo as another human individual, the lack of a settling criterion will not be a solid enough argument to deny its ontological status of individual (and thus contradict his moral attitude). Vice versa, if the subject does not regard the embryo as an individual human, the lack of such a criterion will support his innermost conviction. This fact explains the assertion that the ontological argument, though relevant to the question of ethics, does not truly exhaust it' [12].

mammalian blastocyst during the hatching [13]. The splitting of inner cell mass model can explain some cases of monozygotic twinning following in vitro fertilization [14].

(3) Scientific evidence can in no way and certainly not alone grant the human embryo the ontological status of 'a human being in every sense', i.e. a person, because 'human being' and the 'person' do not belong to the field of biological concepts and are not formal objects of empirical research. Genetics and developmental biology do suggest, however, and with the support of ever-growing research results, that the embryo is none other than an individual of the human species in the initial stage of its life cycle, which will lead it – through a coordinate, continuous and gradual process[3] – to become an adult as we are, because it is already one of us: 'He who will be a man is already man' [16]. But then 'How could a human individual not be a human person?' [8, AAS 80, 79; quoted in ref. 4]. According to common experience and sound thought, 'every separation between individual and person in the human being is arbitrary, a game between philosophy and biological science without true cognitive value' [3].

(4) The recognition of the human embryo and fetus as a human being raises a number of practical questions. Among them, one seems to be crucial in order to deal with other dilemmas: Is the unborn child entitled to the same human rights as we are? The answer to this question depends on which rights we consider and the kind of foundation of rights we lay. The argument is difficult and would require us to go more deeply into the theory of rights. Because of limited time, I shall only outline the natural rights view embraced by Catholic tradition and look briefly into an alternative foundation of human rights.

In the following discussion, the word 'right' is used in its strongest sense to designate that which is categorically or unqualifiedly due to an individual from others. Rights, understood in this sense, cannot be overridden, although the validity of some rights may depend on circumstances. Rights

[3] The essential characteristics of the process of embryo development have been synthesized in the final report of the Committee of Inquiry into Human Fertilisation and Embryology (UK) as follows: 'While, as we have seen, the timing of the different stages of development is critical, once the process has begun, there is no particular part of the developmental process that is more important than another; all are part of a continuous process, and unless each stage take place normally, at the correct time, and in the correct sequence, further development will cease' [15].

whose compelling force is independent of circumstances are considered to be inalienable or fundamental rights. Among them, the right to life of an innocent human being – that is, the right not to have his/her already existing life interrupted by anyone for whatever reason – is almost universally accepted by principle. The absolute inviolability of innocent human life is a moral truth clearly taught by Sacred Scripture, constantly upheld in the Church's Tradition and consistently proposed by her Magisterium: 'The deliberate decision to deprive an innocent human being of his life is always morally evil and can never be licit either as an end in itself or as a means to a good end' [1, 57: AAS 87, 465].

As John Paul II recalled, 'the foundation on which all human rights rest is the dignity of the person' [17]. Human dignity, in turn, rests on the human proper and primordial nature – the 'nature of the human person' [18, p. 51] – which is 'the person himself in the unity of soul and body, in the unity of his spiritual and biological inclinations and of all the other specific characteristics necessary for the pursuit of his end' [19]. The dignity of each and every human being exceeds the value of material objects and living beings because it is deeply rooted in reason and freedom which distinguish man from animals. Thus, 'the dignity of the person is the indestructible property of every human being' [20]. This view is shared by the Universal Declaration of Human Rights, whose preamble recognize the 'inherent dignity and [...] the equal and inalienable rights of all members of the human family' [21].

In a theological perspective, man is 'the only creature on earth whom God willed for its own sake' [18, p. 24]. The meaning of his existence is to be an end in himself, not to be a means for other ends. Man's coming into being does not conform to the laws of biology alone, but also, and directly, to God's creative will, which is concerned with the genealogy of the children of human families. In the biblical narrative, the difference between man and other creatures is shown above all by the fact that only the creation of man is presented as the result of a special decision on the part of God, a deliberation to establish a particular and specific bond with the Creator: 'Let us make man in our image, after our likeness' [Genesis 1:26]. 'The life which God offers to man is a gift by which God shares something of himself with his creature' [1, 34: AAS 87, 439]. God 'willed' man from the very beginning 'in his image and likeness', and 'God "wills" him in every act of conception and every human birth. God "wills" man as a being similar to himself, as a person' [22]. This is true for everyone, including those affected by diseases and disabilities since their prenatal life.

'Man has been given a sublime dignity, based on the intimate bond which unites him to his Creator: in man there shines forth a reflection of God himself' [1, 34: AAS 87, 439]. According to Saint Irenaeus of Lyons, 'man, living man, is the glory of God' [23]. Inscribed in the personal dignity of every human being are its inalienable rights, whose foundation rests on God's 'will' and whose respect and protection is entrusted to man: 'From man in regard to his fellow man I will demand an accounting for human life' [Genesis 9:5].

Life is always a fundamental right of every innocent man.[4] There are no circumstances in which this statement can be overridden. Even when a man has no consciousness of or interest in his life, for the only reason that he is alive life remains his basic and inalienable good on which every other good rests. However, a theory frequently proposed in the context of the abortion debate assume that a being can have rights only if it has or is capable of having 'conscious desires' or 'interests'.[5] On this presupposition, embryos

[4] The expression 'innocent man' (in place of 'man') refers to the case of legitimate defense, 'in which the right to protect one's own life and the duty not to harm someone else's life are difficult to reconcile in practice. Certainly, the intrinsic value of life and the duty to love oneself no less than others are the basis of a true right to self-defense' [1, 55: AAS 87, 451]. Moreover, 'legitimate defense can be not only a right but a grave duty for someone responsible for another's life, the common good of the family or of the state' (Catechism of the Catholic Church, 2265). Unfortunately, sometimes 'It happens that the need to render the aggressor incapable of causing harm sometimes involves taking his life. In this case, the fatal outcome is attributable to the aggressor whose action brought it about, even though he may not be morally responsible because of a lack of the use of reason' [1, 55: AAS 87, 451; 24, 25]. This is the context in which to place the problem of the death penalty. On this matter there is a growing tendency, both in the Church and in civil society, to demand that it be abolished completely.

[5] Among others, the following authors accept the capacity for 'conscious desires' as a necessary condition of possessing rights. Laura Purdy and Michael Tooley [26] hold that 'an organism can have the right to life only if it now possess, or possessed at some time in the past, the capacity to have a desire for continued existence'. Joel Feinberg [27] favors what he calls the 'actual possession' criterion: 'It is because people are conscious; have a sense of their personal identities; have plans, goals and projects; are liable to pain, anxieties and frustrations, can reason and bargain, and so on – it is because of these attributes that people have value and interests, desires and expectations of their own, including a stake in their own futures, and personal well-being of a sort we cannot ascribe to unconscious or nonrational beings... Only because of their sense of self, their life plans, their value hierarchies, and their stakes in their own future can they be ascribed fundamental rights'. In another paper, Feinberg [28] discusses what he calls the 'interest

and fetuses are not entitled to inalienable human rights, including the right to life, integrity and development.

The 'conscious desires' approach to the foundation of rights shows its weakness when faced by the question: What is the source of our moral obligation to recognize and respect the rights of another being? The fact that someone has, or is capable of having, desires and interests of any kind is not obviously a compelling reason for each of us to comply with these desires and protect these interests. A desire or an interest cannot have the character of a right unless it is connected with a certain status of the subject that expressed or can express such an aim. The recognition of a subject's desire or interest as worthy of respect and compliance depends on the correspondence between the desire or interest and the 'intrinsic value' or dignity of the subject. Therefore, neither the presence of desires or interests is a condition for the possession of a right nor the absence of them can exclude the existence of this right.

(5) Today the assertion of the human embryo's right to life, integrity and development is especially pressing because of the extraordinary increase and gravity of threats to the life of individuals and peoples, especially where life is weak and defenseless, such as the unborn one. In addition to the ancient scourges of poverty, hunger, diseases, violence and war, new threats are emerging on an alarmingly vast scale. Besides abortion, a widespread practice that intentionally terminates the life of a human embryo or fetus (both as a result of a surgical or pharmacological direct interruption of pregnancy and a consequence of several post-coital contraceptive procedures), in vitro fertilization and embryo transfer protocols are not exempt of serious and common risks for the integrity and the life of the early human embryo. Threats which are no less serious arise from the field of biomedical research and biotechnology, where experimentation on human embryos is currently being performed in a number of laboratories. In a social and cultural context which makes it more difficult to face and accept aging and suffering, the temptation becomes all the greater to resolve the problem of thus far incurable diseases by harvesting stem cells from human embryos and fetuses in the hope that they will lead to promising cell and gene therapies.

Stem cell research is a new, exciting field of developmental and cell biology, and evidences are growing that a number of patients will benefit from

principle', according to which 'the sort of beings who can have rights are those who have (or can have) interests'. The concept of 'interest', for Feinberg, implies 'conscious desires' [28, p. 49].

possible clinical applications of stem cell culture and differentiation [29–34]. Catholics recognize the great potential for human therapeutics in stem cell research and do not oppose this experimental investigation per se if the cells are obtained from sources such as post-natal tissues, miscarriages, or placental blood. As John Paul II reminded in his address to the 18th International Congress of the Transplantation Society, 'this is the direction that research must follow if it wishes to respect the dignity of each and every human being, even at the embryonic stage' [35]. What is morally unsustainable is the harvesting of stem cells by destruction of human embryos at the blastocyst stage (removal of the inner cell mass), as currently proposed by several investigators and allowed in some countries.

Human embryos created specifically for research – either by in vitro fertilization or nuclear transfer cloning – do not have a different status than embryos created for reproductive purposes. In both cases, if killed in order to obtain stem cells the embryo's life would be treated as a means to an end and its fundamental right to life violated. Even if the embryos are frozen spare embryos that result from in vitro fertilization and will be discarded anyway or parents were to consent to use fresh spare embryos not transferred into the uterus, this would not change the inherent status of the embryos themselves. 'There is no moral or legal basis for subjecting any member of the human species to harm or death in nontherapeutic research based on the prediction that it will die anyway, no matter how certain that prediction may be' [36]. Parents are not ethically or juridically entitled to consent for invasive or destructive nontherapeutic research on their child, even if an unborn one. Some documents who favor or admit embryonic stem cell research, in their concern to stress the value of human life and the importance to consider the moral opinion of many members of the society in which they live, grant that the human embryo – even when subjected to experimentation – should be treated with 'respect' [37; see 38 for the case of experimentation on human embryos]. No one can fail to see that this statement seems to be merely an assurance that the embryos will be destroyed only in 'research that incorporates substantive values such as reduction of human suffering' [37]. 'Respect', understood in this way, is reduced to and used as a weak form of protection that is suitable for an object (however precious, things do not have an intrinsic value) but inadequate for a subject (the value of human beings is not conditional on something other than its intrinsic value). A true respect for a human embryo as a human being cannot override its fundamental right to life, integrity and development, and this commitment to refrain from doing harm is independent of circumstances.[6]

The ethical dilemma posed by stem cell research is a serious and overwhelming one and its solution requires a great sense of responsibility towards the dignity of every human being, including both patients eagerly waiting for a therapy and human embryos and fetuses silently waiting for full development. Currently, the alternative to human embryonic stem cells rests on three different sources of stem cells and pre-differentiated cells: fetal tissues, cord blood, and adult tissues [40–44]. The possibility of differentiating in vitro and in vivo pluripotential cells of different origin, as well as to dedifferentiate and redifferentiate precursor cells into specific lineages, is extensively investigated in several laboratories and the exploitation of the developmental plasticity of some somatic cells is now more than a speculation [45–59].

There is a general moral consensus for harvesting stem cells from cord blood and adult tissues. As to the use of tissues from aborted fetuses, while not in one sense different from the harvesting of organs or tissues from adult cadavers, from the Catholic perspective it is considered immoral when there is complicity with and a possible incentive for elective abortion (spontaneously aborted fetuses do not raise this ethical reservation).

In concluding, I express the hope that, thanks to the work of so many generous and highly-trained people, scientific and clinical research in the field of developmental biology, embryology and obstetrics will grant the human embryo and fetus, both as a subject of inquiry and a patient, the respect and the treatment that is due to a child, even if still unborn. For a responsible practice of human biology and medicine the fundamental criterion is the defense and promotion of the integral good of the human person. Consequently, it is evident that every experimental or clinical procedure performed on the human person is subject to ethical limits: 'What is technically possible is not for that reason alone morally admissible' [8, Introduction, 4: AAS 80 (1988), 76]. These limits do not mortify the great devotion to scientific discovery and clinical care that characterize the biomedical profession. On the contrary, they allow scientists and physicians to participate in the Creator's glance at and care of every human being, especially the weakest and defenseless ones.

[6] No end is believed to be good, such as the use of stem cells for the preparation of other differentiated cells to be used in what look to be promising therapeutic procedures, can justify an intervention of this kind. A good end does not make right an action which in itself is wrong [39].

References

1 Pope John Paul II: Encyclical letter. Evangelium vitae (March 25, 1995), 1995;101:AAS 87, 517.

2 Pope John Paul II: Address to the participants in the study conference on 'The Right to Life in Europe' (December 18, 1987): Insegnamenti X, 1987;3:1446.

3 Cardinal Ratzinger J: Presentation of 'Evangelium vitae' to the journalists accredited to the Holy See. L'Osservatore Romano (Weekly edition in English), April 5, 1995, p 2.

4 Pope John Paul II: Encyclical letter. Evangelium vitae (March 25, 1995), 1995; 60: AAS 87, 469.

5 Second Vatican Ecumenical Council: Pastoral constitution on the Church in the Modern World. Gaudium et spes (December 7, 1965), 14.

6 Pope John Paul II: Apostolic exhortation. Famifiaris consortio (November 22, 1981), 1982;11:AAS 74, 92.

7 Congregation for the Doctrine of the Faith: Declaration: De abortu procurato (November 18, 1974), 1974;12:AAS 66, 738.

8 Congregation for the Doctrine of the Faith: Instruction on respect for human life in its origin and on the dignity of procreation. Donum vitae (February 22, 1987), 1998; I, 1: AAS 80, 78.

9 Thomas Aquinas: Summa theologiae I, q. 29, a. 1–2.4.

10 Ao A, Erickson RP, Winston RM, Handyside AH: Transcription of paternal Y-linked genes in the human zygote as early as the pronuclear stage. Zygote 1994;2:281–287.

11 Fiddler M, Abdel-Rahman B, Rappolee DA, Pergament E: Expression of SRY transcripts in preimplantation human embryos. Am J Med Genet 1995;55: 80–84.

12 National Bioethics Committee: Identity and Status of Human Embryo (June 27, 1996). Rome, Presidenza del Consiglio dei Ministri, Dipartimento per l'lnformazione e 'Editoria, 1996, 5.3.

13 Massip A, van der Zwalmen P, Mulnard J, Zwijsen W: Atypical hatching of a cow blastocyst leading to separation of complete twin half-blastocysts. Vet Rec 1983;112:301.

14 Alikani M, Noges N, Cohen J, Rosenwaks Z: Monozygotic twinning in the human is associated with the zona pellucida architecture. Hum Reprod 1994;9: 1318–1321.

15 Department of Health and Social Security: Report of the Committee of Inquiry into Human Fertilization and Embryology (Chairperson: Warnock M). London, Her Majesty's Stationery Office, London, 1984, 11.19.

16 Tertullian: Apologeticum IX, 8; in Migne (ed): Patrologia Latina, I, 371, 2.3; Corpus Christianorum Latinurum (Brepols, Turnhout) I, 103, 1.35.

17 Pope John Paul II: Post-synodal apostolic exhortation. Ecclesia in America (January 22, 1999), 1999;57: AAS 91, 792.

18 Second Vatican Ecumenical Council: Pastoral constitution on the Church in the Modern World. Gaudium et spes (December 7, 1965).

19 Pope John Paul II: Encyclical letter. Veritatis splendor (August 6, 1993), 1993;50:AAS 85, 1173.

20 Pope John Paul II: Post-synodal apostolic exhortation. Christifideles laici (December 30, 1998), 1989;37: AAS 81, 462.

21 General Assembly of the United Nations: Universal Declaration of Human Rights (December 10, 1948), Preamble.

22 Pope John Paul II: Letter to families. Gratissimam sanae (February 2, 1994), 1994;9:AAS 86, 879.
23 'Gloria Dei vivens homo': Irenaeus of Lyons. Adversus Haereses, IV, 20, 7; in: Sources Chretiennes. Paris, Les Editions du Cerf, 100/2, pp 648–649.
24 Thomas Aquinus: Summa theologiae II-II, q. 64, a. 7.
25 Alphonsus De'Liguori: Theologia morallis 1, III, tr. 4, c. 1, dub 3.
26 Purdy L, Tooley M: Is abortion murder? in Perkins R (ed): Abortion: Pro and Con. Cambridge, Schenkman, 1974, p 144.
27 Feinberg J: Abortion; in Regan T (ed): Matters of Life and Death, ed 2. New York, Random House, 1980, p 270.
28 Feinberg J: The rights of animals and unborn generations; in Blackstone WT (ed): Philosophy and Environmental Crisis. Athens, University of Georgia Press, 1974, p 51.
29 Stocum DL: Stem cells in regenerative biology and medicine. Wound Repair Regen 2001;9:429–442.
30 Keller R: Stem cells on the way to restorative medicine. Immunol Lett 2002;83:1–12.
31 Stanworth SJ, Newland AC: Stem cells: Progress in research and edging towards the clinical setting. Clin Med 2001;1:378–382.
32 Forbes SJ, Vig P, Poulsom R, Wright NA, Alison AR: Adult stem cell plasticity: New pathways of tissue regeneration become visible. Clin Sci 2002;103: 355–369.
33 Luttun A, Carmeliet G, Carmeliet P: Vascular progenitors: From biology to treatment. Trends Cardiovasc Med 2002;12:88–96.
34 Stewart R, Przyborski S: Non-neural adult stem cells: Tools for brain repair? Bioessays 2002;24:708–713.
35 Pope John Paul II: Address to the 18th International Congress of the Transplantation Society (August 29, 2000), 2000;AAS 92, 826.
36 Pellegrino E: Testimony before the National Bioethics Advisory Commission; in: National Bioethics Advisory Commission, Ethical Issues in Human Stem Cell Research, vol III (Religious Perspectives). Rockville, NBAC, 2000, p F–4.
37 Geron Ethics Advisory Board: Research with Human Embryonic Stem Cells: Ethical Considerations. Hastings Center Report, March/April 1999, pp 32–33
38 Council of Europe: Convention on Human Rights and Biomedicine (April 4, 1997), art 18: 'Where the law allows research on embryos in vitro, it shall ensure adequate protection of the embryo'.
39 Pontifical Academy for Life: Declaration on the Production and the Scientific and Therapeutic Use of Human Embryonic Stem Cells. Vatican City, Libreria Editrice Vaticana, 2000, p 15.
40 Weissman IL, Anderson DJ, Gage F: Stem and progenitor cells: Origins, phenotypes, lineage commitments, and transdifferentiations. Ann Rev Cell Dev Biol 2001;17: 387–403.
41 De Wynter EA, Testa NG: Interest of cord blood stem cells. Biomed Pharmacother 2001;55:195–200.
42 Anversa PA, Nadal-Ginard B: Myocyte renewal and ventricular remodelling. Nature 2002;415:240–243.
43 Sanchez-Ramos JR: Neural cells derived from adult bone marrow and umbilical cord blood. J Neurosci Res 2002;69: 880–893.
44 Vats A, Tolley NS, Polak JM, Buttery LD: Stem cells: Sources and applications. Clin Otolaryngol 2002;27:227–232.
45 Clarke D, Frisen J: Differentiation potential of adult stem cells. Curr Opin Genet Dev 2001;11:575–580.
46 Zubair AC, Silberstein L, Ritz J: Adult hematopoietic stem cell plasticity. Transfusion 2002;42:1096–1101.

47 Avots A, Harder F, Schmittwolf C, Petrovic S, Muller AM: Plasticity of hematopoietic stem cells and cellular memory. Immunol Rev 2002;187:9–21.
48 Forbes SJ, Vig P, Poulsom R, Wright NA, Alison AR: Adult stem cell plasticity: New pathways of tissue regeneration become visible. Clin Sci 2002;103: 355–369.
49 Frisen J: Stem cell plasticity? Neuron 2002;35:415–418.
50 Lemischka I: A few thoughts about the plasticity of stem cells. Exp Hematol 2002; 30:848–852.
51 Poulsom R, Alison MR, Forbes SJ, Wright NA: Adult stem cell plasticity. J Pathol 2002;197:441–456.
52 Torrente Y, Belicchi M, Pisati F, Pagano SF, Fortunato F, Sironi M, D'Angelo MG, Parati EA, Scarlato G, Bresolln N: Alternative sources of neurons and glia from somatic stem cells. Cell Transplant 2002;11:25–34.
53 Holden C, Vogel G: Stem cells. Plasticity: Time for a reappraisal? Science 2002;296: 2126–2129.
54 Tsai RY, Kittappa R, McKay RD: Plasticity, niches, and the use of stem cells. Dev Cell 2002;2:707–712.
55 Krause DS: Plasticity of marrow-derived stem cells. Gene Ther 2002;9:754–758.
56 Vescovi A, Gritti A, Cossu G, Galli R: Neural stem cells: Plasticity and their transdifferentiation potential. Cells Tissues Organs 2002;171:64–76.
57 Loeffler M, Roeder I: Tissue stem cells: Definition, plasticity, heterogeneity, self-organization and models – A conceptual approach. Cells Tissues Organs 2002;171:8–26.
58 Hawley RG, Sobieski DA: Somatic stem cell plasticity: To be or not to be. Stem Cells 2002;20:195–197.
59 Theise ND, Krause DS: Toward a new paradigm of cell plasticity. Leukemia 2002;16:542–548.

Rev. Roberto Colombo, PhD

Università Cattolica del Sacro Cuore,
Largo A. Gemelli 1,
IT–20123 Milan (Italy)
Tel. +39 02 7234 2284, E-Mail rcolombo@mi.unicatt.it

Blazer S, Zimmer EZ (eds):
The Embryo: Scientific Discovery and Medical Ethics.
Basel, Karger, 2005, pp 53–73

An Islamic Perspective

Ahmad Natour[a,b,c] Baha'eddin Bakri[d,e]
Vardit Rispler-Chaim[f]

[a]Moslem High Court of Appeals, Jerusalem; [b]Faculty of Law, Tel-Aviv University, Tel Aviv; [c]Natanya Academy College Law School, Interdisciplinary Institute, Herzliya, Israel; [d]Washington College of Law, American University, Washington, D.C., USA; [e]Noon Center for Quranic Researches and Studies, Ramallah; [f]Department of Arabic Language and Literature, University of Haifa, Haifa, Israel

This paper tries to determine when human life begins according to the Islamic tradition. The beginning of life, a fascinating topic that can be studied from various points of view, will be studied here in its Islamic legal and ethical aspects. The paper explores the rulings of the Qur'an and the Sunna, the primary sources of Islamic law, the rulings reached by generations of medieval jurists as they appear in their legal compilations (collectively titled Fiqh – Islamic law), which are also based on the Qur'an and Sunna, and the rulings of contemporary jurists and ethicists (*fatwa*s – legal consultations). The fatwa literature is originally structured in a question-answer format. The jurist who issues a fatwa is called a *mufti*. Fatwa literature has been produced from the ninth and tenth centuries CE to the present. Fatwas often discuss and rule on the pertinent questions of the time. Nowadays fatwas serve as the main channel to assess modern technologies and medical ethics, apart from other topics of interest for Muslims [see ref. 1 for the history and content of the fatwa literature].

This paper discusses mainly Islamic Sunni attitudes. The Sunnis comprise 90% of the Muslims in the world. The Shi'i legal system, although having much in common with the Sunni legal system, has some distinct characteristics whose depiction exceeds the scope of this paper. Occasional references to Shi'i Islam will, however, be made when relevant.

The Sources of Islamic Law

Primary Sources

The Qur'an

The Qur'an, literally meaning reading or recitation, is the book, in Arabic, which sums up the content of God's revelations to the Prophet Muhammad, over a period of about 20 years at the beginning of the seventh century CE (according to some Islamic historical sources the revelation to the Prophet Muhammad continued for 23 years). Muslims believe that the Qur'an is the very word of God, and that it is the source book of Islamic ethics and values. The bulk of the Qur'anic content provides mainly general and moral guidance on what the aims and aspirations of Muslims should be. Matters that rank as legal in the strict sense of the term comprise but 500 out of more than 6,200 verses in total of the Qur'an [2].

The Sunna of the Prophet

Sunna literally means a clear path, and also an established course of conduct. The literary work called Sunna is several volumes containing thousands of short narrative reports (each called a *hadith* – a tradition, a speech, or a story) in which the Prophet is recorded to have done, said, and consented (without words) to certain statements, events, and human deeds. Since the Prophet is believed to have been guided by revelation throughout his prophetic mission, the Sunna gained sanctity, and assumed its role as a holy source of law, close to that held by the Qur'an [3]. The Sunna was transmitted orally by Muslims for about two centuries after the death of the Prophet in 632 CE. It was thereafter collected and codified, mostly in the course of the ninth century CE. The foregoing 200-years interval left enough time for additions, omissions, and misquotations to infiltrate the authentic material, so the final version of the Sunna had to be preceded by a strict process of Hadith criticism.[1]

Secondary Sources

The secondary sources of Islamic law are used to explain the primary sources, and adapt new rulings for cases that are not directly discussed in the primary sources. If the primary sources have a clear text on a given question, no further investigation of the jurists is permitted. Independent investigation by a jurist (*ijtihad*)[2] is acceptable only when the Qur'an and Sunna are silent on some issue. The jurist is then called a *mujtahid* (one who exerts himself to extract a ruling). Additional sources of law have been developed by the jurists to enable them to reach a ruling when the Qur'an or the Sunna does not provide an answer.

Ijma', Consensus

This means that if the jurists of a particular generation are unanimous on an issue, this becomes the law to be followed. This source of law derives its authority from the Prophetic hadith, 'My community will never agree upon an error' [2, p. 223]. One *ijma'* can be overruled only by another *ijma'*.

Qiyas, Analogical Deduction

According to this principle, the jurist can determine the relevance of the ruling in one case (which is mentioned in the primary sources) as valid in

1 This process of criticism examined only the authenticity of the chains of transmitters of the hadiths, and concluded with the acceptance of ten main authentic and trustworthy collections of Hadith, attributed to ten different scholars. The two most famous and reliable of them are those by al-Bukhari and Muslim. Their statements on legal issues are treated as law. See: EI (Encyclopaedia of Islam). v. 'Hadith' by J. Robson, especially pp. 24–27.

2 Literally, *ijtihad* means the effort which needs to be exercised by a jurist to reach a ruling over issues under examination. On the different ranks of *mujtahids* in the Sunni world, as well as on the question whether the activity of *ijtihad* indeed stopped in the Sunni world in the tenth century CE, see a special issue of Islamic Law and Society (published by E.J. Brill, Leiden, The Netherlands) 3/2 1996. Also see EI2 (Encyclopaedia of Islam, second edition) v. '*Ijtihad*' by E. Tyan.

another case (absent from the primary sources), because of similarity in the attribute (reason or case) [2, pp. 83–113]. This principle requires that at least one similar case to the one under examination exists, and for which there is a clear ruling in the holy texts.

Other Sources

These include *istihsan* (equity in Islamic law), *istislah*, or *maslaha* (public interest) and *istishab* (presumption of continuity), *'urf*, and *'ada* (local custom), and more[3]. According to these latter sources of law, if the holy sources cannot provide a solution to a legal question, the fact that the public may benefit, or that justice can be served, or that people are used to behaving in a certain way, while no Islamic dogma is violated, may become a source of authority. Many of the modern technologies, as well as medical treatments, have been accepted and legitimized for devout Muslims by way of these 'other sources'.

There are four schools of law in the Sunni Islamic world (each called *madhhab* – school) and they differ in their degrees of acceptance of the secondary sources of law. The Hanafi school, to which adhere about 50% of the Sunni Muslims in the world today, is the most flexible in that it accepts legislation based on all secondary sources. The Hanbali school hardly resorts to any of the secondary sources and rests mainly on the primary sources. The Shafi'i and Maliki schools take a compromising approach, each adopting some but not all of the secondary sources.

Jurists who have been asked to rule on issues pertaining to the beginning of life have followed in their investigation the above order of sources to reach their conclusions. This is true for jurists in the past as well as the present.

The Origins of Life

The Creation of the Embryo

The Qur'an has dedicated a considerable number of verses to the subject of creation. The term 'creation' (*khalq*) or its Arabic derivatives features more than 260 times in the Qur'an [4]. The first creation is always that of Adam,

[3] On *istihsan* see: [2, p. 22]. On *'ada* see: EI2 (Encyclopaedia of Islam, second edition) v. "Ada' by G.H. Bousquet. On 'urf see EI2 (Encyclopaedia of Islam, second edition) v. "*urf*' by G. Libson and F.H. Stewart.

the first man, the father of humanity (*Abu al-Bashar*), who was created by God from clay. Since the creation of Adam, all people are created in a woman's womb, after safely passing through three formative stages of development, and then the fourth crucial stage of ensoulment, until they are ready to be born.

Qur'an 23, 12–14 summarizes this process of creation as follows:

Verily we created man from a product of wet earth. Then placed him as a drop (of seed) (*nutfa*) in a safe lodging. Then fashioned We the drop a clot (*'alaqa*), then fashioned We the clot a little lump (*mudgha*), then fashioned We the little lump bones, then clothed the bones with flesh, and then produced it as another creation. So blessed be Allah, the best of Creators!

Qur'an 22, 5 provides a similar description of the process: ...'We have created you from dust, then from a drop of seed, then from a clot, then from a little lump of fresh shapely and shapeless, that We may make (it) clear for you. And We cause what We will to remain in the wombs for an appointed time, and afterward We bring you forth as infants, then (give you growth) that ye attain your full strength.'

Qur'an 32, 7–9 speaks of the creation from clay, but also mentions the important stage when the soul is blown into the human:

... and He began the creation of man from clay. Then He made his seed from a draught of despised fluid. Then He fashioned him and breathed into him of His spirit, and appointed for you hearing and sight and hearts... [5].

According to the Qur'an and the Sunna, each of the first three stages of pregnancy, namely the *nutfa*, the *'alaqa*, and the *mudgha*, lasts 40 days, altogether 120 days. The *nutfa* is probably the stage of the zygote, the *'alaqa* is when the embryo clings to the wall of the womb, and the *mudgha*, is when the embryo assumes the shape of a chewed substance[4].

[4] Dr. Muhammad 'Ali al-Bar and other Muslim physicians, respond to the first three Qur'anic stages of creation of the fetus, and say that they happen faster than in the Qur'anic account: the stage of the *'alaqa*, they claim, starts at the sixth day of pregnancy, while the stage of *mudgha* starts at day 20 or 21. The creation of the various organs starts at the end of the second month. At day 35, the *mudgha* is 5 mm long, and it grows to about 3–5 cm until the end of the second month. The creation of all organs ends toward the end of the third month, when the fetus is about 10 cm long and weighs about 55 g. [6, 34–36]. According to Keith L. Moore. Scientific interpretation of references to embryology in the Qur'an. In The Journal of the Islamic Medical Association, January–June 1986, vol. 18, pp 15–16, *mudgha* takes its name from the notion that 'the somites at the back of the embryo somewhat resemble teeth marks in a chewed substance'.

Only after the first 120 days of pregnancy does Allah send the angel that breathes the spirit or soul (*ruh*) into the human body, and consequently it becomes a true human being.

Blowing the Soul into the Embryo (*Nafkh al-ruh*)

The presence of human life or 'personhood' is identified with the presence of the soul in a human being. The fact that one's heart is beating, for example, is not indicative of one's vitality, nor is it proof of the existence of his soul. This circumstance has been applied to cases related to the beginning of life, as well as to cases related to the end of life, when the heart may still be beating but the brain stem is diagnosed as dead [7]. The beating heart is thus no sign of 'personhood'.

The embryo does not acquire the legal effects of being human from its very first creation; this happens only after 120 days of pregnancy have lapsed. From a medical point of view, the presence of *ruh* is marked by voluntary movements of the fetus in the womb and by a speedy development. The external form of the fetus is complete [6].

Mufti al-Sha'rawi, for example, referred to the first 120 days of pregnancy as 'a man in potential' (*insan bil-quwwa*), while after 120 days it becomes 'an actual man' (*insan bil-fi'l*) [8].

The two different statuses of the fetus, before and after 120 days, will have an immense impact on the permissibility to abort fetuses in Islamic law and ethics. The first 120 days, when it is not legally and fully a human, will render the option of premeditated abortion less of a crime. Therefore, when one causes the loss of a fetus younger than 120 days one must pay an indemnity to the parents, especially if the loss resulted from a violent act; still it will be lower than if the fetus had been older than 120 days.

Harm to a fetus caused by a third party after 120 days of its development that results in its premature birth and subsequent death requires blood money (*diya*) to be paid to the mother. If it was aborted dead, a smaller compensation (*ghurra*) is due to her, as the fetus at that stage is believed to be like one of her organs. The various laws concerning the aborted fetus aim to emphasize that every human life is valuable and inviolable. Moreover, a fetus older than 120 days is entitled to certain monetary rights, for example, from its father's bequest, and also to bequeath to others, like every living child [9]. The moment of ensoulment thus constitutes a major divide between the two stages in embryonic development, between the potential of becoming human and the existence of a full human being.

Abortion

In Islamic law and ethics, abortion (*ijhad* or *isqat al-haml*) is not totally banned, nor is it totally allowed. Rulings on abortion significantly differ in the various schools of law. The Shafi'i school sets the boundary between permission and prohibition of abortion at 42 days of pregnancy [10, p. 248]. But not all Shafi'is follow suit. Al-Ghazzali (d.1111 C.E.), for example, did not allow abortion at all (similarly to the Hanbali Ibn Rajab [11]). According to him, fertilization resembles the creation of a contract, and obligations result from the breaking of contracts. But his is a minority opinion. If abortion is conducted with the acquiescence of both spouses and is performed safely, it is permitted by all four schools. However, the schools differ on when during the pregnancy the abortion may be performed.

The Hanafi jurists hold several different opinions, the dominant one being that abortion is permissible until the end of the fourth month. This most lenient approach coincides with the identification of ensoulment at 120 days of pregnancy. The Maliki and Hanbali schools regard abortion as impermissible at any stage, and take an increasingly grave view of the crime with the progression of the pregnancy [10, p. 257].

Modern jurists are also divided on the issue of abortion. Their respective positions are influenced by whether or not they view abortion as similar to infanticide (*wa'd*), a pre-Islamic usage already utterly forbidden in the Qur'an. A possible likeness between the two cases is that in both an existing life is terminated by violence (true for a fetus after 120 days of pregnancy). Others view abortion as similar to coitus interruptus (*'azl*), which is largely ruled 'not recommended' (*makruh*) by Islamic law but seldom prohibited (*haram*). This comparison suits the first 120 days of pregnancy, the stage of a fetus before ensoulment. During this stage the fetus has no life, and the destruction of the embryo can be likened to the spilling of semen (a lifeless material as well). *'Azl* and early abortion aim at the same goal, not to let the semen/the fetus reach the womb/continue its development [12, pp. 8–10].

The present Sheikh al-Azhar, Muhammad Sayyid Tantawi, permits abortion but requires that it be done through a clinically safe method. The Syrian mufti Mustafa al-Zarqa' ruled it 'not recommended'. Other jurists, such as Mahmud Shaltut and Wahba al-Zuhayli, ruled that abortion is impermissible from the moment of creation [6, p. 166]. The previous Sheikh al-Azhar, Jad al-Haqq 'Ali Jad al-Haqq, considered abortion within the first 120 days of pregnancy a means of family planning, hence permissible [12, p. 11].

Al-Sha'rawi was not opposed to abortion during the first 120 days of pregnancy, nor were Sheikh 'Atiyya Saqr and others [12, p. 9].

When the mother's life is at risk all jurists conclude that abortion is mandatory, even if later than 120 days of pregnancy. Being not yet born, the fetus is inferior to its mother, and when it endangers the mother it is the fetus that should be sacrificed. The mother is a living human being, and the fetus, even after 120 days of development, is secondary, as long as its head has not emerged at birth. Saving life is a prime duty in Islamic law and ethics, and the mother's life must therefore be saved, even at the cost of sacrificing her fetus. Not saving the mother's life, or letting mother and fetus die, would be equated with killing her, and no one (physician, husband, a jurist) would be a willing party to such a crime.

Even those who view abortion as a permissible option do not consider it desirable. But in certain cases some jurists may justify abortion.

If the pregnant mother is still breast-feeding an infant, her pregnancy is believed to reduce the quality of her milk, hence to endanger the nursing child's life. In such a case the fetus, who is the unborn child, must be aborted in order to save the life of the existing infant. The living child has priority over the unborn. Others stipulate that abortion is required only if the infant's father is financially unable to hire a wet-nurse [13]. If the baby's source of nourishment is guaranteed the need for abortion is waived. As for the option of buying milk from mothers' milk banks, this is generally undesirable. Since milk banks provide no identification of the mothers who donate the milk, and since there is a prohibition in Islamic law against the marriage of a man and a woman who when they were infants nursed from the same woman, there is reluctance to use these banks. Only a single donation, not on a permanent basis, and only in an emergency, may be allowed [12, pp. 122–125]. With the availability nowadays of artificial baby food formulas on the one hand, and while the health advantages of mother's milk is increasingly emphasized on the other, this dilemma of whether to abort while breast-feeding has to undergo further reassessment.

Parents' poverty, or low standard of living, has for many centuries been the subject of controversy over whether it justifies abortion or not. Those who refuse to take the economic factor into consideration rely on two verses in the Qur'an; these are **6**, 152 and **17**, 31. The first reads: '...and that ye slay not your children because of penury – We provide for you and for them –...' The latter reads: 'Slay not your children, fearing a fall to poverty, We shall provide for them and for you. Lo! The slaying of them is great sin.'

Contemporary jurists, on the issue of poverty, often use the saying 'God's table is wide', implying that God will provide enough food for all His creatures. Those who doubt God's ability to provide for all His creation have lost faith in God. Poverty and richness, it is added, are temporary conditions; they may instantly change with God's will. Others justify abortion for poor parents lest they deteriorate economically, and more especially emotionally and functionally.

Raising children is known to be a difficult task, sometimes a testing period for their parents (*fitna*). Some parents might perhaps opt not to repeat an unpleasant experience. In densely populated countries such as Pakistan it is sometimes advised to keep the family small so as to favor 'quality over quantity' [14]. 'Quality' is usually understood to be good education and a high standard of living. In such countries the demographic tendencies are probably encouraged by the political regime.

Even when quantity is encouraged it is sometimes justified by political arguments. In Egypt, for example, several jurists have urged to keep the birth rates high since the 'nation' needs more working hands and more soldiers [12, p. 13, ff. 28].

If the fetus is diagnosed in the womb as impaired (*mushawwah*), as prenatal screening now allows us to know, is it acceptable according to Islamic ethics to abort it?

Ghanim [6, pp. 183–186] quotes several jurists who condone the abortion of an impaired fetus if it has not yet passed the 120 days of pregnancy, and if the impairment is so serious that it will not allow the person that this fetus will eventually become to live a decent life. It is stipulated that experts must rule on the impairment as incurable, and that a trustworthy medical committee must testify to the severity of the fetal condition. This was the ruling of the Assembly of Islamic Jurisprudence held in Mecca on February 10, 1990; for permission to abort for genetic defects until 120 days, see al-Hashimi [15]. But other voices are sounded on this issue.

Other jurists question whether one human being can decide for another that the latter's life is worthless and that it lacks dignity. Are not the parents and the physicians who favor the abortion of disabled fetuses 'playing God'? Jurists who deny the right to abort an impaired fetus claim that medical knowledge is constantly developing, and the absence of a cure today does not mean that tomorrow one may not be found, even for the worst disease. Besides, it is argued that in most cases it is materialistic considerations and the interest of the family that will have to care for the disabled child take precedence, not the real chances of the disabled fetus/child to survive [6, pp. 183–184; 16, pp. 81–95].

After 120 days of pregnancy the fetus is a human being enjoying his or her rights in full. A person should never be killed merely because he or she is disfigured. The only legal justification to abort after 120 days is if the mother's life is in danger. Compelling needs leading to abortion should actually exist and be clearly evident. They should not be 'possible' or 'anticipated'. It should be known with certainty what the results might be if the compelling condition is ignored and abortion is not opted for [17].

As for fetuses which are the result of rape, the late Sheikh al-Azhar, Jad al-Haqq 'Ali Jad al-Haqq, as well as Sheikh al-Qaradawi and others, ruled that it must not be aborted. The reasons they gave are that the fetus did not perpetrate any crime, so it does not deserve to be killed. Even if the woman was raped by enemies, such as the Croatians in Bosnia or the Russians in Chechnya, the fetus is anyway born a Muslim. (If the father is unknown, the religion of the child is always that of its mother, in this case – Islam.) A Muslim, they continue, may be killed only for a crime he or she has committed. But the fetus of rape is innocent, and therefore deserves to be allowed to live [6, pp. 175–179]. The jurists recommend that women made pregnant by rape persevere and be patient, trust in God, and go on with their daily lives, raising the undesired child, with or without a husband [16, pp. 87–90]. The families of raped women and the surrounding society are urged to accept and succor these women and their children. Young men are encouraged to marry the rape victims so as to prevent the women from becoming sinners and a source of family shame.

The few jurists who do justify abortion in such cases are driven exactly by the latter motives; raped women become social outcasts, and their families usually resort to murdering their daughters to protect the honor and good reputation of the family. At other times the raped woman may choose to commit suicide instead.

Those who rule the abortion of fetuses of rape legitimate, allow it only during the first 40 days of pregnancy [6, p. 177]. In 1999, Sheikh' Ikrima Sabri, the Chief Mufti of the Palestinian Authority, set an important precedent. He permitted Muslim women who were raped in Kosovo to take an abortifacient medicine to terminate the pregnancy. His argument was that this could prevent Muslim women from giving birth to Serbs, especially men, who may be in the future may be enlisted by the Serbs to fight Muslims

[16, p. 88]. His argument stems from political or military considerations, but the precedent has nevertheless been set.

Rulings Concerning Modern Medical Applications

Artificial Insemination
Since adoption is outlawed in Islamic law, artificial insemination has become one of the most helpful means for infertile Muslim couples trying to produce children.

Two types of artificial insemination exist, internal and external.

Internal insemination is defined as injecting a male's sperm into a woman's vagina so that it may reach the ovum and natural fertilization will then take place. This process is allowed only if the sperm is the husband's and the ovum is his wife's, and while their marital contract is valid [18]. Insemination of the wife by her husband's sperm after his death is accordingly not permitted: the marital contract expires with the death of either spouse. Several jurists explained that permission for a wife to use her deceased husband's sperm might be an avenue for other women to conceal illicit sexual conduct, claiming that they became pregnant with their late husband's sperm. This is a possibility, because according to Islamic law, in the year following the husband's death any child born to his wife is considered the late husband's offspring. Contrary to this, on November 16, 1988, Sheikh 'AbdAllah al-Mushidd published a fatwa in which he allowed the wife to use her husband's sperm after his death [12, p. 23].

Artificial insemination with the husband's sperm is allowed because Islamic law recognizes that pregnancy can occur even without penetration. A woman may herself insert her husband's sperm into her vagina.

The use of artificial insemination methods is not viewed as interference with God's will. God created the sperm and the egg, and fertilization will in any case not take place unless God so desires. The medical technique merely facilitates the encounter of sperm and egg. Since artificial insemination does not have a 100% success rate, this proves that God is in charge of the outcome, not the assisting physician. Any pregnancy that does or does not take place is a result of God's will.

The husband's sperm must not be mixed with a donor's sperm, nor should a sperm donation be taken for this purpose from a sperm bank. The introduction of 'foreign' sperm (of a man who is not married to her) into the wife's vagina will constitute adultery (*zina*). This is one of the most heinous crimes mentioned in the Qur'an, and it entails a sentence of death by stoning for the married adulterer or adulteress, and flogging for the unmarried partner to adultery, male or female.

As for the way that the sperm is extracted from the man, by masturbation (*istimna'*), pumping out, or any other means, although not desired these acts are not totally prohibited (they rank as *makruh*) [19][5]. They would make artificial insemination illegal.

Some questions still need to be discussed in this domain. For example, is artificial insemination allowed in the husband's absence or against his will? Can artificial insemination be conducted during the period following a divorce that is not final (*talaq ba'in baynuna sughra*) (a certain period after the divorce)? Would artificial insemination be allowed during the *'idda* (the waiting period of 3 months that a divorcee has to observe, or the 4 months and 10 days that the widow has to wait before remarrying)? The *'idda* means that technically, and with regard to rights and duties, the husband and wife are still married. Most probably artificial insemination would not be permitted during the *'idda* as it should be treated analogously to natural intercourse, requiring the husband's consent.

External artificial insemination or IVF means that the ovum is fertilized in ways different from natural sexual intercourse, and that the fertilization takes place outside a woman's womb, usually in a test-tube at the laboratory.

The original IVF means that the wife's ovum is fertilized by the husband's sperm in a test-tube, and after a few days of development the embryo, when it is about 4–8 cells, it is transplanted into the wife's womb to continue its development till birth. This method can be effective in cases where the wife's fallopian tubes are blocked, and there is no access between the ovaries and the womb. Islamic law has no objection to this method, as long as precautions are taken to guarantee that only the husband's sperm and only his wife's ovum are used in the fertilization process. Any sperm or ovum donated by a third party, not by the husband or the wife, would lead to a situation equal in its sinfulness to adultery, and deserve appropriate punishment; such cases are totally forbidden [20]. The prohibition remains effective whether the fertilized ovum is partially by donor (only the sperm

[5] Masturbation is generally prohibited by all schools of law. But, if lust overcomes a person, and he might therefore fall into adultery, *istimna'* is the lesser evil. It ranks as 'undesirable', but not 'forbidden' [19].

or only the ovum), or if the whole zygote is a donation, and whether the zygote is transplanted after fertilization into the wife's womb or into a surrogate mother's womb [6, pp. 240–241]. Surrogate parenting is not permitted in Islamic law [21]. A child born through a surrogate mother would have to undergo adoption by the biological father to gain social legitimization, but adoption is forbidden, as mentioned. Thus, another sin (adoption) is added to the sin of using a 'foreign' womb in which to transplant the zygote.

For a test-tube fertilization to be legitimate, a trustworthy Muslim physician has to supervise the process. The Muslim physician must verify that neither 'foreign' sperm to the marriage nor a 'foreign' ovum has been involved in the fertilization. Also, in the case of frozen embryos, if fertilization has succeeded and the couple desires no more pregnancies, or one of the spouses has died or the marriage has ended in divorce, the remaining reproductive material must be destroyed. This includes all remaining zygotes, sperm, and ova. The use of these 'superfluous' reproductive materials by other people, not the husband and wife who produced the sperm and the ova, is prohibited, as it leads to a result similar to illicit sexual ties (*zina*). For this reason, sperm banks are entirely outlawed in Islamic law because they do not examine whether blood ties exist between the donor and the recipient. They thereby violate the Islamic determination to preserve lawful blood relations between children and their parents [12, p. 25].

The transplant of a fertilized ovum is possible only while marriage still lasts. After divorce or death the transplant of the zygote into the wife's womb is prohibited [22]. The IVF process, like intercourse, also requires the consent of both spouses.

A few jurists object to the whole process of IVF out of fear that someone might abuse the technology, or someone at the lab might cheat and cause irreversible damage to the pure lineages so cherished by Islamic law and society. Eventually, they maintain, what may have started as a good cause of helping childless couples could open the door to endless risks for the whole of Islamic society [6, pp. 246–247, see also J Islamic Med Assoc (USA) 1987;3:461].

Some of the risks that IVF may entail are:

1 An affluent woman may choose to hire another woman's womb to carry her fetus until birth. Thus, the affluent woman will not have to undergo the hardships of pregnancy and labor, the changes in her external appearance, and especially gaining weight, and losing, at least temporarily, her beautiful figure.

2 While in the natural fertilization process only strong and healthy spermatozoa succeed in penetrating the ovum, in the IVF process even weak and sick sperm cells may end up doing so, hence weak and sick people, carriers of genetic, physical, and mental disorders, might be born. Better then to avoid the process completely, since the outcome might be hazardous. One principle in Islamic law suggests that in order to avoid the damage involved in an idea or a technology, it is sometimes preferable to forgo altogether the benefits that accrue from these same ideas and technologies [23]. Analogously, IVF should be abandoned, even though it may entail some benefits to humans, because it may also entail danger.

Children who are conceived through IVF technology, by one or two 'foreign' donors, namely the donors/owners of sperm and ovum are not married to one another, are considered in Islamic law a *laqit* (foundling), a child whose lineage is dubious. At best they can establish lineage to their mothers, but never to their biological fathers, since no marital bonds connected the owner of the sperm and the owner of the ovum [24]. Needless to say, these children are doomed in respect of their social status.

Cloning

Human cloning is generally banned by most Sunni jurists [25]. There are several explanations for this:

1 It is not healthy to found a society on cloned people; this is also the perception of other religions [26].
2 It is difficult for governments to control the scientific experiments by law, so each laboratory or factory can do whatever it wishes with cloning. It is an opening for the abuse of technology. Therefore, for example, Presidents Clinton, Chirac, and Kohl outlawed human cloning [27].
3 The cell that is chosen for the cloning process is mature. It is not clear what impact this has on the cloned person; it is suspected that he or she might suffer from rapid aging and geriatric diseases at young age [27].
4 If the cloning process fails, what should become of the disfigured persons created? Will they be killed? Will their organs be sold on the organ stock exchange? Will they be displayed in semi-zoos so that others can witness the tragic results of those playing with genes?
5 Cloning reduces humanity to a level of bestiality, deprived of emotions and noble intentions [27].

6 Cloning may produce more health hazards to the cloned person than the natural fertilization.
7 In a normal fertilization process maternal and paternal genetic material becomes mixed so a diversity of individuals are born, and all are stronger and enjoy better disease resistance. Non-sexual reproduction is like taking a picture of another picture; the more times the picture is taken, the less clear it becomes. By analogy, cloning might weaken humankind.
8 Cloning causes a mixture of genealogical lines. From a genetic point of view, the cloned man is like a twin brother of the man he was cloned from (the owner of the cell). The cloned man is not his son, even if the embryo was transplanted into the womb of the latter's wife. Therefore, cloning will never be able to solve the problem of infertile couples, as expected. They will not produce children, only twin brothers and sisters, duplicates of themselves [28].
9 Because of the blurring of genealogical lines, the making of humans through cloning hinders the performance of many religious duties such as marriage, maintenance of children and wives, tracing paternity, inheritance, guardianship, blood ties, and more [29]. Certain parts of Islamic law may even become irrelevant.
10 Cloning is an attempt by scientists to create humans in the lab, while human creation is only possible by Allah, and in a woman's womb [30].
11 Man is not only a sum of genes, but also the product of his family, education, and environment, so that a successful cloning will at best manage to duplicate only one part of human existence, not all of it [28].

Despite the widespread objection to human cloning, a few favor it. These are several Shi'i scholars such as Muhammad Husayn FadlAllah [31], the leader of the Hizbullah group in Lebanon, Sheikh Mustafa al-Harandi [31, p. 18] of Iran, and Sheikh Muhammad Sa'id al-Hakim [31, p. 18] of Najaf, Iraq. Their support for human cloning is interesting and surprising. But it should be remembered that not all Shi'i jurists share their attitude.

Arguments in favor of human cloning:

1 Cloning is not a 'new' creation, but rather a disclosure and an exposition of the secrets of nature, which God Himself has created and made enjoyable for man. Those secrets have existed in the world since Creation. It is man's limited ability that only recently has enabled him to discover these secrets and make use of them.

2 The Qur'an mentions three unusual ways of creation by God, which are different from fertilization of the egg by sperm: Adam, the first man on earth, was created from clay; Hawa, his wife, was created from Adam's rib; and 'Isa (Jesus), was miraculously created in a virgin's womb without having a father. According to this rationale, cloning can be considered one more of these 'unusual' ways.

3 The response to the critique that cloning will enable scientists to select the characteristics of the cloned person is that Islamic law, since its early history, has advised parents on how to secure certain desired qualities in their offspring, through the consumption of certain foods, timing of the intercourse, etc. Predetermination of the cloned person's characteristics is therefore not a new achievement, nor is it prohibited.

4 Islamic law can be applied to the cloned person. Interesting attempts to show that this is workable have been made by al-Harandi on several issues; the issue of inheritance is given below as an example.

5 The cloned child does not qualify as 'a Shar'i child', a child conceived from the merging of his or her mother's egg with the sperm of her lawfully wedded husband, his or her father. Cloning has produced a new form of 'fatherhood' and 'motherhood', so the question arises of how the cloned child will inherit? The Islamic laws of inheritance are prescribed as early as the Qur'an, and they are very precise; a non-Shar'i child is not entitled to a share of his or her 'father's' estate. However, a father, according to Islamic law, has the right to bequeath up to one third of his estate (*wasiyya*, will) to whomever he chooses other than a Shar'i heir. (There is a Prophetic tradition '*la wasiyya liwarith*' (there is no will in favor of an heir); it means that legal heirs cannot be willed to. See on the laws of the will EI2 [32]. See on laws of inheritance EI2 [33].) This third can be allocated to the cloned child so that he or she is not deprived of all financial rights. The general rules of *wasiyya* are true for Sunni and Shi'i schools of law. However, several Shi'i traditions, based on a unique interpretation of Qur'an 2:180, do permit a *wasiyya* to benefit Shar'i heirs, such as one's children or wives. For al-Harandi, a Shi'i jurist, a will in favor of a cloned child can be legitimate, whether the cloned child is recognized as a Shar'i heir (at least to the mother, the donor of the egg) or not. This financial solution, offered by al-Harandi, begs the question of whether there is a father-son relationship at all between the 'father' and the cloned 'son', or of what type of relationship, hence commitments, exist between them. Yet despite the questions left open, the cloned child has been placed

within the consensus. This is indicative that for al-Harandi and his like cloning can be accommodated by Islamic law as an innovative, but at the same time desirable mode of bringing new people to life. After all, al-Harandi concludes in his book, human cloning is no more than utilizing nature's laws, God's laws, to bring a wanted child to life.

Embryo Research

Any type of medical action on human embryos that aims at providing treatment for the embryo itself is definitely permissible. Medical experimentation on the embryos, if it does not adversely affect it, is allowed as well, as long as actions that might harm the embryo are avoided. Medical experiments that may damage the living embryo are strictly prohibited. Also, induced miscarriages for the sake of obtaining organs for transplant were outlawed by the Islamic Assembly of Jurisprudence held in Jeddah in 1990. The Assembly did allow the use of dead embryos' organs in transplants as long as they are not traded commercially [34].

According to other jurists, parts of the embryo may be donated by its father and mother for research if it is younger than 120 days and both parents consent. At that stage the embryo is not yet a human being; it belongs to its parents, and they may do with it as they choose [35]. The donation of living embryos for research purposes is also permissible if it is done when they are in their first stages of development, and no suffering is caused to the mother, the owner of the ovum [36, p. 118]. Another stipulation is that the research be done as early as possible in the development of the embryo: the stage of the *nutfa* is preferable to the stage of the *'alaqa*, and the latter stage is preferable to the stage of the *mudgha* [36, p. 121]. This flexible ruling refers to embryos still in a test tube, frozen embryos, and embryos of natural miscarriages only, not to embryos that would intentionally be aborted to serve as a source of organs for transplant. From the above ruling, one may deduce that research on stem cells, which is conducted on embryos in their very first days after fertilization, when they are not yet human according to Islamic ethics, and not yet implanted in the womb, may win the approval of most Muslim jurists. This assumption is supported by the knowledge that 'superfluous' or 'unnecessary' zygotes are anyway destined for destruction, and no further reproductive role may be assigned to them. The chief stipulation attached to permission to conduct stem cell research is that they will not be used in reproductive processes, only in research, that they will not be used commercially, and that only authorized and supervised medical centers will be allowed to conduct such research [36, pp. 120–126]. But since this research holds so much promise for the discovery of new cures and medicines, and for the welfare of human beings, it is reasonable to anticipate that it will gain more Muslim jurists' approval on the basis of such legal principles as *maslaha* and equity (the secondary sources of Islamic law).

Conclusions

Islamic legal texts, relying on Qur'anic verses and the Sunna, describe in detail the stages in the creation and formation of the embryo. The various understandings of the holy texts lead to different rulings concerning the human embryo. These rulings have always had a direct impact on attitudes to abortion among the jurists.

The Shafi'i school based its ruling that abortion must not be performed later than 40 days after conception on the perception that the formation of the fetus is complete in the sixth week of pregnancy. The Hanafi jurists permitted abortion until the fetus is 120 days old, based on the understanding that ensoulment takes place 120 days after conception. Contemporary jurists are also divided, in keeping with the above views, on whether abortion is permitted at all, and if it is, at what time during pregnancy.

When there is a compelling need, or if there is a justified Shar'i reason, such as danger to the mother's life, abortion of the fetus is permitted even after 120 days of pregnancy. The compelling need should be real, certain, and apparent.

With regard to artificial insemination, internal or external, all methods are legitimate provided that only the spouses contribute to the creation of the embryo. This means that the sperm and ovum must belong to a married couple, and the fertilized ovum must be returned only to the owner of the ovum's womb. No surrogate motherhood is permissible in Islamic law and ethics. Artificial insemination may not occur after the death of the husband, or without his consent.

Human cloning is prohibited by the majority of Sunni and Shi'i jurists as interference in God's creation, and as holding more hazardous than helpful effects on the continuation of humankind; only a very few Shi'i jurists legitimize human cloning.

Embryo research is permissible if it aims at curing the embryo itself, and if the experiments do not harm the embryo. It is forbidden to induce miscarriages in order to obtain fetal organs for transplant. Organs of dead fetuses were already legitimized in 1990 by the Assembly of Islamic Jurisprudence to be used in transplants. But no commercial use of organs is permissible. Parts of embryos and 'superfluous' embryos may be donated for research if those embryos are younger than 120 days and both parents consent. This ruling probably applies only to embryos in test tubes, frozen embryos, and embryos of natural miscarriages.

Research on stem cells, if, as pledged, is strict in using only 'superfluous' 2- to 4-day-old embryos, and probably only those still in test-tubes, has a good chance of gaining Muslim jurists' approval. Other stipulations that may accompany such permission are that both parents consent, that the stem cells are not used for reproduction but only for research, and that the benefits derived from the research will outweigh the detriments.

The tolerance and flexibility of Islamic law that are demonstrated in many of the ethical decisions concerning the beginning of life, abortion, artificial insemination, and embryo research stem from the Qur'anic teaching and the Sunna of the Prophet Muhammad. If these two sources do not provide the precise answer to a newly arising question, and before secondary sources are employed, Muslim jurists have to consider the rule 'Allah desireth for you ease; He desireth not hardship for you...' [Qur'an 2:185]. This verse implies that God aims at the well-being of all humans, not at their suffering. When jurists utilize the secondary sources of Islamic law, especially *maslaha* and *istihsan*, to solve ethical dilemmas, they also respond to God's will.

References

1 Muhammad Khalid Masud, Messick B, Powers DS (eds): Islamic Legal Interpretation, Muftis and Their Fatwas. Cambridge, Harvard University Press, 1996.

2 Wael B Hallaq: A History of Islamic Legal Theories. Cambridge, Cambridge University Press, 1997, vol 37, p 3.

3 Muhammad al-Ghazzali: Hadha Dinuna (This is our faith). Damascus, Dar al-Qalam, 1997, p 209.

4 Muhammad Fu'ad 'Abd al-Baqi: Al-Mu'jam al-Mufahras liAlfaz al-Qur'an al-Karim (The Concordance of the Holy Qur'an). Beirut, Dar al-Fikr, 1987.

5 Mohammed Marmaduke Pickthall (Translator): The Meaning of the Glorious Koran. Washington, The New American Library, 1953.

6 Ghanim U: Ahkam al-Janin fi al-Fiqh al-Islami (The laws concerning the fetus in Islamic law). Kufr Qara' (Israel), Dar al-Huda 2003, pp 35–37.

7 Qararat waTawsiyat Majma' al-Fiqh al-Islami fi Jedda (Decisions and recommendations of the Assembly of Islamic jurisprudence). Beirut, Dar al-Qalam, 1998, decision #17.
8 Al-Sha'rawi. Al-Fatawa. (Fatwas) Cairo, n.d. v.3, 26–27.
9 Ahmad Fathi Bahnasi: Al-Qisas wal-Hudud fi al-Fiqh al-Islami (Criminal justice in Islamic law). Cairo: al-Sharika al-'Arabiyya lil-Tiba'a wal-Nashr 1964, 99–107.
10 Mustafa 'Abd al-Fattah: Jarimat Ijhad al-Hawamil (The crime of abortion of pregnant women). Beirut, Dar Ulu al-Nuha 1996, p 248.
11 Muhammad 'Ali al-Bar: Khalq al-Insan bayna al-Tibb wal-Qur'an (The creation of man between medicine and the Qur'an). Saudi Arabia 1981, p 219.
12 Vardit Rispler-Chaim: Islamic Medical Ethics in the Twentieth Century. Leiden, EJ Brill, 1993, pp 8–10.
13 Mahmud Shaltut: Fatawa. Cairo, Dar al-Qalam, 1960, pp 293–297.
14 Saleem M: Ethical justification of family planning; in: Islamic Studies Journal. Islamic Research Institute. September 1969, v.8/3:253–261.
15 Nisrin bint Muhammad al-Hashimi: Al-I'aqat al-Khalqiyya fi al-Atfal, Asbabuha waRa'y al-Islam fi Turuq al-Wiqaya minha (Physical disabilities in children, the reasons for them, and Islamic views concerning ways to avoid them). London, Dar al-Hikma, 1995, pp 105–106.
16 Vardit Rispler-Chaim: The right not to be born: Abortion of the disadvantaged fetus in contemporary fatwas; in Brockopp JE (ed): Islamic Ethics of Life, Abortion, War and Euthanasia. Columbia, University of South Carolina Press, 2003, pp 81–95.
17 'Abd al-Fattah: Jarimat Ijhad al-Hawamil (The crime of abortion of pregnant women). Beirut, Dar Ulu al-Nuha, 1996, p 284.
18 Assembly of Islamic Jurisprudence, decree #16, 1986, p 34.
19 Ziyad Ahmad Salama: Atfal al-Anabib bayna al-'Ilm wal-Shari'a (Test-tube babies between science and Islamic law). Beirut, Dar al-Bayariq, 1996.
20 Nasr Farid Wasil (the previous mufti of Egypt): 'Amaliyyat atfal al-anabib...halal bishart (Procedures to create test-tube babies...permissible on condition). 'Aqidati March 4, 2003, p 5.
21 Ghazala Javaid: On surrogate motherhood. J Islamic Med Assoc (USA) 1987;19:126.
22 Al-I'tisam. (Egypt) June 1989, pp 38–39.
23 Muhammad Shawqi Ibrahim: Mawqif al-Qur'an al-Karim min Tifl al-Unbub (The Qur'anic position on test-tube babies). Cairo, n.d., p 214.
24 Ghanem Isam: Islamic Medical Jurisprudence. London, Probsthain, 1982, pp 57–58.
25 Assembly of Islamic Jurisprudence in Jeddah, Decree #94 of 1997; in: The Decrees and Recommendations of the Islamic Assembly of Jurisprudence, 1998, p 216.
26 Al-Ra'y al–'Amm: (Egypt) March 15, 1997, p 3.
27 Majma' al-Buhuth al-Islamiyya (Islamic Research Council): Mashru' Bayan al-Istinsakh al-Bashari (The program for human cloning). Majallat al-Azhar 1997;7:1066–1074.
28 Muhammad Sayyid Salama: Al-Istinsakh al-Bayuluji waHimayat Huquq al-Insan (Biological cloning and the protection of human rights). Majallat al-Azhar 1997;8:1249–1253.
29 'Abd al-Qadim Zallum. Hukm al-Shar' fi al-Istinsakh (Islamic law on cloning). Baqa al-Gharbiyya, Maktabat al-Sunna, 1997, pp 9–18.
30 Muhammad Sayyid Tantawi (the present Sheikh al-Azhar): Al-'Alam al-Islami. December 16–22, 1996, p 13.

31 Mustafa al-Harandi: Al-Istinsakh al-Bashari waMawqif al-Shari'a al-Islamiyya (Human cloning and the position of Islamic law). Kuweit, Maktabat al-Alfayn, 1997.
32 Schacht J: The Encyclopedia of Islam, ed 2v. '*wasiyya*' (will).
33 Layish A: The Encyclopedia of Islam, ed 2. v. '*mirath*' (inheritance).
34 Assembly of Islamic Jurisprudence, 1990. Beirut, Dar al-Qalam 1998, p 119, decree #56.
35 Isam Ghanem: Embryo Research: An Islamic Perspective. Med Sci Law 1991;32:14.
36 Muhammad Na'im Yasin: Abhath Fiqhiyya fi Qadaya Tibiyya Mu 'asira (Legal studies of contemporary medical issues). Amman, Dar al-Nafa'is, 2000.

Vardit Rispler-Chaim, PhD

Department of Arabic Language and Literature,
University of Haifa, Mount Carmel, IL–31905 Haifa (Israel)
Tel. +972 4 824 9789, Fax +972 4 824 9710, E-Mail varditrc@research.haifa.ac.il

cells and self-renewal. The isolation, differentiation and culture systems developed for EC cells laid the groundwork for the development of similar methods for ES cells.

By using similar methods to those used to isolate EC cell line, the first ES cell lines were derived from mouse blastocyst in 1981 [6, 7] and the superiority of these cells was revealed: while EC cells tend to demonstrate karyotype instability, ES cells exhibit and maintain normal diploid karyotype during continuous culture. Also, ES cells have better developmental potential, as evident from four main features of mES cells: (1) undifferentiated mES cells consistently contribute to chimeras and particularly to the germ cell line [8]; (2) some mES lines can form entire viable fetuses [9]; (3) subcutaneous injection of mES cells into syngeneic mice induce the formation of teratomas which may include cells of all three germ layers [10], and (4) in vitro aggregations of ES cells result in the formation of EBs with regional differentiation into embryonically distinct cell types [11].

The proven pluripotency of ES cells was used for the development of a variety of in vitro differentiation systems, including induced differentiation systems into hematopoietic stem cell-like cells [12, 13], neural precursors [14, 15], cardiomyocytes [16], and insulin-secreting cells [17, 18]. The availability of such differentiation models and the use of mES cells to promote the research on self-maintenance mechanisms and early mouse development encouraged researchers to isolate ES cells from other species as well. During the last two decades, ES cell lines and ES cell-like lines have been derived from other rodents, such as golden hamsters [19], rats [20] and rabbits [21–23], domestic animal species [24–29] and three non-human primates [30–32]. However, despite the diversity of ES cell lines, it was only mES cell lines which have been reported to demonstrate the complete set of ES cell features, rendering them the most potent research model for ES cell lines.

Differentiation systems are only one method by which ES cells may be obtained. Another source for their isolation is blastocysts produced by the nuclear transfer technique. In this process, a metaphase II oocyte is enucleated, the oocyte's genetic material is removed, and a donor somatic nucleus is inserted either by fusion or injection. The reconstructed oocyte is then activated electrically or chemically, which results in a developing embryo. ES cell lines isolated from nuclear transfer embryos were reported from bovine [33] and mouse [34–36]. The resultant lines and offspring can serve as research models for the studies on reprogramming and imprinting.

Due to the great promise of mES cells as a research tool, great efforts were invested in the derivation of human ES (hES) cells. The first hES cell lines were derived by Thomson et al. [37] in 1998. These lines had been shown to express the main features of ES cells, i.e. prolonged undifferentiated proliferation, self-maintenance, stable developmental potential to differentiate into representative tissues of the three embryonic germ layers both in vivo and in vitro, and exhibition of stable and normal karyotype [37–39]. The availability of hES cell lines provides a unique new tool with widespread potential for both research purposes and clinical applications. hES cells may be utilized in various study areas, such as early human development, differentiation processes, lineage commitment, mechanisms of self-maintenance, gene or protein functions, and drug testing and toxicity. Future development of hES cell differentiation models into specific lineages may lead to their use in cell-based therapy.

Cell-based therapy is the most sought after future application of hES cells. Most chronic human diseases involve the destruction or dysfunction of cells. However, when the main cause of the disease is loss of cells, such as the case of diabetes mellitus or Parkinson's disease, replacement of the lost cells with hES cells may be the optimal solution, as specific cell types will be produced. The proven ability of hES cells to differentiate in vitro into each cell type of the adult body, makes them the optimal source of cells for this purpose. One of the obstacles to utilizing hES for cell-based therapy is graft rejection and donor-recipient compatibility. This problem could be solved by either genetic modification of the HLA antigens or by banking hES cell lines and creating a database of histocompatibility types which will cover large fractions of the population. Recently, the American National Institutions of Health established a task force aiming at characterizing most existing hES cell lines and banking histocompatibility types for worldwide public health use. A third solution may arise from therapeutic cloning of human blastocysts. A recent work by Hwang et al. [40] demonstrated the ability to form human blastocysts by the nuclear transfer technique, and to isolate pluripotent hES cells from these blastocysts. This cloning technology may allow the production of lines by nucleus donation from cell-based therapy candidates. Additional invaluable clinical application of hES cells will be their use as a model for evaluating the efficiency and toxicity of newly developed medicines. The pluripotency of these cells will enable large screening for the effect of new drugs on a variety of tissue types, which will reliably mimic many of the cell-to-cell interactions existing in the human body. The availability of such models may also reduce the need for animals testing.

The formation of hES cells carrying genetic diseases, either by genetic manipulation of the existing lines or by deriving new hES cell lines from surplus sick embryos from preimplantation genetic diagnosis program may add a unique tool for the research on the pathogenesis of genetic diseases. This will enable better understanding of the mechanisms underlining the symptoms of these diseases. Such lines may also be used for the development of gene therapy strategies for these diseases.

Considering all of the above-mentioned advantages, it is clear that hES cells may prove to be a revolutionary tool for clinical research and treatment.

To date, several dozens of apparently normal hES cell lines have been reported worldwide [41]. Their various sources include surplus [37, 39, 42] or low-quality [43] embryos from in vitro fertilization (IVF) programs and embryos produced for research purposes [44], which may raise ethical concerns. The increasing number of available hES cell lines indicates that the derivation of these lines is a reproducible procedure. A recent report put forth the application of the human nuclear transfer technique to rabbit oocytes as a source for deriving hES cell lines for therapeutic application [45] – the hES cell lines produced demonstrated the main features of hES cells. Though possibly useful, the ethical questions arising from this method in respect to therapeutic cloning should be carefully considered.

Derivation of Human Embryonic Stem Cells

Similarly to the isolation of mES cells, there are three methods for the derivation of hES cell lines: immunosurgical isolation, mechanical isolation of the ICM, or the use of intact embryos in whole. The success rates of these procedures reach 30% and 50% for mouse and human, respectively [42, 46].

Immunosurgical Isolation

Immunosurgery was developed during the seventies by Solter and Knowles [47] as a method for the derivation of EC cell lines and for the research on early embryonic development, after which it served as the basis for the first ES cell line derivation from mouse blastocysts [6, 7].

The aim of immunosurgery is to selectively isolate the ICM from the blastocyst. This is done in several stages: first, the glycoprotein outer layer

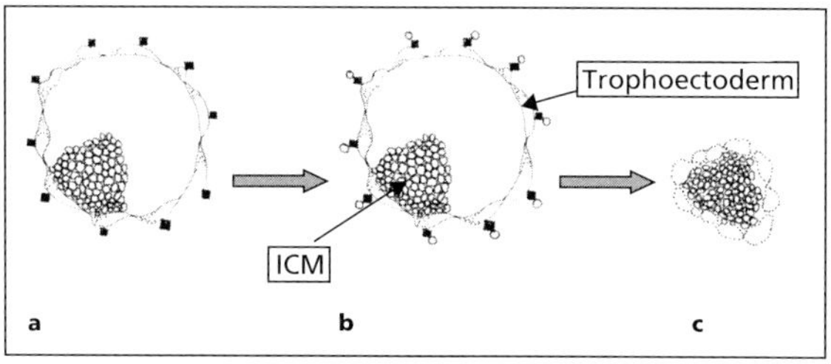

Fig. 1.

Schematic drawing of immunosurgery. **a** Exposed blastocyst incubating in anti-human whole serum antibodies, which recognize and attach to all human cells (*). **b** Further incubation in guinea pig complement-containing medium (/) which lysis all cells marked with the antibodies. **c** The intact ICM surrounded with lysed cells.

of the zona pellucida (ZP) is dissolved by Tyrode's solution or pronase enzyme. Then the exposed embryo is incubated in anti-human whole serum antibodies, which attach to any human cell (penetration of the antibodies into the blastocyst is prevented due to cell-cell connections within the outer layer of the trophoblast). Incubation with guinea pig complement-containing medium which lysis all antibody-marked cells, and the intact ICM is further cultured on mitotically inactivated mouse embryonic fibroblasts (MEFs). These stages are illustrated in figure 1. Since the ZP allows the penetration of both antibodies and guinea pig complement, it may be alternatively removed post lysis by complementary proteins.

Mechanical Isolation

The selective removal of the trophoectoderm layer can also be achieved mechanically. After the embryo is exposed from the ZP, the trophoblast layer is gently removed using 27G needles. As in the immunosurgery method, the last stage comprises of culturing the intact ICM with MEFs. An example of cultured ICM after mechanical isolation is demonstrated in figure 2a.

Plating Intact Embryos in Whole (de novo Isolation)

Contrary to the principal concept of immunosurgery, de novo isolation of hES cell lines does not necessitate the removal of the trophoblasts. Lines can

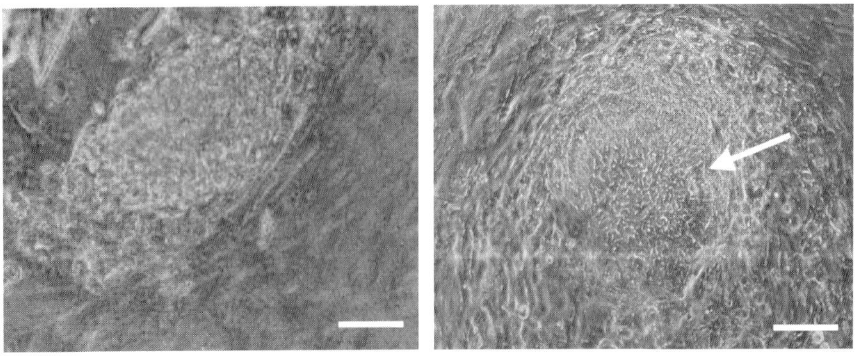

a b

Fig. 2.
ICM cultured with MEFs (**a**) after mechanical removal of the trophoectoderm layer and (**b**) when plated as an embryo in whole. The ICM outgrowth is marked with an arrow [with permission from 74].

be derived simply by plating a zona-free embryo in whole on mitotically inactivated MEFs. The exposed embryo attaches to the feeder layer and flattens, permitting the continuous growth of the ICM, with the surrounding trophoblasts as monolayer. When the ICM reaches a sufficient size, it is removed and propagated (fig. 2b). Although far more straightforward, this method bears the risk of ICM differentiation.

Human Embryonic Stem Cell Culture

The traditional methods developed for culturing EC cells laid the needed infrastructure for the culture of mES cells and later on hES cells. The basic culture conditions of ES cells include MEFs as feeder layer and medium supplemented with fetal bovine or calf serum (FBS). The MEF feeder layer has a dual role, namely to support ES cell growth and to prevent spontaneous differentiation. When cultured in these conditions, ES cells grow as flat colonies with typical spaces between the cells, high nucleus-to-cytoplasm ratio and with the presence of at least two nucleoli (illustrated in fig. 3a). Although they require meticulous care which includes daily medium change, removal of differentiated colonies from the culture and routine passaging every 4–6 days, hES cells can be cultured in large numbers, and frozen and thawed with reasonable survival rates [37, 39, 48].

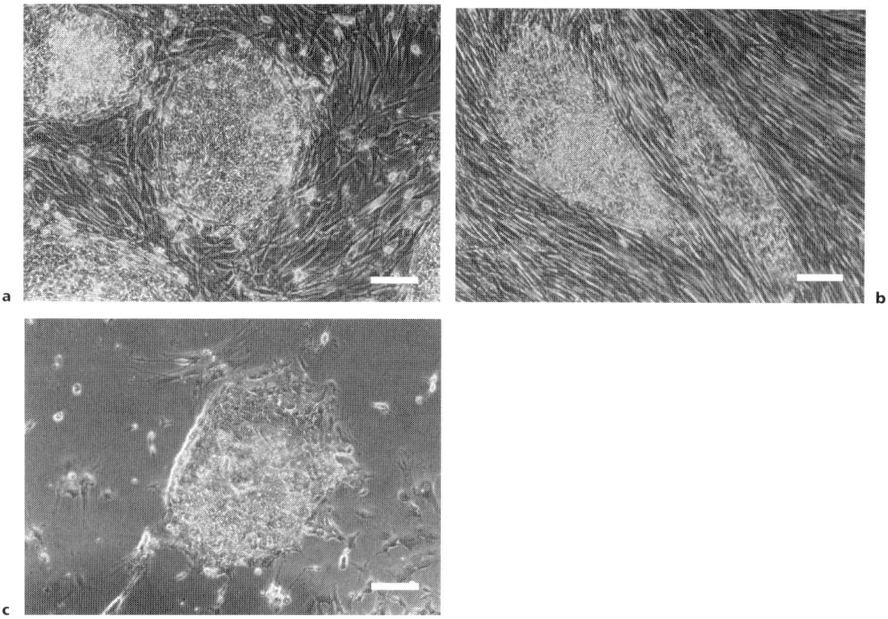

Fig. 3.

hES cell colonies cultured in various culture conditions: with a MEF feeder layer (**a**), with a foreskin fibroblast feeder layer (**b**), and in feeder and serum-free conditions using fibronectin and medium supplemented with TGF-β_1, bFGF and LIF (**c**).

In order to establish a well-defined environment for the culture of both EC and mES cells, a feeder-free culture system was developed. mES cells had been shown to be capable of being cultured continuously as undifferentiated cells without an MEF feeder layer when grown with gelatine and medium supplemented with leukemia inhibitory factor (LIF) [49]. In these conditions, mES cells maintain all their features. In contrast, up until recently, hES cells could be cultured with MEFs only [37, 39]. The possible future uses of hES cells for clinical purposes will require a culture system which will be both well-defined and animal-free. Such culture system will prevent the cells' exposure to animal photogenes and could be accurately repeated.

Since their first derivation in 1998, the culture systems for hES cells have enjoyed three major advances: (1) the ability to grow under serum-free conditions [50]; (2) the use of human feeder layers as substitutes to MEFs

[51–53], and (3) maintenance in an undifferentiated state in feeder-free and serum-free conditions [54, 55].

Two alternatives were suggested as substitute feeders to the MEF feeder layer: human embryo-derived fibroblasts or Fallopian tube epithelial feeder layers [51], and foreskin fibroblasts [52]. Both alternatives were found to support undifferentiated hES cells and the derivation of new hES cell lines [51, 53]. Human serum was used as a replacement for FBS for the formation of animal-free conditions [51]. Furthermore, serum replacement (Invitrogen Corporation®) provides well-defined culture conditions [50, 52]. Using foreskin fibroblasts as feeders, for example, hES cells were cultured for more than 105 passages (over 300 doublings) while exhibiting all their typical features, including expression of typical surface markers and transcription factor Oct4, differentiation into representative tissues of the three embryonic germ layers both in EBs and in teratomas, high telomerase activity and maintenance of normal karyotype (more than 70 consecutive passages) [unpubl. data]. It is noteworthy that the morphology of hES cell colonies grown with foreskin feeder layers is slightly different than that of colonies grown with MEFs in terms of their long and elliptic organization (fig. 3b).

Human feeders have additional advantages. While MEFs proliferate in culture for limited passages only, human feeders (foreskins fibroblasts) can grow to reach up to 42 passages with no difference between the ability of high-passage and low-passage ones to support the growth of hES cells, even after several cycles of freezing and thawing [52]. These feeders may therefore be advantageous when large-scale growth of hES cells is required, such as in the case of therapeutic applications, where not only a large-scale culture system is needed, but also one that is animal-free. The ideal culture method will therefore be the combination of an animal-free matrix and both serum and animal-free medium. The first step towards this solution was reported by Xu et al. [54] who demonstrated for the first time a feeder-free culture system where hES cells were grown on Matrigel, laminin or fibronectin using 100% MEF conditioned medium, supplemented with serum replacement. The major shortcomings of this system are the possible exposure of the cells to mouse pathogens through the conditioned medium, and the absence of a well-defined medium.

A further step forward was achieved by the development of both serum- and feeder-free culture system [55]. Using medium supplemented with serum replacement, transforming growth factor-β_1 (TGF-β_1), basic fibroblast growth factor (bFGF) and LIF, hES cells were cultured for prolonged periods of more than 50 passages with fibronectin [55]. No conditioned medium was used. Cells cultured in these conditions exhibited all ES cell major characteristics. Examples of an undifferentiated hES cell colony grown in such system are illustrated in figure 3c. This method comprises a well-defined culture system which facilitates the future uses of these cells in research practices and provides a safer alternative for future clinical applications. The utilization of an animal-free serum replacement will mark the achievement of the ultimate goal: a well-defined and animal-free culture system for hES cells.

Differentiation Systems for Human Embryonic Stem Cells

As with murine ES cells, when hES cells are detached from the MEF feeder layer and cultured in suspension, they spontaneously create cell aggregates known as embryoid bodies (EBs) [38]. After 24 h in suspension the cells within the EBs organize in two layers, namely an outer layer of endoderm and an inner layer of ectoderm [46]. During the following days a cyst usually forms. Embryonic stem cells within the EBs spontaneously differentiate to cell types from the three embryonic germ layers. Examples for EB development are illustrated in figure 4. Most of the existing methods for directing mES cell differentiation in vitro include the formation of EBs as one of the initial steps, as is the case with differentiation of mES cells into hematopoietic cells [57], neurons [14] and cardiomyocytes [16]. Apparently, the formation of EBs encourages ES cells to differentiate and consequently increases the rate and efficiency of differentiation. hES cells, like mES cells, spontaneously create EBs when cultured in suspension, although these EBs have been found to be somewhat less organized than mES cell-derived EBs [38].

During their 5 years of existence, hES cells have been shown to spontaneously differentiate into cardiomyocytes [58], endothelial cells [59], and insulin-secreting cells [60]. Models for their directed differentiation include neural precursors [39, 61, 62], hematopoietic cells [63, 64], cardiomyocytes [65, 66] trophoblasts [67], hepatocytes [68] and endothelial cells [69]. The fact that an impressive variety of hES cell differentiation models developed in a relatively short time period indicates that the development of differentiation systems similar to those of mES cells is a feasible objective.

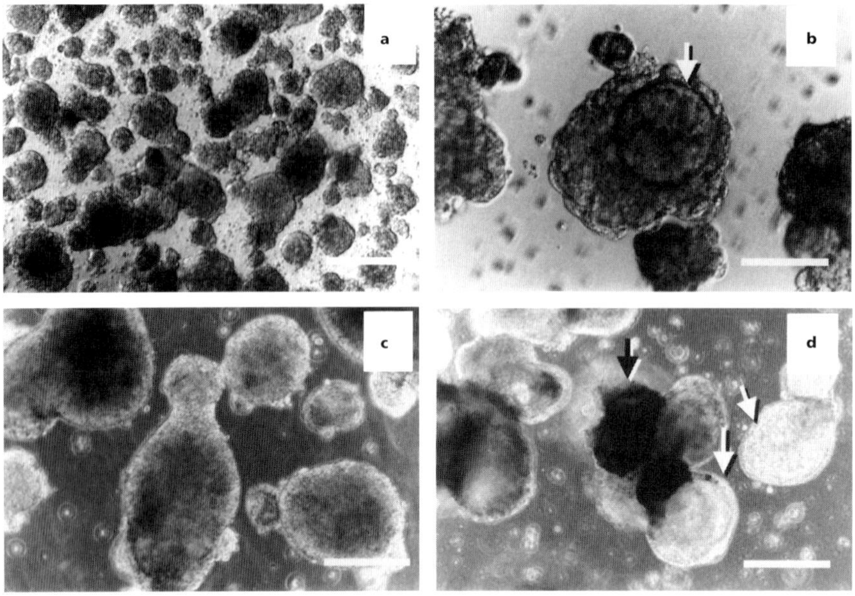

Fig. 4.

EB development. **a** EB formed by H-9 cells following 24 h in suspension. Bar = 100 μM. **b** EB from line I-6 following 48 h in suspension. Note the ectoderm layer (arrow) surrounding the EB. Bar = 75 μM. **c** EB formed by H-9 cells following 4 days in suspension. The EB starts to create a cyst. Bar = 50 μM. **d** EB formed by H-9 cells following 6 days in suspension. Note the well-developed cyst (white arrows) and some melanin-containing cells (black arrow). Bar = 75 μM. From Amit and Itskovitz-Eldor [56].

Similarly to mES cells, hES cells form teratomas following their injection into the hind leg muscle of SCID mice. Within these teratomas, they were shown to differentiate into representative tissues derived from all three embryonic germ layers, including bone and cartilage tissues, striated muscle, gut-like structures, structures resembling fetal glomeruli, neural rosettes, etc. [37, 39]. In some teratomas, hES cells can also create more complex and well-organized organ-like structures, which require cooperation between cells and tissues derived from different germ layers, such as salivary gland-like structures, including the exocrine secretory units and ducts and associated myoepithelial cells, full skin tissues and hair follicles (fig. 5) [42]. The teratoma model therefore serves as an additional method to demonstrate the pluripotency of hES cells.

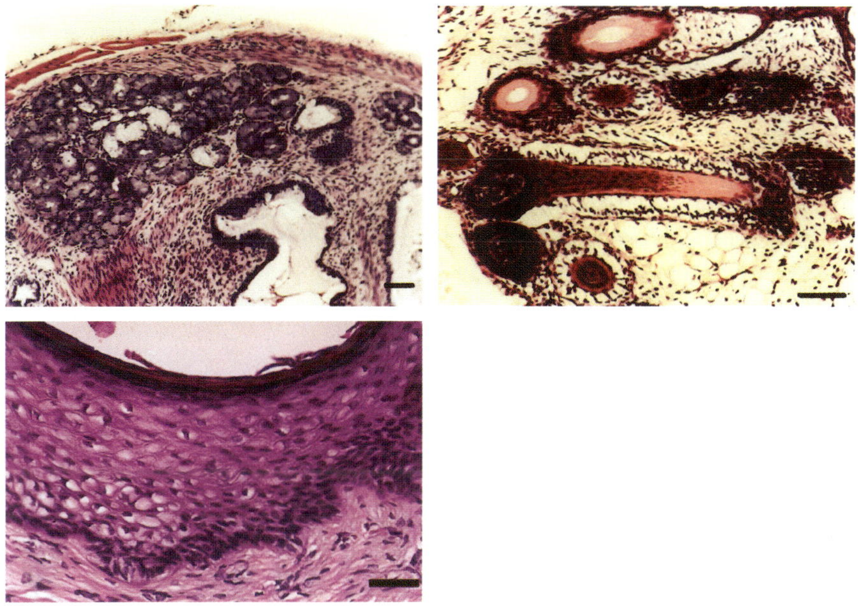

a b c

Fig. 5.

Differentiated hES cells in teratomas. **a** Mixed salivary gland with serous and mucous secretory cells. HE. **b** Group of developing hair follicles. HE. **c** Complete skin tissue. Keratin containing cells facing a large lumen. Bar = 50 μM. **a, b** From Amit and Itskovitz-Eldor [42], and **c** from Amit and Itskovitz-Eldor [56].

Genetic Manipulation of Human Embryonic Stem Cells

One of the most important milestones in the development of research models for mES cells has been the ability to manipulate these cells genetically. Efficient stable transfection methods may be utilized for creating pure populations of cells, directed differentiation, marking of the cells for facilitated recognition in histological slides and the examination of the role of specific genes in embryonic development by gene knockout or over expression methods.

hES cells are easy to transfect and stable transfection protocols were already developed for them. In some, various transfection agents were used [70] while others successfully used lenti-viruses vectors [71, 72].

Another powerful manipulation model is homologous recombination. In mES cell models, homologous recombination was widely used to create knockout mice and to induce differentiation in vitro. The availability of homologous recombination techniques my facilitate the use of hES cells both in basic research and for cell-based therapy. Recently, Zwaka and Thomson [73] demonstrated stable homologous recombination of hES cells by electroporation. Although the success rates were low compared with the existing protocols for mES cells, this study demonstrates that homologous recombination may be introduced to hES cells.

Acknowledgements

The authors thank Mrs. Hadas O'Neill for editing the manuscript and Mr. Assaf Sadeh for hand-sketching figure 1. The research conducted was partly supported by the Fund for Medical Research and Development of Infrastructure and Health Services, Rambam Medical Center, and the Technion Research and Development Foundation, Haifa.

References

1 Reynolds BA, Weiss S: Clonal and population analyses demonstrate that an EGF-responsive mammalian embryonic CNS precursor is a stem cell. Dev Biol 1996;175:1–13.
2 Kahn BW, Ephrussi B: Developmental potentialities of clonal in vitro cultures of mouse testicular teratoma. J Natl Cancer Inst 1970;44:1015–1029.
3 Martin GR, Evans MJ: The morphology and growth of a pluripotent teratocarcinoma cell line and its derivatives in tissue culture. Cell 1974;2:63–72.
4 Evans MJ: The isolation and properties of a clonal tissue culture strain of pluripotent mouse teratoma cells. J Embryol Exp Morphol 1972;28:163–176.
5 Martin GR, Evans MJ: Differentiation of clonal lines of teratocarcinoma cells: Formation of embryoid bodies in vitro. Proc Natl Acad Sci USA 1975;72:1441–1445.
6 Evans MJ, Kaufman MH: Establishment in culture of pluripotential cells from mouse embryos. Nature 1981;292:154–156.
7 Martin GR: Isolation of a pluripotent cell line from early mouse embryos cultured in medium conditioned by teratocarcinoma stem cells. Proc Natl Acad Sci USA 1981;78:7634–7638.
8 Bradley A, Evans M, Kaufman MH, Robertson E: Formation of germ-line chimaeras from embryo-derived teratocarcinoma cell lines. Nature 1984;309:255–256.
9 Nagy A, Rossant J, Nagy R, Abramow-Newerly W, Roder JC: Derivation of completely cell culture-derived mice from early-passage embryonic stem cells. Proc Nat Acad Sci USA 1993;90:8424–8428.
10 Wobus AM, Holzhausen H, Jakel P, Schoneich J: Characterization of pluripotent stem cell line derived from mouse embryo. Exp Cell Res 1984;152:212–219.

11 Doetschman TC, Eistetter H, Katz M, Schmidt W, Kemler R: The in vitro development of blastocyst-derived embryonic stem cell lines: Formation of visceral yolk sac, blood islands and myocardium. J Embryol Exp Morphol 1985;87:27–45.
12 Nakano T, Kodama H, Honjo T: Generation of lymphohematopoietic cells from embryonic stem cells in culture. Science 1994;265:1098–1101.
13 Kennedy M, Firpo M, Choi K, Wall C, Robertson S, Kabrun N, et al: A common precursor for primitive erythropoiesis and definitive haematopoiesis. Nature 1997:386:488–493.
14 Brüstle O, Spiro AC, Karram K, Choudhary K, Okabe S, McKay RDG: In vitro-generated neural precursors participate in mammalian brain development. Proc Natl Acad Sci USA 1997;94:14809–14814.
15 Brüstle O, Jones KN, Learish RD, Karram K, Choudhary K, Wiestler OD, et al: Embryonic stem cell-derived glial precursors: A source of myelinating transplants. Science 1999;285:754–756.
16 Klug MG, Soonpaa MH, Koh GY, Field LJ: Genetically selected cardiomyocytes from differentiating embryonic stem cells form stable intracardiac grafts. J Clin Invest 1996;98:216–224.
17 Soria B, Roche E, Berná G, León-Quinto T, Reig JA, Martín F: Insulin-secreting cells derived from embryonic stem cells normalize glycemia in streptozotocin-induced diabetic mice. Diabetes 2000; 49:157–162.
18 Lumelsky N, Blondel O, Laeng P, Velasco I, Ravin R, McKay R: Differentiation of embryonic stem cells to insulin-secreting structures similar to pancreatic islets. Science 2001;292:1389–1394.
19 Doetschman T, Williams P, Maeda N: Establishment of hamster blastocyst-derived embryonic stem (ES) cells. Dev Biol 1988;127:224–227.
20 Iannaccone PM, Taborn GU, Garton RL, Caplice MD, Brenin DR: Pluripotent embryonic stem cells from the rat are capable of producing chimeras. Dev Biol 1994;163: 288–292 [erratum in Dev Biol 1997;185: 124–125].
21 Giles JR, Yang X, Mark W, Foote RH: Pluripotency of cultured rabbit inner cell mass cells detected by isozyme analysis and eye pigmentation of fetuses following injection into blastocysts or morulae. Mol Reprod Dev 1993;36:130–138.
22 Graves KH, Moreadith RW: Derivation and characterization of putative pluripotential embryonic stem cells from preimplantation rabbit embryos. Mol Reprod Dev 1993;36:424–433.
23 Edwards RG: Personal pathways to embryonic stem cells. Reprod Biomed Online 2002;4:263–278.
24 Notarianni E, Galli C, Laurie S, Moor RM, Evans MJ: Derivation of pluripotent, embryonic cell lines from the pig and sheep. J Reprod Fertil Suppl 1991;43:255–260.
25 Sims M, First NL: Production of calves by transfer of nuclei from cultured inner cell mass cells. Proc Natl Acad Sci USA 1994;91:6143–6147.
26 Wheeler MB: Development and validation of swine embryonic stem cells: A review. Reprod Fertil Dev 1994;6:563–568.
27 Chen LR, Shiue YL, Bertolini L, Medrano JF, BonDurant RH, Anderson GB: Establishment of pluripotent cell lines from porcine preimplantation embryos. Theriogenology 1999;52:195–212.
28 Mitalipova M, Beyhan Z, First NL: Pluripotency of bovine embryonic stem cell line derived from precompacting embryos. Cloning 2001;3:59–67.
29 Li M, Zhang D, Hou Y, Jiao L, Zheng X, Wang WH: Isolation and culture of embryonic stem cells from porcine blastocysts. Mol Reprod Dev 2003;65:429–434.

30 Thomson JA, Kalishman J, Golos TG, Durning M, Harris CP, Becker RA, et al: Isolation of a primate embryonic stem cell line. Proc Natl Acad Sci USA 1995;92:7844–7848.
31 Thomson JA, Kalishman J, Golos TG, Durning M, Harris CP, Hearn JP: Pluripotent cell lines derived from common marmoset (*Callithrix jacchus*) blastocysts. Biol Reprod 1996;55:254–259.
32 Suemori H, Tada T, Torii R, Hosoi Y, Kobayashi K, Imahie H, et al: Establishment of embryonic stem cell lines from cynomolgous monkey blastocysts produced by IVF or ICSI. Dev Dyn 2001;222:273–279.
33 Cibelli JB, Stice SL, Golueke PJ, Kane JJ, Jerry J, Blackwell C, et al: Transgenic bovine chimeric offspring produced from somatic cell-derived stem-like cells. Nature Biotechnol 1998;16:642–646.
34 Munsie MJ, Michalska AE, O'Brien CM, Trounson AO, Pera MF, Mountford PS: Isolation of pluripotent embryonic stem cells from reprogrammed adult mouse somatic cell nuclei. Curr Biol 2000;10:989–992.
35 Kawase E, Yamazaki Y, Yagi T, Yanagimachi R, Pedersen RA: Mouse embryonic stem (ES) cell lines established from neuronal cell-derived cloned blastocysts. Genesis 2000;28:156–163.
36 Wakayama T, Tabar V, Rodriguez I, Perry AC, Studer L, Mombaerts P: Differentiation of embryonic stem cell lines generated from adult somatic cells by ¡¡nuclear transfer. Science 2001;292:740–743.
37 Thomson JA, Itskovitz-Eldor J, Shapiro SS, Waknitz MA, Swiergiel JJ, Marshall VS, et al: Embryonic stem cell lines derived from human blastocysts. Science 1998;282: 1145–1147 [erratum in Science 1998;282: 1827].
38 Itskovitz-Eldor J, Schuldiner M, Karsenti D, Eden A, Yanuka O, Amit M, et al: Differentiation of human embryonic stem cells into embryoid bodies comprising the three embryonic germ layers. Mol Med 2000;6:88–95.
39 Reubinoff BE, Pera MF, Fong C, Trounson A, Bongso A: Embryonic stem cell lines from human blastocysts: Somatic differentiation in vitro. Nat Biotechnol. 2000;18:399–404.
40 Hwang WS, Ryu YJ, Park JH, Park ES, Lee EG, Koo JM, et al: Evidence of a pluripotent human embryonic stem cell line derived from a cloned blastocyst. Science 2004;303:1669–1674.
41 NIH human embryonic stem cell report, 2001.
42 Amit M, Itskovitz-Eldor J: Derivation and spontaneous differentiation of human embryonic stem cells. J Anat 2002;200:225–232.
43 Mitalipova M, Calhoun J, Shin S, Wininger D, Schulz T, Noggle S, et al: Human embryonic stem cell lines derived from discarded embryos. Stem Cells 2003;21:521–526.
44 Lanzendorf SE, Boyd CA, Wright DL, Muasher S, Oehninger S, Hodgen GD: Use of human gametes obtained from anonymous donors for the production of human embryonic stem cell lines. Fertil Steril 2001;76:132–137.
45 Chen Y, He ZX, Liu A, Wang K, Mao WW, Chu JX, et al: Embryonic stem cells generated by nuclear transfer of human somatic nuclei into rabbit oocytes. Cell Res 2003;13:251–263.
46 Robertson EJ: Embryo-derived stem cell lines; in Robertson EJ (ed): Teratocarcinomas and Embryonic Stem Cells: A Practical Approach. Oxford, IRL Press, 1987, pp 71–112.
47 Solter D, Knowles BB: Immunosurgery of mouse blastocyst. Proc Natl Acad Sci USA 1975;72:5099–5102.
48 Reubinoff BE, Pera MF, Vajta G, Trounson AO: Effective cryopreservation of human embryonic stem cells by the open pulled straw vitrification method. Hum Reprod 2001;16:2187–2194.

49 Williams R, Hilton D, Pease S, Wilson T, Stewart C, Gearing D, et al: Myeloid leukemia inhibitory factor maintains the developmental potential of embryonic stem cells. Nature 1988;336: 684–687.
50 Amit M, Carpenter MK, Inokuma MS, Chiu CP, Harris CP, Waknitz MA, et al: Clonally derived human embryonic stem cell lines maintain pluripotency and proliferative potential for prolonged periods of culture. Dev Biol 2000;227: 271–278.
51 Richards M, Fong CY, Chan WK, Wong PC, Bongso A: Human feeders support prolonged undifferentiated growth of human inner cell masses and embryonic stem cells. Nat Biotechnol 2002;20:933–936.
52 Amit M, Margulets V, Segev H, Shariki C, Laevsky I, Coleman R, et al: Human feeder layers for human embryonic stem cells. Biol Reprod 2003;68:2150–2156.
53 Hovatta O, Mikkola M, Gertow K, Stromberg AM, Inzunza J, Hreinsson J, et al: A culture system using human foreskin fibroblasts as feeder cells allows production of human embryonic stem cells. Hum Reprod 2003;18:1404–1409.
54 Xu C, Inokuma MS, Denham J, Golds K, Kundu P, Gold JD, et al: Feeder-Free growth of undifferentiated human embryonic stem cells. Nat Biotechnol 2001;19:971–974 .
55 Amit M, Shariki C, Margulets V, Itskovitz-Eldor J: Feeder and serum free culture system for human embryonic stem cells. Biol Reprod 2004;in press.
56 Amit M, Itskovitz-Eldor J: Human embryonic stem cells; in Veeck LL, Zaninovic M, Zaninovic N (eds): An Atlas of Human Blastocysts. Boca Raton, CRC Press-Parthenon Publishers, 2003, pp 213–229.
57 Keller GM: In vitro differentiation of embryonic stem cells. Curr Opin Cell Biol 1995;7:862–869.
58 Kehat I, Kenyagin-Karsenti D, Snir M, Segev H, Amit M, Gepstein A, et al: Human embryonic stem cells can differentiate into myocytes with structural and functional properties of cardiomyocytes. J Clin Invest 2001;108:407–414.
59 Levenberg S, Golub JS, Amit M, Itskovitz-Eldor J, Langer R: Endothelial cells derived from human embryonic stem cells. Proc Natl Acad Sci USA 2002;99:4391–4396.
60 Assady S, Maor G, Amit M, Itskovitz-Eldor J, Skorecki KL, Tzukerman M: Insulin production by human embryonic stem cells. Diabetes 2001;50:1691–1697.
61 Zhang SC, Wernig M, Duncan ID, BrÜstle O, Thomson JA: In vitro differentiation of transplantable neural precursors from human embryonic stem cells. Nat Biotechnol 2001;19: 1129–1133.
62 Reubinoff BE, Itsykson P, Turetsky T, Pera MF, Reinhartz E, Itzik A, et al: Neural progenitors from human embryonic stem cells. Nat Biotechnol 2001;19: 1134–1140.
63 Kaufman DS, Hanson ET, Lewis RL, Auerbach R, Thomson JA: Hematopoietic colony-forming cells derived from human embryonic stem cells. Proc Natl Acad Sci USA 2001;98:10716–10721.
64 Chadwick K, Wang L, Li L, Menendez P, Murdoch B, Rouleau A, et al: Cytokines and BMP-4 promote hematopoietic differentiation of human embryonic stem cells. Blood 2003;102:906–915.
65 Xu C, Police S, Rao N, Carpenter MK: Characterization and enrichment of cardiomyocytes derived from human embryonic stem cells. Circ Res 2002;91: 501–508.
66 Mummery C, Ward D, van den Brink CE, Bird SD, Doevendans PA, Opthof T, et al: Cardiomyocyte differentiation of mouse and human embryonic stem cells. J Anat 2002;200:233–242.

67 Xu RH, Chen X, Li DS, Li R, Addicks GC, Glennon C, et al: BMP4 initiates human embryonic stem cell differentiation to trophoblast. Nat Biotechnol 2002; 20:1261–1264.

68 Rambhatla L, Chiu CP, Kundu P, Peng Y, Carpenter MK: Generation of hepatocyte-like cells from human embryonic stem cells. Cell Transplant 2003;12:1–11.

69 Gerecht-Nir S, Ziskind A, Cohen S, Itskovitz-Eldor J: Human embryonic stem cells as an in vitro model for human vascular development and the induction of vascular differentiation. Lab Invest 2004;in press.

70 Eiges R, Schuldiner M, Drukker M, Yanuka O, Itskovitz-Eldor J, Benvenisty N: Establishment of human embryonic stem cell-transfected clones carrying a marker for undifferentiated cells. Curr Biol 2001;11:514–518.

71 Ma Y, Ramezani A, Lewis R, Hawley RG, Thomson JA: High-level sustained transgene expression in human embryonic stem cells using lentiviral vectors. Stem cells 2003;21:111–117.

72 Gropp M, Itsykson P, Singer O, Ben-Hur T, Reinhartz E, Galun E, et al: Stable genetic modification of human embryonic stem cells by lentiviral vectors. Mol Ther 2003;7:281–287.

73 Zwaka TP, Thomson JA: Homologous recombination in human embryonic stem cells. Nat Biotechnol 2003;21: 319–321.

74 Amit M, Itskovitz-Eldor J: Isolation and maintenance of primate ES cells; in Lanza R (ed): Handbook of Stem Cells. San Diego, Elsevier, 2004, vol. 2: Embryonic Stem Cells, in press.

Joseph Itskovitz-Eldor, MD, DSc

Department of Obstetrics and Gynecology,
Rambam Medical Center, PO Box 9602, IL–31096 Haifa (Israel)
Tel. +972 4 854 2536, Fax +972 4 854 2503, E-Mail itskovitz@rambam.health.gov.il

Blazer S, Zimmer EZ (eds):
The Embryo: Scientific Discovery and Medical Ethics.
Basel, Karger, 2005, pp 91–106

Stem Cells as Targets for Gene and Cell Therapy

Shimon Slavin

Department of Bone Marrow Transplantation and Cancer Immunotherapy, and Cell Therapy and Transplantation Research Center, Hadassah-Hebrew University Hospital, Jerusalem, Israel

Recent developments of noninvasive and invasive technologies associated with the imaging and sampling of small quantities of body fluids and cells isolated from body fluids and the increasing capacity for interventional procedures based on surgical genetic or cellular manipulations, there has been significant progress in understanding the normal ontogeny and pathology of the unborn fetus. In parallel with better understanding of hematopoietic stem cells on the one hand, and more recently, embryonal stem cells on the other, theoretical options for prenatal interventions may open new horizons for treatment of genetic disorders in utero or even pre-implantation of fertilized eggs, as well as using cells obtained from fertilized eggs at different stages of gestation for genetic and cellular interventions, and for the development of new organ-like cells that may eventually replace the need for perfused organ transplantation. In view of the growing understanding of molecular biology and genetic manipulation of cells and the feasibility to use stem cell therapeutically, and most of all, considering recent discoveries associated with stem cell plasticity, there has been a considerable increase in the therapeutic potential and future horizons of using stem cells in clinical practice with a potential application of stem cell transplantation in the context of the unborn fetus. Indeed, successful clinical application of stem cell transplantation for a large number of malignant and nonmalignant disorders, depends on induction of host-vs.-graft (HVG) unresponsiveness, a process which is best induced in nature by implantation of the fetus into his mismatched mother. Induction of transplantation tolerance such as is the rule when the fetus is conceived, has been the Holy Grail of transplant surgeons and clinicians involved in clinical stem cell transplantation. Hence, better understanding of the maternal-fetal relationship is likely to shed more light into Mother Nature's tools for the induction of unresponsiveness without using aggressive immunosuppressive modalities.

Mixed Chimerism and Bilateral Transplantation Tolerance as the Basis for Therapeutic Allogeneic Stem Cell Transplantation

Allogeneic stem cell transplantation of premature cells derived from the bone marrow compartment, stem cells mobilized from the blood or cord blood stem cells is an important clinical tool for treatment of patients with a wide variety of malignant and nonmalignant diseases. Unfortunately, until recently, stem cell transplantation was still considered a hazardous, expensive and complicated procedure associated with high rates of procedure-related morbidity and mortality. As will be discussed below, we have reason to believe that safer, simpler, and less traumatic and less costly stem cell transplantation procedures may become available in the near future for wider clinical application for a broader spectrum of indications. Our optimism results from the fact that transplantation tolerance to donor stem cells, which seems to be the key element for successful and safe stem cell transplantation, and likewise, unresponsiveness of donor cells against the host, can be accomplished with reduced intensity conditioning and central immunoregulation in the thymus leading to deletion of 'self' or rather of alloreactive T cells, respectively.

There are many accepted indications for transplantation of bone marrow-derived stem cells, and the number of indications is continually increasing. Some of the major indications for bone marrow transplantation for both malignant and nonmalignant diseases and the rationales for choosing these indications are shown in table 1. The indications for

Table 1.

Common indications for allogeneic stem cell transplantation for life-threatening malignant and nonmalignant diseases

- Replacement therapy for diseases caused by deficiency of stem cells (e.g. severe aplastic anemia) or abnormal stem cells (e.g. severe combined immune deficiency)
- Replacement therapy for diseases caused by deficiency of stem cell products (e.g. enzyme deficiency diseases such as Gaucher's disease)
- Replacement of host with donor stem cells in genetic disorders and diseases caused by abnormal stem cells or stem cell progeny (e.g. beta-thalassemia major)
- Replacement of host with donor immunohematopoietic cells in malignant hematologic diseases following eradication of tumor cells of host origin with high dose chemoradiotherapy
- Stem cell transplantation for induction of transplantation tolerance as a platform for allogeneic cell therapy with naïve or specific immune donor lymphocytes
- Elimination of self-reactive lymphocytes in conjunction with autologous stem cell transplantation, or replacement of host with donor stem cells in conjunction with allogeneic bone marrow transplantation for the treatment of life-threatening autoimmune diseases
- Stem cell transplantation for induction of transplantation tolerance to donor organ allografts and xenografts

allogeneic stem cell transplantation are based on the great diversity of stem cell products, as shown in figure 1.

Bone marrow transplantation is associated with high rates of procedure-related toxicity and mortality as well as unavoidable late complications that are frequently caused directly or indirectly by the intensive conditioning administered during the pre-transplant period. Therefore, it would be a major advantage if a safer bone marrow transplantation procedure could be introduced using well-tolerated conditioning. Patients with high-risk hematologic malignancies in particular could benefit from a curative procedure at an early stage of the disease, thus avoiding the need for long-term chemotherapy with all the associated complications. Patients with genetic diseases would also benefit at an early stage of their disease, when the chance for complete cure may be much higher. Obviously, the earliest possible intervention may occur following in vitro fertilization using sensitive polymerase chain reaction (PCR) technology for diagnosis at the stage of a single cell. Early diagnosis of genetic disorders from chorionic villi represents an opportunity for early

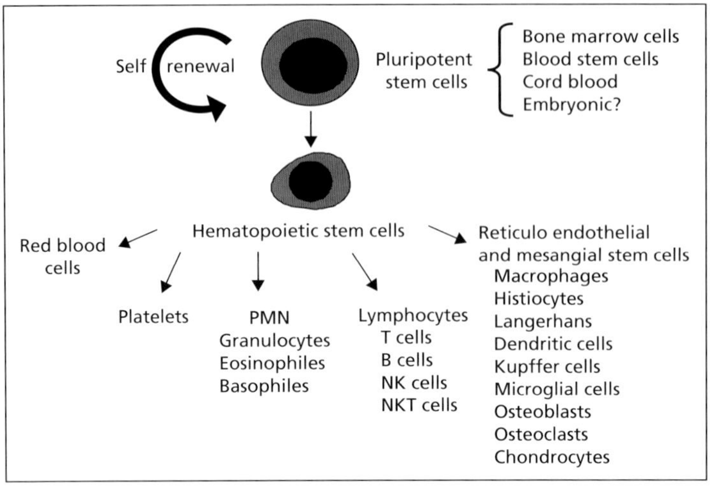

Fig. 1.
Development of the immunohematopoietic system.

diagnosis of certain genetic diseases, as early as 10–11 weeks of gestation, with the option to abort the unborn fetus, if affected with a documented incurable disease, or represents a challenge for intra-uterine stem cell transplantation for treatment of genetic disorders that may be caused by deficient or abnormal stem cell products.

Maternal-Fetal Natural Mixed Chimerism as an Ultimate Model for Induction of Transplantation Tolerance with Nonmyeloablative Conditioning

Transplantation tolerance across the major histocompatibility complex occurs spontaneously in nature, as evidenced by the fact that pregnant females do not reject their conceptus. In fact, as shown by Owen [1] in the 1940s, placental parabiosis in utero leads to permanent mixed chimerism and bilateral transplantation tolerance. These observations instigated one of the most exciting experiments carried out in the 1950s [2]. The experiment by Billingham et al. [2] showed that infusion of parental stem cells into neonates with no exogenous immunosuppressive treatment resulted in mixed chimerism and permanent transplantation tolerance to donor alloantigens. This suggested that there is a window of opportunity, shortly after delivery, during which tolerance can be induced without the need for conditioning. Tolerant recipients were shown to be chimeras with only a small proportion of donor cells. However, without corroborating evidence that transplantation tolerance could be intentionally induced, the approach could not be applied in clinical practice for immunocompetent recipients. Nonetheless, these experiments suggested that stable mixed chimerism is feasible and may be responsible for successful induction of transplantation tolerance to donor alloantigens. In addition, these observations indicated that if antigen specific unresponsiveness can be achieved with nonmyeloablative immunosuppression, it should be possible to accomplish the same goal with minimal or no conditioning, by immune regulation rather than immunosuppression, analogous to the mechanism of unresponsiveness which operates at the stage of 'self/non-self' discrimination and during pregnancy. Since transplantation tolerance is induced by engraftment of stem cells, development of mixed chimerism may be the only critical requirement for induction of HVG and graft-vs.-host (GVH) unresponsiveness.

Starting in 1976, we published a series of papers addressing the feasibility of establishing transplantation tolerance and bilateral tolerance by mixed chimerism in immunologically mature recipients across the major histocompatibility complex [3–8]. Experiments in mice [3–5], rats [6] and dogs [7] showed that following nonmyeloablative conditioning with well-tolerated total lymphoid irradiation (TLI), recipients experienced durable engraftment of donor bone marrow and skin or perfused organ allografts, with no graft-vs.-host disease (GVHD). In mixed chimeras, HVG and GVH were neutralized simultaneously without the need for any post-transplant immunosuppression. However, the mechanisms responsible for the balanced equilibrium in mixed chimeras were not understood [9]. After TLI, circulating and tissue-bound T cells were eliminated [4] and newly formed T cells acquired tolerance to protein antigens [10] and alloantigens [3–8]. Circulating and spleen cells analyzed by FACS before new T cells were detectable were large cells carrying the null phenotype [11]. When T cells reappeared, the large cell subpopulation decreased, suggesting that the latter played some role in the development of the unresponsive state. These large cells were enriched with hematopoietic progenitor cells [12], indicating that, upon maturation in the thymus, any new antigen encountered would be regarded as 'self', resulting in apoptosis of self-reactive T cells.

Following TLI, enrichment with such immature cells enabled the recipients to develop tolerance, mainly as a result of clonal deletion [13]. Following nonmyeloablative conditioning, between the time when no mature T cells are present and the appearance of uncommitted immature cells, allografts or any protein antigen will be regarded as self.

Spleen cells from recipient chimeric mice with intact skin allografts did not cause GVHD and could transfer their specific tolerance to skin allografts in secondary recipients [14]. Tolerant chimeras had large mononuclear 'null' cells (negative for Thy1, CD4, CD8 and Ig) that suppressed 100% MLR [15]. Suppressor cells of MLR were soybean agglutinin positive large cells that looked like stem cells, and had suppressive functions that were identical to those of normal marrow cells. Interestingly, although suppressor cells were present in chimeras, specific unresponsiveness could best be explained by clonal deletion and anergy of residual cells [13, 14].

Ildstad and Sachs [16] and subsequently Sykes and Sachs and coworkers [17–19] showed similar results, except that they used TBI and infused two sets of cells rather than protecting the mouse's own cells and infusing allogeneic lymphocytes. The former studies were continued by Starzl et al. [20] who showed that donor cells could not be detected in non-rejector mice using PCR analysis, implying that even micro-chimerism may enhance graft acceptance and donor tolerance induction. More recently, based on an improved understanding of the mechanism of alloimmune responses and the ability to block the immune response by suppressing costimulation, transplantation tolerance has been induced using truly minimal conditioning [21]. We reasoned that if clonal deletion could not be accomplished by mimicking natural central tolerance induction, there might be other ways to induce donor specific clonal deletion [22]. In clinical bone marrow transplantation, there are two ways to achieve engraftment without GVHD: (1) Complete T cell depletion in both the graft and the host, leading to no GVHD and no rejection, but this requires aggressive hazardous conditioning. (2) Balancing the T cells in the graft and the host to downregulate host anti-donor and donor anti-host alloreactive T cells by a mechanism of veto [9].

However, the optimal way to achieve engraftment without GVHD would be to deplete only the relevant T cells in the graft and in the host, thus inducing apoptosis/cytoreduction of both host-reactive T cells to prevent GVHD and donor-reactive T cells to prevent rejection, respectively.

Studies have shown that reduced intensity conditioning can be very useful in conjunction with clonal deletion [9, 22] or immunoregulation by costimulation blockade [21]. The more effective the conditioning, the better the tolerance induction, with fewer donor cells needed for durable engraftment of donor hematopoietic cells, especially following nonmyeloablative conditioning. In contrast, the more intensive the pre-grafting immunosuppression, the more aggressive the GVHD, suggesting some possible down-regulation between host and donor immunohematopoietic cells. Engraftment could be facilitated by donor T cells, hence, when using T-cell-depleted stem cell allografts to completely prevent GVHD, higher numbers of donor stem cells were required in both mice [24] and man [25]. In summary, mildly immunosuppressed hosts required either higher numbers of donor stem cells or induction of donor-specific clonal deletion. These results suggested that immunosuppression could be achieved without myeloablation in the clinic and that a window of immunosuppression would prevent rejection of donor stem cells required to induce transplantation tolerance.

In the future, treatments based on immunoregulation rather than non-discriminatory elimination of alloreactive cells in the recipient should render patients less prone to infectious complications and secondary cancer. Examples of tolerance induction to autologous as well as allogeneic lymphocytes, respectively, without exogenous immunosuppression include: spontaneous induction of self-tolerance induced by deletion of self-reactive T cells in the thymus; peripheral antigen-dependent anergy that down-regulates potentially self-reactive T cells that may escape central clonal deletion in the thymus; immune recovery of recipients of mismatched bone marrow allografts following T-cell-depleted stem cell transplantation with no GVHD.

Based on experimental data and cumulative clinical experience, it can be concluded that donor alloreactive T cells are most dangerous following intensive conditioning, which includes a combination of immunosuppression and myeloablation. In addition to the degree of mismatching, which determines the alloreactive potential of immunocompetent donor lymphocytes, the intensity of GVHD is also directly proportional to the intensity of the conditioning. Hence, following intensive myeloablative conditioning, control of GVHD may require one of the following approaches: (1) T cell depletion (preferred in mismatched donor-recipient pairs) to control GVHD while avoiding post-transplant immunosuppression; (2) use of non-alloreactive donor T cells for immunological reconstruction and safe adoptive transfer of donor immunity while preventing or minimizing GVHD.

Following nonmyeloablative conditioning, donor T cells can facilitate donor stem cell engraftment with an acceptable risk of GVHD, depending on the intensity of the conditioning, since mixed chimerism may partially protect the host from GVHD. Hence, following NST, when residual T cells of host origin need to be controlled, the role of donor T cells in facilitation of engraftment is much more critical. Accordingly, alloreactive T cells may play an important role in graft facilitation. Under such circumstances, the following can be anticipated:

- T-cell-depleted allografts, or purified stem cells, may be highly susceptible to rejection by residual host T cells escaping immunosuppression, due to lack of the engraftment facilitation effect mediated by immunocompetent donor T cells.
- Engraftment of purified, T-cell-depleted stem cells requires larger doses of donor cells to overcome resistance by host T cells and NK cells and to provide an advantage to donor cells in an anticipated hematopoietic competition between host and donor cells in the bone marrow compartment.
- Veto effects to neutralize residual immunocompetent and alloreactive host lymphocytes can be mediated by alloreactive donor lymphocytes; however, non-alloreactive or tolerant donor T cells cannot facilitate engraftment in the continuous presence of residual alloreactive host T cells.

An inverse relationship exists between the stem cell dose given and the degree of specific HVG unresponsiveness. At a low frequency of cytotoxic T lymphocyte precursor cells (CTLp), very few cells will engraft. At a high percentage of CTLp cells, the chance of achieving mixed chimerism is low, instead full donor chimerism is more likely. The positive and negative roles played by alloreactive T cells in bone marrow transplantation are summarized in table 2.

Based on the above, non-myeloablative stem cell transplantation (NST) resulting in mixed chimerism, rather than full donor chimerism following myeloablative conditioning, may be the safest and optimal method for transplantation of donor stem cells and for induction of bilateral transplantation tolerance. Transplantation tolerance induced by engraftment of stem cells may also provide an opportunity to exploit the anti-tumor potential of alloreactive donor lymphocytes [28] for the treatment of malignant [33, 36–38] and nonmalignant disorders [34, 39].

In conclusion, experimental and clinical application of different treatments to control the immune system, concentrating on minimal conditioning to accomplish bilateral transplantation tolerance of HVG and GVH responses, is the main focus of interest. The goal is to take advantage of

Table 2.
Positive and negative aspects of immunocompetent T cells in bone marrow transplantation

Positive aspects
Protection against infectious complications
Induction of unresponsiveness [26]
Downregulation by host T cells of donor T cells and control of GVHD [27]
Downregulation by donor T cells of host T cells, control of graft rejection and facilitation of engraftment [24, 25]
Reaction against host hematopoietic cells (malignant, genetically abnormal or self-reactive) by donor cells eliciting a graft-versus-malignancy, graft-versus-genetically abnormal stem cells or graft-vs.-autoimmunity effect [28–35]
Negative aspects
T cells are the major obstacles to successful transplantation of bone marrow and organ allografts: host T cells cause rejection and donor T cells mediate both acute and chronic GVHD

immune regulation as a basis for safe and well-tolerated allogeneic stem cell transplantation to be followed by cell therapy. Better approaches for the treatment of malignant and nonmalignant diseases, using immune cells to eliminate, replace or control malignant and nonmalignant cells, will hopefully be developed. In this regard, better understanding of the mechanisms that result in maternal fetal unresponsiveness is likely to provide new clues to clinically applicable modalities for prevention or rejection of bone marrow stem cells and organ allografts, and possibly better potential future applications of stem cells and mesangial stem cells as a source of multipotential stem cells for non-hematopoietic indications associated with stem cell plasticity [40].

Gene Therapy of Genetically Abnormal Stem Cells

As can be seen in figure 1, stem cells are the source of all hematopoietic series circulating in the blood as well as platelets and circulating as well as tissue bound cells products of the reticulum epithelial cell system. Hence, genetic engineering of stem cells by transduction of new genes with a goal in mind to replace missing or abnormal genes can result in production of genetically modified stem cell products. Successful genetic engineering of stem cells may thus lead to permanent replacement therapy, since stem cells have the capacity to renew themselves, thus serving as a constant source of genetically corrected stem cell products. Since many of the genetic disorders associated with abnormal or deficient genes can be diagnosed in utero, early diagnosis on the one hand and availability of vectors with relevant genes may represent a promising therapeutic option for patients with a large number of genetic abnormalities, especially those caused by abnormality of products of stem cells, since correction of such diseases may be accomplished by transplantation of autologous stem cells transduced in vivo with normal gene products. Gene therapy trials have demonstrated the feasibility and safety of engineering hematopoietic stem cells for the treatment of hematopoietic diseases and preclinical animal models and man. Recent improvements in gene transfer to hematopoietic stem cells combined with selective induction of growth and differentiation of such cells, allowed effective transduction of stem cells and consequently normal production of stem cell progeny. Gene therapy of immune deficiency appears particularly attractive for treating genetic disorders where genes were identified, cloned and introduced into vectors that can be used for gene therapy. The first successful gene therapy was reported by Cavazzana-Calvo et al. [41] in patients with a severe combined immune deficiency (SCID) variant due to gamma-chain deficiency (SCID-X1). Unfortunately, although immune deficiency was reversed in a series of 9 of 11 patients [Fischer A, pers. commun.], 2 patients developed lymphoproliferative disorder, which is most likely associated with the gene therapy procedure, most likely autogenesis that resulted in malignant clonal expansion.

Second disease where successful gene therapy resulted in complete reversal of immune deficiency, was in patients with another type of SCID, adenosine deaminase deficiency (ADA-SCID). ADA-SCID is an inherited disorder characterized by lymphopenia, impaired humoral and cellular immune responses, recurrent infections and failure to thrive. ADA deficiency results in accumulation of purine metabolites, especially adenosine, 2-deoxyadenosine and adenine deoxyribonucleotides (dAXP) in cells and tissues. Accumulation of these toxic metabolites results in apoptosis, hence impaired growth and development of T, B and natural killer (NK) cells and results in severe immune deficiency, which results in current infections and death. In addition, ADA deficiency is characterized by renal, hepatic and neurological abnormalities

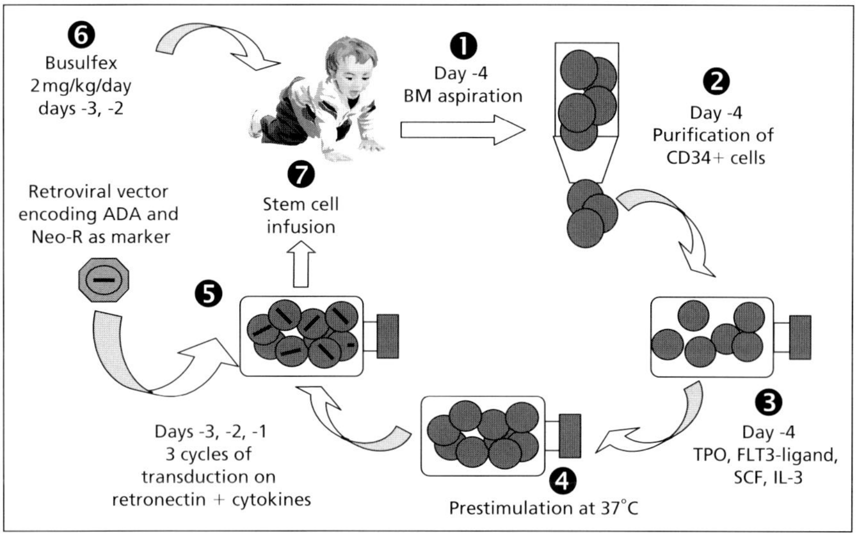

Fig. 2.
Gene transfer protocol into autologous BM CD34+ cells of an ADA-SCID patient.

that suggest that other somatic cells may also be affected by deficiency of ADA gene.

Previous trials to introduce ADA gene into stem cells resulted in very low yield, despite durable expression of the transgene in some cases. Consequently, treated patients continue to be dependent on exogenous supply of the pegilated form of enzyme (PEG-ADA). In a recent study done in collaboration with the Gene Therapy Group of the San Raffaele Gene Therapy Institute in Milano [42], we have introduced a new principle in conjunction with gene therapy of a patient with ADA-SCID. Based on our cumulative experience with hematopoietic reconstitution in patients conditioned with reduced intensity conditioning, it seems obvious that hematopoietic competition plays a major role in determining the proportion of durable engraftment of transplanted stem cells. Consequently, as can be seen in figure 2, we have decided to cytoreduce the patient's own stem cell pool prior to gene therapy with low doses of Busulfan, therefore providing infused transduced autologous stem cells with a biological advantage that will provide them an opportunity to replicate in the bone marrow niche before recovery of patient's own genetically abnormal hematopoietic stem cells. Another principle that was induced into our gene therapy trial was intentional deprivation of PEG-ADA, again, to provide biologic advantage to genetically transduced stem cells that produce the enzyme and thus will have a biologic advantage that will give them a better chance in hematopoietic reconstitution with genetically abnormal host stem cells. As detailed in a recent publication [42] and in 3 additional patients treated thus far based on the same principle [Aiuti A, pers. commun.], complete reversal of immune deficiency was accomplished with no procedure-related toxicity or any appreciable complications. Our first patient, now 3 years out, maintains normal life with no susceptibility to infections. The patient never received PEG-ADA, neither before nor after transplantation and did not require any medical care. Normal number of lymphocytes and lymphocyte subsets was documented with 100% transduction of B and T cells and some other subsets of stem cells, again suggesting transduction of stem cells with successful multi-lineage gene therapy. Our patient developed spontaneous antibodies to chicken pox following an epidemic of chicken pox in the neighborhood and developed no signs of disease, suggesting that her immune system was functional.

Taken together, it seems that gene therapy may already provide a realistic tool for treatment of patients with immune deficiency, thus suggesting that it may become an acceptable treatment of choice for other genetic disorders associated with deficiency of well-defined gene products.

Conclusions

Stem cell transplantation represents an effective modality for the treatment of a large number of disorders caused by deficient, abnormal or malignant products of stem cells. Methods for accomplishing successful stem cell transplantation in clinical practice are constantly being improved and current methods based on reduced intensity conditioning, or nonmyeloablative conditioning in preparation for stem cell transplantation (NST), suggest that allogeneic stem cell transplantation can be accomplished safely in all age groups, including patients with poor performance status. Further approaches for amplifying the graft-vs.-malignancy effect on the one hand, while developing better methods for control of graft-vs.-anti-host responses, still represent a challenge for future studies. Gene therapy of autologous stem cells was shown to be effective, thus suggesting that alternative strategies may exist in the future for treatment of diseases that require stem cell transplantation, either normal allogeneic or genetically modified autologous, depending on the type of disease and availability of a suitable donor. Since stem cell transplantation also represents a form of gene therapy, the whole genome is introduced rather than well-defined genes. The biology of stem cells and hematopoietic stem cells will be better understood and as newer modalities will be developed for earlier diagnosis of disease susceptibility or onset of disease, such modalities may be utilized early on in the stages of delivery or possibly even by intra-uterine testing of the unborn fetus. Successful intra-uterine stem cell transplantation has already been reported in several cases of immune deficiency, where rejection of donor stem cells was prevented by the basic disease. Better understanding of the mechanisms of paternal-fetal relationship and naturally induced tolerance during pregnancy is likely to provide newer concepts for safer transplantation in patients in need of allogeneic stem cells. In the future, embryonal stem cells may also be used as an imaging clinical tool or as a source for determining somatic or hematopoietic stem cells.

Acknowledgements

We would like to thank the following for their ongoing support: The Szydlowsky Foundation; Donald & Ronne Hess; The Gabrielle Rich Foundation; Fig Tree Foundation. The work was carried out at The Danny Cunniff Leukemia Research Laboratory.

References

1 Owen RD: Immunogenetic consequences of vascular anastomoses between bovine twins. Science 1945;102:400.
2 Billingham RE, Brent L, Medavar PB: Actively acquired tolerance to foreign cells. Nature 1953;172:606.
3 Slavin S, Strober S, Fuks Z, Kaplan HS: Long-term survival of skin allografts in mice treated with fractionated total lymphoid irradiation. Science 1976;193: 1252–1254.
4 Slavin S, Strober S, Fuks Z, Kaplan HS: Induction of specific tissue transplantation tolerance using fractionated total lymphoid irradiation in adult mice: Long-term survival of allogeneic bone marrow and skin grafts. J Exp Med 1977;146:34–48.
5 Slavin S, Fuks Z, Kaplan HS, Strober S: Transplantation of allogeneic bone marrow without graft vs. host disease using total lymphoid irradiation. J Exp Med 1978; 147:963–972.

6 Slavin S, Reitz B, Bieber CP, Kaplan HS, Strober S: Transplantation tolerance in adult rats using total lymphoid irradiation (TLI): Permanent survival of skin, heart and marrow allografts. J Exp Med 1978;147:700–707.
7 Howard RJ, Sutherland DER, Lum CT, et al: Kidney allograft survival in dogs treated with total lymphoid irradiation. Ann Surg 1981;193:196–200.
8 Slavin S: Total lymphoid irradiation. Immunol Today 1987;3:88.
9 Prigozhina T, Gurevitch O, Slavin S: Non-myeloablative conditioning to induce bilateral tolerance after allogeneic bone marrow transplantation in mice. Exp Hematol 1999;27:1503–1510.
10 Zan-Bar I, Slavin S, Strober S: Induction and mechanism of tolerance to bovine serum albumin after total lymphoid irradiation (TLI). J Immunol 1978; 121:1400–1404.
11 Weigensberg M, Morecki S, Weiss L, Fuks Z, Slavin S: Suppression of cell mediated immune responses following total lymphoid irradiation (TLI). 1. Characterization of suppressor cell of the mixed lymphocyte reaction. J Immunol 1984;132:971–978.
12 Slavin S, Seidel HJ: Hematopoietic activity in bone marrow chimeras prepared with total lymphoid irradiation (TLI). Exp Hematol 1982;10:206–216.
13 Morecki S, Leshem B, Weigensberg M, Bar S, Slavin S: Functional clonal deletion versus active suppression in transplantation tolerance induced by total lymphoid irradiation (TLI). Transplantation 1985;40: 201–210.
14 Morecki S, Leshem B, Eid A, Slavin S: Alloantigen persistence in induction and maintenance of transplantation tolerance. J Exp Med 1987;165: 1468–1480.
15 Slavin S, Strober S: Induction of allograft tolerance after total lymphoid irradiation (TLI): Development of suppressor cells of the mixed leukocyte reaction (MLR). J Immunol 1979;123:942–946.
16 Ildstad ST, Sachs DH: Reconstitution with syngeneic plus allogeneic or xenogeneic bone marrow leads to specific acceptance of allografts or xenografts. Nature 1984;307:168–170.
17 Sykes M, Chester CH, Sachs DH: Protection from graft-vs.-host disease in fully allogeneic chimeras by prior administration of T cell-depleted syngeneic bone marrow. Transplantation 1988;46:327–330.
18 Sykes M, Sachs DH: Mixed allogeneic chimerism as an approach to transplantation tolerance. Immunol Today 1988;9:23–27.
19 Sykes M, Sachs DH: Bone marrow transplantation as a means of inducing tolerance. Semin Immunol 1990;2:401–417.
20 Starzl TE, Demetris AJ, Murase N, Trucco M, Thomson AW, Rao AS: The lost chord: Microchimerism and allograft survival. Immunol Today 1996;12:577–584.
21 Werkerle T, Kurtz J, Ito H, et al: Allogeneic bone marrow transplantation with co-stimulatory blockade induces macrochimerism and tolerance without cytoreductive host treatment. Nat Med 2000;4:464–469.
22 Prigozhina T, Gurevitch O, Zhu J, Slavin S: Permanent and specific transplantation tolerance induced by a non-myeloablative treatment to a wide variety of allogeneic tissues. Transplantation 1997;63:1394–1399.
23 Storb R, Yu C, Barnett T, et al: Stable mixed hematopoietic chimerism in dog leukocyte antigen-identical littermate dogs given lymph node irradiation before and pharmacological immunosuppression after marrow transplantation. Blood 1999;94:1131–1136.

24 Bachar-Lustig E, Rachamim N, Li HW, Lan F, Reisner Y: Megadose of T cell-depleted bone marrow overcomes MHC barriers in sublethally irradiated mice. Nat Med 1995;1:1268–1273.
25 Reisner Y, Martelli MF: Bone marrow transplantation across HLA barriers by increasing the number of transplanted cells. Immunol Today 1995;16:437–440.
26 Waldmann H, Cobbold S: How do monoclonal antibodies induce tolerance? A role for infectious tolerance? Ann Rev Immunol 1998;16:619–644.
27 Weiss L, Slavin S: Prevention and treatment of graft vs host disease by down-regulation of anti-host reactivity with veto cells of host origin. Bone Marrow Transplant 1999;23:1139–1143.
28 Slavin S, Naparstek E, Nagler A, et al: Allogeneic cell therapy with donor peripheral blood cells and recombinant human interleukin-2 to treat leukemia relapse post allogeneic bone marrow transplantation. Blood 1996;87: 2195–2204.
29 van Besien K, Sobocinski KA, Rowlings PA, et al: Allogeneic bone marrow transplantation for low-grade lymphoma. Blood 1998;92:1832–1836.
30 Or R, Mehta J, Naparstek E, Okon E, Cividalli G, Slavin S: Successful T cell-depleted allogeneic bone marrow transplantation in a child with recurrent multiple extramedullary plasmacytomas. Bone Marrow Transplant 1992;10:381–382.
31 Tricot G, Vesole DH, Jagannath S, Hilon J, Munshi N, Barlogie B: Graft-versus-myeloma effect: Proof of principle. Blood 1996;87:1196–1198.
32 Eibl B, Schwaighofer H, Nachbaur D, et al: Evidence for a graft-versus-tumor effect in a patient treated with marrow ablative chemotherapy and allogeneic bone marrow transplantation for breast cancer. Blood 1996;88:1501–1508.
33 Childs RW, Clave E, Tisdale J, Plante M, Hensel N, Barrett J: Successful treatment of metastatic renal cell carcinoma with a nonmyeloablative allogeneic peripheral-blood progenitor-cell transplant: Evidence for a graft-versus-tumor effect. J Clin Oncol 1999;17:2044–2049.
34 Kapelushnik J, Or R, Aker M, et al: Allogeneic cell therapy of severe beta thalassemia major by displacement of host stem cells in mixed chimera by donor blood lymphocytes. Bone Marrow Transplant 1996;19:96–98.
35 Slavin S, Nagler A, Varadi G, Or R: Graft vs. autoimmune lymphocytes (GVA) following allogeneic bone marrow transplantation in a patient with chronic myelogenous leukemia and severe systemic psoriasis and psoriatic polyarthritis. Exp Hematol 2000;28: 853–857.
36 Slavin S, Nagler A, Naparstek E, et al: Nonmyeloablative stem cell transplantation and cell therapy as an alternative to conventional bone marrow transplantation with lethal cytoreduction for the treatment of malignant and non-malignant hematologic diseases. Blood 1998;91: 756–763.
37 Nagler A, Slavin S, Varadi G, Naparstek E, Samuel S, Or R: Allogeneic peripheral blood stem cell transplantation using a fludarabine-based low intensity conditioning regimen for a malignant lymphoma. Bone Marrow Transplant 2000;25:1021–1028.
38 Slavin S: Immunotherapy of cancer with alloreactive lymphocytes. Lancet Oncol 2001;ii:491–498.
39 Slavin S, Nagler A, Aker M, Shapira M, Or R: New frontiers in cancer therapy; in Giralt S, Slavin S (eds): Non-Myeloablative Stem Cell Transplantation (NST). Oxford, Darwin Scientific, 2000, pp 83–91.
40 Körbling M, Katz RL, Khanna A, et al: Hepatocytes and epithelial cells of donor origin in recipients of peripheral-blood stem cells. N Engl J Med 2002;346:738–746.

oocyte by nuclear transfer and its in vitro culture to the blastocyst stage without implantation in a uterus. It is an area of research aimed at allowing major therapeutic advances that may save the lives and alleviate the suffering of patients with severe diseases, hence its usual denomination as 'therapeutic cloning'.

ES cells have been studied in mouse and their transplantation has been tested in several animal models of diseases, and shown to have the potential to cure diseases. Since 1998, research on the development of human ES cell lines in the USA, Sweden, Australia and Israel has indicated that there is an enormous potential for Medicine. The research on ES cells in Israel is particularly strong and has been highlighted by the journal *Science* [1]. The Rambam Hospital and Technion Rappaport Institute groups of Prof. Joseph Itskovitz-Eldor, Karl Skorecki and Lior Gepstein have obtained differentiation of human ES cells into insulin-producing cells and cardiomyocytes that in the future could be used for diabetes and myocardial repair [2, 3]. The groups of Drs. Benjamin Reubinoff and Tamir Ben-Hur at the Hadassah Medical Center have obtained differentiation of human ES cells into neuronal progenitors, aiming at transplantation for neurological diseases. At the Hebrew University, the laboratory of Dr. Nissim Benvenisty has transfected human ES cells with gene constructs that can increase their safety and therapy potential.

Since the existing human ES cell lines were not produced under conditions suitable for clinical use (which would require avoiding animal serum or feeder cells), scientists will need to isolate more human ES cells. The main source will continue to be supernumerary embryos (blastocysts) remaining after completion of in vitro fertilization treatments and that may be donated by the parents for therapeutic research. There will also be attempts to produce 'autologous' ES cells from 'cloned' blastocysts by transferring into oocytes the nucleus of a somatic cell taken from a prospective patient. This latter technology is still in its infancy but one recent report from South-Korea [4] claims success in developing human oocytes fertilized by nuclear transfer until they reached the 5-day blastocyst stage and in deriving an ES cell line from the inner cell mass.

One should keep in mind that research on fertilization of oocytes by nuclear transfer has a number of important medical applications and is not only for the production of autologous transplantable tissues. Thus, elucidating the reprogramming of the chromosomal DNA, which is needed to allow it to initiate early embryo development, has importance for research on aging, cancer and cell differentiation.

Ethical Debates on Human Embryo Stem Cells and Therapeutic Cloning

Human ES cell lines can be derived without use of cloning technologies, but cloning could add the important advantage of obtaining autologous ES cells.

The ethical debates on these two procedures, although distinct, are nevertheless related.

Opinions on Human ES Cell Research in Various Countries

Ethical debates have surrounded the development of human ES cell research. The first publication [5] in 1998 by Thomson's group at Madison University in collaboration with Itskovitz-Eldor from Technion's Rambam Hospital described the derivation of ES cells from supernumerary IVF human embryos, i.e. those which remained after a successful treatment for infertility and would no longer be used and for which the only alternative was frozen storage or destruction. Such supernumerary IVF embryos, donated with the informed consent of the parents, have been the source of the about 70 lines of human ES cells that are part of the world Registry compiled in 2001 by the US National Institutes of Health (NIH) [6]. The present status in the USA is that scientists working with federal funding (in the USA or abroad) can use the human ES cell lines from the Registry but cannot produce new cell lines of the same type. This restriction may not apply to private companies.

In 2001, the International Bioethics Committee (IBC) of UNESCO issued a report [7] on the Use of Embryonic Stem cells in Therapeutic Research [McCall-Smith A, Revel M: rapporteurs] which was adopted by the Intergovernmental Committee (IGC) and by the General Conference of the 170 member States of UNESCO. The report establishes that a pluralism of opinions exists, including the opinion to allow donation of supernumerary embryos:

'Every society has the right and the duty to debate and decide upon the ethical issues with which it is confronted. The IBC recognizes that human embryonic stem cell research is a subject on which it is desirable for a debate to occur at a national level to identify which position on this issue is to be adopted, including abstaining from this research... Whatever form of research involving embryos is allowed, steps should be taken to ensure that such research be carried out within the framework of a state-sponsored regulatory system that would give due weight to ethical considerations and set up appropriate guidelines. When authorization of donations of supernumerary pre-implantation embryos from IVF treatments for therapeutic embryonic stem cell research is under consideration, particular attention should be given to the dignity and rights of both parental donors of embryos.'

A similar pluralistic position was expressed by the European Group on Ethics in Science and New Technologies (EGE) [8] in November 2000: 'The derivation of stem cells from embryonic blastocysts raises the issue of the moral status of the human embryo. In the context of European pluralism, it is up to each Member State to forbid or authorize embryo research. In the latter case, respect for human dignity requires regulation of embryo research and the provision of guarantees against risks of arbitrary experimentation and instrumentalization of human embryos.' Many European countries have made such bioethical provisions and authorized the use of supernumerary embryos. The ethical evaluation has been particularly intense in the UK culminating in approval by the House of Lords [9]. The Commission of the European Communities has extensively reviewed the ethical and legal positions of different countries on the issue of human embryonic stem cell research [10].

The ethical position of individual societies and countries on deriving stem cells from supernumerary embryos, which puts an end to their capacity to develop, derives from considerations on the moral status of pre-implantation embryos, and is contingent to religious, cultural, philosophical and sometimes constitutional considerations in diverse societies. The magister of the Catholic Church [11] is that the personal status of a human being is acquired at the moment of fertilization of the oocyte; the Holy See does not authorize IVF, among others because it would necessarily create embryos in excess so that not all could fulfill their potential to become human beings. A fortiori, it condemns ES cell production from blastocysts, or research on such cells derived by third parties, and of course cloning for ES cell research. That a pluralism of opinions exists on the moral status of the embryo is shown by the fact that many countries in the Christian sphere of influence authorize IVF because of its therapeutic value in the treatment of infertility. It must be realized that accepting IVF has implied accepting research for improving the IVF reproductive technique, for example the in vitro culture of embryos for about a week in order to select the embryos with the highest chances of implantation, discarding some that are unsuitable. Other research on preimplantation embryos led to new medical procedures, such as ICSI (sperm injection into oocytes to treat male infertility) or PGD (preimplantation genetic diagnosis to help carriers of severe genetic diseases select embryos not affected by the disease and discard the affected ones). The moral questions on the status of the pre-implantation embryo posed by these IVF procedures are not different from those on ES cell derivation from embryos created for IVF but which are no longer destined for implantation and can be used for medical therapeutic aims to develop methods to save the lives of others. In some countries there is nevertheless a pluralism of opinion on whether or not to authorize these individual procedures or research, leading to situations which are not always consistent. In France, IVF for procreation is permitted but the derivation of human ES cells was forbidden for a long time (in July 2004, the French Senate suspended for a period of 5 years the ban on ES cell research from human embryos when this research is considered to be of valuable use for major therapeutic progress and on the condition that it cannot be pursued by an equally efficient alternative method).

Particularly interesting is the situation in Germany, where derivation of human ES cells is not permitted. Germany has an Embryo Protection Law (1992) that aims to protect human life from the early embryo stage. Before April 2002, it would have been legally possible to import ES cells, taking advantage of the NIH Registry of 2001. However, it was considered that allowing importation might incite other persons working abroad to produce ES cells and thereby to destroy embryos, and that this was a criminal act under the German Law. Following intense debate, a Stem Cell Import law was passed in the Bundestag that prohibits the import and use of human stem cells, but allows some exceptions if the ES cells were derived under strict bioethical control from spare (supernumerary) embryos and if the ES cell lines were made before 1/1/2002. There has been intense interest from the German Science Ministry in the bioethical regulations for ES cell research in Israel, and the possibility to import ES cells from Israeli laboratories, principally that from the Rambam Hospital. A German-Israel symposium organized by GIF, July 8–10, 2002 in Heidelberg was dedicated to an in-depth examination of the ethical and legal positions in Germany and in Israel on ES cell research. This symposium examined the achievements of scientists in the two countries and the possibilities of collaborations in the field of ES cells therapeutic applications. Such international meetings are of utmost importance for a true understanding of the ethical and legal positions taken by different countries on the issue of human ES cell research. Reaching such understandings will be one of the functions of the International Stem Cell forum created in 2004 by a number of national academies.

Ethical Opinions on Human ES Cell Research in Israel

The Bioethics Committee of the Israel National Academy of Sciences and Humanities[1] issued a report on The Use of Embryonic Stem cells for Therapeutic Research [12] in August 2001, circumscribing the ethical questions in the context of Jewish law, as compared to Christian and Moslem religious views.

Judaism places a high value on the religious obligation of treating serious illness even if it requires transgression of religious commands such as the sanctity of Sabbath. This stems from a deep respect of human life and of the human person, as has been restated by many modern Rabbinic authorities (Posekim), starting with Rabbi Moshe Feinstein and Israel Chief Rabbi Goren. The obligation of saving life cannot obviously be done at the expense of another life. However, in Judaism, the obligation of saving the life of a pregnant mother, or preventing grave damage to her health, is viewed as taking precedence over any moral status of the embryo, up to the moment of birth. With respect to the embryo prior to implantation, it is further viewed that there is no potential for the fertilized egg or the blastocyst to initiate pregnancy and develop to birth unless there is a parental decision to do so. These moral stances have been the basis for authorizing IVF and related medical procedures (ICSI, PGD), often with religious consent and with moral consistency. These views on respect of human life and dignity were taken into consideration in the report.

In the report, specific recommendations on human ES cell research stemming from these moral considerations were layed out. In brief, the report states that 'within the framework of IVF treatments, it will be permissible to donate supernumerary embryos that are no more destined to implantation, and this specifically for the purpose of therapeutic research'. It also states that there must be regulations to insure free and informed

[1] The Bioethics Committee is pluridisciplinary and includes ethics philosophers (Prof. Asa Kasher and David Heyd), a Rabbi and physician (Dr. Mordechai Halperin), jurists (Judge Shoshana Berman, Prof. Amos Shapira, Adv. Gali Ben-Or), geneticists/bioethicists (Prof. Hermona Soreq, Dr. Efrat Levi-Lahad, Prof. Michel Revel, Chair) and Academy officers (Prof. Alex Keynan and Dr. Yossi Segal).

consent for the donation, respect of human dignity, autonomy and liberty of the donors. The regulations should protect the rights of parents who find embryo research unacceptable. There should be a separation between the medical team responsible for the IVF treatment and the medical and scientific teams involved in ES cell research who receive the donation. Preimplantation embryos should not be sold or bought; imperatives of justice and equality in the access to the modern medical technologies such as ES cell research must be upheld. Research involving the derivation of stem cells from human embryos should be scrutinized meticulously in order to avoid unethical aims, and the medical applications of human ES cell research must be restricted to well-identified therapeutic aims.

The report also supports the continuation of research into other sources of human stem cells, including adult stem cells, which are often proposed as alternatives to those derived from supernumerary embryos.

Ethical Views on Cloning to Obtain Autologous Embryo Stem Cells

As indicated above in the scientific medical aspects of ES cell research, the subject of the so-called therapeutic cloning should be understood as a part of the research aimed at producing transplantable tissues which would be compatible (autologous) to the patient in need of the transplant. In this procedure, fertilization by nuclear transfer is used only to obtain blastocysts from which ES cells can be derived (in vitro and without implantation in utero). It is important to view this procedure in the larger framework of human ES cell research, in order to avoid confusion in the use of the term 'human cloning'. Once the moral principles on which derivation of human ES cell are accepted, there is only the need to consider the particular ethical issues in ES cells stemming from cloning technologies.

In one sense, the ethical issues may be considered less severe than with IVF supernumerary embryos. The 'cloned' blastocysts that would be used are a priori not destined to implantation in utero and reproduction, but the purpose here would be a different purpose, namely ES cell therapeutic research. In addition, there would be no question of ending a potential to life, since this potential would not exist. In fact, the Israel Law 'Prohibition of Genetic Intervention 5759–1998' – (which was renewed for another 5 years in 5764–2004) stipulates that embryos produced by the cloning technology shall not be implanted in utero for reproductive cloning. (The same Law also prohibits germ-line gene modification, while appointing a committee to follow the progress in medical sciences and to advise the Health

Minister on whether important beneficial medical applications may not eventually derive from these technologies, justifying making exceptions to the Law).

Why can it be ethically acceptable to a priori 'create' blastocysts by nuclear transfer in order to derive ES cells for therapeutic purposes? This is because sperm and intact ova are not used and the process differs from reproductive IVF. In IVF, the purpose is procreation justifying the use of sperm which the Jewish law forbids to waste in vain. IVF embryos should not be created a priori for any end other than reproduction, otherwise the embryo becomes a means and not an end in itself. Only when some of these embryos cannot be used for initiating a pregnancy do they become supernumerary and such blastocysts may then be donated for therapeutic research. In the case of blastocysts made by cloning (nuclear transfer), the reproductive end is not a priori an accepted purpose and using these blastocysts for ES cell derivation does not imply altering the end for which they are produced.

In the world, one of the major objections that has been raised against 'therapeutic cloning' is that if research on producing human blastocysts by nuclear transfer would be authorized, it would not be possible to control whether this research would not be a first step towards reproductive cloning. This is the major objection raised by President G.W. Bush in his February 9, 2002 address asking for a ban on all forms of cloning research. He stated: 'Anything besides a total ban on human cloning would be unethical, it would not be implementable, one would not know which embryo is a clone or when such embryos are implanted.'

However, from the ethical point of view, the same objections may be raised against IVF or any medical practice. Medical ethics have allowed us to set up strict regulations which ensure control over which sperm is used to fertilize which oocyte and to ensure that the embryos produced in vitro are implanted in the mother to whom they belong and in a precisely determined number. This strict control over the medical practice of IVF has shown that it is possible to entrust physicians to act responsibly (a recent case in the UK where an embryo from another couple was mistakenly born from the wrong mother has not led to banning IVF). In Israel, utmost care is taken; in certain hospitals each IVF process is witnessed with the help of the religious Puah organization. Strict implementation of a ban that would not permit reproductive cloning should be possible while allowing the beneficial research on 'therapeutic' cloning to proceed.

The Unesco IBC report on Human ES cells [7] concludes that 'nuclear transfer should be used only for therapeutic research'. It, therefore, considers that such research is not in contradiction with the Universal Declaration on the Human Genome and Human Rights and the clause against reproductive cloning therein. The IBC reports puts forward the argument that the benefits of the procedure (of nuclear transfer to produce embryonic stem cells) can take precedence over the fears deriving from this 'slippery slope' argument (i.e. that one type of scientific activity should be banned because it is close to another unauthorized practice). The role of bioethics is to define the limits of the permissible and not to ban upfront and completely medical advances that may save lives and alleviate suffering.

The research on human ES cells from blastocysts produced by nuclear transfer holds the highest promises for obtaining transplantable tissues that would not be rejected by the patients. This has led the US National Academy of Sciences in its January 2002 document on Cloning [13] to recommend that: 'research on approaches that prevent immune rejection of stem cells and stem cell-derived tissues should be actively pursued. These scientific efforts include the use a number of techniques to manipulate the genetic makeup of stem cells, including somatic cell nuclear transfer'.

Ethical debates are still ongoing in many countries that have authorized human ES cell research. In Europe, most of these countries have prohibited or tend to prohibit cloning for ES cells. At the European Union, the Group on Ethics of Science [8] 'considers that, at present, the creation of embryos by somatic cell nuclear transfer for research on stem cell therapy would be premature, since there is a wide field of research to be carried out with alternative sources of human stem cells (from spare embryos, fetal tissues and adult stem cells)'. Most of this does not really answer the quest for autologous ES cells. The UK is for the moment the only European Member State with a specific law that permits the creation of human embryos by fertilization or by somatic cell nuclear transfer [14]. The UK authorized this research in an extension of its Human Embryology Act that has been approved by the House of Lords. On August 11, 2004, it was announced that the UK Human Fertilization and Embryology authority (HFEA) has approved an application for making human blastocysts by cloning with the purpose of producing autologous ES cells for therapeutic research on diabetes. In the USA (see above), the Senate is still considering whether the ban on cloning should include cloning to produce stem cells. In Australia, a recent decision was to support a ban on Reproductive Cloning but not to include nonreproductive cloning research. Canada does not allow cloning to produce ES cells.

At the United Nations there are demands to extend the proposed UN International Convention against Reproductive Cloning to ban any research on cloning, even for therapeutic ends, such as for producing autologous ES cells. An initial proposal by France and Germany, also supported by Japan, would ban human cloning for the purposes of reproduction. A second draft resolution submitted by the USA, Costa Rica and other countries at the 57th session of the General Assembly Sixth Committee, would ban all forms of cloning and would include a ban on research: '... States shall not permit any research, experiment, development or applications ... of any technique aimed at human cloning'. This position appears extreme to many who consider that research on cloning may lead in the future to medical discoveries that will be beneficial not only for ES cell therapeutical applications in Regenerative Medicine but also for understanding the processes of DNA reprogramming which are relevant to cancer and to cell differentiation. In view of these contradictory positions, the UN Sixth Committee voted in December 2003 to delay a decision for at least 2 years.

Situation of Cloning to Produce Stem Cells in Israel

From the legal point of view: the Israel Law 'Prohibition of Genetic Intervention 5759–1998', while prohibiting the creation of a 'complete human being' by reproductive cloning, does not rule out producing cloned embryos that will not be implanted'. This was confirmed during the parliamentary process which led to the renewal of the Law in 2004 for another 5 years, and the text was modified to specify that what is prohibited is the implantation of a 'cloned' embryo in a uterus for reproductive purposes. The penalty for violating the Law was also made more severe, in view of the dangers in the reproductive cloning technology.

The Bioethics Committee of the Israel Academy of Sciences and Humanities in the recommendations of its August 2001 report [12] concluded that it 'considers it ethically permissible to experiment with new in vitro technologies to produce ES cells, such as reprogramming somatic cell nuclei by transfer into enucleated oocytes (so-called therapeutic cloning without reproductive purposes)'. The Committee based its recommendation on ethical grounds many of which were exposed above, including those related to ES cells from supernumerary IVF embryos. However, the production of cloned blastocysts for ES cell research must be viewed as experimental and be strictly supervised and regulated.

The position of the Bioethics Committee is also based on Jewish Law, as stated in its above quoted report under Halachic Conclusions [p. 12, paragraph 4]: 'The creation of any embryo for such research purposes is prohibited. Nevertheless, the creation of in vitro pre-implantation embryos for research should be allowed if it is probable that this research will help save human life. This includes creating embryos by the cloning technology.' As in the UK, the opinion in Israel is that the respect for human life and human dignity is not violated by authorizing research that has the potential to alleviate suffering of patients, provided it is carried out under strict bioethical regulations.

In its report, the Bioethics Committee of the Israel Academy defines [12] a number of guidelines for the strict monitoring of this research. The research and therapeutic applications of nuclear transfer (cloning) to produce stem cells must be done (and can be done) with complete respect of human dignity.

Strict regulations should ensure that the numerous human oocytes needed for cloning research are obtained with respect of the bioethical regulations set up for IVF. A new Israeli Law is being prepared on oocytes donation for reproductive purposes [15]. This Law will also address the question of oocytes donations for research, or the use of oocytes that are unfit for IVF purposes and could be donated for research including research on cloning for ES cells. The ethical rules for organ transplants are in this sense a model: These are donations and not commodities.

In the future, there may also be other methods to obtain cytoplasts (enucleated cells) suitable for research on cloning for ES cell research, such as cytoplasts from existing ES cell lines. Human oocytes could also be produced by maturating in vitro cells from ovary biopsies or producing oocytes from ES cell cultures [16]. Methods to obtain ES cells that would be more efficient than nuclear transfer could eventually be developed reducing the number of human oocytes needed. Parthenogenesis, for example, is presently under study [17].

The guidelines on ES cell research proposed by the Israel Academy Bioethics committee [16] have moved to the stage of implementation. The Health Ministry's National Helsinki Committee for Genetic Research in Humans has, since January 2003, proceeded along these guidelines in dealing with specific research applications from Israeli scientists on new ES cell production from supernumerary IVF embryos, some of which were approved. The Helsinki Committee has also examined applications on cloning for ES cells, although no approval was yet given (up to July 2004).

Impact of the Possible International Convention against Human Cloning on the Situation in Israel

The final form of the International Convention, which is now being discussed at the UN, will probably not be known for several years. Several scenarios must be taken into account. If the UN convention is limited to reproductive cloning, it will most likely be a ban without a time limit. The question will, therefore, arise of whether Israel should change the present legal situation. Based on the ethical and philosophical principles that led to opt for a time-limited moratorium on any medical application of reproductive cloning, it would appear justified to continue to have a time-limited prohibition. The Israel Law 'Prohibition of Genetic Intervention' having a built-in periodical review process of the scientific, medical and ethical situation, allows to renew the moratorium as many times as needed. This position can be defended on moral grounds, since, practically, the effect of the ban is the same whether it is time-limited or not. The difference is that there is no upfront condemnation of an entire area of scientific inquiry. If, in the distant future, some important medical applications of the technology will become apparent as a result of animal experimentation, which will also be proven safe and efficient, it is likely that the International Convention may also be reexamined.

Another scenario is if the International Convention stipulates a total ban, including cloning for stem cells or for other research purposes. In this case, Israel will not be the only country confronted with the dilemma of whether or not to allow the continuation of nonreproductive cloning research. There will probably be a concerted review of the situation in all countries, such as the UK, where cloning for stem cell research is permitted. Much will depend on whether or not the medical promises of cloned stem cells will be such that banning the research will appear less ethical than allowing it to proceed. The majority of Israel's bioethicists would prefer that in the UN debate Israel should side with those nations who do not want a total ban on all forms of cloning.

References

1 Vogel G: Stem cells: In the Mideast, pushing back the stem cell frontier. Science 2002;295:1818–1820.

2 Assady S, Maor G, Amit M, Itskovitz-Eldor J, Skorecki KL, Tzukerman M: Insulin production by human embryonic stem cells. Diabetes 2001;50:1691–1697.

3 Kehat I, Kenyagin-Karsenti D, Snir M, et al: Human embryonic stem cells can differentiate into myocytes with structural and functional properties of cardiomyocytes. J Clin Invest 2001;108:407–414.

4 Hwang WS, Ryu YJ, Park JH, et al: Evidence of a pluripotent human embryonic stem cell line derived from a cloned blastocyst. Science 2004;303:1669–1674.

5 Thomson JA, Itskovitz-Eldor J, Shapiro SS, et al: Embryonic stem cells derived from human blastocysts. Science 1998;282: 1145–1147.

6 National Institutes of Health: NIH Human Embryonic Stem Cell Registry. http://escr.nih.gov/

7 United Nations Educational Scientific and Cultural Organization (UNESCO): Reports of the International Bioethics Committee. http://www.unesco.org/ibc

8 European Union: European Group on Ethics. Opinion No.15. Ethical Aspects of Human Stem Cell Research and Use. 14 November 2000. http://europa.eu.int/european_group_ethics/docs/avis15_en.pdf paragraph 2.4.

9 House of Lords Select Committee: Report on Stem Cell Research. February 2002 http://www.parliament.the-stationary-office.co.uk/pa/ld200102/ldselect/ldstem/83/8301.htm

10 Commission Staff Working Paper: Report on human embryonic stem cell research. http://europa.eu.int/comm/research/press/2003/pdf/sec2003–441 report_en.pdf

11 Pontificia Academia Pro Vita: Declaration on the production and the scientific use of human embryonic stem cells, 2000.

12 The Bioethics Committee of the Israel National Academy of Sciences and Humanities. The Use of Embryonic Stem cells for Therapeutic Research, 2001. http://www.academy.ac.il/bioethics.html or at stwww.weizmann.ac.il/bioethics

13 US National Academy of Sciences: Scientific and medical aspects of human reproductive cloning, 2002. http://www.nationalacademies.org/

14 Commission Staff Working Paper: Report on human embryonic stem cell research. http://europa.eu.int/comm/research/press/2003/pdf/sec2003–441report_en.pdf

15 Israeli Ministry of Health: National Statutory Committee for the Issue of Oocyte Donation. http://www.health.gov.il/units/egg_cont/law.htm

16 Hubner K, Fuhrmann G, Christenson LK, et al: Derivation of oocytes from mouse embryonic stem cells. Science 2003;300:1251–1256.

17 Cibelli JB, Grant KA, Chapman KB, et al: Parthenogenetic stem cells in nonhuman primates. Science 2002; 295:779–780.

Michel Revel, MD, PhD

Department of Molecular Genetics, Weizmann Institute of Science,
PO Box 26, IL–76100 Rehovot (Israel)
Tel. +972 8 934 2101 / +972 8 934 2103, Fax +972 8 934 6106,
E-Mail michel.revel@weizmann.ac.il

Blazer S, Zimmer EZ (eds):
The Embryo: Scientific Discovery and Medical Ethics.
Basel, Karger, 2005, pp 120–142

The Unborn Child: Scientific Discovery, Medical and Ethical Dilemmas

Round Table Discussion

Moderator and Editor

Karl L. Skorecki

Participants

Alan R. Templeton Jeffrey M. Drazen Michel Revel
Roberto Colombo Ahmad Natour Avraham Steinberg

On 12 of November 2002, an unprecedented and unique opportunity presented itself to conduct a round table discussion with spontaneous participation from an eclectic group of scholars, addressing a series of questions. These questions relate to some of the most exciting and challenging ethical dilemmas facing scientists and medical researchers. The audience for the round table discussion also included an impressive cross-section of participants of diverse backgrounds, ranging from social work to molecular biology, from religious law to clinical practice, and represented a fine example of civil discourse conducted at the highest and most meaningful level. In fact, several of the round table discussants and participants, commented that this level of civil discourse could not have taken place in most constituencies around the world, for fear of disorderly and disruptive interruption representing prior prejudices and biases. The success of this round table discussion represented a microcosm of the success of the conference upon which this monograph is based – and reflects the thoughtful input of the participating scholars. The round table discussants were Professor Alan Templeton, Professor Jeffrey M. Drazen, Professor Michel Revel, Father Professor Don Roberto Colombo, and Kadi Ahmad Natour, many of whom have also contributed an additional written paper. It was my great privilege to moderate this round table discussion and to summarize the essential contents and opinions. In addition, the questions posed before the participants, have been sent to Professor Rabbi Avraham Steinberg, who has contributed his written input, which has been incorporated as an appendix into this chapter.

Framework Questions

The Round Table Discussion was based on the framework of a series of questions posed by the moderator, and which are summarized as follows:

- *'Slippery Slope': Potential Unwanted Outcomes of Emerging Technologies.* One of the major ethical arguments in considering the adoption of novel clinical or research initiatives and guidelines, particularly pertaining to reproductive technologies and genetics, emanates from fear of the 'slippery slope'. As usually presented, this argument raises the concern that although breaking through a given barrier which may be ethically acceptable in its own right, such a breakthrough may lead to a loosening of regulatory impediments and thus facilitate subsequent actions of questionable ethical validity or societal concern. In each of their own areas of expertise, the participants were asked to describe their concept of the 'slippery slope' and its implications, if any, for unwanted societal outcomes of emerging technologies and initiatives discussed at the conference. To what extent are the participants' opinions and points of view influenced by this argument, and how can unwanted outcomes be preempted without jettisoning an otherwise meritorious initiative?

- *Scientific Imperative vs. Societal Responsibility.* A related dilemma pertains to the balance between the 'scientific imperative' to uncover and report scientific truth on the one hand, with the sometimes conflicting concept of 'societal responsibility', in which potential harmful outcomes can emerge from the application or interpretation of such discoveries. Is the balance to be achieved within this apparent dichotomy an issue that should be left within the domain of the scientific community or does it require the input of other elements in society?
- *Interaction of Research Scientists with the Media.* Tied in with this dilemma is a definition of the role and interface of enthusiastic research scientists with the press and public. Is it within the mandate of Institutional Review Boards to extend their reach beyond the traditional mandate of protecting the patient as a research subject, and extend this to the broader mandate of potential future societal harm, and the extent to which this can be defined?
- *'Ignorance is bliss' or 'A little knowledge is a dangerous thing' are two famous sayings.* Are we currently really in a position where we are ready and willing to learn and apply to the clinical arena as much as technology allows about the relationships between genotypic variation (at the level of DNA sequence) and phenotypic variation (differences in individual appearance, behavior, disease predisposition and response to drugs)?
- *'Lingua medica' – refers to the appropriate use and distortions that sometimes confuse our thinking based on medical terminology.* For example, there has been a significant level of confusion in the definitions and distinctions between such terms as 'therapeutic cloning', 'reproductive cloning', and 'somatic nuclear transfer'. It has been recently suggested that the more appropriate terminology of 'somatic nuclear transfer' be used instead of 'therapeutic cloning' to distinguish this from the quite different process of 'reproductive cloning'. Would a more rigorous definition of the terms sharpen the ethical, legal and theological discourse, especially pertaining to questions concerning the status of the embryo?
- *Evolutionary implications of germline intervention.* Currently in Israel there is a 5-year moratorium banning reproductive cloning and germline gene intervention. What are the scientific and evolutionary implications to the future of human diversity, and human disease burden of interventions such as germline therapy?

It should be noted that the constraints of time did not permit all of these questions to be addressed in a systematic and comprehensive manner by all the participants. The participants were free to look at the entire spectrum of questions, and in their comments to extrapolate where relevant, to other questions or related issues. Furthermore, the transcripts of the Round Table Discussion have been edited in conjunction with the participants, and the text represents a paraphrase of their verbal comments following revision.

Prof. Revel: The slippery slope issue is of course a philosophical concept, stating that if you take the first step in a certain direction you may have no way to stop and thus will proceed and slip into actions that are either immoral or illegal or both. Now, this concept is only theoretical, and I strongly believe that the function of bioethics is to provide the safeguards or guidelines that will prevent us from slipping. In my view, a function of the Bioethics Committees – which around the world are pondering ethical issues on genetics, stem cell research or cloning – is to define the 'limits of the permissible' in the applications of the scientific research. That means to define a strong position onto which to hold, in order not to slip on the slippery slope. Many people think that the only solution is to ban upfront new technologies because their development will necessarily lead us to unwanted use. But in my opinion, we do not have to fear such a slippery slope. What we have to do is to develop the strict ethical guidelines that will prevent unwanted applications, but allow mankind to benefit from what is permissible in the scientific advance.

Prof. Templeton: I agree with the point of view that was just articulated. I don't think we can be afraid of the slippery slope, but I do think we have to acknowledge that it is a danger. In my talk I tried to emphasize that biology does not provide any clear thresholds. We are dealing with a continuum. We need to constantly reevaluate where we place ethical thresholds on this biological continuum because the technology is ever changing. As our technology changes, our options change, the side effects change, the implications change. Therefore, we are not so much on a slope as we are on a pathway that is moving constantly. It's more like surfing, which is what we have been doing here at this conference. How do we stay in the right place, when the wave is always dynamic, both from the biological point of view, and the technological point of view? I think we have to keep in mind that the ethics are also a dynamic process. The ethical answers that we have today may be totally inappropriate a decade from now. So we have to put a framework in place that will constantly reevaluate our ethical positions on these issues, so that we don't end up in a slippery slope situation, or we don't 'wipe out' as we surf on the often turbulent waves of change.

Kadi Natour: As a matter of fact I am really afraid of the slippery slope in this field, because of what technology can do to human society. But this is not confined to the field of the medical research, but also to any field of our life. So we need to develop our lives to work in order to improve our condition, but at the same time define the constraints. So, I do believe that we need codes of ethics in order to regulate all of these activities. Religion can be one of the most important instruments in order to provide such guidelines and control this activity.

Prof. Drazen: I am less pessimistic about the slippery slope. I think, as Dr. Revel said, that if we don't take a step forward for a fear of what might happen, we may never take a step forward. So I think that when I find myself on a physical slope, that maybe I should not be on, I take it a little bit at a time. Then, I stop and assess whether I am in the right place. And if not, I quit, and if things are going 'okay', I'll take another look. But the critical issue is to make sure that you look, and to make sure that it is not just you yourself that is doing the looking. You need to have people who are dispassionate who are looking with you, because any scientist who is successful is not dispassionate about his or her work. And so, after you have gone a little bit on the slope, it is time to have a meeting about this, and say: 'this is where I have been, and this is where I think I am going'. And I think that has benefit, and here is the potential benefit that others need to weigh in to make sure that you are not intellectually out of control. It is important to ensure that the researcher is not blinded to factors that should be seen but are not always seen. But I think if we do not move at all, we will remain where we currently are. We must move forward.

Prof. Skorecki: Prof. Revel, I would like to point to a concrete example. I know that in the report on 'The Use of Embryonic Stem Cells for Therapeutic Research' published in 2001 by the Bioethics Committee of the Israel Academy of Sciences and Humanities, a point is made that the slippery slope question is actually the issue which divides trivial nonmedical use of stem cell research from life-saving research.

Prof. Revel: Maybe I should rephrase the question a little differently. Can cloning for medical research be allowed without fear that it will lead to reproductive cloning? There is a consensus today that reproductive cloning, i.e. use of the cloning technique to try to give birth to a child, would be medically extremely dangerous as seen from the accumulated experience in animal cloning. For that reason, reproductive cloning should not be permitted. Now, some may see the use of so-called 'therapeutic' cloning for producing embryonic stem cells – which may allow the production of life-saving transplants that (due to cloning) will not be rejected by the patient's body – as one step on the road that could potentially lead to reproductive cloning. This is an example of the slippery slope argument. More specifically, the slippery slope argument in this case would posit that if we allow scientists to experiment with nuclear transfer for producing stem cells, they may discover the way to make reproductive cloning safer, better, and more acceptable. This causes fear among those who oppose any research on reproductive cloning. So we have here a clear case of the slippery slope argument. The answer, as set in the Israel Law on Genetic Intervention (as renewed in 2004), is to prohibit implantation in utero of an embryo that is produced by cloning technology. Thereby, as proposed in our report, we can prevent slipping on the slippery slope and allow scientists to work on fertilization by somatic nuclear transfer limited only to production of cloned blastocysts in vitro, with the purpose of deriving cloned embryo stem cells. However, we should note that today this research meets other ethical problems, namely the source of the numerous oocytes needed.

Prof. Skorecki: Perhaps in light of your comment, let us just step out of the order of the questions in the list for a minute, and go right to the last issues related to germline therapy at the level of the fertilized egg. What are the evolutionary implications, ethical implications, including all the way to reproductive cloning, and the effect of scientific terminology on ethical positions. You used the phrase 'therapeutic cloning', which in the minds of many who read about it, confuse this term with reproductive cloning. Would someone please like to address this question? Perhaps Prof. Colombo, I know you have thought about these issues and perhaps wish to comment.

Prof. Colombo: Thank you for giving me the opportunity to address that. From a strictly scientific point of view I disagree with what has been proposed this morning from the developmental, evolutionary points of view. I would like to say that the evolutionary point of view is not the only biological view. I would like people here not go home with the idea that the evolutionary point of view on fertilization is the only scientific point of view. If we examine books on developmental biology and embryology, I think most will agree that fertilization is the beginning of organ development. Let us take the book by Scott Gelbert. Scott Gelbert is a well-recognized authority. His book is translated all over the world. You can find in chapter two, entitled: 'Fertilization, the beginning of new organs' the first paragraph which documents and provides evidence that the beginning of the development of every sexually reproducing organism is fertilization, with no doubt. Books on embryology state that the beginning of a fetus is embryonic development, and the beginning of embryonic development is fertilization or nuclear transfer. Thus, it is evident that there is not one biological point of view of this. The only distinction between therapeutic cloning and reproductive cloning will see this as devoid of any scientifically identical ground. If we look at what happens if you transfer the nucleus of the somatic cell into an enucleated oocyte, either you don't have any development because the yield of the process is very low, or you have the development of an embryo, which is identical to embryo development by sexual gametogenesis and fertilization. If you take a group of blastocysts, you cannot distinguish which blastocysts were obtained by fertilization and which were derived by nuclear transfer. How could you distinguish these two? Is there any means to distinguish these two kinds of embryos as two distinct types of entities, or are they the same type of entity? And so, if we take an embryo which is aimed at development, like in IVF, why should we not utilize an embryo which was produced by nuclear transfer?

Prof. Templeton: I did try to be careful that I was providing an evolutionary perspective and indicated that there are many other perspectives. I think it's really important in a conference like this to acknowledge multiple perspectives. This allows us to see that there are many different ways of looking at the same problem. And in fact, the evolutionary perspective was an important one to bring to your attention precisely because many of you were not familiar with it. It is not mentioned in the textbooks that you read. But yet, the evolutionary perspective is a valid one that should make us think. Until we can see this breadth of perspectives, our own thinking is limited and narrow. In order to be able to address ethical issues, we have to take a very broad perspective and to realize that there is a diversity of life on earth, but there is also a diversity of opinion among humans on these issues. We need to incorporate this diversity into our thinking. So, I am not claiming that what I presented was the only way of looking at it. Rather, the evolutionary perspective is a way that I think has some validity, and that should at least raise questions. Whether it provides answers or not, it is the question which needs to be debated here. So I do not disagree with anything you said. Yes, I was providing one of many perspectives, but I think it is an important one. Concerning the use of gene therapy to change the germline, and therefore incorporate engineered genes into the kind of evolutionary continuum that I talked about, one of the big problems right now is that most gene therapy addresses one gene at a time, and here we have the problem. What happens if we take one gene at a time, even if we have a good study with strong statistical significance, maybe even published in the *New England Journal of Medicine*? When we make the transition from a genetic study to germline gene therapy, we place this gene into the context of a highly genetically variable and evolving population. How the engineered gene behaves in the population can be quite different than its behavior in a scientific study. I can give you an example of the pitfalls of this approach. In looking for genes for coronary artery disease, some case-control studies done in the 1980s looked at the apolipoprotein E gene in hyperlipidemics. Three common alleles of ApoE were identified that are polymorphic in human populations, named the '2', '3' and '4' alleles. In the case control study, the frequency of the '2' allele was close to 90% in type III hyperlipidemics compared to 8–9% in the general population. Therefore, the conclusion was that the '2' form is a 'bad' allele. This is the allele that you don't want. Let us suppose that we had the technology at that time to change everybody with a type '2' allele to a type '3', the so-called 'good' allele from that study. What would have been the impact? Well, our group has performed longitudinal forward prospective studies on that, and now we know that among the people bearing the '2' allele, 98% of them do not suffer from hyperlipidemia, and in fact on average, they have lower cholesterol levels. Only 2% of them become type III hyperlipidemics, and now we know in part that's due to epistasis with other genes that are found in some populations but not others. This is what occurs when you do a case-control study that is biased in its sampling. How many people actually have type III hyperlipidemia? It is a very small proportion. When you study that very nonrepresentative portion of the population, you can get highly significant and completely valid scientific results that are a disaster if you apply them to the general population. And remember, when we are talking about germline changes, we are talking about introducing a gene into a population, not just about a therapy for an individual. Therefore, the population context is very important. In fact there is no single gene that uniformly increases or decreases risk for coronary artery disease. They simply do not exist. And so, right now I would say in terms of the ethical argument, our knowledge of genetic systems is really in a very primitive state. We know a lot about what an individual gene does in a particular context, but what we really need to know is how multiple genes come together in the context of a population, subject to many environmental influences. And we really have very little work in that area, and that's what we need to be concerned about, if we are going to think about anything approaching germline therapy. I don't see us even being close to that stage at this point. So, you made the distinction between a eugenic and a genetic kind of issue, and I say we should avoid any eugenic type of mentality right now, because we are simply ignorant. And whether we ever want to, even if we develop the required knowledge, I think that is an ethical issue itself. Quite frankly, I would be very reticent about such an approach.

Prof. Revel: Thank you. If I may, I want to relate to what Reverend Colombo has said. Prof. Colombo made the argument that one cannot distinguish between a cloned embryo, or blastocyst, and one that was obtained by normal fertilization. There is a debate ongoing in the United Nations following a German-French initiative to establish an International Convention against human reproductive cloning, i.e. using the cloning procedure to give birth to a baby. The reasons for that are various and, as I said already, the consensus today is that – from the medical safety point of view – reproductive cloning should not be permitted. However, there is an initiative from the USA which is supported by the Holy See, to ban all forms of cloning, including the possibility of cloning in vitro for obtaining cloned embryonic stem cells. Moreover, this latter initiative seeks to ban all forms of *research* that could possibly lead to reproductive cloning. The reason which was given, as heard from President G.W. Bush himself in a White House address, is that one could not distinguish between an embryo that was generated by cloning and an embryo that has been generated by sperm fertilization, and who knows what the physicians are doing in the back rooms of the hospitals and laboratories, there will be no control and no way to know what is going on. Therefore, it is preferable to ban everything, including research on nonreproductive (therapeutic) cloning. I think this position is difficult. As much as I can understand, the position of the Holy See opposes embryo stem cell research (without cloning) because it involves destruction of a preimplantation IVF embryo, even if it is supernumerary (remaining in excess after completion of the IVF treatment) and the only alternative for this embryo is to be kept frozen indefinitely or destroyed. The Catholic Church considers that full human life begins from fertilization. But with cloning, one is not dealing with an embryo that can become a human being, since the law in almost every country today prohibits reproductive cloning. So, I am afraid that one is again a victim of the slippery slope argument. One is trying to prevent research, aimed at developing the cloning technology for embryonic stem cells – in order to produce autologous tissues that could be used in patients without risk of immune rejection – because one is afraid of not being able to distinguish what the physicians are doing. I believe that the Editor-in-Chief of the *New England Journal of Medicine*, in this panel, will agree that physicians have ethical responsibility in what they are doing, otherwise they will not dare to send their articles to his journal (except cases of unprofessional conduct which are to be punished). I think we have a here real problem of mistrust of the medical and scientific profession. And this is something which should be looked at seriously.

Prof. Drazen: That should be a topic for the next conference.

Kadi Natour: I am not sure there is a clear difference between these concepts. I think that cloning in principle is against our known beliefs, because it is an unnatural way of bringing people to the world. I think it alters the concept of human life. I shall give you some examples of what will happen if this technique of cloning takes place in the future. What might happen is that the marriage rules and laws of family provenance might become disrupted. There are more responsible means of dealing with the matter of the infertile couples, and related problems. This is not the proper way to deal with the problem, because maybe you generate more problems than are solved.

Prof. Revel: In relation to what Kadi Natour just said, there is nevertheless the consideration that if reproductive cloning were to become medically safe and efficient, it could be used to alleviate the suffering of some couples who are unable to procreate otherwise, and would not want to use a sperm bank or the donation of oocytes from a source outside the couple. If the cloning was safe and efficient, many Rabbis in Israel would consider it to be preferable to the use of a sperm bank, because in an anonymous sperm donation from a bank there is a danger that, unknowingly, a brother and a sister might marry and procreate. Although this is unlikely to happen, the anonymous nature of the sperm donation makes it theoretically possible, and this is enough to raise religious concerns. Cloning, from such a Rabbinical point of view, would be safer because the baby would be a 'genetic' twin to the father or mother donor of the somatic nucleus, and therefore his identity would be known. It is open to discussion, of course, if the offspring would be really the son or the twin brother, but filiation and parenthood are much more than how the child was created: as in other IVF procedures, the child would be loved and desired by the family. I do not know whether reproductive cloning could ever become a technology that would be safe and efficient, but certainly we should not disregard it off hand for certain potential specific and limited medical applications. At present and because the animal experience shows the cloning method to be dangerous, it is unethical to consider its use in humans. Israel has a law prohibiting cloning of a complete human being for 5 years (the Law was renewed in 2004). The law does permit the cloning of preimplantation embryos for nonreproductive purposes, such as cloned embryo stem cell research.

Prof. Skorecki: I would like to ask Prof. Drazen to respond to the following question please. What is the Editor's position when he receives a paper which has been submitted for review and has passed Institution Review Board approval, but is highly ethically charged, under debate at the United Nations or under debate worldwide?

Prof. Drazen: The honest approach is that editors make their independent decision about the utility and the appropriateness of the ethical review, and about ten times a year we reject papers that are otherwise scientifically sound and have been approved by review boards, but where we feel that that process was not well thought out. The obvious, but extreme example is that if we got a paper from Josef Mengele about his experiments, it would have been approved by the local board, but would be banned from publication. So we make it our job to decide on our own and the key points are: were patients aware that they were in the research protocol; did they know about the alternative management approaches for their condition; did they know the risks and benefits; and did they enter the protocol, as far as you can tell without cooption of any kind. We need to make those decisions ourselves as an independent body, and we do that all the time. And as I said, over the course of a year we reject about ten papers that people say were approved, and we always get appeals from the authors. The editorial process is confidential, so I can't give you specific examples. The common case would be an ongoing clinical trial. It may happen that during a 10-years duration trial, evidence is forthcoming from another source that suggests an alternative treatment for the condition for which the trial participants have been enrolled. The evidence may be very compelling, and not just from a single source. From my perspective, the trial can continue, if the patients were informed clearly about the availability of a new therapy. But unless they have been informed, even if the trial has only begun, and there is something new out there that the participants should know about, they should be given the option to drop out without any negative consequence to the participants in making the decision to drop out. So, it is our job as editors to make up our own minds about it. And I think the rules are fairly standard, and we don't want somebody else making decisions for us.

Prof. Revel: If I may, I would like to answer the other question that was asked about ethics committees. I think there is a slight distinction between the Helsinki review boards, especially those in local hospitals, and a bioethics committee. The bioethics committees are, by definition, multidisciplinary. Therefore, the number of scientists in these committees does not exceed the number of lawyers, of philosophers and of religious representatives. All have equal representation, and for this reason such bioethics committees are better equipped to deal in-depth and at length with societal questions and values. On the other hand, the primary role of the Helsinki committees is to ensure that the study and procedure designs will be implemented with all the ethical controls and supervision that are required. To give an example, a decision was made *in principle* in Israel, allowing experimentation regarding somatic nuclear transfer for the cloning of blastocysts for purposes of stem cell research. However, this research would require many oocytes because the technique is extremely inefficient. Therefore, the Helsinki committee did not give *practical* approval to this research. There is a need to monitor the source of oocytes and ensure that scientists will do only what is permitted and not beyond that. Is monitoring possible? There exists, for example, in Israel a voluntary IVF monitoring system to ascertain that the sperm is from the husband and the egg is from the wife, and that there is no mismatching of sperm and egg in IVF procedures. I believe that it is possible to have a monitoring system also for the cloning research, and it is the role of the Helsinki Committee to set-up such a monitoring for protecting the rights of participants. There are difficult issues involved with cloning for embryo stem cells, one being the right of women donating the oocytes. In Israel, such voluntary donations are being arranged for IVF treatment of infertile women, but donations for research have not been yet arranged. With goodwill and a positive outlook on the life-saving aspect of the research, it should be possible to find the appropriate solution.

Prof. Skorecki: As a corollary, I would like to raise as a topic for future discussion or audience participation the following question: should institutional review boards and hospital ethical committees, address only what is there primary mandate today, which is protection of the human subject in research, or should their role be extended to issues of the possibility of societal harm to a group that is being studied? Perhaps this can be developed into a topic for a future conference.

Audience Discussion

Prof. Skorecki: Thank you to the round table participants. I would now like to open the round table to discussion and participation by members of the audience.

Amos Shapira, for Tel-Aviv University School of Law: My question is whether you addressed economic interests and political interests. What is the media's position with regard to biotechnological research in general, and stem cell research in particular? From what I have heard, we may have a clash between values – religious values, humanistic values, freedom of research, questions of monitoring etc., but what about other interests, that we all know play a role – institutional interest, economic interests and political interests? Don't they deserve some realistic appraisal in such a debate?

Prof. Skorecki: Some of the speakers in their lectures addressed economic issues. A few spoke about politics and the role of politicians, who we know stand behind a lot of what we do and adjudicate. The Minister of Health was here yesterday. In spite of this, I would like to ask if any members of the panel would like to address the question by Prof. Shapira about political and economic implications.

Prof. Colombo: Instead of replying to your question, I would like to raise my own question at this point. What is the value of human life? How do you value this? Could you put this on a par with economic interests, or with other kinds of interests? Are economists willing to take into account that their own lives and the lives or their wives or sons, as a mere economical wage or something more than an economical object.

Prof. Skorecki: Maybe Prof. Revel can comment on this as well. It does deal with the issue of the infinite value of human life and the obligations of society. To what extent does society have to delve into its collective resources to save one individual human life? This leads us to a thoughtful discussion about this issue. Does anyone else wish to comment?

Prof. Templeton: When people think of the economic issues at stake, they think of the tradeoffs between the cost of therapy and the potential benefits to human life. But there is another aspect that was actually hinted at this morning, or at least mentioned, that we need to be concerned about, and that's the commercialization of these technologies. For example, about a month ago in St. Louis, there was an ad in a newspaper called the 'The Jewish Light' circulating amongst the Jewish community. A company was saying they would send you a kit with which you could do a cheek cell swab, and then they would send you back information about Tay-Sachs, cystic fibrosis, and many other genetic diseases, as well as whether you are a Cohen or a Levi. I have a friend at the University of Michigan who monitors such ads, and it is amazing how many private companies are now offering DNA testing for all sorts of purposes. Some of these companies deal with ethnicities, some deal with genetic diseases. There is actually a lot of profit to be made in this area, and for this reason people are going into it. The problem is that this area has not yet been regulated. This brings us to the issue of counseling. How do we really equip people to deal with the facts? They receive a test and it says they are a carrier of Tay-Sachs. How do they interpret this information? What do they do with this information? We have to keep in mind that this genetic technology is rapidly becoming commercialized, and is being used for all sorts of purposes, some that seem very remote from why they were originally developed. There are strong economic issues driving this. So, should we be concerned about this? Should this be regulated? Or does this imply that basically anyone in the United States, for example, can get genetic testing done privately?

Prof. Skorecki: This question related also to the media and the relationship between science, research and the media. Most of the journals, including the *New England Journal of Medicine* have very clear-cut rules. Still, enthusiastic researchers at the time and shortly after publication feel free to express their opinions in the media. Is there any further thought from the scientific journals, including the *New England Journal of Medicine* other than imposing strict moral rules, to limit authors of edited and reviewed publications from direct contact with the public.

Odette Leviztky from the Ethics Department at Tel-Hashomer Medical Center and Bar-Ilan University: I'd like to thank the speakers for the wonderful presentation. I think this conference brings us issues that are politically and emotionally loaded. In an ethical discussion, it is very important to be sensitive to the use of language and the choice of terminology. I think that the choice of the title, 'The Unborn Child', is very charged. I think it means taking a stand in the politically ongoing debate between 'pro life' and 'pro choice'. I would like to raise this issue of the choice of the title. As a woman, I would like to emphasize the fact that this unborn fetus, not child, can only exist inside my body. Therefore, any decision regarding its testing, its continued or interrupted existence, has everything to do with my autonomy and my body integrity. Eggs, required for research must be extracted from my ovaries. I found this perspective lacking from our discussions here. A second issue that I find problematic is that during 2 days of conference, we have heard 22 male speakers and only 2 female speakers, and I find that unfortunate.

Prof. Skorecki: Thank you for the comment. I don't think the participants of the round table are the ones to address your important comment, since they are not the organizers. I don't know if any of the organizers wish to address these very important, well-taken points. I think a lot of thought went into the title, and you can see it comes across quite differently in Hebrew than in English. These are important issues of semantics which

I also alluded to earlier. Reproductive cloning, fetal cloning, stem cells – there is no question that language carries with it value-laden connotations and implications. Does anyone wish to make a comment? We thank you for these insights and perhaps they can be used in organizing future conferences.

Moshe Friedman from the Medical Genetic Department in Sheba Hospital and member of the Supreme Helsinki Committee on Genetics: I would like to raise the issue of the slippery slope. I think that we have made considerable progress down the slope. Scientists should not be called upon to set the boundaries, but rather philosophers or religious advocates or legal counselors. The reason I am mentioning this is because reproductive cloning has actually been practiced. Not exactly in the way we consider it now, but it was practiced by the Germans in the Lebensborn Farms whereby they selected people whom they considered to be ideal prototypes of the Aryan race. Now, what we are doing is in some way a relaxation of selection in the Darwinian way of thinking, and I think we have far too little knowledge to allow these things to take place at the present. I think a lot has to be learned before we know something about gene interaction, and to where it may lead us. The problem is that if anything goes wrong, it would be better to occur in civilized progressive countries. Once you unleash this technology, it may lead to wrongful use in modern societies. That is where the real risk lies. It is like nuclear technology, which was developed for peace but was put to use for war, and it is a great risk to all of mankind.

Prof. Skorecki: I think that relates to one of the points raised earlier – social responsibility versus scientific imperative – can we ever use these kind of arguments to legally limit the progress of scientific discovery? Would anyone like to comment?

Prof. Revel: I think that the comparison and judgment of true medical practices on the same level as Nazi crimes is not productive. Hypothetically, medical use of reproductive cloning would be only for individual cases in order to alleviate suffering or to allow procreation, when no other technology can be used. In addition to cases of infertility that have no other cure, cloning may also be applied in certain cases of carriers of genetic diseases in order to have children free of this disease. For a couple that discovers that one of them is a carrier of Tay-Sachs mutation, it may be possible to have offspring who are not carriers, by reproductive cloning of the healthy parent. I think it is difficult to compare these medical applications to the atomic bomb: the nuclear weapons were right from the start developed to kill, to destroy and to win wars. Researchers who work on cloning technologies consider it a means to a cure, a medical technology. Of course, one can misuse any medical technology and the Nazi German doctors, if they can be called that, have shown that medicine can be distorted for inhumane criminal purposes. That is why after the Second World War, the World Medical Association proclaimed the Helsinki Declaration to ensure that no human experimentation be done without informed and free-willing consent, without autonomous decision and participation on the part of the patient. I think this is the safeguard that will prevent us from slipping on the slope that you are referring to. We have to weigh up the risks and the benefits. Risks always exist, but adherence to Bioethics Norms should enable mankind to avoid these risks.

Moshe Friedman: May I comment about what you said please. The problem didn't exist only in Germany. I must remind you that in the United States, the Supreme Court actually, Justice Holmes, allowed the sterilization of under-privileged people. After this ruling, tens of thousands of people were sterilized in the United States. Next, there was a pathologist in Chicago, whose name I don't recall at the moment, who openly declared that he was performing euthanasia. Let me remind you that enforced sterilization laws existed in Europe until the 1960s. So what I am talking about is not a theoretical threat at all. It is a realistic problem, and our moral dilemma is very real, and we must be very careful in authorizing these technologies. Of course I do not oppose helping a childless couple or curing a disease, but I am afraid of wrong applications. I must remind you that euthanasia is practiced now in China and in Singapore, and sex selection is practiced in India and in other countries. This is a real threat and is not a figment of the imagination.

Prof. Revel: Let me return to Prof. Shapira and concern about the economic aspects. He touched on a very important issue, which may have two sides. One is undoubtedly that society should make every effort to provide medical aid and therapeutic drugs to everyone, in particular developing countries in the Third World, at an affordable price. The price and availability of medications is a real moral and ethical issue for the World, which until now has not been well addressed. On the other hand, one has to recognize that if we want new medications, new drugs, one has to allow commercial pharmaceutical companies to make profits. For honest disclosure, let me say that I am involved with some pharmaceutical products myself. I believe that questions of Intellectual Property can be handled in an ethical and moral fashion. Recently, some international organizations have proposed to prevent patents on DNA. A total ban would be wrong, because if we want investments in making new drugs or developing new medical technologies, we have to let them be patented. Patents are the tools found by society to encourage companies to disclose their research. What should be prevented are patents which are not formulated in a way that describes a new product, which are not new inventions, but merely describe the DNA sequence. This should not be permitted, because it does not disclose a medical use and may prevent others from doing so. In many areas of medical research there may be economic interests, but these ought not to come in place of the real moral values of medical research, which seek to save the life and the health of the individual human being.

Prof. Skorecki: We have heard from a number of speakers that technology and science are not in themselves lacking in ethical values. In fact, the example given in the previous question in some countries is a case in point wherein sex selection is a very low technology practice. I think we understand what we are talking about. So we can obviously talk about this a great deal more, but I'd like to leave time for two final questions or comments please.

Roni Dayan, Faculty of Life Sciences – Bar Ilan University: We might find ourselves practicing gene therapy in many cases in a few years in the future. My question is, to what extent should we consider the implications with respect to increasing defective genes in the population when we practice gene therapy as opposed to the process of natural selection.

Prof. Templeton: That's an old question which has come up many times. Haldane actually answered it in the 1940s on a radio show, and gave an excellent answer. He said that the impact of modern medicine has been the substantial decrease of genetic disease. The reason is that when you look at genetic diseases, for many of them the effect that we associate with the disease phenotype is recessive. But the evolutionary dynamics of the gene is actually determined more by what it does in the heterozygote condition. In fact you can show, using the equations of population genetics, that it's almost irrelevant whether the gene was lethal or semi-lethal in the homozygous condition. The recessive disease is just a 'side effect'; it is the effect of the gene in the heterozygote that dominates in determining its frequency in the population. Haldane pointed out that the most common genetic diseases in humans are common because they are advantageous in heterozygotes, often because of resistance to some infectious disease. So, for example, individuals who are heterozygous for sickle-cell anemia are resistant to malaria, whereas homozygotes suffer from the genetic disease of sickle-cell anemia. The control of malaria diminishes the beneficial effect of the heterozygote state for sickle cell disease. This in turn leads to an evolutionary reduction in the frequency of the mutant allele. Hence, the impact of medicine in this case is to alter the evolutionary pressures to diminish the frequency of the genetic disease of sickle-cell anemia. So we need to keep this in mind when we are looking at genetic disease, the primary focus from the medical point of view may be distinct from the point of view of evolution. Most genetic diseases actually have a very minor contribution to Darwinian selection. The genetic disease is not what the genes are there for; it's not why they are being selected. In fact, the decision to treat the medical conditions in heterozygous individuals who are far more common than homozygotes results in more selection against the genetic disease. The eugenic arguments that modern medicine is somehow destroying the gene pool of humanity do not have any merit.

Janise Plag, a pediatrician in Meir Hospital, and in private practice in the Chicago area: I'd like to ask, in term of reproductive cloning – let's assume that cloning can be made safe in the short term, still the determination of its safety in the long term, will take many years. In the interim, is it fair to subject a child to potential unknown future complications because of the couple's desire to have a child? So, is it possible to ensure that cloning is safe without first crossing ethical boundaries?

Kadi Natour: I think it's not fair in order to please ourselves, to carry out experiments on others, in other's bodies and to play with others lives. So, I do believe that this is very dangerous, and we should consider it as individuals and as foundations and as a society. I am afraid that these questions have a lot of aspects, not only from the religious or human points of view. And if I follow the answer to Prof. Shapira's question, from the political, social, and economical point of view, this subject is very controversial. What happens, for example, when these projects are funded by the state. All of us agree that this research and projects should be funded by the state. The state has its budget from all the citizens, and this is a very big question. Other questions concern the 'industry' of having children in this way. Who will have the control of this? The state or private foundations, or what exactly. Who will run this business? And there could be a possibility of having children for rich people, and the poor people will have no possibility to benefit. And I think it's a very tough question that we have to face bravely and before we slip, we have to deal with it.

Prof. Colombo: I would like to stress that the question is a worldwide process, because it raises the point of view of cloning the human being. In many cases, we heard the points of view of couples who are childless. We heard the point of view of a patient who is waiting for a new cure for his disease. But we use the term therapeutic cloning in a way that is contrary to good clinical practice. Because in good clinical practice rules, the therapeutic experimentation is a trial, whose potential benefit is for the subject himself, not for others. This is why we use therapeutic experimentation, therapeutic trials. In this case 'therapeutic' is misleading because it refers the benefit to other people and not to the subject himself.

Prof. Revel: I agree with Prof. Colombo. The words 'therapeutic cloning', which were coined by R.P. Lanza in *Nature Medicine* in 1999 is not a good term. Better speak of cloning for producing embryonic stem cells that are autologous to the patient in need of a cell transplant, and have the advantage over regular embryonic stem cells that the transplant will not be subject to immune rejection. The purpose is therapeutic, as in other types of transplantation from a donor to a recipient, for curing a patient or saving his or her life. The same therapeutic ethical principles which permit harvesting of vital organs or vital cells from a body that has no potential for life of its own, as after brain death, are for many valid as well for supernumerary embryos that remain after a successful IVF treatment and have no more life potential since the parents have completed their plans for pregnancies. It may be argued that cloning of any type is subjecting the human embryo to instrumentalization. Two remarks are in place. First, the teachings of the Catholic Church that the fertilized egg is a human person also led to prohibit in vitro fertilization for the purpose of reproduction. A fortiori then, embryo stem cell or cloning research is unacceptable. But for those who accept IVF as a therapeutic answer to infertility, is there necessarily a danger of instrumentalization? In 1982, I attended a meeting at the Vatican. It was said that IVF is against human dignity, that one should not be born out of a 'test tube'. It was stated that humans should be procreated in an act of love, and not in a test tube. It was said that IVF would lead to terrible abuse, commercial exploitation and that it would destroy family values. We see today all over the world, and in Israel which is one of the leaders in IVF, that IVF can be done under ethical conditions for the medical benefit of countless infertile couples. We should learn from the IVF experience, and see that new technologies should not be immediately banned because we are afraid of them. It should be the vocation of bioethics to find a way to make the best use of new medical technologies, as was the case for IVF.

Appendix

Brief Comments on the Round Table Discussion
Prof. Steinberg: Unfortunately, I was absent from the important round-table discussion. Many fundamental and weighty issues were raised and discussed by the participants. I would like to briefly comment on some of these issues.

One of the principles discussed at length at the round table discussion was the issue of the slippery slope. This is indeed a serious argument concerning the limits of implementation of scientific discoveries, but one should not abuse it. I suggest the following points for argumentation: on the one hand, every new discovery may lead to unwanted and even dangerous consequences. There is no good without bad. Hence, taking the argument of the slippery slope to its extreme would lead to a total ban on science and to a complete cessation of the implementation of scientific discoveries. Using this argument in this way one should stop using cars because they are the number one killers in modern societies, and go back to horse and buggy. On the other hand, totally disregarding the dangers of the slippery slope and letting scientists go totally free without any restrictions may indeed lead to unwanted consequences that should be prevented. Therefore, both extreme approaches are wrong.

Since almost all values and implementations bear relative significance and since in many instances different and opposing values lead to different implementations, society must balance between them. This, obviously, is a difficult way to adopt because it will certainly lead to debates and strong disagreements, but it seems to me to be the only reasonable way. For the sake of striking such a morally defensible balance it seems to me that one should take into account the expected benefits and risks as well as the prospect of societal ability to restrict, control and regulate the processes so that benefit will be maximized and damage and danger will be minimized. In the process of accepting or rejecting a proposed significant scientific discovery a multidisciplinary committee should try to foresee the potential advantages as well as damages and disadvantages as best as possible and control, restrict and regulate the discoveries for the benefit of mankind.

In this sense, genetic innovations, gene therapy, stem-cell research and cloning are not different from others major advancements in science throughout human history. Obviously, the aspect of slippery slope is valid only if the first steps are not considered inherently wrong. Hence, those who believe that therapeutic cloning is inherently wrong should ban it as such, but they cannot argue the slippery slope argument. However, for those who argue that there is no inherent moral and/or religious wrong in human cloning, but agree that at this stage of the scientific development there are serious ethical problems with the potential outcome of reproductive cloning, should allow therapeutic cloning without fear of slipping into reproductive cloning. This argument is based upon the enormous potential good of therapeutic cloning combined with appropriate societal legal and moral regulations to prevent reproductive cloning. In other words, the combination of the benefit of therapeutic cloning that much outweighs the risks of slipping into fertility cloning, with the societal restrictions, control and regulation against slipping into fertility cloning forms a defensible ethical balance in this situation. One still may argue that some irresponsible and criminal scientists will abuse the permission to produce a cloned blastocyst for stem cell use and proceed to reproductive cloning. This, however, is in my view an unbalanced use of the slippery slope argument, because this is true for every societal permission of implementing innovative scientific discoveries.

The same holds true for the distinction between somatic gene therapy and germline gene therapy. Whenever genetic therapy will become a reality, it might be quite appropriate to use it for somatic changes because of its enormous healing potential, but ban the use of such technology for germline changes because of its potential damage to generations. Once again, one should not use the argument of slippery slope to ban somatic gene therapy, because on balance the benefits to society by using somatic gene therapy combined with societal enforcement of appropriate regulations and restrictions against germline gene therapy should outweigh the fear of slippery slope.

As we know from history it is almost impossible to halt scientific advantages through ethical or legal constraints. Total banning of scientific discoveries usually leads to underground developments which cannot be controlled or regulated. It is much wiser to proceed with caution and with overt societal checks-and-balances, so that science and society will be able to maximize benefits and minimize damages.

Karl L. Skorecki, MD, FRCP

Department of Nephrology and Molecular Medicine,
Rambam Medical Center,
PO Box 9602, IL–31096 Haifa (Israel)
Tel. +972 4 854 3250, Fax +972 4 854 2946, E-Mail skorecki@techunix.technion.ac.il

Blazer S, Zimmer EZ (eds):
The Embryo: Scientific Discovery and Medical Ethics.
Basel, Karger, 2005, pp 143–165

Are Genes Our Destiny?

Implications and Ethical Limitations of Genetic Determinism in Medicine and Behavioral Sciences

Michel Revel

Department of Molecular Genetics, Weizmann Institute of Science, Rehovot, Israel

The Need for Bioethics

Bioethics has the vocation to ensure that the much-needed advancements in life sciences, together with their applications in medicine, be solely instruments to promote human welfare and human dignity. Bioethics encompasses the ethical, legal, social and cultural dimensions of the life sciences and the technologies associated with them. In doing so, bioethics fulfills today a predominant role to guarantee protection of human rights and fundamental freedoms in a time of major scientific advances in human genetics and reproduction. Operationally, the task of bioethics is *defining the limits of the permissible* in the applications of scientific and biotechnological advances to human beings. Knowledge itself ought not to be limited and, therefore, the function of bioethics is not to ban upfront research into new technologies but to define the limits within which, if at all, these new scientific means may be applied and for what purpose.

The public has to be educated about science. Every advancement of science and technology raises anew the question of what are we to do with our increased power over nature. A task of the ethics of science is to take care not to 'demonize' science, presenting its power as a danger to human cultural values, as a demon that wants to take control over human free choice of action or as a Promethean revolt [1]. Science alone does not answer the question of what to do with the knowledge it generates – it is not in itself a moral value. Rather, the human cultural values in their ethical, legal, philosophical and often religious dimensions are the tools which help determine how to use knowledge for good purposes. The biblical image of the 'Tree of Knowledge of Good and Evil' [Genesis chap. 2] is already a warning to mankind that knowledge (science) may be used for good as well as for evil, and because science is morally neutral it should not be consummated without the 'Tree of Life' [Zohar Bereshit, Folio 33b], which is the symbol of all higher moral values sustaining human life (as they are expounded in the biblical message, Torah).

Hence, bioethics is by essence pluridisciplinary based on the interactive discussions between scientists, lawyers, philosophers, teachers of religions and public figures. Almost all over the world, bioethics committees have been established and operate at various levels: at the international level, for example UNESCO's International Bioethics Committee [IBC], at the level of national bioethics committees, which translate the general principles and formulate policies for each country, and at the local level in many hospitals and medical centers where the policies need to be implemented. The ideal form of these debates is the search for a consensus by what has been called 'the ethics of discussion' that, as put by the German philosopher Jurgen Habermas, is 'a consensus that cannot be achieved by force, no matter how much deductive logic or empirical proof are involved' [2]. The consensus is not reached by saying: 'I have scientific proof' or 'here is a philosophical proof or religious proof that what I am saying is correct'; consensus is also not a compromise, but rather a synthesis, a sublimation of the discussion to a point where all can live with the resolutions. Often, particularly at the international level, the resolutions are pluralistic, leaving open several options such as to use or not to use the technology.

At this meeting on 'The Unborn Child: Scientific Discovery, Medical and Ethical Dilemmas', we heard how different the positions of representatives of three religions (Judaism, Islam and the Catholic Church) may be, illustrating how complex and difficult, but also how necessary, is the task requested from bioethics committees to reach a consensus and formulate acceptable policies.

The Human Genome Project: A Revolution in Biotechnology and Medicine

In the mid-1980s, an international effort was initiated to determine the DNA sequences present in the 23 pairs of chromosomes which carry human heredity. The Human Genome Project, officially completed in 2002, is bound to revolutionize our understanding of human biology and tremendously expand the medical applications of genetics. Of the estimated 25,000 genes dispersed along the human DNA molecules, only about 10% are known as genes whose alterations cause hereditary genetic diseases. Best identified are the monogenic diseases linked to changes in a single gene, but most of the common human diseases are multigenic (resulting from interactions between several genes) and multifactorial (resulting from complex interactions of genes and environmental factors). Completion of the Human Genome Project is only the start of exciting research into the function of each of the genes which direct the development of the human embryo, fashion the body organs, the immune system and the human brain. The significant degree of polymorphism in many human genes and intergenic chromosomal segments (about 0.1% variation in the 3 billion nucleotides composing the genome) allows defining the genome of every individual. By comparing DNA from large numbers of individuals who suffer from a certain disease to an equally large number of donors who do not suffer from this disease, it is possible to establish statistical association between a certain genotype and the probability to acquire this disease. These genetic association studies [3] have more statistical power than the classical linkage studies, and are particularly important for multigenic and multifactorial diseases, such as cardiovascular diseases, asthma, diabetes, schizophrenia and other psychiatric syndromes.

Genetic Testing and Genetic Counseling

Through knowledge of gene configurations associated with diseases, physicians will be able to make more exact diagnoses but there will be also increasing interest in testing for these genes before a disease occurs, and before birth or before conception (preimplantation genetic diagnosis or PGD). Although of enormous beneficial potential for the prevention of serious genetic diseases, the expansion of such predictive medicine also raises ethical challenges particularly if the significance of certain genetic predispositions is not well understood, if the genetic penetrance is low or if the gene may predispose to a disease appearing late in life. Moreover, the very definition of what is a serious genetic disorder may be sometime subjective [4], and some may desire to use genetics in order to select for characteristics that have no immediate medical significance. Many of these inevitable practical difficulties in prenatal or preimplantation genetic diagnosis (PGD) may be alleviated by appropriate genetic counseling that must accompany genetic testing. This genetic counseling has to follow well-defined ethical guidelines. It should respect the autonomy of the person, especially that of a mother when the question arises whether to continue or interrupt pregnancy because of a gene alteration in the embryo. The counseling must be nondirective but informative and adapted to the cultural environment of the counselee. When possible, it should be given by physicians with a comprehensive intent to treat, and avoid being only a description of the statistical chances of disease. 'High-street' or 'supermarket' gene testing (as practiced for blood pressure) would not be appropriate in human genetics, for which a personal and intimate counseling is essential. Results of prenatal genetic tests should be confidential to the mother, who will then decide to whom the information should be passed on. Ideally, the information will be jointly discussed by both parents. The right 'not to know' the result of a test should be preserved, in particular for members of families where all relatives of the proband are requested to be tested.

Genetic testing ought to remain voluntary, with informed personal consent, and with free individual decision regarding the actions to be taken as an outcome of the test. The decision of whether to continue or interrupt pregnancy when a genetic disease or malformation is diagnosed rests ultimately on the mother-to-be who is required to make an individual decision after being given expert genetic counseling. One of the ethical issues in the Human Genome Project, particularly in its impact on prenatal and preimplantation genetic diagnosis, is to avoid any risk of returning to eugenic practices [5]. The fear is not unreasonable. In the early 20th century, in advanced countries including USA and Scandinavia, the Eugenics theories and movement sought to eliminate social 'undesirables' by controlling human breeding, and these theories ultimately served the objectives of Nazi Germany for 'cleaning out' contaminating elements – first the mentally retarded and chronically sick, later the Jews and other 'inferior' people [6]. However, as pointed out by F.D. Ledley, there is 'an essential distinction between eugenics and genetics in the ... importance ascribed to individual welfare relative to society' [7]. The danger of eugenics is fundamentally linked to the power given to the State, or to society at large, of dictating a genetic policy and imposing decisions about human reproduction. Medical genetics can remain free of eugenic danger as long as it is only the individual concerned (the mother) who makes a free and informed decision about procreation. Involvement of the State in genetics, even for economic motives, should be therefore a source of concern and this applies as well to insurance companies and employers who seek access to genetic information. An International Declaration on Human Genetic Data adopted by UNESCO (October 16, 2003), and legislation in several countries including Israel (Genetic Information Law, 2000, dealing with confidentiality of genetic samples and data), set out the rules for protection of identified genetic information, i.e. information or DNA samples that can be traced to the individual being tested. These jurisdictions are essential to protect the rights of individuals against any genetic discrimination or other societal pressures (justified needs for DNA testing in criminal procedures being also addressed in these documents).

The advances in prenatal medical genetics, offering increasing number of technologies and tests for genetic diseases, should not and have not resulted in more abortions. In fact, the experience shows that before the advent of a test, families at risk had less children either avoiding pregnancy or interrupting it because of doubt [8]. Access to reliable genetic tests allows more secure procreation. As an example, prenatal testing for β-thalassemia in Cyprus and Sicily has actually reduced the number of abortions in carrier families (which was 75%). This may be taken as a justification for the decision to screen the entire population for carriers of the mutations, and for requiring prospective couples to be tested and informed of whether both are carriers [9]. Although screening of entire population poses ethical problems (lack of voluntary and free consent to be tested), the Cyprus experience shows that 90% decrease in birth of children suffering from this severe blood disease can be achieved while respecting human dignity thanks to the collaboration of educators and the Church with physicians. Premarital screening of adolescents is also being used by groups of orthodox Jews in which marriage is pre-arranged and the matchmaker receives confidential information from the testing agency Dor Yesharim on whether or not the prospective groom and bride may be both carriers of the Tay-Sachs mutation or four other prevalent severe genetic diseases. Nevertheless, population screening for genetic characteristics must be subject to intense ethical scrutiny and done only when justified by the desire of the population to avoid continuous suffering from a severe affliction prevalent in the population. Otherwise, screening should be restricted to genetic diseases that can be cured or prevented by medication or appropriate diets, such as is the case for phenylketonuria (PKU) for which screening at birth is done almost worldwide.

The Ethical Complexity of Genetic Testing

As already mentioned, the definition of what is a serious genetic disorder in the unborn child is often subjective and depends on individual decisions of the prospective parents [4]. This is particularly true for malformations and handicaps: who can decide objectively what is acceptable and what is not? The fact is that there are two extreme views of genetic testing. On the one hand, Associations of Handicapped advocate 'the right to be different', and demand from Society the right to be respected and accepted as being different. In this view, the existence of a genetic test or other mean of prenatal diagnosis should not be an incentive for interrupting pregnancy, and Society has the duty to make all the investments necessary to allow an active participation of the handicapped in normal professional life. At the other extreme, some would say: every birth with a genetic defect is an error of prenatal diagnostic as evidenced by lawsuits for 'Wrongful Life' against the geneticist or even against the parents. The claim in these lawsuits sounds like 'it would be better not to have been born', even though the judicial process is essentially about financial compensation for the suffering child. The famous Perruche case led the French Parliament in 2002 to negate the right to claim that it would have been better not to be born, except in cases where a professional malpractice on the part of the geneticist or the genetic counselor can be proven. The truth is that real life lies somewhere between these two extreme viewpoints. It is important to give consideration to the life experience and opinions of disabled persons. In real life, many handicapped would rather say: 'Thank God that my parents did not take the genetic test and make a decision to abort me because, despite my severely impaired condition, I know today all what I would have missed would I not have been born'.

Genetic testing is not about seeking an 'ideal genetic make-up' or an ideal baby. Some fear that the multiplication of genetic tests may distance the mother from her fetus. Too often today, mothers avoid an affective relation to the fetus before being certain that he has no genetic defect: a sort of 'tentative pregnancy' [10]. The unborn child is not a consumer-good, which is accepted only if defect-free (or returned to the manufacturer). Parents confronted with the news that the fetus has a malformation or will be handicapped need time to reflect and eventually undergo a mental process of 'adoption' of the diseased child. This process, whatever the conclusion reached – to accept or not the pregnancy – evolves within the framework of an appropriate genetic counseling. In general, it is important to understand that prenatal genetic diagnosis, at least with the present technologies, cannot ensure a perfect genome and even if in the future the DNA chip technology will allow a genomewide testing of all genes, the question will remain of whether the goal of genetics is to eliminate all 'bad' genes. The very notion of 'good' and 'bad' genes does not have a scientific basis. Many pathogenic gene variants have been selected for, rather than being just accidental. Eradicating the mutation for sickle cell anemia, which in the heterozygote state protects against Malaria, may be dangerous. It can be assumed that many such gene mutations afford the carrier some advantage, not evident today, resulting in our considering the mutation only for its pathogenic effect in the homozygote state. The cystic fibrosis mutation is known today as a disease, but may afford in carriers a protection against cholera. Eradicating these mutations from the human species may be dangerous in some environments and at some times in human history. One should not eradicate gene variants from the human genetic pool, as one eradicated the smallpox virus (and even this has proven dangerous against the threat of biological warfare). With all the undeniably beneficial progress in human medical genetics, the public needs to know that there is no ideal human genome. As put by the Quebec Genetic Group: 'It is important to conceive man in his complexity and originality, to recognize that all humans carry abnormal recessive genes and susceptibility genes (5–30 in each of us). No one can be qualified as genetically sane or genetically deficient'.

The limits of genetic testing are also determined by the risks. It does not make sense to test for rare syndromes (occurrence of 1/5–10,000) if the risk of spontaneous abortion after amniocentesis is higher (1/2–400). Families or ethnic groups at risk ought to be tested for severe diseases, but testing in the public at large is justified only if the frequency and the severity of the disease are similar to the risk or higher. Predictive genetic testing in asymptomatic individuals poses complex ethical questions, in particular if there is no effective intervention to prevent or treat a disease [11]. This becomes even more complex in the unborn child and different categories of genetic tests need different ethical evaluation. Genetic alterations causing severe diseases, often lethal in childhood, raise little ethical concern but prenatal diagnosis for late-appearing diseases – that will affect the individual after 40 or 60 years – poses much more difficult ethical questions. Genes that cause a predisposition to a disease, increasing its risk but not determining absolutely the disease to occur – as is the case for many cancer genes – raise additional queries. Finally for multigenic and multifactorial diseases, including mental disorders such as schizophrenia, and the most common cardiovascular affections, it is not clear what the predictive value of the genetic test is, since it appears almost impossible to predict all the interactions between the genetic condition, the environment, the nutrition and other modalities of life [12].

Should One Use Genetic Testing for Nonmedical Reasons?

The Council of Europe's Convention on Human Rights and Biomedicine (art.12) states: 'Tests which are predictive of genetic disease or which serve either to identify the subject as a carrier… or to detect a predisposition to a disease may be performed only for health purposes or for scientific research linked to health purposes, and subject to appropriate genetic counseling'. Genetic testing is primarily intended as a mean to improve the medical condition of the individual tested, or for research aimed at the same purpose. These limits of genetic testing are being challenged by the progress in prenatal and preimplantation diagnosis.

Consider the cases in which PGD is performed to select for embryos that will be HLA-matched in order to be a donor of cord blood stem cells (or bone marrow cells) for a diseased sibling, suffering for example of Fanconi anemia [13]. While the medical aim is evident, it may be argued that the medical benefit is for the sibling and not for the embryos being subjected to selection. In some cases, the PGD is done to ensure that the embryo itself does not have the genetic disease and in addition that it is HLA-matched, but one can envisage diseases such as leukemias where the PGD selection will be done solely for HLA matching. The crucial ethical argument will then be to ascertain that the parents really desire another child, that he will be an end in himself and in no way just a mean to save the life of the diseased sibling (or parent). The Jewish bioethicist Rabbi Moshe Tendler has stated that if the child is desired anyhow there is nothing wrong in having him also be a donor to save another life. As Jewish law emphasizes that the health of the mother takes precedence over the unborn child (necessitating abortion to save her physical or her mental health), it may also be argued that the mother's anguish at having an older child dying from a disease while she plans another pregnancy is a strong enough medical motive to authorize the procedure.

Sex-selection by PGD poses much more difficult ethical queries. In the case of sex-linked genetic diseases, such as X-chromosome-linked hemophilia, PGD may be used in order to ensure that the embryo is a girl and will not suffer from the disease. The medical aim is evident and justifies the risk to the mother who will have to undergo IVF to perform the PGD. This is preferable to the trauma of abortion, especially in families at high risk where the same situation arises at each pregnancy. However, when sex selection is done for family balancing or to satisfy a preference of the parents for one or the other gender, there is no real medical aim. The risks to the mother involved in IVF treatment are not justified, and moreover the selection by PGD is now being done between equally healthy embryos, just because some are not of the preferred gender. Many bioethicists, including John A. Robertson [13], find this a very controversial application of modern genetic testing, even if there is no real danger of causing a great disparity in the sex ratio of the population (such as occurred in China and India by a variety of abortion methods). Following a case in Israel, for which selection of a girl embryo was authorized by the Health Ministry to avoid revealing that a child born to a man living in a very religious closed community was conceived from a sperm donor (as the boy would not have been a Cohen [priest] like his father), the Health Ministry asked for guidelines from two Bioethical Committees in Israel. The guidelines now state that gender selection by PGD will be authorized only for medical reasons such as sex-linked diseases. However, in rare instances, where the sex-selection is motivated to avoid serious threat to the mental health of one or both parents, or of the child to be born, the case will be brought to a National Board of experts, including clinical psychologists, this board having the authority to authorize gender selection by PGD in exceptional cases. In cases in which PGD is done anyhow for diagnosis of a genetic disease, and the sex of the embryos is known anyhow, the guidelines recommend that a request for sex selection be considered more favorably by the board, provided there is also the above mental health threat. A minority view expressed was that in such cases where the risks of IVF are taken anyhow for medical reasons, the desire for sex selection be granted without need for approval by the board.

Genetic testing by PGD (or otherwise) for nonmedical reasons should be strictly monitored as they open the door to the 'baby on order' or designer genetics, where parents may 'dream' to use genetic for selecting physical characteristics or character traits in their offspring. Sex selection may itself be apprehended as a genetic selection for behavior, although it is clear that social attitudes and expectations play an important role in the different behavior of the two genders [13]. Indeed, there is danger in an excessive belief in genetic determinism, i.e. giving genetics excessive weight in shaping the human person to the point where the environment, life style and education are underestimated. It is essential to realize that the human genome project is necessarily a reductionist approach to human nature, an approach with obvious benefits for mankind but which cannot and ought not to be viewed as explaining all human nature. A pertinent example of the ethical queries raised by the new power of human genetics, and the illusions it may help create, is the emerging field of behavioral genetics.

Behavioral Genetics

Let us try first to define what behavioral genetics really is. How does it differ from other areas of human genetics? The Nuffield Council on Bioethics recently issued a report on 'Genetics and human behavior: the ethical contex' [14], presenting the scientific data and their implications up to 2002. Much of the present discussion is based on this report.

Behavioral genetics is an attempt to locate specific genes or groups of genes associated with behavioral traits and to understand the complex relationship between genes and the environment. Complex, because in most cases multiple genes will interact to fashion our behavioral tendencies. Complex, because in all likelihood, the lessons of behavioral genetics will not be understood without referring to the environment and conditions in which a human lives.

Examples of the aspects of human personality under study are intelligence (elaborated on below), musical abilities, sexual orientation, susceptibility to aggressiveness or other antisocial conducts, and tendencies towards extraversion or novelty seeking. There are of course many other types of behavior that can be studied in the human species, some being found also in animals thereby raising the question of how much we humans are determined by our biological nature and how much of our behavior can be controlled by human freewill and intellect. Intelligence encompasses probably one of the more specific aspect of human behavior, but one which cannot be separated from the influence of education and environment.

Behavioral Genetics: Distinction from Medical Genetics

A second characteristic of behavioral genetics, as defined here, is that it differs from research into the genetic bases of diseases and disorders. In the case of behavioral genetics researchers investigate aspects of our personalities not actually diseases or disorders; it is important to stress this difference, because there are diseases of behavior that are investigated in the framework of medical genetics, but behavioral genetics deals with nonpathological variance.

The meaning of genetic variation between humans is best illustrated by a bell-shaped curve describing the distribution of a trait over an entire population. There are some cognitive traits which are 'species universals' – for example language learning. Every human knows to speak (excluding again pathological conditions) and this can be defined as a nonvarying trait (or genetic characteristic). Then there are rare disorders, which are clustered at one very extreme end on the bell curve, affecting only a very small part of the population. Examples may be severe retardation and early-onset Alzheimer's disease. Pathologies due to mutation in a single gene may give a similar extreme bias in distribution. Next, there are traits which are more frequent and be found in a sizeable part of the population on one side or the other of the bell curve, representing common mild disorders, such as mild retardation or learning disabilities – and are likely to result from multiple genes. But, as already stated, behavioral genetics deals with the normal distribution of traits, for example cognitive abilities, that vary within the normal range in the middle of the bell curve. By assigning a quantitative value to each group over the curve, one attempts to define 'quantitative traits'. The gene loci that may affect the variance are named quantitative trait loci or QTLs. This affords a quantitation of behavior (as one would quantify height or weight). But it is a normal variation and what is being studied is actually where in this variance one or another individual in a population would be.

Two methodological remarks may be useful. First, the analogy with height and weight are in place because there are upper and lower limits to what is considered as the normal range. Moreover, these limits vary with the epoch: a child with short stature that in the past may have been considered normal may today receive growth hormone treatment, and the limit at which obesity is considered pathological and requiring treatment is lower than it was before. The definition of the normal range is not absolute, but nevertheless there is a normal range in which a medical intervention would be considered improper. These considerations apply of course to the definition of the normal range of behaviors as well.

A second remark is that research on the genetics of QTLs is rapidly evolving thanks to the advent of genetic 'association' studies [15]. These make use of large-scale, population-based DNA collections which allow associating genetic polymorphisms (variations among individual genomes) with diseases but also with normal phenotypic characteristics (including behaviors). As an example of medical application the Israeli company IdGene compared genomewide scans for single nucleotide polymorphisms (SNPs) on almost 1,000 DNA from schizophrenia patients to 3,000 controls and discovered a significant association between schizophrenia and a given form of catechol-O-methyltransferase, an enzyme producing a neurotransmitter [16]. However, the probability of diseases such as schizophrenia is the result of many genes (multigenic) and also of interactions with the environment (multifactorial). Two other genes were already found associated with schizophrenia [17]. Studies done before by linkage analyses on small families or groups could not show these associations because they lacked the statistical power provided by the large numbers of DNA samples. As of today, there are population based large collections of DNA samples in several countries [18], the UK Biobank aiming to collect 500,000 samples. These advances will most likely be instrumental in the attempts to identify genes that vary with behavior. Simply as an example, a genetic association was claimed for cigarette smoking [19], this of course being clearly only one of the many different factors, both genetic and environmental, that influence smoking behavior.

To reiterate, behavioral genetics is distinct from genetics of human disease because it deals with nonpathological variance within the normal range. There are diseases of behavior but these pathologies are being studied as part of clinical genetics and, as explained above, the genetic basis for diseases of behavior is different from just a variation in abilities over the population.

General Ethical Issues in Behavioral Genetics

A critical view of behavioral genetics cannot ignore that it raises ethical issues. The central topic of behavioral genetics is the heritability of variance among individuals, and of course between groups, implying an inescapable social impact of the research. In a sense, it is assigning a value, a certain quantity, and inevitably a certain quality to the uniqueness of the individual. In ethical terms, to the statement that every human being is unique, we might have to add that some are more unique than others, some are better than others as a result of the QTLs assigned to their personality.

However, it is not the study of behavioral genetics that poses the main ethical queries but the applications that these studies may have. Given that the scientific enquiry is justified, there are likely to be purposes and outcomes deserving a serious ethical reflection. One purpose of knowing about the genetic basis of behavior could be intervention or treatment, for example preventing aggressive behavior by using medication or by attempts to change the socioeconomic environment. A more problematic purpose might be that of selection, for example using prenatal genetic testing or even PGD in order to test or screen for certain behavioral traits in the unborn child. Next we may want to stream children in school on the basis of intelligence and aptitude as we predict them from a genetic test. This surely should switch on some ethical red lights. Other purposes may be the screening of employees or job seekers to exclude those with traits that the employers consider undesirable. Insurers may seek genetic information about behavior and personality traits in order to estimate the risk of giving an insurance policy. Yet another purpose may be to claim diminished legal responsibility for one's actions or to mitigate punishment for criminal behavior by saying 'I was made like that', 'I was born like that' and therefore I am not responsible for my action, I do not bear moral responsibility. These implications of behavioral genetics, distinguish it not only from the genetics of diseases but also from social application of genetics such as geographic genetics or study of the migration of human populations, etc. Clearly, there are some words of caution which need to be said about behavioral genetics.

First of all, it is important to reaffirm that it is a legitimate area of research. Certainly one should let this research go on and investigate the genetic basis for various human behaviors – range of behavioral skills and even intelligence (IQ). But at the same time it is capital to say that extreme care is required in the interpretation of the results. Quoting Lewis Wolpert

[20]: 'Scientists have the obligation to examine the social implications of their work. It matters a great deal if complex behavioral characteristics are treated as being controlled by genes and behavioral influences are ignored. Scientists have an obligation to make the reliability of their views in these sensitive social areas clear to the point of overcautiousness'. The social implications of behavioral genetics are very powerful and the interpretation of the results is often careless. We see how quick the press is to speak of 'the gene for aggressiveness' or 'the gene for criminality' or the 'alcoholism gene', even a 'gene for monogamy' based on the length of time a male rodent spends copulating with the same female. Indeed, scientists have an obligation to make the reliability of their views in these sensitive social areas clear to the point of overcautiousness – it is not even enough to be cautious. When scientists identify a genetic variation that affects behavior, they must tell us how much it affects the behavior, how much of the variance among the human population is accounted for by the gene variation and whether the effect of the gene is likely to be influenced by environment, education, socioeconomic status, etc. This all the more because the interpretation may depend on social outlook and may influence political decisions.

Heritability of Intelligence: The Ethical Context

A good example of these dilemmas is the heredity of intelligence in all its implications. Evidence for a heritable component in intelligence or IQ level is rather strong (monozygotic twin studies indicating a heritability[1] of 0.5–0.7), and the hunt for QTLs of cognition is underway [21]. But the question is whether one should try to improve intelligence by genetic changes and selection or by better education and living conditions? As a matter of fact, the hereditarian theory of IQ did not emerge from knowledge of specific genes or the human genome project. It came out of the 19th century eugenic movement and in 1904, Charles Spearman invented a value called '*g*' for general intelligence or general cognitive ability, a single parameter claiming to correlate various mental tests that often produce different scores on children or adults. This *g* factor became a tool in eugenics and in 1940 the controversial British scientist Cyril Burt made political use of *g* for

[1] Heritability is the proportion of variation in the population which is attributable to genetic influences. A value of 0.6 means that 60% of the variation in a trait across a population (bell-shaped curve) is the result of differences in their genotypes.

screening and assess children, as a result of which only 20% of the children were sent to grammar school preparing for university while 80% were relegated to technical or secondary modern school as unfit for higher education. Such prospective screening makes a sociopolitical statement, namely that it is better to make a selection of children than to invest in trying to educate those who may have difficulties in the education system. Burt's approach was opposed in particular by L. Thurstone who showed that there is not one dominant innate *g*, but rather multiple primary mental abilities (PMA), making it much harder to predict success or failure. However, he was not really believed. In 1979, the American scientist Arthur Jensen revived the *g* factor in a book 'Educability and Group Differences' claiming that children from some ethnic groups are innately unfit for education. In the same vein are many of the ideas developed by Hernstein and Murray [22] in 'The Bell Curve: Intelligence and class structure in American life' where African-Americans are reported to have an average lower IQ than white Americans. Many critics pointed out that this may be due to the fact that the IQ testing is biased by culture and environment.

A most outspoken opponent to the misuses of the research on heritability of intelligence, outlined above, has been Stephen Jay Gould, one of the greatest experts on evolution and biology in the 20th century. In his book 'The Mismeasure of Man' [23], Gould criticizes the hereditarian theory of IQ and especially the *g* factor, depicting it as 'a reification of a single number used to rank people on a unilinear scale of intellectual worth'. Nevertheless the concept of an innate and genetically based *g* survives and was reaffirmed in a December 2001 *Nature Neuroscience* article [24] co-authored by Robert Plomin, a leading expert on behavioral genetics. This article is a comment on a study by Thompson et al. [25] published in the same issue comparing by magnetic resonance the volume of gray matter areas in the brain of genetic (monozygotic) twins versus non-genetic twins, and correlating these volumes with the *g* value. Gray matter volume in several areas of the brain cortex showed a much higher correlation in genetic twins leading the authors to conclude that there is a high heritability for gray matter volume. Given a correlation between brain volume and *g* of about 0.4 (40% of individuals with larger brains have higher *g* scores) it is proposed that 'given the high heritability of variance of gray matter volume in the new paper, it seems likely that its association with *g* is also mediated genetically rather than environmentally'. Plomin favors the 'hypothesis of genetic *g*' – that the same genetic factors affect diverse cognitive abilities. Whether this study really takes into account environmental influences on *g* and IQ remains debatable. The genetic and non-genetic twins were matched for duration of cohabitation and parental social class. An important question is whether the correlation with IQ would still be significant if the twins were raised apart since IQ of genetic twins are different if adopted in families of different socioeconomic environment (see below).

Another conclusion drawn by Plomin from the similarity in gray matter volume in genetic twins is that the density of neurons, the gray matter, may not be easily modified by experience. This contrasts with the views of many neurobiologists who, like Jean-Pierre Changeux, consider that the connections (synapses) between neurons are very much influenced by learning and training, and that neuron connections are made and destroyed all the time, and therefore are not genetically predetermined. Yes, there is a 'genetic envelope' but the neuron connections are malleable, mostly made by learning and destroyed if there is no learning. Even if the numbers of neurons are genetically determined that does not mean that the functions of the brain (related to the connections between the neurons) are pre-determined. It certainly does not mean that the cognitive functions could not be changed by better education.

The Report of the Nuffield Council for Bioethics [14] addresses the issue of the heritability of brain volume and its implication for cognitive abilities: 'The only securely replicated correlation is that between IQ and the overall volume of the brain – where the correlation is about 0.4. But we do not know whether that effect is genetic: improved nutrition and a more stimulating environment will both cause a significant increase in the volume of the rat's brain and improve their learning ability, and it is entirely possible that these and other environmental variables have a similar impact on the human brain [26]'. As a matter of fact, it appears unlikely that the volume of the brain is affected solely by genes because in animals the brain becomes bigger if the animals are trained and are given more exercise. Even with the important study of Thompson et al. [25] showing that the volume of certain cortical areas correlates better with intelligence, it is reasonable to say that this area of genetic research requires considerably more detailed studies before firm conclusions can be drawn. Overcautiousness is required.

Medical genetics has made very important discoveries on the genetic basis of diseases affecting intelligence, such as mental retardation due to fragile X chromosome and others. But it is important to note that, despite a better understanding of mental retardation, not a single gene involved in the development of mental retardation has been shown to be associated with the normal variation in IQ. The basis for the observed normal range of IQ variance cannot be reduced to a single cause. This emphasizes further the necessary distinction between medical genetics and behavioral genetics.

Is It All in Our Genes? – An Important Ethical Debate

The complexity of the concept of 'heritability' for intelligence and IQ has been particularly emphasized by Lewontin et al. [27] in 'Not in our genes'. This book examines in detail the meaning of heritability, i.e. genetic variance divided by the total variance (genetic plus environmental). For IQ, most studies show that the genetic variance contributes about 50% of the IQ variance. But one often makes the mistake to believe that heritability means unchangeability. In fact, adoption can increase IQ – on the average – from 86 points to 117 points, most likely as a result of a change in familial and socioeconomic environment. Non-adopted siblings of low socioeconomic level fail a year of school at a rate of 56%, but this rate can decrease to 13% for an adopted sibling. Even for children who are genetics twins and have a similar IQ, where they are educated has a major influence on their success in school. The real question is then: if IQ levels are heritable, is this heritage also irreversible? Lewontin makes the interesting remark that the heritability of arithmetic skills has been changed by the pocket calculator – you may be unable to calculate rapidly but once you are given a pocket calculator there is no difference between you and a very gifted arithmetician. Environment can change intelligence. As noted by Plomin and Kosslyn [24], even the heritability of *g* measured in twin studies is changing from infancy (20%) to childhood (about 40%) to adulthood and old age (about 60%). Could that be related to higher learning capacities and higher receptivity to environmental clues in the young? – We do not know.

Gould [23] in the Mismeasure of Man further points out fundamental difficulties in the concept of IQ heritability. One is that human uniqueness lies in the flexibility of what our brains can do: 'What is intelligence if not the ability to face problems in an unprogrammed manner?'. When we say that the innate IQ predicts human intelligence, we overlook the fact that flexibility, creativity, much more than a given ability, are the hallmark of human intelligence. We are not born with a fixed capacity but we have flexible potentials. The question, says Gould, is not the classical opposition of biological nature versus cultural nurture. Rather it is that in the study of man's biological nature there are two conflicting theories: one of biological potentiality versus another claiming biological determinism. Both are biological theories. There is nothing compelling in the theory of genetic determinism. Genes do not determine but give potentials and this is particularly true for the interaction of brain with environment. There is nothing compelling in the theory that personality traits and cognitive ability are genetically determined. Data on twins with identical genomes indicate that genes account for 0.5 of the variance in general cognitive ability, while shared and nonshared environmental agents account for 0.33 and 0.17 of the variance (with an error of measurement of 0.1). Thus, genetic twins are correlated 50% in their intelligence, but still the environment contributes another 50%. A 50% correlation is high, it is more than fraternal twins (~25%) but it is by far not 100%: genetic twins are not the same person. If one could safely clone two individuals they would not be the same person, not have the same personality traits, not more than genetic twins. Great caution must be taken to understand what these percentages mean: the influences of the genes and of the environment cannot be compared by such statistics, because they are of different nature. Enough to say that genes beneficial in one environment may be poor in another.

The fundamental issue at stake is: how much are we determined by our genes? For behavioral genetics this is indeed a crucial question. Attempting to simplify genetic data that are obviously complex, the media often propagate the idea that there is a gene for aggressiveness, a gene for criminality and so on for different human behaviors. What the data really say at best is that having a certain form of a gene contributes X percent to predisposition to a certain behavior, most genes affecting behavior having only small effects (usually up to 5%). Furthermore the effects of two genes are in general not additive, that is to say that inheriting two genes that act on a certain behavioral trait does not mean that the effect of one will be added on top of the effect of the other. In one of the seminal studies on behavioral genetics authored by Israeli and USA researchers [28], a certain form of a gene encoding a receptor for the neurotransmitter dopamine was found associated with novelty seeking (curiosity, impulsiveness, as based on a self-reported yes/no questionnaire) so that this genotype accounted for 3–4% of the overall variation in novelty seeking. Confusion can occur when such important results are reviewed under the title 'Genes for personality traits' [29], which may be understood by laypersons in a deterministic sense. The same can be said for association between a serotonin transporter gene and neuroticism or a dopamine transporter and the post-traumatic stress syndrome [30]. In the latter case, the contribution to behavior was 3–8% and the Israeli psychiatrist who made this discovery said that the help of the family or the social worker will usually be more important than the genetic contribution. Such statements are very important for the general public to escape the delusion of genetic determinism and are probably relevant in the study of most personality traits.

A feature of behavior which should be stressed is that genetically-based differences in behavior are nevertheless malleable. In a classical experiment by the anthropologist Franz De Waal [31], two species of aggressive and of peaceful macaque were clustered in the same cage. When the peaceful Bonono macaques had a fight, their characteristic behavior was to end the fight very quickly by having instead sexual contacts, what we would call love-making. The aggressive macaques learned quickly, in about 6 months, and began to behave in this peaceful way. Hence, even if genetics establishes that a behavior – including aggressiveness – is related to certain genes, this does not mean that it is determined and unchangeable by learning.

Sociobiology and Human Cultural Values

Contemporary thoughts about behavior have been much influenced by sociobiology and Edward O. Wilson's [32] theory that many of the human behaviors, noble ones such as altruism and the will to defend the weaker, but also male domination and xenophobia, are rooted in biology and Darwinian selection, rather than being the results of culture and ideologies. To explain the natural selection of altruism, in which the altruist individual would be unable to transmit the genes which caused him to sacrifice his life for the sake of others, sociobiology proposes that the selection acts at the level of the whole group because altruism benefits the collective. Similarly, homosexuality – implying as well no gene transmission – would benefit the group by increasing the number of adults who can protect the progeny of others. Feeling that extending observations on animal societies to human nature may overlook important aspects of human culture, Gould [33] among many others [11] presents arguments to escape the determinism of sociobiology, that our biology determines our social behavior:[2] 'Human

[2] Some would extend the 'bio' too far: even bioethics is understood by some as meaning that ethics is the result of our biology and controlled by genes.

behavior is adaptive. But adaptation in humans may arise by the alternative route of non-genic, cultural evolution'. In Life's Grandeur he writes [33]: 'The most impressive contrast between natural evolution and cultural changes lies embedded in the major fact of our history. We have no evidence that the modal form of human bodies or brains has changed at all in the past 100,000 years ... but cultural change, on a radical other hand, is potentially Lamarckian in basic mechanism. Any cultural knowledge acquired in one generation can be directly passed to the next by what we call, in a most noble way, education. ... This uniquely and distinctively Lamarckian style of human culture inheritance gives our technological history a directional and cumulative character that no natural Darwinian evolution can possess.' On behavior, Gould [35] asks for holding the middle road: 'Modern biology provides a model standing between the despairing claim that biology has nothing to teach us about human behavior and the deterministic theory that specific items of behavior are genetically programmed by the action of natural selection'.

The much heralded Human Genome Project may itself encourage reductionist views of human nature, and Lewontin [34] forewarns that the inherent ethical issue to the whole human genome project is to escape a determinism, categorizing of humans according to their genetic makeup, or in his words: 'say when we know the molecule that makes up all our genes, we will know what it is to be human'. Philosophers and men of religion have, over the centuries, labored on attempts to define the human with its interfacing intellect, spirit and physical body. Paleohistory, structural analysis of myths and psychoanalysis have sketched a complex image of the human mind and soul. Genetic determinism would be a poor substitute indeed. Even our forefathers had a better understanding of the limits of inborn fate. In the Talmud [35], there is a discussion about astrology or horoscopes and the belief that man's fate is determined at birth: '... a man born under the sign of Mars will be bloodlusty (violent, aggressive). Rabbi Ashi says he may become a barber (surgeon of that time), or a murderous brigand, or [he may become] a butcher or a circumciser'. That is he can use his bloodlust for good or for bad purposes. A commentary on this text in the 14th century [36] gives it a truly modern meaning with implications for human behavioral genetics: 'If all is fate, where is moral responsibility? But innate fate only predisposes, it does not determine. Man's spirit can either overcome the drive or use it for good and not for evil.' Genetics may predispose some to a toughened, more aggressive temper but man has free will, moral responsibility, and he can decide to use his predisposition to be a surgeon and not a murderer. In 'Not in our Genes' [15] the same thought is expressed in this way: 'Human actions are consequences of immense arrays of interacting causes ... [if] constrained by a single cause ... we are no longer free.'

Bioethics and the Genetics of Man and His Behavior

The Universal Declaration on the Human Genome and Human Rights has given, I believe, the right platform on which to approach the complexity of human behavioral genetics, by clearly stating that genes alone do not suffice to define a human being. Thus, in Article 2a: '*Everyone has a right to respect for their dignity and for their rights regardless of their genetic characteristics*'. There should be no discrimination based on genetics, and that should apply to use of behavioral genetics for streaming children in schools, and other kinds of discriminations. Furthermore, in Article 2b: '*That [human] dignity makes it imperative not to reduce individuals to their genetic characteristics and to respect their uniqueness and diversity*'. The behavior of any human being can similarly not be reduced to his genetic make-up but depends on his intellect and freewill. Culture, education and social environment have a major impact as indicated in Article 3: '*The human genome, which by its nature evolves, is subject to mutations. It contains potentialities that are expressed differently according to each individual's natural and social environment including the individual's state of health, living conditions, nutrition and education*'.

There may be few areas where an in-depth bioethical reflection is more needed than the application of human genetics to behavioral traits. The power to analyze the influence of genes on personality and behavioral tendencies is almost at hand. There will be a growing demand for using genetic screening methods in order to produce design babies, along parent's or society's wishes. It is capital to keep a comprehensive view of human life, an encompassing experience of complex interactions. Not only do genes and environment interact, but the human brain in its flexible predisposition is the centre where culture and nature meet to shape behavior.

Let us keep clearly in mind the limits of genetic determinism in medicine and in behavioral sciences.

References

1 Revel M: Flame from ashes. Haaretz Daily (English edition). Friday May 4, 2001.
2 Habermas J: De l'ethique de la discussion. Paris, Editions du Cerf, 1992. (Specific quote is in: Changeux JP, Ricoeur P: La Nature et la Regle. Paris, Editions Odile Jacob, 1998, p 264.)
3 Cardon LR, Bell JI: Association study designs for complex diseases. Nat Rev Genet 2001;2:91–99.
4 Wertz DC, Knoppers BM: Serious genetic disorders: Can or should they be defined? Am J Med Genet 2002;108: 29–35.
5 Garver KL, Garver B: The Human Genome Project and Eugenics Concerns. Am J Hum Genet 1994;54:148–158.
6 Kuhl S: The Nazi Connection: Eugenics, American Racism and German National Socialism. Oxford, Oxford University Press, 1994.
7 Ledley FD: Distinguishing genetics and eugenics on the basis of fairness. J Med Ethics 1994;20:157–164.
8 Revel M: Genetic Counseling. Proc IntBioethics Committee of UNESCO, Third Session, September 1995, vol I, chap 2.
9 Cao A: Carrier screening and genetic counselling in beta-thalassemia. Int J Hematol 2002;76(suppl 2):105–113.
10 Rothman BK: The Tentative Pregnancy: How Amniocentesis Changes the Experience of Motherhood. New York, Norton, 1993.
11 Evans JP, Skrzynia C, Burke W: The complexities of predictive genetic testing. BMJ 2001;322:1052–1056.
12 Sing CF, Zerba KE, Reilly SL: Traversing the biological complexity in the hierarchy between genome and CAD endpoints in the population at large. Clin Genet 1994;44: 6–14.
13 Robertson JA: Extending preimplantation diagnosis: The ethical debate. Hum Reprod 2003;18:465–471.
14 Nuffield Council on Bioethics: Genetics and human behavior: the ethical context. http://www.nuffieldbioethics.org/behavioralgenetics/index.asp
15 Bird T, Jarvik GP, Wood NW: Genetic association studies. Neurology 2001;57: 1153–1154.
16 Shifman S, Bronstein M, Sternfeld N, et al: A highly significant association between a COMT haplotype and schizophrenia. Am J Hum Genet 2002;71:1296–1302.
17 Chumakov I, Blumenfeld M, Guerassimenko O, et al: Genetic and physiological data implicating the new human gene G72 and the gene for D-amino acid oxidase in Schizophrenia. Proc Natl Acad Sci USA 2002;99:13675–13680. Erratum in: Proc Natl Acad Sci USA 2002;99:17221.
18 http://stwww.weizmann.ac.il/bioethics. Reports of the Bioethics Committee of the Israel Academy of Sciences and Humanities. Report on Population-based large-scale collections of DNA samples and databases of Genetic Information.
19 Sabol SZ, Nelson ML, Fisher C, et al: A genetic association for cigarette smoking behavior. Health Psychol 1999;18:7–13.
20 Wolpert L: The Unnatural Nature of Science. London, Faber & Faber, 1992, p 163.
21 Gottesman I: Twins: En route to QTLs for cognition. Science 1997;276:1522–1523.
22 Hernstein RJ, Murray C: The Bell Curve: Intelligence and Class Structure in American Life. New York, Simon & Schuster Adult Publishing Group, 1995.
23 Gould SJ: The Mismeasure of Man. New York, Norton, 1996, pp 234–320.
24 Plomin R, Kosslyn SM: Genes, brain and cognition. Nat Neurosci 2001;4: 1153–1154.

25 Thompson PM, Cannon TD, Narr KL, et al: Genetic influences on brain structure. Nat Neurosci 2001;4:1253–1258.
26 Renna JM, Rosenzweig MR: Enriched and Impoverished Environments. New York, Springer, 1987.
27 Lewontin RC, Rose S, Kamin LJ: Not in Our Genes. New York, Panthon Books, Random House, 1984, pp 83–129.
28 Benjamin J, Li L, Patterson C, Greenberg BD, Murphy DL, Hamer DH: Population and familial association between the D4 dopamine receptor gene and measures of novelty seeking. Nat Genet 1996;12: 81–84.
29 Benjamin J, Ebstein RP, Lesch KP: Genes for personality traits: implications for psychopathology. Int J Neuropsychopharmacol 1998;1:153–168.
30 Segman RH, Cooper-Kazaz R, Macciardi F, et al: Association between the dopamine transporter gene and posttraumatic stress disorder. Mol Psychiatry 2002;7: 903–907.
31 De Waal F: Good Natured – On the origin of Justice and Injustice in Human Beings and other Animals. Cambridge, Harvard University Press, 1996.
32 Wilson EO: On Human Nature. Cambridge, Harvard University Press, 1988.
33 Gould SJ: Life's Grandeur – The spread of excellence from Plato to Darwin. London, Vintage, 1997, pp 217–230.
34 Lewontin R: The Doctrine of DNA. London, Penguin Books, 1993, p 14.
35 Jewish Babylonian Talmud: Tractate Shabbat. Folio 156a.
36 Rabeinou Nissim: Derashot Ha-Ran. Hadroush hashemini.

Michel Revel, MD, PhD

Department of Molecular Genetics, Weizmann Institute of Science,
PO Box 26, IL–76100 Rehovot (Israel)
Tel. +972 8 934 2101 / +972 8 934 2103, Fax +972 8 934 6106,
E-Mail michel.revel@weizmann.ac.il

Blazer S, Zimmer EZ (eds):
The Embryo: Scientific Discovery and Medical Ethics.
Basel, Karger, 2005, pp 166–201

Preimplantation Genetic Diagnosis

Avi Tsafrir Yoel Shufaro
Alex Simon Neri Laufer

IVF Unit, Department of Obstetrics and Gynecology,
Hadassah Hebrew University Medical Center, Jerusalem, Israel

Preimplantation genetic diagnosis (PGD) is an early method of prenatal diagnosis, in which genetic material from an oocyte or an embryo is examined during in vitro fertilization (IVF) prior to embryo replacement. Only embryos free of targeted genetic abnormalities are selected for transfer back to the uterus. The first clinical use of PGD, described in the beginning of the 1990s, was determination of sex in order to avoid replacement of male embryos in cases of X-linked diseases [1]. In 1992, the first live birth was reported following PGD for an autosomal-recessive disorder, cystic fibrosis [2]. In the mid-1990s, the use of fluorescent in situ hybridization (FISH) with chromosome-specific probes became common for PGD, and surpassed Mendelian indications in frequency. Initially, PGD was developed as an extended mode of prenatal diagnosis for embryos with single gene disorders, and it thus spared women from the consequences of standard prenatal diagnosis methods such as chorionic villous sampling (CVS) or amniocentesis, usually preformed in the second trimester. Using PGD, the stress resulting from the unknown genetic status of the embryo and the difficult decision regarding termination of the affected pregnancy, which some couples find unacceptable, could potentially be avoided.

Although introduced as a tool for prenatal analysis of embryos at high risk for genetic diseases, PGD has been suggested as a treatment for infertility in certain conditions. Since some forms of reproductive failure such as repeated pregnancy loss and advanced maternal age are closely linked with embryonic chromosomal aberrations, embryo screening for aneuploidies by PGD may be beneficial for these indications as well, in order to improve IVF success rates. The ultimate goal of PGD as a treatment for infertility would therefore be selection and transfer of genetically normal embryos, increased pregnancy rates, fewer abortions, fewer multi-fetal pregnancies, and finally, delivery of a single, healthy baby.

Advanced technology and the pooling of knowledge from several disciplines are essential for the success of PGD. Therefore, close collaboration between fertility clinicians, clinical embryologists and clinical and molecular geneticists is required. Accordingly, PGD is currently performed in a limited number of fertility centers worldwide. Providing knowledge regarding the genetic status of embryos, ethical dilemmas such as defining the proper indications for genetic analysis of embryos and social sex selection demand urgent discussion and decision. In this chapter we will review genetic, embryologic, and clinical aspects of PGD. Ethical aspects of this subject will be discussed as well.

Reproductive Genetic Risk

PGD can be applied to three types of genetic disorders in order to prevent the implantation of abnormal embryos, the need to terminate pregnancies and the birth of abnormal offspring. Different types of genetic assays need to be designed and performed for each group of disorders.

The first type is recessive X-linked disorders which are heterogeneous or cannot be attributed to a single gene defect, such as Duchene muscular dystrophy (DMD), in which the birth of a diseased offspring can be totally avoided by the transfer of female embryos only. Historically, the first PGD application was sex selection for such a purpose [1]. The second type includes defined single gene disorders, autosomal-dominant (AD), autosomal-recessive (AR), or X-linked recessive (XR), which are associated with known amplifiable mutations, or can be distinguished by genetic linkage. In the case of AD disorders such as Huntington's disease or Marfan syndrome, the inheritance of a single affected allele results in an abnormal phenotype. Therefore, around 50% of the offspring of an affected individual are expected to inherit at least one mutated allele and become affected as well. In the case of AR disorders such as cystic fibrosis (CF), Tay-Sachs and sickle-cell anemia, only individuals inheriting two mutated alleles will become affected and statistically, even if both parents are mutation carriers, 25% of their offspring will actually be affected. Only women can be healthy carriers of X-linked recessive mutations; male carriers will always be affected. Presuming the father is healthy, half of the male offspring (25% of the total number) born to carrier women will inherit a single mutated allele and will be affected. The third type of disorder involves healthy individuals with balanced chromosomal rearrangements. A percentage of the gametes produced by these individuals is likely to be unbalanced, giving rise to embryos with large-scale deletions or an excess of genetic material. Even if compatible with life, unbalanced genomes are associated with severe anomalies.

Clinical and Technical Procedures

In vitro Fertilization

By definition, IVF is necessary for PGD, in order to provide embryos or oocytes for genetic analysis prior to implantation. Basically, no changes in the basic *clinical* elements of the IVF routine are needed in a PGD cycle: ovarian stimulation using various protocols, oocyte collection, and embryo replacement to the uterine cavity after fertilization occurred in vitro. It should be emphasized that the IVF procedure is not risk-free to the patient. Adverse events such as side effects of hormonal treatment, ovarian hyperstimulation syndrome, complications of anesthesia and invasive procedures for oocyte collection are not rare. Certain obstetric complications such as preterm labor may be higher in IVF pregnancies compared with naturally conceived gestations [3]. Some medical, developmental and psychological concerns regarding IVF babies have not been fully settled yet [4]. Couples who are offered PGD and therefore IVF, but do not require assisted reproduction treatments for other indications, should be fully informed of the issues and understand these aspects when considering PGD, as well as the cost of this intervention.

Biopsy Methods

One necessary challenge for successful PGD is the collection of an element of the oocyte or embryo containing genetic material, without causing damage to the embryo or the biopsied cell. Introduction of micromanipulation techniques to the embryology laboratory, which became standard in the mid-1990s for performing intracytoplasmic sperm injection (ICSI) procedures, enabled successful biopsies using several approaches.

Polar Body Biopsy

The polar bodies may be considered useless genetic material which are extruded during meiosis I and II, and are therefore available for genetic analysis of the female gamete. The first polar body (PB1) is a by-product of the first meiotic division, and contains a double signal for each chromosome. In case of meiosis I errors, such as chromosomal nondisjunction or chromatid missegregation, other signal patterns will occur. The genotype of the oocyte will be the opposite of the PB1 genotype. In contrast, the genotype of the second polar body, when examined by FISH, will normally show one signal for each chromosome. Deviation from this pattern suggests meiosis II errors. Technically, the common method for mechanical breaching of the zona pellucida (ZP) is by using fine needles, possibly with introduction of a biopsy pipette [5]. Another alternative is the use of laser [6].

Blastomere Biopsy

Blastomere biopsy at the cleavage stage is the most extensively used method for PGD. The eight-cell stage embryo was found to be most suitable for biopsy in early studies, since the cells are still totipotent. Removal of cells earlier than this may reduce the inner cell mass from which the embryo is derived [7–10]. However, sister blastomeres could not express totipotency with further embryonic development. According to Edwards and Beard [11], four-cell mouse embryos have three totipotent cells and one trophectoderm cell. At the eight-stage cell, similar control would produce five inner cell masses of germline precursors, and three trophectoderm cells. Blastomere reduction might therefore endanger the embryo by reducing the number of cells essential to form a particular cell line.

The first technical step in the procedure is to create a hole in the ZP. The most popular method is to apply a thin stream of Tyrode's solution to the ZP. The ZP is dissolved and a hole is made. A considerable amount of cell

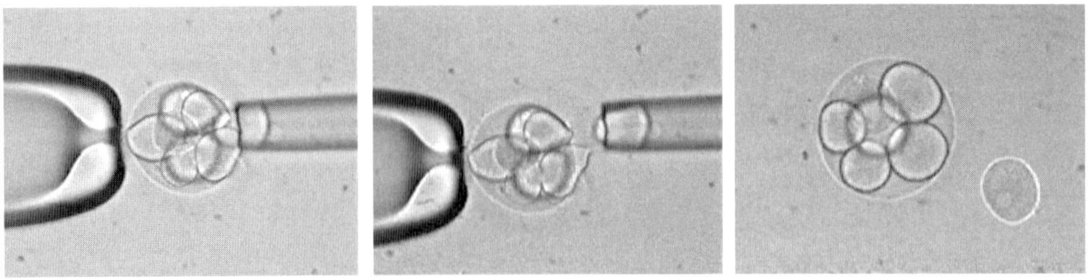

a b c

Fig. 1.
Embryo biopsy. Sequential photographs of an embryo biopsy. An 8-cell embryo is held by a holding pipette (on the left), the zona pellucida is opened and a single blastomere is aspirated (**a**, **b**) out of the embryo without damaging it (**c**).

damage during this step is possible. The use of laser technology enables precise and safer ZP hatching, and is used successfully for PGD purposes [12, 13]. The purpose of the next step is to remove one or two blastomeres. In the aspiration method, a biopsy pipette is introduced through the hole created in the ZP and cells are gently aspirated partly into the pipette, then the pipette itself is retrieved (fig. 1). Another technique described is the extrusion method, in which gentle pressure is applied on a perpendicular point to the opening in the ZP, in order to squeeze out the blastomeres [14].

Blastocyst Biopsy
The blastocyst is the last stage of embryo development in which biopsy can be preformed. The obvious advantage is the number of cells available for examination. A second advantage is the option to analyze trophoblasts and avoid biopsy of the embryo proper. In contrast, few embryos reach the blastocyst stage in vitro, and very little time is left for analysis before transfer of the embryos to the uterus. A possible solution for this problem would be cryopreservation of the blastocyst, though no PGD pregnancies using this approach have been reported so far. The second major drawback is the fact that trophoblasts are often multi-nucleated or in syncitium, which make them not suitable for genetic analysis.

Cryopreservation of Biopsied Embryos
Embryo cryopreservation is routinely performed in IVF treatments, in order to avoid replacement of multiple embryos and therefore multi-fetal pregnancies, without discarding good quality embryos. Not all embryos are

suitable for transfer after this process, and reported frozen-thawed embryo survival rates are 30–70% [15]. Less frequently, cryopreservation of supernumerary biopsied human embryos may be sometimes necessary in order to avoid transfer of multiple healthy embryos. Another benefit would be to gain time for further genetic analysis. Using standard cryopreservation protocols for biopsied embryos clearly results in lower embryo survival rates, probably because of the hole in the zona pellucida formed during biopsy [16, 17]. Only few successful pregnancies from biopsied, cryopreserved embryos have been reported so far [18]. However, some leading groups currently report on promising survival rates using different cryopreservation protocols [19].

Comparison of Biopsy Methods
The main advantage of polar body biopsy is the fact that no effect on embryo viability is expected and indeed, the percentage of embryos entering cleavage was not reduced after this procedure [20]. However, polar body analysis provides no information regarding abnormalities of paternal origin, or late post-zygotic events. Sexing is also impossible with polar body biopsy. Early reports on polar body biopsies concerned the first polar body only. It has been realized that a nondetected allele dropout can occur and result in misdiagnosis. Therefore, consecutive biopsies of the first and second polar bodies are preferred in order to gain better control over such events [21]. These limitations are solved by a cleavage-stage biopsy. An important limitation of this approach results from the high mosaicism rate in cleaving embryos [22, 23]. This fact can lead to the misdiagnosis and replacement of abnormal embryos. Another disadvantage is the limited amount of tissue available for diagnosis. Short time for genetic analysis is the major limitation in blastocyst biopsy, considering low survival rates in biopsied embryos following cryopreservation. Clearly, cleavage stage embryo biopsy remains the main approach for removal of DNA for genetic analysis [24]. According to the 2001 PGD consortium report, based on data collected from PGD cycles performed in the years 1999–2001, almost all biopsies were performed on cleavage stage embryos, with few being performed on polar bodies, and none on blastocysts [25].

Genetic Analysis

The major obstacle towards the performance of reliable PGD is the ability to reach an accurate molecular or cytogenetic diagnosis based upon the DNA content of a single cell. The introduction of polymerase chain reaction

(PCR) in the mid-1980s provided a successful method for selective DNA amplification up to a quantity upon which reliable molecular diagnosis could be performed [26]. In addition, FISH enabled the determination of the presence, absence and number of chromosomes or chromosomal fragments of interest. More complex variations of these basic techniques have been developed in order to bypass their initial limitations, increase sensitivity and specificity, and to correctly diagnose more complex conditions [27]. Novel methods for the purpose of a more accurate, rapid and simultaneous diagnosis of several conditions are being developed and will be described.

Polymerase Chain Reaction

Single copy mutation diagnosis is feasible only if the investigated sequence is amplified to a number of copies sufficient for molecular analysis. This amplification is performed using PCR. In this cyclic reaction, the genomic DNA is first denatured by heating it into two separate strands. A pair of short DNA fragments homologous to the sequence flanking the investigated area (primers) is added and allowed to anneal to the homology site after the temperature is lowered. Once the primers have attached to their homology sites they can be extended by a thermostable (*Taq*) DNA polymerase to form two new complementary DNA strands. The two identical double strands, created from a single double strand, can be denatured again and go through another amplification cycle as described. In this manner the number of DNA molecules is exponentially increased in every cycle [5]. The PCR cannot be extended to infinity, limiting the number of amplicons that can be created from a single copy. As the cycle number increases, the efficacy gradually declines. This phenomenon occurs due to a decrease in *Taq* polymerase activity and trimming of the amplicons' edges by the *Taq* polymerase itself. This problem can be solved by performing a two-step nested PCR [5, 27–29]. In the first step, a large amplicon defined by two outer primers is amplified by PCR. In the second step, the PCR product is further amplified using a second set of inner primers that anneal to nontrimmed sites (fig. 2). This results in a high efficacy amplification of the area between the inner primers [28].

The next step following DNA amplification is the analysis of the amplified product (amplicon) for mutation presence. Traditionally, the PCR products are separated by electrophoresis and are detected by radioactive labeling, ethidium bromide or silver staining. In disorders caused by

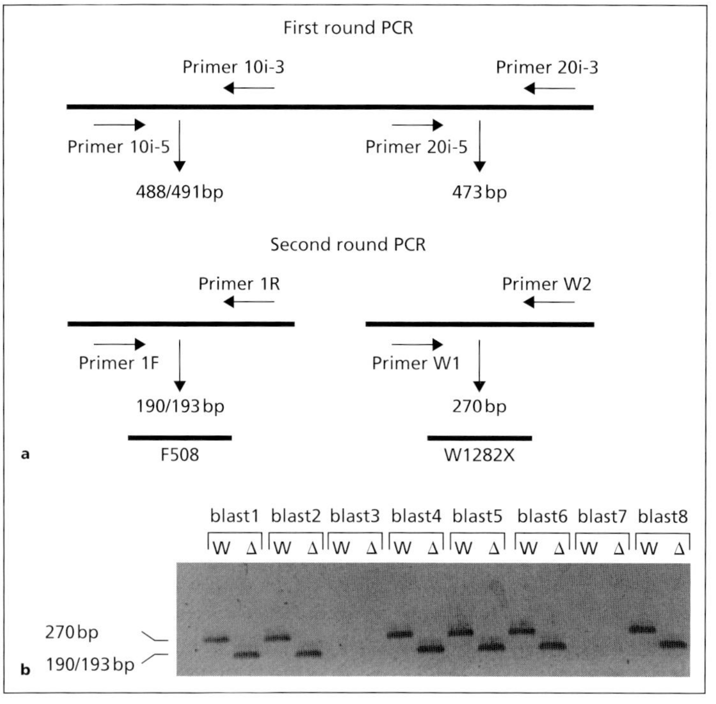

Fig. 2.

PGD of 2 cystic fibrosis mutations by multiplex nested PCR analysis. **a** Schematic representation of multiplex nested PCR for simultaneous amplification of ΔF508 and W1282X CF mutations [adapted from Avner et al: Hum Reprod 1994;19:1676–1680]. **b** Gel electrophoresis of the amplification products from 8 blastomeres. ΔF508 is detected as a 190- to 193-bp band (Δ) and W1282X is detected as a 270-bp band (W). Blastomeres 3 and 7 are not mutation carriers and blastomeres 1, 2, 4, 5, 6 and 8 carry both mutations.

deletions of large segments (like DMD and spinal muscular atrophy – SMA), the PCR can be designed to amplify the deleted sequence. In such a case, the absence of an amplicon following PCR should be diagnostic to the existence of the deletion. In disorders in which the mutated allele is significantly larger than the normal one (such as fragile X and myotonic dystrophy), primer location can be selected to produce amplicons of different sizes – distinguished by electrophoresis. However, in most cases, a mutation-carrying amplicon cannot be distinguished from its normal parallel based on size only. In these instances, the mutation can be detected by direct sequencing,

Any X-linked disorder which cannot be correctly diagnosed by single cell PCR can be prevented by (female) sex selection. Potentially, the expected 1:1 sex ratio can be shifted towards more female embryos by enrichment of the X-chromosome-bearing spermatozoa in a cell sorter. This step could increase the final number of selected embryos available for transfer [27]. The X and Y chromosomes are detected by two color-distinguished probes targeted against their centromeres. A third chromosome is also detected in this manner and serves as a ploidy control, making misdiagnosis in this system very unlikely [35] (fig. 3a).

FISH can also be used in order to determine the copy number of any chromosome. A very reliable test is produced by directing two differently labeled probes against the tested chromosome, in addition to a probe against another chromosome for ploidy control. Risk factors for producing chromosomally abnormal fetuses include prior delivery of a chromosomally abnormal child and advanced maternal age. Although very rare, germline mosaicism cannot be completely excluded. PGD by FISH can be designed to select only euploid embryos (for the tested chromosome) for uterine transfer [36]. This approach can be broadened to analyze more chromosomes in cases of advanced maternal age or repeated implantation failure, in order to increase the reproductive success rate. This strategy, known as PGD for aneuploidy screening (AS), was shown to decrease the abortion rate and increase the number of ongoing pregnancies and deliveries [37].

FISH can also be used in order to detect embryonal chromosomal translocations, with the use of specific probes or a combination of sub-telomeric and centromeric probes [38]. Generally, one of the parents is a healthy carrier of a balanced translocation, and a substantial proportion of the produced gametes are genetically unbalanced. As a result, a large part of the embryos are destined to be genetically unbalanced, ending in miscarriage, abortion or an abnormal child. Reciprocal transformations, which are the commonest form of chromosomal anomalies, are an exchange of terminal segments between two chromosomes. They are generally family unique [27]. Reciprocal translocations can be diagnosed by FISH using probes spanning and flanking the breaking area [29, 34, 38]. Such an approach is accurate and even distinguishes between embryos carrying balanced translocations and those with a normal chromosome arrangement. This approach is time consuming and expensive due to the need to design a specific probe for each translocation.

A more general approach uses probes specific for the (distal) subtelomeric region of the chromosomes involved, in combination with probes

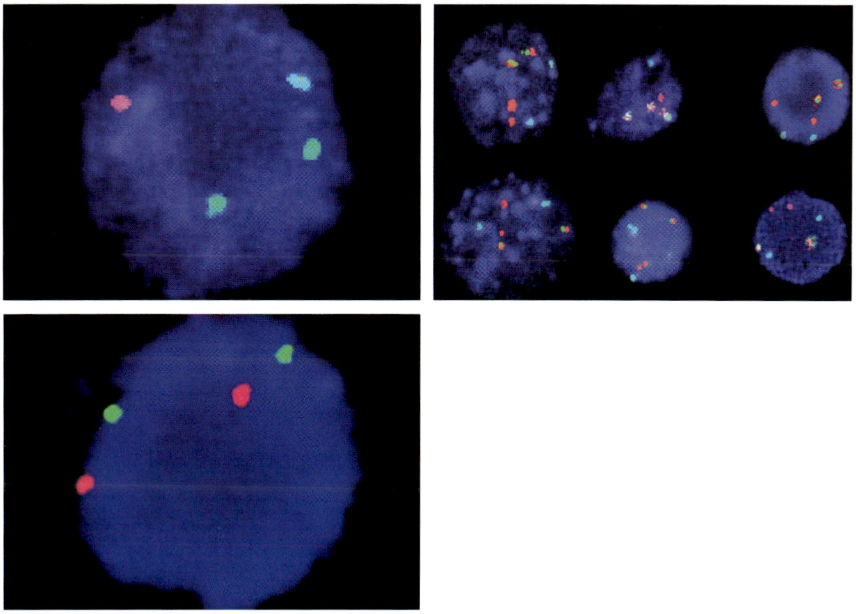

a b c

Fig. 3.

Fish images of human blastomeres. **a** Demonstrating the presence of 4 chromosomes; X (red), Y (marine) and 18 (green). **b** One of the parents is a carrier of a balanced reciprocal translocation; 11q:9q. The red labeled probe is against the 9q telomere, the marine probe hybridizes with chromosome 9 centromere, and the multi-colored probe is specific for 11q. All blastomeres hybridize twice with each probe, indicating that none of them is unbalanced. A formal metaphase spread karyotype is required in order to distinguish between the balanced translocation and the normal state. **c** One of the parents has a balanced Robertsonian translocation between chromosomes 13 and 14. The red-labeled probe is specific for a telomeric portion of chromosome 14 distal to the translocation. The green-labeled probe hybridizes with a domain on chromosome 13 proximal to the translocation. FISH reveals that this blastomere originates from a balanced embryo, which has no missing chromosomal segments. This FISH analysis does not distinguish between a normal nontranslocated state and a balanced translocation.

for the centromeric region of the same chromosomes. These probes are readily available and do not have to be specifically designed. This approach distinguishes only between unbalanced and balanced genomes, not between balanced translocation and the normal state [27, 29, 34, 38] (fig. 3b). Robertsonian translocations are a centric fusion of two acrocentric chromosomes, which occur in a few well-defined sites. Unbalanced gametes of balanced carriers lack or have an excess of entire chromosomal arms, making PGD by FISH using chromosome enumerator probes quite straightforward (fig. 3c) [27, 29, 34].

Comparative Genomic Hybridization

Conventional FISH methods can be used to analyze for the presence of only a few chromosomes. Full chromosomal karyotype analysis is feasible only in metaphase spreads which are very difficult to obtain from embryonic blastomeres. Comparative genomic hybridization (CGH) is a molecular technique that simultaneously evaluates the entire genome from a single cell for aneuploidy and genetic imbalances and can be performed on interphase nuclei. Following whole genome amplification during which the tested DNA is labeled with a fluorescent dye, it is mixed with DNA from a reference cell labeled with a different dye. The mixture is then hybridized together to an existing normal metaphase spread. The relative fluorescent intensity of each dye is detected by a digital camera, and compared to that of the other dye. The major benefit of this approach is aneuploidy screening for all chromosomes and detection of relatively minor (>20 Mbp) imbalances, overcoming the limitations of FISH chromosomal probes [5, 27, 29]. Indeed, in the first described case of pregnancy following pre-implantation confirmation of euploidy by CGH, other embryos regarded as chromosomally normal by FISH were found to be aneuploid by CGH [39]. However, since the performance of CGH requires three days, embryo cryopreservation is mandatory, reducing the number of viable embryos for transfer. It should also be taken into account that CGH detects only relative hybridization mismatches. In the case of complete polyploidy, a balanced normal hybridization with the reference DNA will occur, giving an apparently normal result [5, 27, 29].

Clinical Aspects and Outcomes of PGD

Since PGD is currently performed in a limited number of specializing centers, and in a relatively small number of cycles, most information is provided by the European Society of Human Reproduction and Embryology (ESHRE) PGD consortium. After collecting data from 25 centers, 1561 PGD cycles carried out from 1999 to 2001 were summarized [25]. Eighty-two percent of the cycles were referred because of genetic risk and 14% for

Table 1.

Referrals (%) for PGD according to indication: the PGD Consortium Report, 1999–2001 (n = 1,561)

Chromosomal	41
X-linked	19
Autosomal recessive	19
Autosomal dominant	16
Social sexing	2
Other and unknown	3

Adapted from the PGD consortium data collection, 2002 [25].

aneuploidy screening. Forty-one percent of cycles were conducted for chromosomal abnormalities such as structural abnormalities including translocations and aneuploidies and 54% for monogenic disorders (table 1).

About one-third of 426 PGD cycles performed during 2001 were for infertile patients. Zona drilling was performed equally either by laser or Tyrode's. Almost all biopsies were performed on cleavage stage embryos, with a success rate of 99% for 2,844 embryos. A diagnosis was achieved in 85%. 997 (17%) embryos were found suitable for transfer. The overall pregnancy rate of PGD cycles was 19% per oocyte retrieval. This rate is not significantly different from the overall success rate of IVF today.

Sexing for X-linked diseases was almost always performed by FISH. Monogenic diseases were evaluated by PCR. In almost all PCR cycles, ICSI was used to achieve fertilization, in order to avoid sperm contamination. PGD was only used in 2001 for 35 different monogenic diseases (table 2).

The most common autosomal-diseases evaluated were myotonic dystrophy and Huntington's disease. Common autosomal recessive conditions examined were cystic fibrosis, β-thalassemia and spinal muscular atrophy. Fragile X syndrome, Duchenne/Becker muscular dystrophy and hemophilia were the common sex-linked conditions evaluated. The ESHRE PGD consortium reported on 451 clinical PGD pregnancies so far [25]. Of those, 68% resulted from FISH cycles and the rest from PCR cycles. The clinical abortion rate in the first trimester was 11%. Information on complications in pregnancy and delivery was completed on 157 pregnancies. This complication rate was comparable to the

Table 2.

Main referrals (%) for monogenic diseases: the PGD Consortium Report, 1999–2001 (n = 838)

Autosomal recessive	
Cystic fibrosis	13
Thalassemia	6
Spinal muscular atrophy	6
Other	9
Autosomal dominant	
Myotonic dystrophy	11
Huntington's disease	9
Charcot-Marie-Tooth disease	21
Other	9
X-linked	
Fragile-X syndrome	9
Duchenne/Becker's	8
Muscular dystrophy hemophilia	3
Other	15

Adapted from the PGD consortium data collection, 2002 [25].

complication rate in non-PGD cycles, considering that about 1 in 4 pregnancies was multi-fetal. In a report from Chicago, summarizing deliveries of 102 babies from PGD cycles with polar body biopsy, no adverse neonatal or congenital anomalies were noticed [40].

PGD as a Treatment for Reproductive Failure

It has been long known that the major cause of recognized pregnancy loss is chromosomal abnormality of the embryo, which is estimated as close to 70% [41] Using FISH, PGD analysis has shown that 50–70% of IVF embryos are chromosomally abnormal [42, 43]. High rates of chromosomal abnormalities have been found in inner mass cells of blastocysts [44]. Since FISH examined only a few, specific chromosomes, the real abnormality rate may be even higher. On the other hand, the selection bias of the population referred to IVF and especially PGD, and the possible effect of ovulation induction and other interventions may increase the abnormality rate compared with naturally conceived pregnancies. Moreover, morphologically abnormal and slow-growing embryos have high rates of aneuploidy, and lower chances for a successful pregnancy [45]. It is likely that chromosomal abnormalities are responsible for a substantial proportion of implantation failures. In the routine practice of IVF, several morphological criteria are routinely used for selection of best embryos for transfer. Preimplantation chromosomal analysis may aid in the selection of normal embryos, and increase pregnancy rates for patients undergoing IVF. This procedure has been designated as PGD-AS (aneuploidy screening). Although initially described as a method for early diagnosis of genetic disorders, the majority of published PGD cycles are performed for aneuploidy screening or improvement of IVF outcome. According to the PGD consortium data, almost 50% of PGD cycles were referred for aneuploidy screening. However, no clear benefits of this technique have been proven so far in terms of increasing pregnancy rates, and large prospective studies are required for proper evaluation of the PGD-AS approach. Patients offered this technique should be aware that normal embryos might be excluded from the initial cohorts due to the mistaken diagnosis. Additionally, the contribution of specific individual chromosomal aneuploidies in embryos is not yet clear. Research in this area may aid in the design of specific application of FISH for the most common abnormalities.

PGD for Advanced Maternal Age

As a result of various social processes, many women delay their first reproductive attempts to their late 30s and early 40s. Pregnancy rates decrease dramatically in these years, both naturally and using assisted reproductive technology treatments [46]. Reproductive maternal aging is characterized not only by a decrease in ovarian reserves, but also in increased aneuploidy rates of embryos. PGD studies bring new insight and estimations regarding the magnitude of this phenomenon, both at the oocyte and at the embryo levels. In the largest PGD series reported, polar bodies from 6,733 oocytes from women aged 35 years and older were analyzed [47]. On the basis of FISH analysis for five chromosomes, 52% of oocytes were aneuploid. Gianaroli et al. [48] summarized their experience of analyzing 2,231 embryos from women aged 36 and older by FISH for 5–9 chromosomes. The chromosomal abnormality rate was 69%. Munne et al. [49] found that

26% of 180 embryos analyzed in women aged 40–41 were aneuploid, compared with 8% in 154 embryos for women aged 25–34 years. One should keep in mind that all these studies were performed on infertile couples that had some indication to warrant this procedure. However, it appears logical to assume that aneuploidy screening of embryos may improve implantation and pregnancy rates. Moreover, transfer of euploid embryos may reduce miscarriage rates which may be as high as 50% over 40 years of age [50]. One significant limitation to this approach is the small number of embryos produced in IVF cycles in aging women. For example, in our experience, in 1,176 non-PGD IVF cycles in 353 women aged 40 years and older, 26% did not have any embryos for transfer [unpubl. data]. The average number of embryos for those who had any was only 2.6 per cycle. Obviously, this basic problem cannot be solved by any approach based on embryo pre-selection.

Clinical experience of PGD-AS for advanced maternal age has been applied so far in thousands of treatment cycles [51]. Gianaroli et al. [52] prospectively randomized women aged 36 or older undergoing IVF to PGD of nine chromosomes or assisted hatching alone, which served as controls. Significantly higher implantation rates were noticed in the study group. In a later, retrospective summary from the same center, the clinical pregnancy rate resulting from transfer of euploid embryos to patients belonging to this age group was 27%, and the take-home baby rate was 20% per patient. In a multi-center retrospective study, 117 women aged 35 underwent embryo screening for 4–8 chromosomes [37]. The study group was matched retrospectively for controls. Although no increase in pregnancy rates was noticed, pregnancy loss rates and therefore ongoing pregnancy and delivery rates were higher in the study group. In a smaller report, an encouraging pregnancy rate of 25% in patients aged 36–45 years and older who had PGD-AS was noticed [53]. A significant reduction in miscarriage rates of patients aged older than 35 undergoing PGD-AS was observed in a leading American center. There was also a reduction in the expected rate of chromosomally abnormal conceptions, from an expected rate of 3.2% according to maternal age to 0.8% [49]. According to the PGD consortium report in 2002, 101 PGD cycles referred for aneuploidy screening due to advanced maternal age, defined as ≥35, were performed. The clinical pregnancy rate was 28%. However, in a recent prospective, randomized trial, the results were less convincing. Nineteen patients over 38 years of age who underwent IVF were randomized to PGD or to routine IVF cycles [54]. Fifty-four percent of 41 embryos analyzed for nine chromosomes were abnormal.

There was a trend for a higher pregnancy rate in the PGD group (43 vs. 25%), but the numbers were too small to reach statistical significance. Overall, it appears that advanced age women benefit from aneuploidy screening for selection of best embryos for transfer.

Repeated Pregnancy Loss

About 15–20% of clinical pregnancies end in miscarriage. Most of these cases are sporadic, but some couples suffer from repeated pregnancy loss. Even after an intensive work-up, no explanation for this failure is found in many of these patients. Since the most common reason for sporadic pregnancy loss is chromosomal abnormality of the fetus, PGD for aneuploidy screening has been proposed as a logical treatment approach for this frustrating condition. Indeed, embryos of 71 recurrent miscarrying couples had a high rate of chromosomal abnormalities, when analyzed by PGD [55]. Moreover, all embryos were abnormal in 22% of the overall treatment cycles in this group. In another summary, 89 embryos from 14 young women with a history of repeated abortions were analyzed by PGD. Only 30 were chromosomally normal. Four pregnancies were achieved in eight transferred cycles, and no abortions occurred [48]. In 2001, 45 cycles were reported by the PGD consortium for this indication, defined as more than two miscarriages in a patient with a normal karyotype. The clinical pregnancy rate was 28%.

In the first prospective, randomized trial published so far, 19 patients with RPL, defined as over two spontaneous pregnancy losses were randomized to PGD or controls [54]. There was a trend for a higher pregnancy rate in this group (64 vs. 38%), but the numbers were too small to draw a conclusion.

Repeated Failed IVF Treatment

Occasionally, a young patient with normal appearing embryos did not conceive as expected after repeated embryo transfer cycles. Currently, no specific explanation for this failure is known for many of these women, but some authors define this situation as implantation failure [56]. There is some evidence that embryos derived from these patients have a high rate of chromosomal abnormalities. The analysis of embryos from a small group of patients with implantation failure and transfer of at least one chromosomally normal embryo improved pregnancy rates [56]. In a large retrospective summary, 70 young patients with repeated IVF failures (≥3 cycles) underwent PGD-AS. Approximately 59% of their embryos were chromosomally abnormal. The pregnancy rate in 77 cycles in which normal embryos were transferred was 35%, and a take-home baby rate per patient was 34%. In contrast, the PGD consortium reported 117 treatment cycles performed for repeated IVF failure, commonly defined as at least three IVF attempts. The striking result was a pregnancy rate as low as 11% per embryo transfer. In a small prospective, randomized trial, 19 patients with repeated IVF failure, defined as over two failed cycles (this contradicts what you say above about repeated IVF failure being at least three IVF attempts), were randomized to PGD or controls [54]. Nineteen of 28 embryos analyzed for nine chromosomes were abnormal. PGD offered no benefit in that group. In the IVF repeated failure groups, factors other than embryo aneuploidy, such as endometrial function may be the main cause for infertility.

Disadvantages Associated with PGD

Embryo Damage during Biopsy

Possible damage to embryos can occur as a result of the biopsy procedure itself or due to reduction in embryonic cell mass, as mentioned above. Cell loss of one or two cells did not seem to affect embryo development until the blastocyte stage. In one large series, less than 1% of 4248 embryos have been damaged during the biopsy procedure [49]. The damage of the biopsy procedure, if any, to the process of implantation is unknown. There is no clear evidence that biopsied embryos have lower implantation rates than nonbiopsied ones. Regarding PGD-AS, it is possible, theoretically, that the transfer of selected embryos increases implantation rates and the overall balance is in favor of PGD selection, at least in advanced age patients. In one large series, PGD for women over 40 years of age increased implantation rates in about 7% as compared with controls [49]. Another possible disadvantage is reduction in numbers of normal embryos not transferred as a result of misdiagnosis as abnormal embryos. Specifically, the frequency of embryonic mosaicism may be more common than in live births; perhaps aneuploid cells are selected against resulting in disappearance of the lineage during further embryonic development [57, 58].

Accuracy of PGD

Cases of misdiagnosis and replacement of abnormal embryos have been reported since the introduction of PGD into practice [1, 52]. For example, in one large single center report, 1 out of 26 live babies was affected by spinal muscular atrophy [59]. The cause of this failure is unclear. In another report summarizing 29 pregnancies tested prenatally, in a large series of 183 PGD cycles in a single center, one pregnancy was terminated for misdiagnosis of Huntington's disease [60]. Another example is false abnormal diagnosis rate, which means that normal embryos are not transferred to the uterus. In one leading PGD center, the false normal diagnosis rate was 2% [49]. Since single-center experience is relatively small even in the most active of PGD programs, definite estimation of PGD accuracy is problematic. Different approaches and indications for prenatal and postnatal genetic tests further increase this difficulty. Until now, the PGD consortium included confirmed prenatal diagnosis of 187 PGD pregnancies (table 3). The indications for these tests were not recorded. Six misdiagnosed pregnancies occurred. In addition, two misdiagnoses have been recorded postnatally. According to the latest report, the total rate of misdiagnoses can be calculated as 1.8%, and is higher in the PCR than in the FISH group. Analysis of spare embryos which were not transferred in the PGD-AS group revealed that the original result could not be confirmed in 8% [25].

Both amniocentesis and chorionic villi sampling use hundreds of fetal cells for diagnosis, while PGD analysis depends on FISH or DNA amplification of one or two cells from each embryo. Since most diagnoses are based on a single blastomere, mosaicism is another possible explanation for this inaccuracy. Additional possible mechanisms for diagnostic errors have been discussed above.

Mosaicism is not uncommon in cleavage stage embryo, and examination of a single blastomere might therefore result in misdiagnosis [61]. One approach to overcoming this difficulty is sampling of two blastomeres from each embryo, and transfer of embryos from which two normal similar results were obtained. Indeed, some groups analyze two cells from each embryo

The use of PGD for medical purposes such as screening for aneuploidy, for normal chromosome structure and for Mendelian disorders, is ethically and legally acceptable. The ethical debate revolves around whether it is appropriate to extend these indications to other medical and nonmedical conditions.

PGD for Late-Onset Conditions

Thanks to our ever-increasing knowledge in cancer biology and genetics, it is recognized that people who carry specific gene mutations are susceptible to developing a malignancy later in life. Examples of this include the BRCA1, BRCA2 and P53 mutations whose carriers have a high rate of breast and ovarian cancer. In the future, other malignant and nonmalignant traits, such as retinitis pigmentosa, retinoblastoma, familiar polyposis, Lynch syndrome and neurofibromatosis [68, 69], all of which are associated with gene mutations, will be suitable for genetic testing.

Once the mutation is defined, PGD could allow us to verify that pregnancies are free of these mutations and even prevent the implantation of embryos with these predisposed medical conditions. In fact, it has been reported that PGD was used in order to avoid pregnancies with a P53 mutation [70, 71] and with Alzheimer's [72] and Huntington's disease traits [73].

The argument to justify the use of PGD for diseases that will develop only later in life is that these medical conditions are considered life threatening and extremely debilitating and should be preventable if possible.

Since the early embryo is not yet considered to be a human being and lacks independent rights, the couples' right to choose to have a healthy child is a main issue that cannot be ignored.

Parents have a strong desire to have a healthy child and avoid the burden of continued monitoring, emotional threat and physical suffering that comes with an unhealthy child. Moreover, having a child with an inherited susceptibility to cancer could affect their decision to reproduce [66]. If PGD can offer a better life for them and their unborn children, they should be advised of the procedure's existence. Couples should be informed of the benefits that PGD offers as well as its risks and disadvantages, thus enabling them to implement their rights.

When discussing the prevention of the birth of a fetus that has tested positive for a late-onset disease like Huntington's disease to a parent who is affected with that disease, there are two parts to the ethical issue in question. First, will the affected parent be able to raise the child and second, are the physicians acting responsibly knowing that the child might lose a parent to the disease while he is still a dependent. These arguments, however, can be extended to other medical conditions as well: performing intrauterine insemination on an HIV-positive woman, performing IVF treatment on cancer patients or treating a spouse who is sentenced to life imprisonment. Despite the latter ethical argument, physicians treat these patients, stressing the fact that the child will be born into a loving home and supportive environment and that patients have the right to choose what is best for them. Therefore, PGD for late-onset diseases should be considered ethically acceptable because it will prevent grief and unnecessary suffering for both the child and parents.

PGD for susceptibility conditions is legal in the USA and may be consistent with the statutory guidelines of Israel and other countries in Europe. Therefore, it should be permitted [66].

PGD for Gender Selection

PGD for gender selection is a relatively simple, reliable and established procedure that involves the karyotyping of the sex chromosomes only. It is, however, extremely controversial and exemplifies the divergent ethical positions in the USA and Europe.

Gender selection is requested by two categories of patients. The first group is composed of couples who aim to select the sex of their first child and would mostly select for a male offspring and the second group involves those who already have a child and wish to have another child of the opposite gender.

The main arguments for permitting gender selection are:

1 Gender selection is in agreement with the patients' autonomy and serves the desires of couples that have a strong preference for their offspring's sex. Parents have great discretion in decisions of procreation; sex selection may be viewed as an extension of these procreative liberties. The liberty to make one's own reproductive choices covers the liberty to select the sex of one's children in the same way that one has the liberty to decide how many children to have, when to have them, and whether to have them at all.

2 In countries where abortions or infanticide of females is practiced (illegally, but widely) such as in India, PGD will prevent these abhorrent interventions [74]. In certain cultures it is important to have a first male child

because of his special legal and traditional standing in matters such as inheritance. Again, it is preferable to have PGD for sex selection and destroy embryos than to concur silently with late sex selection (by chorion villous biopsy (CVS) or ultrasonography) and subsequent abortion.

The main arguments against the procedure:

1 Sex selection is an issue of human rights and viewed as a sexist act. It is regarded as a discriminatory procedure mostly against women and undermines the Universal Declaration of Human Rights of 1948 that entails nondiscrimination on the grounds of sex. Discrimination against women is widespread worldwide and the procedure may accentuate these trends.
2 The children born as a result of gender selection may be expected to act in a gender specific way and may disappoint their parents if they fail to do so.
3 PGD is meant for preventing disease and gender cannot be termed a 'disease'.
4 Embryos of the unintended sex will have to be discarded. It is not clear whether the need for gender variety in some families overshadows the necessity to destroy embryos for that purpose.
5 Gender selection will offset the balance between the sexes with fewer women than men. In India and China an underground practice of feticide and sometimes infanticide is practiced and has become a national crisis in these countries. Estimates of the number of female fetuses being destroyed every year in India vary from two to five million and its application has modified the normal ratio of males to females in some provinces from 1.05:1 to 1.2:1 [75]. A response to this argument is that the cost of a PGD is currently prohibitive enough to prevent its wide use and therefore has a negligible effect on this ratio. However, the demand in some cultures may drive prices down and increase the demand and contribute significantly to these disparities [76].
6 Diversion of medical resources for nonmedical purposes is especially strong in countries where medicine is socialized and threatens to drain substantial resources from the medical system.
7 Sex selection may be viewed as a first step towards genetic enhancement. The use of PGD for the selection of gender of the opposite sex for the second child is not considered sexist and will not affect the balance between sexes. A couple who wishes to have children of both genders does so because of the different rearing experiences between the genders [66, 77]. From the cultural point of view, it is the attitude of the

American Society for Reproductive Medicine (ASRM) that 'desiring the different rearing experiences that one has with boys and girls does not mean that the parents, who have already had children of one sex are sexists or likely to devalue one or other sex' [78]. ASRM had initially taken the position that preconception gender selection would be acceptable for purposes of gender variety but not for the first child [78]. This stance has changed and the revised position of the ethics committee of ASRM currently is that 'The committee reaffirms its previous conclusion that initiating IVF and PGD solely for nonmedical gender selection generally, for example, for the first child, should be discouraged.' It also concludes that initiating IVF and PGD solely to create gender variety in a family should at this time also be discouraged [79]. In spite of this position it is not prohibited to perform this procedure in the USA and it is currently estimated that at least five clinics are offering sex selection for nonmedical reasons in the USA and at least 40 babies were born following this procedure [80]. In Israel, the Ministry of Health gave permission for our program to use PGD to select a girl for a couple using anonymous donor sperm to solve a specific problem in Jewish law [81]. In this case the spouse of an azoospermic male member of the Jewish Priesthood (designation: Cohen, based on the biblical tradition of direct paterineal descent from Aharon the biblical high priest) underwent donor insemination. The birth of a male child would have resulted in a situation in which certain synagogue rituals restricted to members of the Jewish priesthood would not be permissible to the child, and hence result in a potentially awkward and embarrassing situation for the father, wherein the confidential information that the child was by donor insemination would be made public. This was circumvented by the permission granted on the part of the Ministry of Health to have only female embryos implanted. As a result the couple had a female daughter and the embarrassing disclosure of sperm donation was circumvented. Currently, however, the procedure has been temporarily suspended for further use until a ministerial regulation is issued.

In India a program in Mumbai is providing sex selection by PGD. It published its experience on the birth of 22 boys from sex selection for family balancing [82]. The ESHRE PGD consortium has reported on 28 pregnancies from three centers outside Europe. Since the procedure is not prohibited in Jordan, it may be that one of these centers is from a program in that country.

In contrast to the three countries (USA, India, Jordan) in which gender selection is not prohibited, the European stance on this issue is clearly negative. The Council of Europe (1996) in Article 14 of the Convention on Human Rights and Biomedicine declared that 'The use of techniques of medically assisted procreation shall not be allowed for the purpose of choosing a future child's sex except where a serious hereditary sex-related disease is to be avoided.' The European Society of Human Reproduction and Embryology (ESHRE) Ethics Task Force 5 could not reach a unanimous decision: 'Two positions can be distinguished: those opposed to every application of sexing for nonmedical reasons and those who accept sex selection for family balancing' [67]. In spite of this ambiguous position, the procedure is illegal in Belgium, France, Germany, Netherlands, Spain, and Sweden. The procedure is also illegal in Japan, two states in Australia, Canada and in the United Kingdom.

In conclusion, the option for sex selection has become a reality available through the combination of IVF and molecular techniques. The procedure seems to be relatively simple, safe and accurate. On the one hand, the preference of males as the first child may be perceived as sending a message to society that women have a suboptimal worth. On the other hand, selecting the sex of the second child for family balancing may obviate these objections provided that (a) the balance of sex ratio will be kept in each center; (b) embryos of the undesired sex would be donated, and (c) the procedure would be paid for by the patients themselves.

PDG for Human Leukocyte Antigen Matching for an Affected Child

Transplantation of hematopoietic stem cells (HSCT) is the only known cure for a number of diseases. The first couple to request this procedure was a couple from Colorado USA who used IVF and PGD to produce embryos that were then screened to determine which future child would be a stem cell and bone marrow donor for their daughter. The couple's daughter, 6-year-old Molly Nash was born with Fanconi's anemia. This is a rare autosomal recessive disease characterized by aplastic anemia, brittle chromosomes and the variable presence of skeletal, cardiac, and renal anomalies. Affected persons have acute myelogenous leukemias and other cancers. Patients do not survive to adulthood. The only proven long-term cure of the bone marrow manifestations is a successful allogeneic hematopoietic HSCT.

Best results have been achieved with human leukocyte antigen (HLA) genotypically-identical sibling donors. HSCT using nongenotypically identical donors is associated with poor survival. Mollie lacked an HLA-identical related donor and PGD was used to select an embryo that was both unaffected by Fanconi's anemia and HLA – identical with Mollie. After 5 cycles of IVF with the transfer of 7 embryos over a span of 4 years, a successful pregnancy occurred. The umbilical cord blood of the healthy infant – Adam – was harvested at birth in 2000 and used as the source of HLA-identical hematopoietic stem cells to reconstitute normal hematopoiesis in his affected sister. A month after Adam's delivery, the patient underwent HSCT and is currently well with normal hematopoiesis [83, 84]. In this case, the first selection for which the preimplantation diagnosis was used was directed at embryos without the anemia and the second selection was for typing of the healthy embryos according to HLA types.

Following the Nash case, a British couple, the Hashmis, whose son Zain suffered from β-thalassemia, was allowed by the HEFA in 2001 to undergo the same procedure. HEFA in principle allows the use of PGD-HLA provided that each application is considered on a case-by-case basis. This position was challenged by a group objecting to the procedure on the grounds of 'absolute respect' for the human embryo that won a high court ruling that HEFA had exceeded its powers. HEFA appealed this decision together with the Department of Health and the decision was overturned by the High Court who wrote that, 'whether the pre-implantation genetic diagnosis has the purpose of producing a child free from genetic defects, or of producing a child with stem cells matching a sick or dying sibling, the IVF treatment that includes the diagnosis constitutes treatment for the purpose of assisting women to carry children' [85].

The main objections raised against the procedure mentioned above are:

1 *Instrumentalization*

This is the main argument opposing this type of request. The selection is made for characteristics (HLA) that are useful only to others. The embryo itself does not benefit from the selection. The child becomes an instrument to cure others. A counter-argument could be that parents who want to have another child anyway have an obligation to try and rescue their sick child. It is highly unlikely that the parents would treat the child as merely a tissue donor and their efforts on behalf the affected child are an expression of their concern for their children and confirm their intention to treat the donor child as equal to the existing one.

2 *The best interest standard*
A major problem for cases which deal with incompetent persons (in this case – embryos) as volunteers is whether the intervention serves their best interest. When it can be shown that the procedure serves an interest of the person, than he is not regarded only as a means. Those in favor of PGD-HLA suggest looking at the family as a whole and arguing that the future child has an interest to grow up in an intact family. It is the best interest of the donor that his or her sibling will be healthy and alive because this has a major impact on the happiness of the family and the atmosphere he will grow in. Giving bone marrow causes minimal harm to one child in order to save the life of another. The enormous benefit to the recipient coupled with the low risk to the donor makes the donation ethically correct and acceptable. If parents can decide that an existing child should undergo an operation in order to donate bone marrow to a sibling, it is difficult to claim that they cannot desire that their future offspring would, likewise, be a HSC donor for a sibling [86].

3 *Feelings of the child*
It could be argued that a heavy emotional burden is placed on the donor child. The bone marrow transplant may not succeed which may in turn create feelings of guilt and failure. The counterargument to this line of reasoning is that the child will be very young when the donation is performed and all the potential negative effects of a failed donation would be diluted by the time the child is old enough to understand his participation in the event.

4 *The fear of a slippery slope*
There is a potential slippery slope for patients to choose other characteristics. That is why Adam Nash was labeled in lay journals and newspapers as a 'designer baby'. This fear can be avoided by professional or legislative control.

The second case of PGD-HLA was the birth of Jamie Whitaker in London 2003 who was described as Britain's first 'savior sibling'. Jamie's brother, Charlie, aged 4, has Diamond-Blackfan anemia, a rare blood disorder that requires him to undergo a blood transfusion every 3 weeks. His only chance of living beyond 30 years of age and the only hope of successful treatment was HSCT of a perfect tissue match. The parents sought permission in the United Kingdom for PGD-HLA but were denied it by the HEFA. In this case, the HEFA's ruling was based on the fact that the risk of another child developing Charlie's condition was so small, there was no potential benefit to the future sibling himself. They then went to the USA where two embryos were selected to provide a match for Charlie.

The British Medical Association subsequently reassessed its support for the selection of embryos in cases where siblings are seriously ill or dying and declared that, 'As doctors we believe that where technology exists that could help a dying or seriously ill child, without involving major risks for others, then it can only be right that it is used for this purpose. The welfare of the child born as a result of the treatment is of crucial importance, but in our view this is not incompatible with allowing the selection of embryos on the basis of tissue type' [87].

In conclusion, the conception of a child in order to save another is morally defensible on condition that the operation that will be performed on the future child is equally acceptable for any living child. The creation of the donor child goes hand in hand with a respect for its autonomy and inherent value.

PGD for Nonmedical Traits

PGD was initially developed in order to prevent the birth of an affected child. One cannot, however, ignore the fact that once the technique is available and genetic traits of personality characteristics will be established, couples might seek PGD for nonmedical indications. These may include eye and hair color, intelligence, height, beauty, sexual orientation and other desired phenotypes. In such a scenario, physicians will be facing the ethical problem of producing a designer baby that would match the couple's wish. Currently, the discussion on whether to permit PGD for such indications seems to be redundant because the genetic traits of these characteristics are yet unknown and most probably, unlike Mendelian traits, are determined by multiple unidentified genes. Nevertheless, ethical discussions on this issue should be encouraged. If such a selection of embryos would be permitted, it harbors the risk of interfering with nature by producing 'designed' children. Preferring a specific phenotype and creating it raises problems such as intensifying discriminations between subjects, unrealistic expectations of parents from such a child, and the psychosocial effects on the designed child.

Although the question of 'designed' children upon request seems currently irrelevant, there are some hypothetical and nonhypothetical cases that can exemplify the ethical problems with a nonmedical PGD request.

A request from a couple with hereditary deafness to have a child without a hearing loss would sound logical and acceptable because 'hearing' is considered normal. A dilemma might arise if a nonhearing child is preferred. The couple might claim that the child will be born into a committed environment to deafness and will have an easier time adapting. In that case, the question is whether such a request serves best the benefit and interests of the child. This ethical problem was discussed widely when a deaf lesbian chose to use sperm from a deaf donor to increase the possibility of having a nonhearing child [88, 89]. While some bio-ethicists found such a request to be understandable [88], others found it unacceptable [90]. Similar dilemmas, stressing the psychosocial effects on the child, his welfare and rights in contrast to the parents' requests are interestingly presented by others discussing the achondroplasia trait [27] and the hypothetical option of PGD for selecting for perfect pitch [66].

While most of the nonmedical uses of PGD are currently irrelevant, witnessing the rapid developments in the field of genetics and molecular biology should provoke debate. Such debate will help to define the public stance on these issues and assist in crystallizing guidelines for these potential interventions of the future.

Future Directions

In the second decade of the PGD era, future advances are expected in all aspects of this modality. More data is required to confirm safety and efficiency of different biopsy methods. Improvements in culture media and cryopreservation protocols will enable further genetic analysis by use of time-consuming techniques such as comparative genomic hybridization. This is one option in the desired move towards full karyotype analysis. Large cohorts and longer follow-up of PGD pregnancies and deliveries are needed in order to assess the safety of PGD. Clinical information, obtained by randomized clinical trials, will aid in defining which infertile couples could benefit from aneuploidy screening. DNA microarray is a potentially useful method of genetic molecular analysis in PGD. This technique offers several advantages, such as screening for diseases which are genetically heterogeneous, and replacement of metaphase spreads currently needed for CGH. However, serious limitations such as the amount of genetic material in one blastomere, the reliability of the data and the high cost prevent this technique from being used in clinical PGD at present [91].

References

1 Handyside AH, Kontogianni EH, Hardy K, Winston RM: Pregnancies from biopsied human preimplantation embryos sexed by Y-specific DNA amplification. Nature 1990;344:768–770.

2 Handyside AH, Lesko JG, Tarin JJ, Winston RM, Hughes MR: Birth of a normal girl after in vitro fertilization and preimplantation diagnostic testing for cystic fibrosis. N Engl J Med 1992;327: 905–909.

3 Olivennes F, Fanchin R, Ledee N, Righini C, Kadoch IJ, Frydman R: Perinatal outcome and developmental studies on children born after IVF. Hum Reprod Update 2002;8: 117–128.

4 Lambert RD: Safety issues in assisted reproductive technology: Aetiology of health problems in singleton ART babies. Hum Reprod 2003;18: 1987–1991.

5 Yaron Y, Gamzu R, Malcov AV: Genetic analysis of the embryo; in Gardner DK, Weissman A, Howles CM, Shoham Z (eds): Textbook of Assisted Reproductive Techniques: Laboratory and Clinical Perspectives. London, Martin Dunitz, 2001, pp 319–333.

6 Montag M, van der Ven K, Delacretaz G, Rink K, van der Ven H: Laser-assisted microdissection of the zona pellucida facilitates polar body biopsy. Fertil Steril 1998; 69:539–542.

7 Nijs M, Van Steirteghem AC: Assessment of different isolation procedures for blastomeres from two-cell mouse embryos. Hum Reprod 1987;2:421–424.

8 Tarin JJ, Conaghan J, Winston RM, Handyside AH: Human embryo biopsy on the 2nd day after insemination for preimplantation diagnosis: Removal of a quarter of embryo retards cleavage. Fertil Steril 1992;58:970–976.

9 Mottla GL, Adelman MR, Hall JL, Gindoff PR, Stillman RJ, Johnson KE: Lineage tracing demonstrates that blastomeres of early cleavage-stage human pre-embryos contribute to both trophectoderm and inner cell mass. Hum Reprod 1995;10:384–391.

10 Hardy K, Martin KL, Leese HJ, Winston RM, Handyside AH: Human preimplantation development in vitro is not adversely affected by biopsy at the 8-cell stage. Hum Reprod 1990;5:708–714.

11 Edwards RG, Beard HK: Oocyte polarity and cell determination in early mammalian embryos. Mol Hum Reprod 1997;3: 863–905.

12 Boada M, Carrera M, De La Iglesia C, Sandalinas M, Barri PN, Veiga A: Successful use of a laser for human embryo biopsy in preimplantation genetic diagnosis: Report of two cases. J Assist Reprod Genet 1998;15:302–307.

13 Joris H, De Vos A, Janssens R, Devroey P, Liebaers I, Van Steirteghem A: Comparison of the results of human embryo biopsy and outcome of PGD after zona drilling using acid Tyrode medium or a laser. Hum Reprod 2003;18:1896–1902.

14 Staessen C, Van Assche E, Joris H, et al: Clinical experience of sex determination by fluorescent in-situ hybridization for preimplantation genetic diagnosis. Mol Hum Reprod 1999;5:382–389.

15 Gerris J, De Neubourg D, De Sutter P, Van Royen E, Mangelschots K, Vercruyssen M: Cryopreservation as a tool to reduce multiple birth. Reprod Biomed Online 2003;7: 286–294.

16 Magli MC, Gianaroli L, Fortini D, Ferraretti AP, Munne S: Impact of blastomere biopsy and cryopreservation techniques on human embryo viability. Hum Reprod 1999;14:770–773.

unclear. Some investigators believe that the pathogenesis is related to obstruction of lymphatic drainage. The finding of nuchal translucency was regarded in the past as local pathology. However, it is now well established that this finding represents an important marker of fetal chromosomal anomalies (mainly Turner's syndrome and trisomies 13, 18, 21). Furthermore, it is also a significant marker of other fetal structural anomalies, mainly of the cardiovascular system.

There are two methods of fetal ultrasonographic examination – the transabdominal scan which is performed at mid and late pregnancy, and the transvaginal scan which is performed in early pregnancy. Currently, most sonographers are familiar only with the older technique of transabdominal scanning, which is easier to perform. The more advanced technique of transvaginal scanning, necessitates a greater level of skill and better spacial orientation, and was therefore, adopted only by a subset of sonographers. However, it should be noted that transvaginal ultrasound examination in the early second trimester of pregnancy (<17 weeks' gestation) offers several important advantages:

1 Early ultrasound examination may increase the detection rate of chromosomal abnormalities. There is now mounting evidence that transient anomalies such as nuchal edema, pyelectasis or hyperechogenic bowel which are observed mainly in early pregnancy serve as markers of a possible chromosomal anomaly. Due to their transient nature, these anomalies may disappear later in pregnancy (>17 weeks' gestation) and thus would be missed if early scanning was not performed.
2 Several fetal organs are visualized more clearly in early gestation. For instance, the fetal hands tend to be open with extended fingers in early pregnancy, making evaluation of the fingers quite simple at this stage. In contrast, as gestation advances, the fists are usually clenched and evaluation of the fingers becomes more difficult. Another example is the examination of the fetal heart. Absence of ossification of the ribs, spine and upper limbs in early gestation, enables examination of the fetal heart in various planes. In contrast, at later stages of gestation, with increased ossification, the available planes of imaging become fewer in number.
3 Early detection of structural anomalies preserves the entire spectrum of therapeutic options, including amniocentesis for chromosomal studies or therapeutic abortion. Early termination of pregnancy using dilatation and curettage is less dangerous than dilatation and evacuation or even

administration of vaginal prostaglandin together with intravenous oxytocin, which are performed in mid-gestation. It also usually has a less detrimental psychological impact on the mother.

4 Early identification of fetal gender may be essential in the diagnoses of linked disorders or to define the zygosity in cases of multiple pregnancy.
5 In cases of severe fetal malformations, early detection may prevent unnecessary invasive procedures such as amniocentesis for advanced maternal age, cervical suture for an incompetent uterine cervix, or tight glucose control for diabetes.
6 Safe selective reduction of a malformed fetus in cases of high-order multiple gestations.
7 Several structural abnormalities are known to be associated with chromosomal disorders. For instance, congenital heart disease, hydronephrosis, omphalocele, clubfoot, single umbilical artery, and growth deficiency. Early detection of these anomalies improves parental counseling and the possibility to perform diagnostic procedures.

In our department, we adopted the transvaginal technique in 1987. Since then, one sonographer (Dr. Moshe Bronshtein) has performed a detailed evaluation of more than 46,000 fetuses. The population consists of self-referred patients who are interested in the early ultrasonographic detection of fetal anomalies or patients who are referred by their physician for the same purpose or for a second opinion. This large series reflects the tendency to perform a detailed targeted ultrasonographic examination of almost every pregnant woman in our practice area. About 88% of the women are at low risk for fetal developmental anomalies, hereditary or congenital syndromes, whereas 12% are at increased risk (exposure to medications, family history of congenital malformations, consanguinity). The examination is most often performed at 14–16 weeks' gestation. Women are advised to have a second scan (transabdominal) at 24–26 weeks' gestation. The second scan is recommended because some fetal anomalies such as hydrocephalus, absence of corpus callosum or some types of dwarfism may present only in the second half of pregnancy.

During the years in which transvaginal scanning was performed, we found it difficult to provide appropriate parental counseling in some cases because of the following reasons:

a Isolated abnormal findings in which the literature reveals a large spectrum of possible clinical manifestations and outcome.
b Lack of data in the literature regarding sonographic findings first observed by us.

- c Limited information on the natural history of known anomalies in cases detected in early pregnancy.
- d Disagreement between the literature and our clinical experience regarding the outcome of fetuses in several anomalies.

This chapter summarizes some of our studies, in which we tried to address these issues. Obviously these studies represent a continuous process of a learning curve, and therefore, the sizes of the different series and the time periods differ among the studies.

Isolated Abnormal Findings in which the Literature Reveals a Large Spectrum of Possible Clinical Manifestations and Outcomes

The depiction of an isolated malformation with a large spectrum of possible clinical manifestations and outcomes precludes precision in parental counseling. The anxious parents actually get a large amount of data but without specific implication regarding their own fetus. Since the familial pattern of many anomalies is not yet well established, we considered the possibility that asymptomatic parents of a fetus with a solitary ultrasonographically detected structural malformation may have the same anomaly without even being aware of it. The novel concept of parental imaging is of potential utility with respect to anomalies, where parents may benefit from an encouraging example regarding the quality of life in adulthood.

Parental Imaging May Help in the Assessment of Abnormalities of Uncertain Prognosis

In cases where an isolated fetal anomaly with an uncertain prognosis was observed (i.e. anomalies which on the one hand had been reported in normal persons, but on the other hand had also been associated with adverse clinical outcome) parents were offered: (a) amniocentesis or cordocentesis depending on gestational age; (b) relevant imaging examination of the parents. Ultrasound examinations were offered to both mothers and fathers in any case where malformations were detected in the fetal abdomen. In cases where CT or MRI examination was relevant (mainly in cases of central nervous system anomalies), the test was first offered to the father.

Table 1.

Cases in which parental imaging was offered after detection of a solitary fetal anomaly

Ultrasonographic findings	Number of cases detected	Cases of similar parental finding (gestational week)	Parent with similar finding
Severe anomalies			
Isolated agenesis of corpus callosum	6*	1, male (27)	mother
Agenesis of lower part of the vermis	3	1, female (23)	father
Enlarged cisterna magna	2	1, female (21)	mother
Agenesis of kidney in female fetus	7	1, female (14)	mother
Mild-moderate anomalies			
Horseshoe kidney	11	1, female 1, male (14)	father mother
Bilateral, large renal calyces (Megacalycosis)	1	1, female (23)	father
Dysmorphic and septated bladder	2	1, male (22)	mother

* In 2 cases parents did not agree to an imaging procedure.

If no anomaly was found in the father, the mother was counseled and informed about the possible adverse effects of the imaging procedure in pregnancy.

In cases where one of the parents was found to have the same anomaly as the fetus and in which pregnancy was continued, meticulous follow-up, postnatal physical examinations and appropriate imaging procedures were performed in the infants.

During the study period, structural abnormalities were detected in 295 fetuses of the 14,118 fetuses which were scanned (2.09%). Solitary anomalies with an uncertain prognosis were detected in 32 cases. Fetal anomalies were divided into two categories, severe and mild-moderate, based on potential prognosis regarding future disability [3] (table 1).

The dilemmas we faced in the parental counseling of these 32 cases were as follows:

Agenesis of Corpus callosum

The prevalence of agenesis of the corpus callosum is 2–3% in developmentally disabled patients [4]. However, studies have been conducted mainly in symptomatic patients, and the prevalence of agenesis of corpus callosum in the general population is unknown. Furthermore, the outcome in cases of an isolated finding of this anomaly has not been defined. A familial pattern of the disorder has been reported in a small number of cases. The mode of inheritance was either autosomal-dominant, autosomal-recessive, or X-linked-recessive. Only 44 cases with prenatal sonographic diagnosis of isolated agenesis of corpus callosum in which parents decided to continue pregnancy have been reported. Following delivery, 10 of these fetuses were found to be severely developmentally disabled. The other 34 newborns were considered normal. However, the follow-up in most of these cases was only for few months or few years and sufficient data on the long-term outcome of these children at school age are not available [5, 6]. In our series, the only case in which pregnancy was continued after the detection of agenesis of corpus callosum was a case where the same anomaly was also detected in the clinically healthy mother.

Agenesis of Lower Part of the Vermis

In partial agenesis of the vermis, the neurologic findings result from abnormalities in the cerebellar hemispheres and nuclei and associated brainstem pathways. Some cases of an isolated finding detected prenatally, were normal. However, the reported follow-up only ranged from 8 weeks to 4 years [7]. A familial pattern of this anomaly has been described. The major clinical features were normal intelligence, delayed achievements of motor milestones, truncal ataxia and nystagmus. Most affected individuals were females; however, males were more severely affected [8]. Of special concern is the familial variety, the Joubert syndrome, which is inherited as an autosomal-recessive disorder and presents as alternating periods of hyperpnea and apnea, ataxia, abnormal eye movements and mental retardation [9]. At present, partial agenesis of the vermis is the only sonographic finding that may be detected in the fetus with this syndrome. Our series included a single case in which the anomaly was detected in a female fetus as well as in her clinically healthy father.

Enlarged Cisterna magna

Enlargement of the cisterna magna is one of the major categories of posterior fossa CSF collection. This condition is mainly secondary to cerebellar atrophy

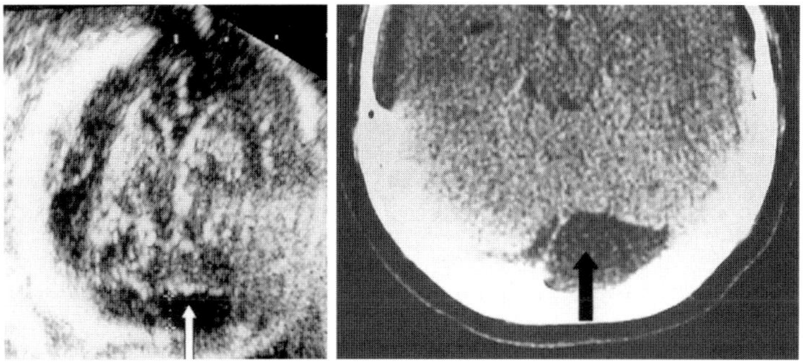

Fig. 1.
Left: Mega cisterna magna (white arrow) detected sonographically in a 15-gestational-week male fetus. Right: Maternal MRI showing an enlarged cisterna magna (black arrow).

or hypoplasia (which is a frequent finding in trisomies), or communicating hydrocephalus. Isolated cisterna magna enlargement has been reported both in asymptomatic and symptomatic patients. In symptomatic individuals, the clinical presentation included hypotonia, tremor, neuropsychiatric symptomatology and nonprogressive macrocephaly. Bodensteiner et al. [10] found developmental and neurological abnormalities in 10 of 14 (62%) patients. It is of interest that the neurologic findings were not specifically localized to the posterior fossa. The authors therefore concluded that the finding of an isolated enlarged cisterna magna may be a marker for abnormal brain function due to subtle disturbances in brain development. Different results were reported by Haimovici et al. [11]. In this report, 15 fetuses with an isolated enlarged cisterna magna were found to be phenotypically normal at delivery. Follow-up (2–69 months) conducted on only 8 of these infants revealed that all infants were clinically normal. None of the published cases of an isolated finding of an enlarged cisterna magna had a familial tendency. In our series, in one of the two cases which were detected, the mother also had an enlarged cisterna magna (fig. 1).

Agenesis of Kidney in the Female Fetus
Unilateral renal agenesis is seen in about 1 in 1,000 live births. It is associated with various structural anomalies in the genitourinary, skeletal,

cardiovascular, gastrointestinal, central nervous and respiratory systems [12]. It should be noted that it is difficult to detect with ultrasound, some of the known associated anomalies (e.g. ventricular septal defects). A familial mode of unilateral renal agenesis has been reported [13]. A primary concern in females with unilateral renal agenesis is the possible association with vaginal atresia or agenesis, and rudimentary uterus (Rokitansky sequence). This anomaly may cause major reproductive, emotional and sexual problems. At present the fetal uterus and vagina cannot be imaged by ultrasound. Therefore, unilateral renal agenesis may be the only ultrasonographic feature pointing to the possible occurrence of this anomaly in the female fetus. In the current series, other than the case in which the mother had also a unilateral renal agenesis, all other families decided to terminate pregnancy.

Diagnostic procedures were offered to the families in all 32 cases of these anomalies, and performed in one or both parents in 30 cases. The other two families refused to undergo an imaging procedure.

In 8 cases, the same anomaly was noted in a healthy parent, and all these pregnancies were carried to term. These cases, 4 with a severe anomaly and 4 with a mild-moderate anomaly are summarized in table 1. In 5 cases the same anomaly was found both in the fetus and mother, and in 3 cases the same anomaly was found both in fetus and father. Karyotyping demonstrated a normal chromosomal analysis in all 8 fetuses. The prenatal diagnosis was confirmed upon postnatal examination, and all the newborns were found to be clinically well.

In all these 8 cases, parents indicated that they would have chosen to terminate pregnancy if a similar anomaly would not have been found in one of them. In contrast, in all 12 cases with severe anomalies in which the same anomaly was not detected in either parent, the parents requested termination of pregnancy. This included three cases of agenesis of the corpus callosum, 2 cases of partial agenesis of the vermis, 1 case of enlarged cisterna magna and 6 cases of unilateral renal agenesis in female fetuses.

Concerning the minor-moderate anomalies detected, an imaging procedure was performed on the parents in all 14 cases (table 1), and a similar malformation was detected in 4 of the parents. Of the 10 cases in which the same anomaly was not detected in the parents, 9 couples decided to continue the pregnancy, the prenatal diagnosis was confirmed after delivery and the children were clinically well. In 1 case of a horseshoe kidney, the parents decided to terminate the pregnancy. Of note, this mother stated she would have continued the pregnancy if a horseshoe kidney had been detected in either parent.

The main issue which arose regarding the cases in the mild-moderate category reported in the current series are as follows:

Horseshoe Kidney. This renal anomaly has been reported in 7% of girls with Turner syndrome. Wilm's tumor is 2–8 times more frequent in children with horseshoe kidney than in the general population [12]. The anomaly is associated with an increased incidence of urological disorders. Only one case of familial occurrence could be found in the literature accompanied by abnormal glucose tolerance and hypertension in adults [13].

Bilateral Large Renal Calyces (Megacalycosis). Megacalycosis is a congenital non-obstructive dilatation of the calyces without pelvic or ureteric dilatation. It is usually unilateral but can be bilateral and was reported to be associated with other anomalies such as megaureters, Hirschsprung's disease and the Schinzel-Giedion syndrome [14]. Familial megacalycosis has been reported [15].

Dysmorphic Gallbladder. Dysmorphism of the fetal gallbladder has been observed in fetuses with chromosomal abnormalities and other structural malformations [16]. It may cause symptoms due to calculi or infections later in life. No familial tendency was reported.

As noted, only two families out of 32 cases refused to undergo an imaging procedure. Both these cases were in fetuses with agenesis of the corpus callosum. The reason for refusal was not because of the nature of the requested imaging procedure (CT or MRI). In one family, the father, who is a physician, claimed that even if such an anomaly would be detected in parents, there would be no guarantee that the same benign clinical presentation in the parents would apply to the fetus. In the second family, the first son who had mental retardation was found during childhood to have absence of the corpus callosum. In two consecutive pregnancies male fetuses with agenesis of the corpus callosum were detected. Both pregnancies were terminated upon parental request. In the fourth pregnancy a female fetus with a normal corpus callosum was born. The parents didn't undergo any imaging procedure because they were reticent with respect to their own findings.

The familial occurrence of some anomalies presented in our study has previously been noted in only a few case reports [8, 13–15]. This paucity of information may not necessarily reflect the actual incidence or extent of familial occurrence of the given conditions, but rather failure to search for a corresponding anomaly in other family members. Our results may indicate that some isolated structural anomalies, which were usually believed not to be of familial origin, are probably of familial and possibly hereditary origin. The increased use of prenatal sonographic examinations will continue to provide us with more information regarding such isolated anomalies in the general population and within families, as well as information on the clinical presentation of these abnormal findings through different generations.

The fact that the parent with the same finding leads a normal fruitful life may be a reassuring indicator, and its role in influencing parental decision making should be considered. However, it is of importance to note that parents should be informed that it is yet unclear if the same structural anomaly will have a similar clinical presentation and prognosis in different generations, or whether the clinical course may worsen in a subsequent generation due to the phenomenon of genetic anticipation, in which the clinical expression is more severe with progressive generations.

Lack of Data in the Literature Regarding Sonographic Findings First Observed by Us

During the years, several such puzzling anomalies were observed. Among others, these include a human tail, a fetal 'mustache' and hyperechogenic foci in the thalamus. This last anomaly will be discussed here in more detail because of its involvement in the central nervous system.

Isolated Hyperechogenic Foci in the Fetal Thalamus in Early Pregnancy

The thalamus is the major relay station for most sensory impulses that reach the primary sensory areas of the cerebral cortex from the spinal cord, brain stem and midbrain. It contributes to motor function by transmitting information from the cerebellum and basal ganglia to the primary motor area of the cerebral cortex.

Linear echogenic structures reminiscent of the shape of a chicken leg, representing echogenic blood vessels in the thalamus and basal ganglia have been described in the fetus [17] and in newborn infants [18]. These linear or branching linear areas of echogenicity have been suggested to represent calcifications [19], or vasculopathy [19, 20]. Different underlying diseases have been suggested, such as congenital infections (bacterial, viral, protozoal) [18–20], chromosomal aberrations (trisomy 13, trisomy 21), asphyxia, non-immune hydrops, and fetal alcohol syndrome [18–20]. However, the underlying pathology was not revealed in all the reported cases.

In our series of 46,244 pregnancies, we observed 9 fetuses (1 in 5,138 pregnancies) who had a hyperechogenic focus (mass) in the thalamus [21]. The size of the foci ranged from 2 to 4 mm and they differed in their features from the previously reported linear echogenic structures of the thalamus. Review of the literature revealed no other reports on such echogenic foci in the fetal thalamus. Two of the fetuses had multiple malformations and pregnancy was terminated. In the other 7 cases there were no other structural anomalies. The karyotype was normal and serologic studies revealed no evidence of recent infection. In all these 7 fetuses, the hyperechogenic foci in the thalamus disappeared on repeated scans performed at 18–22 weeks' gestation and all of them were healthy at delivery. Long term follow-up to the age of 9 years was obtained and no signs of abnormality or developmental disorders were observed.

Our experience indicates that isolated hyperechogenic foci in the thalamus detected in the early second trimester of pregnancy are benign and transient. Extensive targeted ultrasonographic examination, serologic tests for infections, amniocentesis for karyotyping, and cytomegalovirus cultures should be performed in every case. In the absence of associated anomalies, these foci seem to be harmless, will disappear later in the second trimester and carry a good prognosis. However, because there are no other reports in the literature and our series is still small, more data are needed to further validate our current conclusion.

Limited Information on the Natural History of Various Known Anomalies in Cases Detected in Early Pregnancy

There are several anomalies in which the natural history has been reported in cases detected in the second half of pregnancy. However, there is only limited data on the significance of these same anomalies when detected in early pregnancy. We present here two examples of such anomalies.

Fetal Omphalocele Detected In Early Pregnancy

Omphalocele is the most common major congenital abdominal wall defect [22]. In this anomaly the intra-abdominal viscera herniate into the base of the umbilical cord. The prevalence of omphalocele varies considerably in the literature, ranging between 0.8 and 3.9 per 10,000 births [23]. It is known to be a part of 48 different anomaly syndromes. Associated structural anomalies were noted in 27% [28] to 91% [29] of fetuses, and abnormal chromosomes were observed in 20–50% of cases, mainly trisomies 13 and 18 [24, 25].

The exact mechanism leading to omphalocele is controversial. During normal embryonic life, a rapid elongation of the gut and its mesentery characterizes development of midgut. As a result of this rapid growth and simultaneous expansion of the liver, the abdominal cavity becomes too small to contain all the intestinal loops and they enter the extra-embryonic coelom in the umbilical cord. This process of physiological umbilical herniation occurs during the sixth week of development. During the tenth week, the intestines return into the abdominal cavity. This process is called the reduction of the midgut hernia, and is completed at 12 weeks' gestation. It was suggested that omphalocele may result from either failure of the intestinal loops to re-enter into the abdominal cavity, or failure of the embryonic lateral folds to fuse in the midline [26].

The sonographic detection of herniation of intestinal loops into the umbilical cord in early pregnancy raises a dilemma regarding the exact nature and significance of the finding – Does this finding present a malformation or only a delay in the physiological process of the midgut herniation?

We detected an omphalocele in 38 fetuses of 43,896 pregnancies (an incidence of one in 1,155 pregnancies) at 12–16 weeks' gestation. No case of false-negative diagnosis was recorded in this series [27].

Associated structural anomalies were observed on initial scanning in 22/38 (58%) fetuses. An abnormal karyotype was found in 11 of 18 of the fetuses where chromosomal analysis was available. Termination of pregnancy was performed on parental request in 21 fetuses.

In 16/38 fetuses, the omphalocele was a solitary structural finding; all 16 had normal karyotype analysis. In 8 of these fetuses, the abdominal wall defect was small, contained only few intestinal loops and disappeared on repeated scanning between 20 and 24 weeks' gestation.

Of the remaining 8 fetuses with isolated omphalocele, there was 1 case of missed abortion, 1 case of termination of pregnancy and 6 cases of postnatal surgery for the correction of the abdominal wall defect.

The underlying reason for transient omphalocele is yet not clear. It is possible that this phenomenon represents a physiological process of midgut herniation. Review of the literature reveals few reports of transient omphalocele detected at 14 and 15.5 weeks' gestation with a favorable outcome [28, 29].

Despite the fact that in our series there was not one case of an abnormal karyotype in fetuses with an isolated omphalocele, we still believe that karyotyping should be offered to all patients – because our series was too small to draw a definite conclusion regarding the possibility of an abnormal karyotype in such fetuses.

One should be aware that it might be difficult to detect in utero all syndromes associated with omphalocele; for instance, the Beckwith-Wiedemann syndrome. It is not clear at which gestational age the classic signs of this syndrome, such as macroglossia, are apparent on ultrasound examination, and there are even reports of late manifestation of the characteristic findings of this syndrome after delivery [30].

In conclusion, fetuses with a solitary finding of intestinal herniation into the umbilical cord and a normal karyotype have a favorable prognosis. Parents should be counseled about the following possibilities: (a) The fetus has an omphalocele that will be surgically corrected after delivery. (b) The fetus has a transient omphalocele, which may disappear during gestation. (c) The fetus may have a rare syndrome that cannot be definitively diagnosed in utero at present. A follow-up throughout gestation and even after delivery is warranted.

Simple Renal Cysts Detected in Early Pregnancy

Renal cystic diseases in children comprise a relatively common and heterogeneous group of disorders that may be genetic or hereditary, developmental or acquired. Depending on the underlying condition, renal cysts may be multiple or solitary [31, 32]. Most solitary cysts are structurally simple and benign. However, simple renal cysts in children may be associated with other structural or chromosomal abnormalities and, occasionally, with neoplastic processes [31–33].

Simple renal cysts may be detected at any age, including the neonatal and fetal period [33, 34]. Data on sonographic diagnosis of simple renal cysts in the fetus are scarce [34].

We detected 28 fetuses with a simple renal cyst out of 29,984 consecutive pregnancies, giving an incidence of 1 in 1,071 pregnancies. All these cysts were in the cortex of the kidneys and maximal diameter varied between 2.1 and 4.0 mm. No other renal or structural anomalies were observed in these fetuses [35].

In 24 fetuses, the simple renal cysts resolved by 20–24 weeks' gestation and postnatal follow-up sonography was normal. In 3 fetuses, the cysts were still present on repeated sonograms at 22–24 weeks' gestation. In 2 of these cases the cysts were also observed at birth and were still present at the age 3 and 6 years, respectively. There was an additional fetus in our series which had a solitary cyst that met the sonographic criteria of a simple renal cyst at 14 weeks' gestation. Sonography at 18 weeks' gestation revealed 4 noncommunicating cysts of varying size in the same kidney which also had a hyperechogenic appearance. A diagnosis of unilateral multicystic dysplastic kidney was suggested and confirmed after birth. All patients with a diagnosis of fetal simple renal cyst, except for the patient with the multicystic dysplastic kidney (a disease with a high percentage of potential problems, such as reflux in the contralateral kidney, hypertension, Wilm's tumor), thrived well and had no urinary tract infection, impairment of renal function or other urinary tract abnormalities.

In conclusion, a complete sonographic survey of all fetal organs as well as chromosomal analysis is indicated when a simple renal cyst is detected in a fetus. In the absence of structural malformations and chromosomal aberrations, most cysts resolve before birth. However, patients should be observed closely with serial antenatal and postnatal ultrasound. Considering the transient nature, it is possible that fetal simple renal cysts detected in early pregnancy represent a distinct entity within the spectrum of cystic kidney diseases.

Disagreement between the Literature and Our Clinical Experience Regarding the Outcome of Fetuses in Several Anomalies

Once the prognostic significance of an ultrasonographic finding has been established in the literature, it becomes a cornerstone in the parental counseling. However, our clinical experience regarding the prognostic value and meaning of certain ultrasonographic findings oppose the accepted concept. Therefore, we conducted some long-term prospective studies to reevaluate the real meaning of these findings, and offer a more accurate prognostic prediction.

Nonvisualization of the Fetal Gallbladder in Early Pregnancy
The exact incidence of agenesis of the gallbladder is unknown, mainly because the estimated incidence has been calculated from reviews of cases reports. Since the description of agenesis of the gallbladder by Bergman in 1701, only 413 cases have been reported up to 1999 [36]. Small gallbladders have been observed in neonates with cystic fibrosis and there are anecdotal reports of hypoplastic gallbladder in trisomy 18 and 21.

Some investigators have found that the inability to visualize the gallbladder may indicate fetal anomalies, while others have reported a high rate of nonvisualization of the gallbladder in fetuses with normal outcome [16, 37, 38]. Therefore, we looked for the fetal gallbladder in 29,749 consecutive pregnancies at 14–16 weeks' gestation. The gallbladder was not visualized in 34 fetuses, giving an incidence of 1 in 875 pregnancies [39].

In all fetuses in which the gallbladder was not detected, amniocen-tesis was offered to the parents. A search for cystic fibrosis, hepatic enzyme tests, and chromosomal analyses were performed. A postnatal ultrasonographic search for the gallbladder was done. In neonates in whom the gallbladder was not detected, a repeat sonogram was performed at the age of 1 year.

Of the 34 fetuses with a nonvisualized gallbladder, 14 fetuses had associated structural and chromosomal anomalies, while 20 fetuses had nonvisualization of the gallbladder as an isolated finding.

All 20 fetuses with a nonvisualized gallbladder as an isolated finding had a normal karyotype. In 14 of them hepatic enzymes were available for analysis revealing a normal level in all cases. Of interest, in 13 of those fetuses with an isolated finding, the gallbladder was detected later in pregnancy or after birth.

In summary, the gallbladder can be observed in almost all fetuses in early pregnancy. Nonvisualization of the gallbladder in early pregnancy deserves special attention, since almost 40% of these fetuses have associated anomalies. It may also be a marker of cystic fibrosis or external biliary atresia. However, nonvisualization of the gallbladder, especially in fetuses in which this phenomenon is a solitary finding, may be associated with a normal outcome. Furthermore, in some cases it will be possible to depict the gallbladder later during pregnancy or after birth.

Isolated Large Fourth Ventricle in Early Pregnancy

The fourth ventricle is a rhomboid-shaped cavity lying on the posterior aspect of the pons. An enlarged fourth ventricle may be encountered in several malformations, most commonly the Dandy-Walker malformation, Dandy-Walker variant and Vermian-Cerebellar hypoplasia.

We detected 21 fetuses with an enlarged fourth ventricle as a solitary central nervous system finding out of 14,000 consecutive early pregnancies, an incidence of approximately 1:670 pregnancies. All fetuses had a normal karyotype.

Associated minor structural anomalies were detected in five fetuses. The cerebellum had a normal appearance in all 21 fetuses and its size was appropriate for age. At 22–23 weeks' gestation all fetuses were found to have a normal-sized fourth ventricle. This was confirmed again by ultrasonography after delivery. Nineteen infants who were followed up to the age of one year had a favorable outcome with no signs of developmental disorders. Two other infants were lost to follow-up after delivery [40].

During the study period we had seven additional fetuses with an enlarged fourth ventricle that also had other anomalies of the central nervous system. Pregnancy was terminated in all these cases.

Our clinical experience shows that many sonographers and obstetricians tend to make the diagnosis of Dandy-Walker malformation in cases of an enlarged fourth ventricle even though other markers of the malformation are not observed. Many terminations of pregnancies have been performed in such cases. However, as has been shown in our series, the detection of an enlarged fourth ventricle in early pregnancy as a solitary finding, in the presence of a normal cerebellum, may represent a normal anatomical variant. A sonographic follow-up is warranted in these fetuses in order to avoid a false-positive diagnosis of a central nervous system anomaly.

Persistent Intrahepatic Right Umbilical Vein in the Fetus

At about the mid-fourth week of gestation there are two umbilical veins, left and right. During the sixth gestational week, the right umbilical vein usually degenerates, leaving only a left umbilical vein to carry all the blood from placenta to fetus. The persistence of a right umbilical vein has been previously considered as an uncommon condition.

Jeanty [41] gathered only a dozen instances reported in the literature since 1826, and added 6 new cases. Associated anomalies were found in all published cases and in three of Jeanty's own 6 patients, suggesting that persistent right umbilical vein might be an ominous prenatal finding. Following Jeanty's report, further series indicated that it was not that rare [42, 43]. However, data on incidence of associated significant congenital malformations were inconsistent, ranging from 11 to 50%.

We made a sonographic diagnosis of a persistent intrahepatic right umbilical vein in 69 fetuses out of 30,240 consecutive pregnancies, an incidence of 1 in 438, all in low-risk pregnancies. In 60 of 69 cases (87%), the persistent intrahepatic right umbilical vein was an isolated finding with no other malformations [44].

Among the other 9 fetuses, 3 had structural anomalies and 6 had transient sonographic anomalies that disappeared later in pregnancy. Karyotyping showed normal chromosomal analyses in all nine fetuses.

The presence of right umbilical vein in 1:438 pregnancies in our series was similar to the incidence reported in other series. However, we found severe malformations in 1.4% of cases, compared with up to 50% of cases in the literature. Our study was not a population-based study; therefore, bias was possible in incidence of associated anomalies. However, all our cases were detected in low-risk pregnancies.

We believe that an extensive targeted ultrasonographic examination should be done whenever the condition is identified, and chromosomal studies are warranted in every fetus in which associated ultrasonographic abnormalities are detected. In the absence of associated malformations, a persistent intrahepatic right umbilical vein is usually an innocuous condition and carries a good prognosis.

Conclusion

The field of intrauterine sonographic detection of fetal anomalies has dramatically improved during the last decades, and there is a constant increase in the number of malformations observed in utero. Nonetheless, we must remain vigilant and cautious about the interpretation of these ultrasonographic findings. Further studies and meticulous continuous examination of data are the cornerstones of reliable parental counseling. An appropriate counseling process may lower parental fear and confusion, and help in providing the best available management plan for the sake of both the fetus and his parents.

References

1 Romero R: Routine obstetric ultrasound. Ultrasound Obstet Gynecol 1993;3: 303–307.

2 Grandjean H, Larroque D, Levi S: The performance of routine ultrasonographic screening of pregnancies in Eurofetus study. Am J Obstet Gynecol 1999; 181:446–454.

3 Bronshtein M, Zimmer EZ, Blazer S: Imaging studies of parents of fetuses with sonographic anomalies of uncertain prognosis. JAMA 2001;285:737–738.

4 Bogen JE: The callosal syndrome; in Heilman KM, Valenstein E (eds): Clinical Neuropsychology. Oxford, Oxford University Press, 1993, pp 337–371.

5 Vergani P, Ghidini A, Strobelt N, et al: Prognostic indicators in the prenatal diagnosis of agenesis of corpus callosum. Am J Obstet Gynecol 1994;170:753–758.

6 Gupta JK, Lilford RJ: Assessment and management of fetal agenesis of the corpus callosum. Prenat Diagn 1995;15:301–312.

7 Keogan MT, DeAtkine AB, Hertzberg BS: Cerebellar vermian defect: Antenatal sonographic appearance and clinical significant. J Ultrasound Med 1994;13:607–611.

8 Fenichel GM, Phillips JA: Familial aplasia of the cerebellar vermis: X-dominant inheritance. Arch Neurol 1989;46:582–583.

9 Joubert M, Eisenring JJ, Robb JP, Andermann F: Familial agenesis of the cerebellar vermis: A syndrome of episodic hyperpnea, abnormal eye movements, ataxia and retardation. Neurology 1969;19:813–825.

10 Bodensteiner JB, Gay CT, Marks WA, Hamza M, Schaefer GB: Macro cisterna magna: A marker for maldevelopment of the brain? Pediatr Neurol 1988;4:284–286.

11 Haimovici JA, Doubilet PM, Benson CB, Frates MC: Clinical significance of isolated enlargement of the cisterna magna (>10 mm) on prenatal sonography. J Ultrasound Med 1997;16:731–734.

12 Gonzalez R: Urologic disorders in infants and children; in Behrman RE, Kliegman RM, Arvin AM (eds): Nelson Textbook of Pediatrics, ed 15. Philadelphia, Saunders 1996, pp 1527–1553.

13 Boatman DL, Hawtrey CE: Familial horseshoe kidney: A case report. J Iowa Med Soc 1973;63:399–401.

14 Herman TE, Sweetser DA, McAlister WH, Dowton SB: Schinzel-Giedion syndrome and congenital megacalyces. Pediatr Radiol 1993;23:111–112.

15 Lam AH: Familial megacalyces with autosomal recessive inheritance. Report of 3 affected siblings. Pediatr Radiol 1988;19:28–30.

16 Bronshtein M, Weiner Z, Abramovici H, Filmar S, Erlik Y, Blumenfeld Z: Prenatal diagnosis of gall bladder anomalies – Report of 17 cases. Prenat Diag 1993; 13:851–861.

17 Estroff JA, Parad RB, Teele RL, Benacerraf BR: Echogenic vessels in the fetal thalami and basal ganglia associated with cytomegalovirus infection. J Ultrasound Med 1992;11:686–688.

18 Weber K, Riebel Th, Nasir R: Hyperechoic lesions in the basal ganglia: An incidental sonographic finding in neonates and infants. Pediatr Radiol 1992;22:182–186.

19 Ben-Ami T, Yousefzadeh D, Backus M, Reichman B, Kessler A, Hammerman-Rozenberg C: Lenticulostriate vasculopathy in infants with infections of the central nervous system, sonographic and Doppler findings. Pediatr Radiol 1990;20:575–579.

20 Teele RL, Hernanz-Schulman M, Sotrel A: Echogenic vasculature in the basal ganglia of neonates: A sonographic sign of vasculopathy. Radiology 1988;169:423–427.

21 Bronshtein M, Zimmer EZ, Auslender R, Blazer S: Isolated hyperechogenic foci in the fetal thalamus in early pregnancy. Ultrasound Obstet Gynecol 2001;17:333–334.

22 Stoll C, Alembik Y, Dott B, Roth MP: Risk factors in congenital abdominal wall defect (omphalocele and gastroschisis): A study in a series of 265,858 consecutive births. Ann Genet 2001;44: 201–208.
23 Barisic I, Clementi M, Hausler M, et al: Evaluation of prenatal ultrasound diagnosis of fetal abdominal wall defects by 19 European registries. Ultrasound Obstet Gynecol 2001;18: 309–316.
24 Gilbert WM, Nicolaides KH: Fetal omphalocele: Associated malformations and chromosomal defects. Obstet Gynecol 1987;70:633–635.
25 Tan K, Kilby MD, Whittle MJ, Beattie RB, Booth IW, Botting BJ: Congenital anterior abdominal wall defects in England and Wales: 1987–1993. Br Med J 1996; 313:903–906.
26 Moore KL, Persaud TVN: The digestive system; in Moore KL, Persaud TVN (eds): The Developing Human, Clinically Oriented Embryology. Philadelphia, Saunders, 1998, pp 271–302.
27 Blazer S, Zimmer EZ, Bronshtein M: Fetal omphalocele detected in early pregnancy: Associated anomalies and outcome. Radiology, in press.
28 Achiron R, Soriano D, Lipitz S, Mashiach S, Goldman B, Seidman DS: Fetal midgut herniation into the umbilical cord: Improved definition of ventral abdominal anomaly with the use of transvaginal sonography. Ultrasound Obstet Gynecol 1995;6: 256–260.
29 Bromley B, Benacerraf BR: Transient omphalocele. J Ultrasound Med 1992;12:688–689.
30 Chitayat D, Rothchild A, Ling E, et al: Apparent postnatal onset of some manifestations of the Wiedemann-Beckwith syndrome. Am J Med Genet 1990;36: 434–539.
31 Watkins SL, Avner ED: Renal dysplasia and cystic disease; in Holliday MA, Barratt TM, Avner ED (eds): Pediatric Nephrology, ed 3. Baltimore, William & Wilkins, 1994, pp 467–490.
32 Becker N, Avner ED: Congenital nephropathies and uropathies. Pediatr Clins N Am 1995;42:1319–1341.
33 McHugh K, Stringer DA, Hebert D, Babiak CA: Simple renal cysts in children: Diagnosis and follow-up with US. Radiology 1991;178:383–385.
34 Herman TE, Siegel MJ: Renal cysts associated with Turner's syndrome. Pediatr Radiol 1994;24:139–140.
35 Blazer S, Zimmer EZ, Blumenfeld Z, Zelikovic I, Bronshtein M: Natural history of fetal simple renal cysts detected in early pregnancy. J Urol 1999;162:812–814.
36 Singh B, Satyapal KS, Moodley J, Haffejee AA: Congenital absence of the gall bladder. Surg Radiol Anat 1999;21:221–224.
37 Chan L, Rao BK, Jiang Y, Endicott B, Wapner RJ, Reece EA: Fetal gallbladder growth and development during gestation. J Ultrasound Med 1995;14:421–425.
38 Hetzberg BS, Kliewer MA, Maynor C, et al: Nonvisualization of the fetal gallbladder: frequency and prognostic importance. Radiology 1996;199: 679–682.
39 Blazer S, Zimmer EZ, Bronshtein M: Nonvisualization of the fetal gallbladder in early pregnancy: Comparison with clinical outcome. Radiology 2002; 224:379–382.
40 Bronshtein M, Zimmer EZ, Blazer S: Isolated large fourth ventricle in early pregnancy: A possible benign transient phenomenon. Prenat Diagn 1998;18: 997–1000.
41 Jeanty P: Persistent right umbilical vein: An ominous prenatal finding? Radiology 1990;177: 735–738.

The communicative process of genetic counseling differs from other health care counseling in that it typically incorporates the entire family. This is because genes are transmitted through families and because certain conditions are revealed through the family history. Within families, certain members may be affected by, at risk for, or caring for someone with a genetic condition. Prenatal genetic counseling represents a unique situation further complicated by the fact that there is an unborn child involved in the process. However, the subject matter ultimately remains the family and its cultural, social and economic background [1].

It is therefore of prime importance that this service being provided in an environment that is responsive not only to the clinical situation but also to the psychological, and cultural needs of all parties involved. This is particularly important since genetic counseling addresses issues such as reproduction, sexuality, health, disease, and disability, relate to individual and group perceptions, beliefs and practices which are fundamentally influenced by culture. Furthermore, genetic counseling is increasingly becoming a cross-cultural issue as certain subpopulations tend to be more commonly afflicted by genetic disorders than others due to ethno-cultural isolation and intermarriage [2].

A local example for such an ethno cultural isolate is the highly inbred, traditional community of the Arab-Bedouin of the Negev, the southern region of Israel. This population illustrates the cultural characteristics and the problems encountered in utilizing modern genetic services that, to a very large extent, are interrelated.

The Negev Bedouin population of about 130,000 people, is characterized by a high and increasing birth rate (fig. 1), high prevalence of consanguineous marriages (fig. 2) that correlates with high rates of birth defects and genetic diseases (fig. 3), high infant mortality rates compared to the Jewish population (fig. 4) mainly due to birth defects and genetic disorders in consanguineous families (fig. 5) and low level of formal education among women (table 1). Less than 40% of the male population graduated from high school and about 20% only have an elementary school education. Although most pregnant women do visit prenatal care clinics, they tend to do it rather late in pregnancy so prenatal genetic diagnosis is not a relevant option any more (fig. 6). When prenatal genetic testings are being used in this population they are mostly restricted to the noninvasive ones (triple screening and fetal sonography) and significantly lag behind the rates of use in the Jewish population. Rates of amniocentesis among older women are very low but increase upon obtaining an abnormal result of the triple test

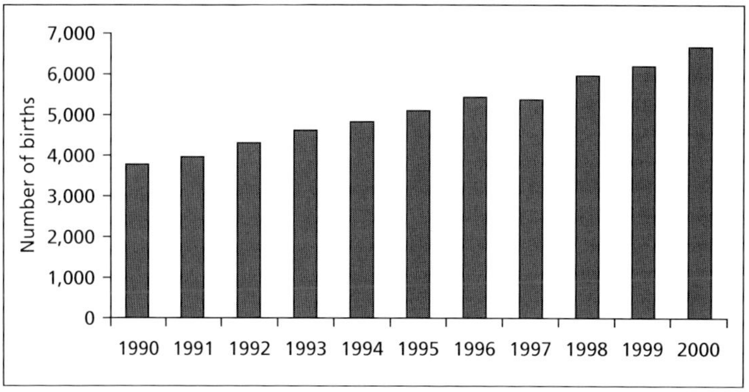

Fig. 1.
Births in the Negev Bedouin population, 1990–2000.

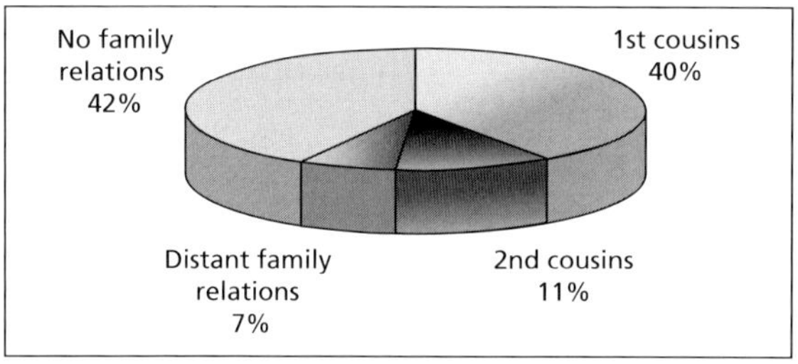

Fig. 2.
Reported consanguineous marriage among Negev Bedouin population, 1990–2000 (n = 879).

(table 2). Utilization rates increase with a history of a previously unsuccessful pregnancy and correlate, to a certain extent, with higher education of husbands and in few cases with women's exposure to western culture while working outside of home. Primigravida women were more compliant than multigravida women on all indices checked (fig. 7). The use of at least one prenatal diagnostic procedure highly correlates with an existing unhealthy child (fig. 8). These facts, no doubt, make the point that there are some inherent barriers that prevent from the use of and complying with genetic counseling for prenatal diagnosis in this specific ethno cultural isolate [3].

The central obstacles in the provision of accessibility to genetic counseling are rooted in communication, language, culture, economics and education.

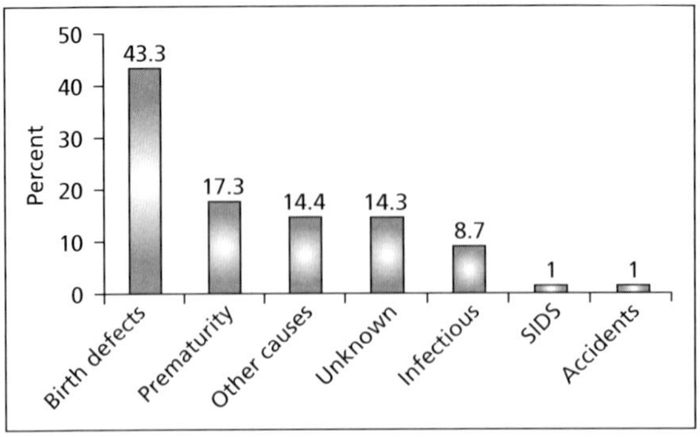

Fig. 3.
Causes of infant mortality in the Bedouin population (%).

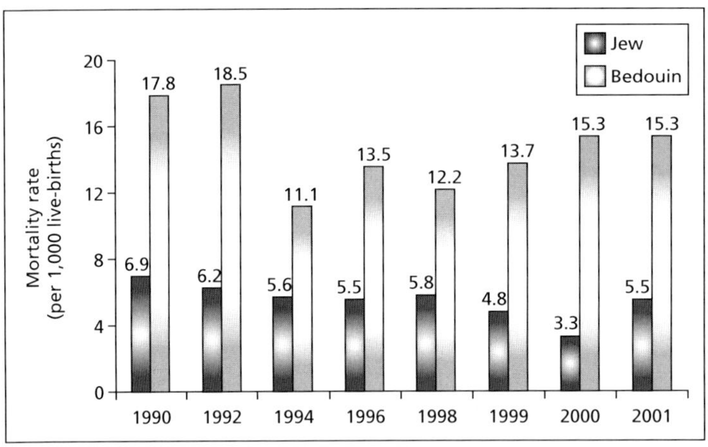

Fig. 4.
Infant mortality rate in Bedouins and Jews in the Negev, 1990–2001.

Ethno cultural distinctiveness is perhaps the greatest barrier to receiving care. Patients can have their own cultural interpretation for the cause of birth defects and genetic disease as well as culturally founded concepts of health, illness and disability [4]. The use of home remedies and folk medicine can also 'interfere' or even hinder the efficient use of prescribed recommendations.

Misconceptions regarding involved medical procedures, including prenatal diagnosis, values placed on the size of the family and preferred

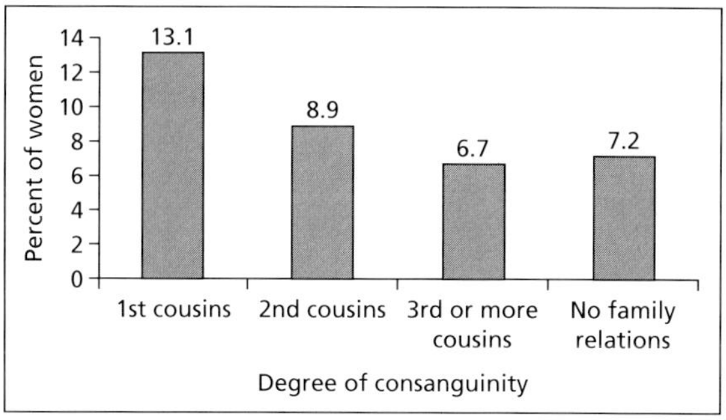

Fig. 5.

Bedouin women reporting congenital anomalies in previous births (at least one) by degree of consanguinity (n = 835).

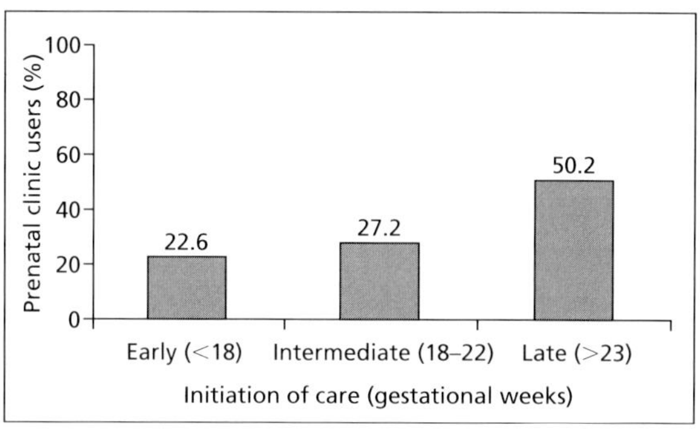

Fig. 6.

Utilization of prenatal services of the Bedouin women who visited prenatal care clinics at least once during pregnancy (n = 972; 89 vs. 99% in the Jewish population).

gender of offspring, religious and societal considerations, inclusion of extended family or community members in medical decision making, distrust with formal systems of health services, apprehension regarding genetic stigmatization and its consequences in terms of prospects for marriage and preservation of family structure – all of these present serious barriers for seeking genetic counseling and using genetic services [5].

In addition, and of further complexity, is the fact that the ethos of nondirective counseling, a basic western concept of the genetic counseling process [6],

Table 1.

Education levels of Bedouin women in the Negev

Educational level	%
Never studied	49.5
Less than primary school	25.7
Primary school	5.4
High school – not completed	8.9
High school completed	6.9
Higher education	3.5

Source: Cwikel J: Health and Welfare Study of Bedouin Women of the Negev. Center for Women's Health studies and Promotion, Ben Gurion University, 2000.

Table 2.

Utilization of prenatal diagnostic procedures among Bedouin women (n = 978)

Procedure	%
Triple test or amniocentesis	22.6
Fetal sonography	42.7
At least one of the previous procedures	48.9
Amniocentesis among eligible by	
Age (>35 years)	8.9
Abnormal result of triple test	57.6

can seem confusing and unfamiliar to some ethno cultural groups and can have adverse effects as to what is expected by them from medical professionals or from individuals perceived to be in a position of authority [7].

Serious barriers also appear on the part of the providers: lack of knowledge of the individual characteristics of patients and their special needs, stereotypic expectations of patients and their decisions, lack of appropriate dynamics and comprehension when using translators, lack of awareness of cultural values and responses, lack of understanding that behavior can be intra- and interculturally specific, provision of services as per values of Western medicine, e.g. excluding extended family members, the use of

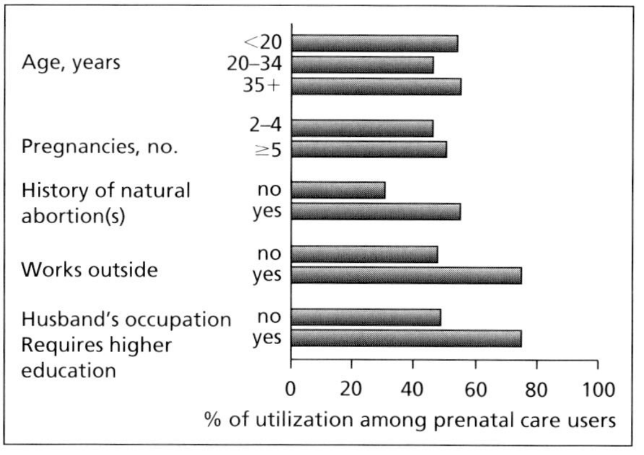

Fig. 7.

Utilization of at least one diagnostic procedure in Bedouin women by demographic and obstetric characteristics (n = 854).

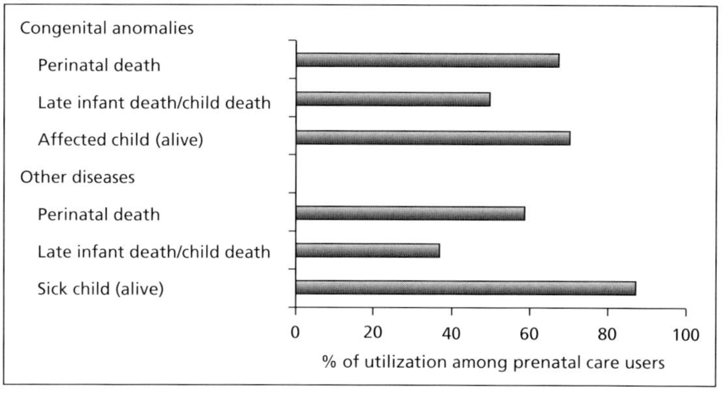

Fig. 8.

Utilization of at least one diagnostic procedure in Bedouin women by mortality and morbidity in previous births (n = 854).

counselors of genders that might cause discomfort for certain ethno cultural groups and other various misunderstandings of traditional norms and values that are incongruent with the 'standard view' of genetic counseling [7].

Ethno cultural barriers to genetic counseling can result in: a decreased utilization of services, miss-termed 'poor compliance' with genetic counseling and specific recommendations and testing, unelected birth of a child

Cross-cultural genetic counseling is a great challenge that necessitates basic knowledge, understanding and in many instances identification with the patient's needs. Therefore, the training of counselors from within a given community seems an appropriate solution, which, nevertheless, is not always simple [18]. A more realistic approach adopted in several communities is the role of a community based assistant genetic counselor from within the ethno cultural group who is not a formally professional but acquires, through appropriate training, certain basic knowledge and skills to provide counseling on routine genetic issues [4, 5]. This practice has shown to improve compliance with the use of genetic services and recommendations.

Mainstream genetic counseling should be familiar with cross-cultural techniques and adopt specific guidelines when working with counselees from diverse backgrounds. Some of these should be:

1 Establishing and maintaining trust.
2 Respecting and acknowledging beliefs and practices concerning the presented problem.
3 Giving attention and respect to expressed suspicion or distrust.
4 Supporting the inclusion of other elected members in the counseling process.
5 Being sensitive to situations where a counselee may be subjected to the possibility of stigmatization, rejection or violence.
6 Providing sufficient guidance so to enable the formulation of an acceptable plan of action embodied in the counselee's beliefs, values and circumstances.
7 Using as much as possible professional interpreters, preferably experienced with respect to genetic counseling.

Our own experience with providing genetic counseling to the Negev-Bedouin population further supports the effectiveness of adopting such guidelines. Over the past decade we have established an infrastructure of community based genetic counseling services aimed at the reduction of birth defects and hereditary diseases in this population. This includes the training of local assistant-genetic counselors and genetic health educators from within the community that provide readily accessible and culturally appropriate genetic information in the Arab language. These nonprofessionals, trained and coached by certified genetic counselors, interact with women visiting the mother and child clinics in the community, visit families in their homes and help spreading accurate information and correct misconceptions and wrong beliefs regarding genetic diseases and prenatal diagnosis. In addition, the program has developed educational genetic curriculum for high school students that has been recognized by the Ministry of Education and has been adopted by most schools in the community. Various educational meetings and workshops have been conducted for community leaders, both nonmedical professionals and leading religious figures. A doco-drama ('Aysha') featuring the potential ill effect of consanguinity and the availability of specific testing for devastating genetic diseases has proven very instrumental in conveying overt and hidden messages in a culturally appropriate setting. The program also includes a component of carrier testing for various genetic diseases which was piloted in several tribes. Here again, community participation in the decision of the most suitable way to conduct such screenings, as well as the actual execution of the projects, was a major consideration in the designing process and the operating stages.

Reducing genetic disorders in the Negev-Bedouin population is a long term goal. Its accomplishment involves many factors other than this ongoing prevention program. However, some results can already be observed in terms of increasing openness to seek genetic counseling and consider prenatal and carrier screening tests especially in families with serious genetic diseases. This is, to a large extent, the result of creating the appropriate sociocultural environment in which the population is being approached by its own people that are sensitive to and aware of their specific needs, in their own language and usually in their own community setting. Moreover, this kind of approach helps empowering the community by realizing the potential of capable individuals that when properly trained, can serve as a self support group to promote addressing pressing issues such as the communal burden of genetic diseases.

And, finally, there is a specific issue that needs further consideration. Most contemporary discussions address cross-cultural issues from the perspectives of presumably defined ethno cultural groups. However, the reality is far more complex. Even within defined groups, there are differences among members related to education, socioeconomic status, societal status within the culture group, and extent of intercultural interactions. Each of these factors creates complex dynamics of self-identity, beliefs and affiliations that transcend those discussed under the unitary ethno cultural categories. These issues should be recognized and addressed appropriately. This makes the task of cross-cultural genetic counseling even more complicated but at the same time interesting and challenging.

References

1 Weil J: Multicultural education and genetic counseling. Clin Genet 2001;59:143–149.

2 Mittman I. Crombleholme WR, Green JR, Golbus M: Reproductive genetic counseling to Asian-Pacific and Latin American immigrants. J Genet Counsel 1998;7: 49–70.

3 Weitzman D, Shoham-Vardi I, Elbedour K, Belmaker I, Siton Y, Carmi R: Factors affecting the use of prenatal testing for fetal anomalies in a traditional society. Community Genet 2000;3:61–70.

4 Punales-Morejon D, Penchaszadeh VB: Psychological aspects of genetic counseling: Cross-cultural issues. Birth Defects Orig Artic Ser 1992;28:11–15.

5 Dixson B, Dang JO, Cleveland PRM: An educational program to overcome language and cultural barriers to genetic services. J Genet Counsel 1992;1:267–274.

6 Wolff G, Jung C: Nondirectivness and genetic counseling. J Genet Counsel 1995;4:3–25.

7 Wang V, Marsh F: Ethical principles and cultural integrity in health care delivery: Asian ethno cultural perspectives in genetic services. J Genet Counsel 1992;1: 81–92.

8 Andrews L: Public choices and private choices: Legal regulations of genetic testing; in Murphy T, Lapp M (eds): Justice and the Human Genome Project. Berkley, University of California Press, 1994, pp 46–75.

9 King P: The past as prologue: Race, class and gene discrimination; in Annas G, Elias S (eds): Gene Mapping: Using Law and Ethics as Guides. Oxford, Oxford University Press, 1992, pp 94–111.

10 Weil J, Mittman I: A teaching framework for cross-cultural genetic counseling. J Genet Counsel 1993;2:159–169.

11 Sue DW, Sue D: What is cultural competence? in Sue DW, Sue DJ (eds): Counseling the Culturally Different: Theory and Practice, ed 4. New York, Wiley, 1998, pp 17–25.

12 World Health Organization (WHO): Community Control of Genetic and Congenital Disorders. Alexandria, EMRO Technical Publications, 1997, series 24. .

13 World Health Organization (WHO): Community Approaches to the Control of Hereditary Diseases. Unpublished WHO document HMG/AG/85.10. Geneva, Hereditary Diseases Program, 1985.

14 Ioannou P: Thalassemia prevention in Cyprus: Past, present and future; in Chadwick RF, Shickle D, ten Have HAMJ, Wiesing U (eds): The Ethics of Genetic Screening. Amsterdam, Kluwer Academic Publishers, 1999, pp 55–67.

15 Abeliovitch D, Quint A, Weinberg N, et al: Cystic fibrosis heterozygote screening in the orthodox community of Ashkenazi Jews: The Dor Yesharim approach and heterozygote frequency. Eur J Hum Genet 1996;4:77–82.

16 Gamberini MR, Lucci M, Vullo C, Anderson B, Canella R, Barrai I: Reproductive behavior of families segregating for Cooley's anemia before and after the availability of prenatal diagnosis. J Med Genet 1991;28:523–529.
17 Bassetti S: Culturally relevant genetic counseling: Nurses play a critical role in helping women and families. AWHONN Lifelines. 2002;6:254–257.
18 Darr A: Consanguineous marriage and genetics: A positive relationship; in Clarke A, Parsons E (eds): Culture, Kinship and Genes. London, MacMillan, 1996, pp 83–97.

Rivka Carmi, MD

Dean, Faculty of Health Sciences, Ben-Gurion University of the Negev,
PO Box 653, IL–84105 Beer Sheva (Israel)
Tel. +972 8 623 9068, Fax +972 8 647 7632, E-Mail Rcarmi@bgumail.bgu.ac.il

Blazer S, Zimmer EZ (eds):
The Embryo: Scientific Discovery and Medical Ethics.
Basel, Karger, 2005, pp 236–258

The Fetus with a Treatable Endocrine and Metabolic Disorder

Guy Rosner[a] Shay Ben Shachar[a]
Yuval Yaron[a,b] Mark I. Evans[c]

[a]Prenatal Diagnosis Unit, Genetic Institute, Tel-Aviv Sourasky Medical Center, and
[b]Department of Obstetrics and Gynecology, Tel-Aviv University, Tel Aviv, Israel;
[c]Institute for Genetics and Fetal Medicine, St. Luke's Roosevelt Hospital Center, Columbia University, New York, N.Y., USA

The achievements of the Human Genome Project have provided mapping of many disease-associated genes and enabled better modes of diagnosis and primary prevention. However, some metabolic and endocrine disorders such as congenital adrenal hyperplasia (CAH) and cardiac arrhythmias may also be amenable to pharmacological interventions [1, 2]. This chapter will focus on the fetus with an endocrine or metabolic defect for which intrauterine pharmacological therapy may be possible. In addition, neural tube defects and the use of folic acid supplementation will also be described.

Endocrine Disorders

Adrenal Disorders

Congenital Adrenal Hyperplasia

Treatment of CAH during the fetal life is a well-described and excellent example of the pharmacological prevention of a birth defect. CAH consists of a group of metabolic disorders all characterized by enzymatic defect in the steroidogenetic pathway. As a result of the enzyme defect, and in order to maintain cortisol production, there is a compensatory increase in ACTH secretion which leads to overproduction of the steroid precursors in the adrenal cortex – hence the adrenal hyperplasia. All forms of CAH are inherited in an autosomal-recessive manner. The phenotype of each form is determined by the severity of the cortisol deficiency and the nature of the steroid precursors which accumulate proximal to the enzymatic block.

The most common abnormality, responsible for >90% of patients with CAH is caused by a deficiency of the 21-hydroxylase (21-OH) enzyme. Other, less common causes for CAH include deficiencies in 11β-hydroxylase, 17-hydroxylase, and 3β-hydroxysteroid-dehydrogenase. Diminished 21-OH activity results in the accumulation of 17-hydroxyprogesterone (17-OHP) as a result of its decreased conversion to 11-deoxycorticosterone. The excess 17-OHP is then converted via androstenedione to androgens, the levels of which increase by as much as several hundred-fold (fig. 1). The excess androgens cause virilization (abnormal development of masculine characteristics in a female) of the undifferentiated female external genitalia. The degree of virilization may vary from mild clitoral hypertrophy to complete formation of a phallus and scrotum. In contrast, genital development in male fetuses is normal. The excess androgens cause postnatal virilization in both genders and may manifest in precocious puberty.

The 'classical' form of CAH involves a severe enzyme deficiency or even a complete block of enzymatic activity, which is associated in two-thirds to three-fourths with salt-loss that may be life threatening. The classical form is easy to recognize in female newborns but may be overlooked in males which may present at a later stage with severe dehydration and even demise. The estimated incidence of classical CAH is 1:5,000–1:60,000, depending on the ethnic background. The 'non-classical' attenuated form of 21-OH deficiency results in partial blockade of the enzymatic activity and is usually clinically apparent as simple virilization in women only later in life. It is estimated to occur in ~3.5% in Ashkenazi Jews and ~2% in Hispanics [3].

The gene for 21-OH is in close linkage to the HLA major histocompatability complex on the short arm of chromosome 6 [4]. The gene for 21-OH (CYP21B) has now been mapped, allowing direct mutation analysis in informative families [5].

Historically, in the late 1970s and early 1980s, diagnosis of CAH was made on amniocentesis by the finding of elevated levels of 17-OHP in the

There is agreement that the treatment requires a professional team that includes an expert high-risk obstetrician, a pediatric endocrinologist, genetic counselor and a molecular genetic laboratory.

Thyroid Disorders

Hypothyroidism

Congenital hypothyroidism affects about 1:3,000–1:4,000 infants [10]. About 85% of the cases are the result of thyroid dysgenesis, a heterogeneous group of developmental defects characterized by an inadequate amount of thyroid tissue. Congenital hypothyroidism is only rarely associated with errors of thyroid hormone synthesis, TSH (thyroid-stimulating hormone) insensitivity, or absence of the pituitary gland. Fetal hypothyroidism may not necessarily manifest in a goiter before birth since maternal thyroid hormones may cross the placenta. Congenital hypothyroidism presenting with a goiter can be found in only about 10–15% of cases, with an estimated prevalence of 1:30,000–1:50,000 live-births [11]. Fetal goitrous hypothyroidism is caused in most instances by maternal exposure to thyrostatic agents used to treat maternal hyperthyroidism [12]. These drugs include propylthiouracil (PTU), the inadvertent use of radioactive ^{131}I in the pregnant women or iodide exposure. Maternal ingestion of amiodarone (antiarrhythmic drug) or lithium (drug for people with mood disorders) may also cause hypothyroidism in the fetus. Finally, fetal hypothyroidism may result from the transplacental passage of maternal blocking antibodies (known as TBIAb or TBII) or rarely due to rare defects in fetal thyroid hormone biosynthesis [11].

Fetal goiterous hypothyroidism may lead to severe fetal and neonatal consequences. An enlarged goiter may cause esophageal obstruction which may lead to polyhydramnios, which may result in preterm delivery or premature rupture of membranes. Rarely, a goiter may even lead to high-output heart failure due to high vascular flow in the goiter [13]. A large fetal goiter can cause extension of the fetal neck leading to dystocia in labor. The effects of the fetal hypothyroidism itself may be devastating. Without treatment, postnatal growth delay and severe mental retardation may ensue. Even with immediate diagnosis and treatment at birth, long term follow up of children with congenital hypothyroidism has demonstrated that they have lower scores on perceptual-motor, visuospatial, and language tests [14].

In suspicious cases, an extensive maternal and family history should be obtained. In patients with a positive history, maternal thyroid hormone levels, as well as blocking immunoglobulin levels should be measured. In addition, all women with a history of any thyroid disease (both hypothyroidism and hyperthyroidism) are advised to have monthly fetal ultrasound scans to screen for fetal goiter, polyhydramnios, or fetal tachycardia [15].

Occasionally, fetal goiterous hypothyroidism may be identified by an ultrasound performed due to increased uterine size caused by polyhydramnios secondary to esophageal obstruction and impaired swallowing. Sometimes, a fetal goiter may be discovered incidentally on a routine scan. Before the advent of cordocentesis, amniotic fluid levels of TSH and FT4 (free thyroxine) were used as potential indicators of fetal thyroid function. However, these proved to be inconsistent [16]. With cordocentesis, fetal thyroid status can be directly and accurately evaluated; fetal response to therapy can therefore be reliably measured using available appropriate nomograms for fetal serum levels of FT4, total T4 (thyroxine), free T3 (triiodothyronine), total T3, and TSH [15, 17]. In utero treatment was initially suggested by Van Herle et al. [18] using intramuscular injection of levothyroxine sodium. Subsequent studies, however, have indicated that intra-amniotic administration of thyroxine may be superior and can lead to resolution of the polyhydramnios as well. The dose of the injected drug may be refined using the fetal thyroid profile in the amniotic fluid and the thyroid size [19]. The doses commonly used for treatment range from 200 to 500 mg intra-amniotically every week. With this regimen, fetal goiters have been shown to regress, hyperextension of the fetal head has been shown to resolve and fetal and newborn TSH levels have normalized [19].

Hyperthyroidism

Neonatal hyperthyroidism is rare with an incidence of 1:4,000–1:40,000/live-births [10]. Fetal thyrotoxic goiter is usually secondary to maternal autoimmune disease, principally Graves' disease or Hashimoto's thyroiditis. As many as 12% of infants of mothers with a known history of Graves' disease are affected with neonatal thyrotoxicosis, which may occur even if the mother is euthyroid [20]. As with hypothyroidism, inherent to the underlying mechanism is the transplacental passage of maternal IgG antibodies. In this case the antibodies, known as TSAb or (TSI), are predominantly directed against the TSH receptor.

Usually, the investigation of fetal hyperthyroidism begins only after the discovery of fetal goiter. Often, the goiter is diagnosed on ultrasound in patients referred due to elevated thyroid stimulating antibodies. In some cases, fetal goiters are realized serendipitously on routine ultrasonography. Others may be discovered in patients referred for scan because of polyhydramnios. Beside the risks related to the goiter itself, untreated fetal hyperthyroidism may be associated with a mortality rate of 12–25% due to high-output cardiac failure [21]. Once a fetal goiter is identified, biochemical evaluation is indicated. Historically, amniotic fluid levels of TSH and FT4 were used as potential indicators of fetal thyroid function. These, however, proved inconsistent in that amniotic fluid levels of these hormones do not always correlate with their serum levels. Some controversy still exists regarding their use; however, they may be of some benefit in centers that do not have available cordocentesis [16]. As previously stated, cordocentesis allows reliable assessment of fetal thyroid status TSH [15, 17], and treatment can be planned accordingly.

Once the diagnosis of fetal hyperthyroidism is confirmed, fetal treatment should be initiated. Authors have attempted treating fetal hyperthyroidism with maternally administered antithyroid drugs. Porreco has reported maternal treatment of fetal thyrotoxicosis with the antithyroid drug propylthiouracil (PTU), which lead to a good outcome [22]. The initial dose used was 100 mg p.o. three times a day, which was later decreased to 50 mg p.o. three times a day. Wenstrom et al. [21] described a favorable outcome using maternal methimazole to treat fetal hyperthyroidism in a patient who could not tolerate PTU. Hatjis [23] also treated fetal goitrous hyperthyroidism with a maternal dose of 300 mg PTU. This patient, however, required supplemental synthroid (levothyroxine sodium) to remain euthyroid. There was good fetal outcome in this case as well.

Inborn Errors of Metabolism

Methylmalonic Acidemia

The methylmalonic acidemias (MMA) are a group of enzyme-deficiency diseases inherited in an autosomal-recessive manner resulting from one of several genetically distinct etiologies. Some cases are caused by mutations in the gene encoding methylmalonyl-coenzyme A mutase while others are due to a defect that reduces the biosynthesis of adenosylcobalamin from vitamin B_{12}. The disease is characterized by a wide clinical spectrum ranging from a benign condition to a fatal neonatal disease. In the severe form, MMA is characterized by severe metabolic acidosis, developmental delay and biochemical abnormalities that include methylmalonic aciduria, long-chain ketonuria, and intermittent hyperglycinemia. Patients with defects in adenosylcobalamin biosynthesis may respond to administration of large doses of vitamin B_{12}, which may enhance the amount of active holoenzyme (mutase apoenzyme plus adenosylcobalamin). A proposed mechanism for the neurological abnormalities observed in methylmalonic acidemia was suggested by a group of Brazilian investigators who administered methylmalonic acid to rats during the first month of their life [24]. A significant diminution of myelin content and of ganglioside N-acetylneuraminic acid was noted in the cerebrum.

More than 20 years ago, Ampola et al. [25] were the first to attempt prenatal diagnosis and treatment of a vitamin B_{12}-responsive variant of MMA. They followed the pregnancy of a patient who had previously suffered the loss of a child to severe acidosis and dehydration at the age of 3 months. The diagnosis of MMA was made posthumously by chemical analysis of blood and urine. In the subsequent pregnancy, amniocentesis at 19 weeks revealed elevated methylmalonic acid in the amniotic fluid. Cultured amniocytes also demonstrated defective propionate oxidation and undetectable levels of adenosylcobalamin. When adenosylcobalamin was added, normal succinate oxidation and methylmalonyl-coenzyme A mutase activity were noted. These studies established that the fetus also suffered from MMA apparently due to deficient synthesis of adenosylcobalamin. It was already known that fetal MMA is associated with increased methylmalonic acid excretion in the maternal urine. Indeed, Ampola et al. [25] documented increased methylmalonic acidemia in maternal urine at 23 and 25 weeks' gestation. Late in the pregnancy, cyanocobalamin (10 mg/day) was administered orally to the mother in divided doses. The treatment only marginally altered the maternal serum vitamin B_{12} level. However, there was a slight reduction of maternal urinary methylmalonic acid excretion that remained severalfold above normal. At approximately 34 weeks' gestation, 5 mg of cyanocobalamin per day was administered intramuscularly. The maternal serum vitamin B_{12}, level then rose gradually to more than sixfold above normal and was accompanied by a progressive decrease in urinary methylmalonic acid excretion. Maternal urinary methylmalonate was only slightly above the normal range when delivery occurred at 41 weeks. Amniotic fluid methylmalonic acid concentrations were three times the normal mean at 19 menstrual weeks and four times the normal mean at term, despite prenatal treatment. Postnatally, the diagnosis of methylmalonic acidemia was confirmed. The infant suffered no acute neonatal complications and had an extremely high serum vitamin B_{12} level. Long-term postnatal management involved protein restriction; however, no continuous vitamin B_{12} treatment was required. In this instance, prenatal treatment certainly improved the fetal and, secondarily, the maternal biochemistry. Whether there was any significant clinical benefit to the fetus by in utero treatment cannot be assessed adequately. It seems likely that reducing the fetal burden of methylmalonic acid should have some beneficial effect on fetal development and could reduce the risks in the neonatal period.

Andersson et al. [26] followed a cohort of eight children with MMA for an average of 5.7 years. Congenital malformations were described, reinforcing the deleterious effects of prenatally abnormal cyanocobalamin metabolism. Growth was significantly improved in most cases after initiation of therapy postnatally and in one case microcephaly resolved. However, developmental delay of variable severity was always present regardless of treatment onset. These data suggest that prenatal therapy of MMA may be effective and perhaps ameliorate some of the prenatal effects. Evans et al. [27] documented the changing dose requirements necessary over the course of pregnancy to maintain adequate levels of vitamin B_{12}. They sequentially followed maternal plasma and urine levels in a prenatally treated pregnancy. Data such as these suggest that modulation of maternal-fetal pharmacological interchange of therapeutic drugs will be difficult to control precisely.

Multiple Carboxylase Deficiency

Biotin-responsive multiple carboxylase deficiency is an inborn error of metabolism caused by diminished activity of the mitochondrial biotin-dependent enzymes (pyruvate carboxylase, propionyl-coenzyme A carboxylase and α-methylcrotonyl-coenzyme A carboxylase). The condition may arise from mutations in the holocarboxilase synthetase (HCS) gene on chromosome 21q22.1 or the biotinidase gene localized to chromosome 3p25 [28–32]. Affected patients present as newborns or in early childhood with dermatitis, severe metabolic acidosis, and a characteristic pattern of organic acid excretion. It has been demonstrated that metabolism in patients or in their cultured cells can be restored toward normal levels by biotin supplementation. Prenatal diagnosis can be made by demonstration of elevated levels of typical organic acids (3-hydroxyisovalerate, methylcitrate) in the amniotic fluid or in the chorionic villi. However, the existence of a mild form of HCS deficiency can complicate prenatal diagnosis as organic acids level in amniotic fluid might be normal [33]. Therefore, prenatal diagnosis must be performed by enzyme assay in cultured fetal cells in biotin-restricted medium.

Roth et al. [34] treated a fetus without the benefit of prenatal diagnosis in a case in which two previous siblings had died of multiple carboxylase deficiency. The first had died within 3 days of birth and in the second, the diagnosis of biotin-responsive carboxylase deficiency was made posthumously. Since the mother was first seen at 34 weeks' gestation, prenatal diagnosis was not attempted. Because of severe neonatal manifestations in previous offspring and due to the probable harmlessness of biotin – oral administration was begun at a dose of 10 mg/day. There were no apparent untoward effects; maternal urinary biotin excretion increased by a factor of approximately 100 during biotin administration. Nonidentical twins were subsequently delivered at term. Cord blood and urinary organic acid profiles were normal, and cord blood biotin concentrations were four to seven times greater than normal. The neonatal course for both twins was unremarkable. Subsequent study of the cultured fibroblasts of both twins indicated that the cells of twin B (but not of twin A) had virtually complete deficiency of all three carboxylase activities. Genetic complementation studies confirmed that despite the normal clinical presentation during the newborn period, twin B was homozygous for the disease mutation. Packman et al. [35] have also reported prenatal diagnosis and treatment of biotin-responsive multiple carboxylase deficiency for a mother who had previously given birth to a male with the neonatal-onset form of this disease. In the subsequent pregnancy, maternal urine organic acid profiles were normal. Carboxylases activities were assayed in cultured amniotic fluid cells obtained by amniocentesis at 17 menstrual weeks. In biotin-restricted medium, the amniotic cells demonstrated the characteristic severe reduction in carboxylase activities. Since these initial reports of prenatal administration of biotin to fetuses affected with this disorder, other cases have been published [33, 36, 37], further provided compelling evidence that biotin administration antenatally is effectively taken up by the fetus and prevents functional deficiency of the carboxylases in an affected newborn. No toxicity from treatment was observed. However, because experience with this treatment is confined to a small number of cases, it is reasonably to carry out prenatal diagnosis and only then to initiate treatment with biotin in any affected fetus.

Smith-Lemli-Opitz Syndrome

Smith-Lemli-Opitz syndrome (SLOS) is a dysmorphological syndrome first reported in 1964 [38]. Features include characteristic facies, growth and mental retardation, and anomalies of the heart, kidneys, central nervous system, and limbs. Cleft palate, postaxial polydactyly, 2–3 syndactyly of the toes and cataracts are often seen in affected patients. The 2–3 syndactyly of the toes is very specific for this disorder and is seen in >90% of affected patients. Affected patients typically present with a narrow forehead, ptosis, anteverted nares, low-set ears, and micrognathia.

Males may present with ambiguous genitalia. In contrast with CAH, patients with SLOS are deficient in cholesterol and therefore lack steroid precursors. This leads to lack of androgens which results in under-masculinization of the male genitalia. Patients with the severe form of the syndrome present not only with these dysmorphological findings but also with a high rate of neonatal mortality [39]. The incidence of SLOS is estimated to be 1:20,000–1:40,000 live-births [40], and it appears to be most common in Caucasian populations of North European origin, with an estimated carrier frequency of 1:70 [41]. In 1993, the etiology of SLOS was discovered to be an inborn error of cholesterol biosynthesis due to a deficiency of the enzyme 7-dehydrocholesterol-Δ-7-reductase [38, 41–44]. The gene for 7-dehydrocholesterol-Δ-7-reductase has been localized to chromosome 11q12–13 [44].

As a result of this enzymatic defect, there is a characteristic biochemical pattern of reduced cholesterol levels and elevated 7- and 8-dehydrocholesterol levels (7-DHC and 8-DHC, respectively) in all body fluids and tissues including red blood cells, fibroblasts, amniotic fluid and chorionic villi. The values observed in affected patients may be extremely variable. The diagnosis is made primarily by the presence of the cholesterol precursor, 7-DHC, and not by the deficiency of cholesterol. Unaffected individuals have levels of 7-DHC and 8-DHC of less than 1 mg/dl whereas patients with SLOS usually have levels of 7–20 or greater. Clinical manifestations correlate with cholesterol levels. Severely affected patients have very low levels of total cholesterol (usually

<10–15 mg/dl), while those with more mild manifestations may present with levels of 40–70 mg/dl. Prenatal diagnosis of SLOS has been available since 1994 by either amniocentesis or chorionic villus sampling [45–47].

Since identification of the cholesterol metabolic defect in SLOS, a treatment protocol has been attempted providing exogenous cholesterol. This form of therapy has now been provided to many patients with SLOS for the past several years in many centers in the United States and internationally [48–50], with the goal of raising cholesterol levels and decrease the precursors, 7-DHC and 8-DHC. It has been shown that dietary cholesterol supplementation can restore a normal growth pattern in children and adolescents with SLOS, alleviate behavioral abnormalities and improve general health [48–50].

Fetal therapy strategies may theoretically include providing cholesterol to the mother or to the fetus. The former, however, is not possible because cholesterol does not cross the placenta well in the second trimester and there is lack of evidence that it crosses the placenta in the third trimester. Moreover, cholesterol is available only in a crystalline form, which cannot be given intravenously or intramuscularly. Furthermore, it is impractical to inject cholesterol into the amniotic fluid because it would precipitate. However, cholesterol can be given to the fetus by giving fresh-frozen plasma in the form of LDL-cholesterol. The group at Tufts University has attempted treatment antenatally in several affected fetuses. In cases where treatment was started late in pregnancy, the results were inconclusive. Although few descriptions of fetal therapy for SLOS exist, the latest report of antenatal treatment comes from that same group of investigators [51]. Therapy was begun at 34 weeks' gestation and resulted in increased fetal cholesterol levels and red blood cell mean corpuscular volume with subtle improvement in fetal growth, as assessed by consequent fetal weight plots. However, no significant change in 7-DHC and 8-DHC levels was observed, further emphasizing the inconclusiveness of that treatment. However, the main point is that since significant development of the central nervous system and myelination occurs prior to birth it is reasonable to assume that providing cholesterol to the fetus, as early as possible would result in the most benefit clinically.

Galactosemia

Galactosemia is an inborn error of metabolism caused by diminished activity of the enzyme galactose-1-phosphate uridyltransferase (GALT).

been a great deal of controversy regarding the benefit of folate supplementation for the prevention of NTDs [58–60]. Finally, in 1991, a randomized double-blinded trial designed by the Medical Research Council Vitamin Study Research Group demonstrated that preconceptual folate reduces the risk of recurrence in high risk patients [61]. Subsequently, it was shown that preparations containing folate and other vitamins also reduce the occurrence of first time NTDs [62]. In response to these findings, guidelines were issued calling for consumption of 4.0 mg/day folic acid by women with a prior child affected with a NTD, for at least 1 month prior to conception through the first 3 months of pregnancy. In addition, 0.4 mg/day folic acid is recommended to all women planning a pregnancy to be taken preconceptually. The data on NTD recurrence prevention is now very well established, and became routine for high risk cases. As of January, 1998, the United States Food and Drug Administration has mandated that breads and grains be supplemented with folic acid. The impact of food fortification with folic acid on NTDs birth prevalence during the years 1990–1999 was evaluated by assessing birth certificate reports before and after mandatory fortification [63]. It was found that the reported birth prevalence of NTDs decreased by 19%. It is important to note that the continuing decline in NTDs rates are estimated to be due to the introduction and increased utilization of prenatal diagnosis, recommendations for multivitamin use in women of childbearing age, and the population-wide increases in blood folate levels since food fortification was mandated [64].

Folate plays a central part in embryonic and fetal development because of its role in nucleic acid synthesis mandatory for the widespread cell division that takes place during embryogenesis. Folate deficiency can occur because of low dietary folate intake or because of increased metabolic requirement as seen in particular genetic alterations such as the polymorphism of the thermolabile enzyme methyltetrahydrofolate reductase (MTHFR). A metabolic effect of folate deficiency is homocysteine elevation in blood. As mentioned, the thermolabile variant of MTHFR 677TT, is a known risk factor for NTDs. However, evidence regarding a second polymorphism in the same gene, 1298AC, does not support its role in NTDs [65]. Additionally, numerous studies analyzing MTHFR variants have resulted in positive associations with increased NTD risk only in certain populations, suggesting that these variants are not large contributors to the etiology of NTDs [66]. Therefore, it seems less likely to advise parents prospectively to test for MTHFR variants. Reinforcement to the assumption that additional candidate genes other than MTHFR may be responsible for an increase risk to NTDs comes from the NTD collaborative group of Duke University [67]. 175 American Caucasians NTD patients and their families were examined for the thermolabile variant of MTHFR. Although a significant association has been found comparing patients and controls, no such association was found in patients' parents. Two other key enzymes in the metabolic pathway of homocysteine are methionine synthase (MTR) and methionine synthase reductase (MTRR). Recently reported, MTR and a specific (A66G) MTRR polymorphisms have been found to be associated with increased risk for NTDs. Interestingly, the NTDs risk was not influenced by maternal preconception folic acid intake at doses of 0.4 mg/day. However, due to limited sample size further studies are needed in order to draw meaningful inferences [68]. Other candidate genes suggested as risk factor for NTDs (mainly spina bifida), are polymorphisms in the mitochondrial membrane transporter gene UCP2 [69]. Despite previous studies suggesting zinc deficiency to play a role in the etiology of NTDs [70, 71], further studies found this observation inconclusive [72, 73]. Methionine deficiency might be involved in NTDs as 30–55% reduction in the risk of having NTD associated pregnancy was reported when methionine intake was greater then the lowest quartile of intake, with further reduction in risk with greater methionine intake [74]. In conclusion, preconception intake of folic acid alone or as multivitamin supplementation reduces the risk of recurrence and first time NTDs. Additionally, folic acid-multivitamin supplementation reduces the occurrence of other congenital anomalies such as seen in the urinary tract (e.g. vesicorenal reflux, horshoe kidney and others), in the cardiovascular system (e.g. conotruncal heart defects), and anomalies involving the limbs and face (orofacial clefting).

Pharmacologic Approaches

It might be appropriate to consider suppressing excessive cholesterol production prenatally in severe hypercholesterolemia when a safe and effective agent for accomplishing this becomes available (although there is no clear evidence for hypercholesterolemic prenatal damage). If cysteamine or related agents were to prove an effective treatment for lethal variants of cystinosis, prenatal therapy might be considered, because excessive and possibly harmful cystine accumulation is evident even in cystinotic fetuses.

Cysteamine levels have been detected in chorionic villi, and significant elevations even at 10 weeks' gestation have been hypothesized. Inhibitors of γ-glutamyltranspeptidase, if safe, would elevate intracellular glutathione levels and inhibit oxoproline production in glutathione synthase deficiency, thereby averting the characteristic neonatal acidosis. In theory, it would be desirable to minimize copper accumulation in Wilson disease as early as possible. If and when reliable prenatal diagnosis of Wilson disease is possible, cautious administration of penicillamine prenatally might be considered. This would be a double-edged sword, however, as the teratogenic potential of penicillamine would demand careful evaluation. Batshaw et al. [75] have treated certain urea cycle defects by administering arginine and benzoate. Since hyperammonemia in some of these entities develops very acutely after birth, it might be desirable to consider pretreating the fetus with these compounds just prior to or during labor to minimize postnatal hyperammonemia [75]. Conversely, it may be desirable to consider drug avoidance as an approach to fetal treatment. For example, fetuses with glucose-6-phosphate dehydrogenase deficiency are sensitive to a variety of drugs that induce hemolysis. It would probably be appropriate to avoid administering such agents to women carrying or known to be at risk for carrying fetuses deficient in glucose-6-phosphate dehydrogenase.

Umbilical cord catheterization under ultrasound guidance may lead to the development of other types of fetal treatment [76]. Systems such as gene replacement are being developed for certain lysosomal storage disorders. Progress is being made in postnatal experimental models on the administration of thymic cells for certain immune deficiency states, bone marrow transplantation for a variety of genetic disorders, and gene transfer. The development of better and earlier techniques for prenatal treatment will be complex, especially with regard to gene transfer; but progress will be made, and access to the fetal vasculature may be required for these methods to have a chance for success.

Bone marrow transplantation or thymic cell infusion is actually only a specialized example of organ transplantation. In the future, fetal organ transplantation may become possible and may open many prospects for surgical treatment of certain biochemical genetic disorders.

One can also speculate about the therapeutic possibilities involving compounds administered directly into the amniotic fluid or into the fetal intestinal tract. It might be possible, for example, to administer thyroid hormone in this fashion or to prevent meconium ileus in cystic fibrosis by instilling not yet determined enzymes into the fetal intestinal tract.

Ethical Considerations

A number of ethical considerations come to mind when discussing the fetus with a treatable endocrine or metabolic disorder, vis-à-vis intrauterine pharmacological treatment. Prenatal diagnosis of fetal endocrine or metabolic disorders is valuable, when this allows implementation of effective treatment or in decision making regarding termination of pregnancy. Certainly, for a select number of disorders, timely implementation of treatment offsets the harmful effects. Some disorders, however, may not be severe enough to merit termination of pregnancy or consider intrauterine treatment. Fetal treatment may have serious adverse effects on maternal health (e.g. steroid administration in CAH) or repeated intra-amniotic injections (e.g. thyroid hormones) which may expose the mother to infection. Thus, the risk of adverse effects to the mother should be weighed against the severity of the fetal/neonatal disorder. Another dilemma is the need to initiate therapy prior to prenatal diagnosis (as in CAH). In such cases, treatment may eventually prove to be unnecessary. As discussed in this chapter, in some conditions, fetal treatment is successful and results in the birth of healthy newborns. This highlights the question whether termination of pregnancy should be considered as an alternative to intra-uterine treatment. Does the availability of successful treatment restrict the woman's autonomy in the decision making process? Preimplantation genetic diagnosis may circumvent some of these dilemmas as it avoids the need for termination of pregnancy by assuring that only unaffected embryos are implanted. This option, however, raises the spectra of 'designer babies'. In centers dealing with fetal treatment, it is advisable to establish a multidisciplinary committee, entrusted with the task of discussing ethical issues of treatment, bearing in mind the unique aspects of each case.

Conclusion

While a multitude of metabolic disorders exist, prenatal treatment for most has never been attempted or considered. The discovery of new disease associated genes and prenatal carrier testing may in the future allow preconceptual carrier detection, without the tragedy of first having an affected child. This may provide targeted therapy in families who chose to continue the pregnancy and offer the prospect of improved outcome by ameliorating at least some of the prenatal deleterious effects of the metabolic disease.

36 Thuy LP, Belmont J, Nyhan W: Prenatal diagnosis and treatment of holocarboxylase synthetase deficiency. Prenat Diagn 1999;19:108–112.

37 Thuy LP, Jurecki E, Nemzer L, et al: Prenatal diagnosis of holocarboxylase synthetase deficiency by assay of the enzyme in chorionic villus material followed by prenatal treatment. Clin Chim Acta 1999;284:59–68.

38 Smith DW, Lemli L, Opitz JM: A newly recognized syndrome of multiple congenital anomalies. J Pediatr 1964;64:210–217.

39 Curry CJR, Carey JC, Holland JS: Smith-Lemli-Opitz syndrome – type II: Multiple congenital anomalies with male pseudohermaphroditism and frequent early lethality. Am J Med Genet 1987;26:45–57.

40 Opitz JM: RSH-SLO ('Smith-Lemli-Opitz') syndrome: Historical, genetic, and development considerations. Am J Med Genet 1994;50:344–346.

41 Kelley RI: Diagnosis of Smith-Lemli-Opitz syndrome by gas chromatography/mass spectrometry of 7-dehydrocholesterol in plasma, amniotic fluid and cultured skin fibroblasts. Clin Chim Acta 1995;236: 45–58.

42 Kelley RI: A new face for an old syndrome. Am J Med Genet 1997;65:251–256.

43 Tint GS, Irons M, Elias E, et al: Defective cholesterol biosynthesis associated with the Smith-Lemli-Opitz syndrome. N Engl J Med 1994;330:107–113.

44 Waterham HR, Wijburg FA, Hennekam RCM, et al: Smith-Lemli-Opitz is caused by mutations in the 7-dehydrocholesterol reductase gene. Am J Hum Genet 1998;63:329–338.

45 Gelman-Kohan Z, Nisani R, Chemke J, Appelman Z, Rappaport S, Hegesh E: Prenatal detection of recurrent SLOS type 2. Am J Hum Genet 1990; 47:A57.

46 Hobbins JC, Jones OW, Gottesfeld MD, Persutte W: Transvaginal ultrasonography and transabdominal embryoscopy in the first-trimester diagnosis of Smith-Lemli-Opitz syndrome, type II. Am J Obstet Gynecol 1994;171: 546–549.

47 Sharp P, Haan E, Fletcher JM, Khong TY, Carey WF: First trimester diagnosis of Smith-Lemli-Opitz syndrome. Prenatal Diagn 1997;17:355–361.

48 Irons M, Elias E, Tint GS, et al: Abnormal cholesterol metabolism in the Smith-Lemli-Opitz syndrome: Report of clinical and biochemical findings in 4 patients and treatment in 1 patient. Am J Med Genet 1994;50:347–352.

49 Irons M, Elias ER, Abuelo D, et al: Treatment of Smith-Lemli-Opitz syndrome: Results of a multicenter trial. Am J Med Genet 1997;68: 311–314.

50 Elias ER, Irons MB, Hurley AD, Tint GS, Salen G: Clinical effects of cholesterol supplementation in six patients with the Smith-Lemli-Opitz syndrome (SLOS). Am J Med Genet 1997;68:305–310.

51 Irons MR, Nores J, Stewart TL, et al: Antenatal therapy of Smith-Lemli-Opitz syndrome. Fetal Diagn Ther 1999;14: 133–137.

52 Elsas LJ: Prenatal diagnosis of galactose-1-phosphate uridyltransferase (GALT) deficient galactosemia. Prenat Diagn 2001;21:302–303.

53 Chen YT, Mattis'on DR, Feigenbaum L, et al: Reduction in oocyte number following prenatal exposure to a high galactose diet. Science 1981;314: 1145–1147.

54 Bandyopadhyay S, Chakrabarti J, Banerjee S, et al: Prenatal exposure to high galactose adversely affects initial gonadal pool of germ cells in rats. Hum Reprod 2003;18:276–282.

55 Frey L, Hauser WA: Epidemiology of neural tube defects. Epilepsia 2003;44(suppl 3):4–13.
56 Smithells RW, Nevin NC, Seller MJ, et al: Further experience of vitamin supplementation for prevention of neural tube defect recurrences. Lancet 1983;i:1027–1031.
57 Smithells RW, Sheppard S, Schorah CJ, et al: Possible prevention of neural tube defects by preconceptual vitamin supplementation. Lancet 1980;i:339–340.
58 Mills JL, Rhoads GG, Simpson JL, et al: The absence of a relation between the periconceptional use of vitamins and neural-tube defects. N Engl J Med 1989;321:430–435.
59 Mulinare J, Cordero JF, Erickson JD, Berry RJ: Periconceptional use of multivitamins and the occurrence of neural tube defects. JAMA 1988;260: 3141–3145.
60 Schulman JD: Treatment of the embryo and the fetus in the first trimester: Current status and future prospects. Am J Med Genet 1990;35:197–200.
61 MRC Vitamin Study Research Group: Prevention of neural tube defects: Results of the MRC vitamin study. Lancet 1991; 338:132–137.
62 Czeizel AE, Dudas I: Prevention of the first occurrence of neural-tube defects by preconceptional vitamin supplementation. N Engl J Med 1992;327: 1832–1835.
63 Honein MA, Paulozzi LJ, Mathews TJ, Erickaon JD, Wong LY: Impact of folic acid fortification of the US food supply on the occurrence of neural tube defects. JAMA 2001;285: 2981–2986.
64 Olney RS, Mulinare J: Trends in neural tube defect prevalence, folic acid fortification, and vitamin supplement use. Semin Perinatol 2002;26:277–285.
65 Parle-McDermott A, Mills JL, Kirke PN, et al: Analysis of MTHFR 1298AC and 677CT polymorphisms as risk factor neural tube defects. J Hum Genet 2003;48:190–193.
66 Finnell RH, Shaw GM, Lammer EJ, Volcik KA: Does prenatal screening for 5,10-methylenetetrahydrofolate reductase (MTHFR) mutations in high-risk neural tube defect pregnancies make sense? Genet Test 2002;6:47–52.
67 Rampersaud E, Melvin EC, Siegel D, et al: Updated investigations of the role of methylenetetrahydrofolate reductase in human neural tube defects. Clin Genet 2003;63:210–214.
68 Zhu H, Wicker NJ, Shaw GM, et al: Homocysteine remethylation enzyme polymorphisms and increased risks for neural tube defects. Mol Genet Metab 2003;78:216–221.
69 Volocik KA, Shaw GM, Zhu H, et al: Risk factors for neural tube defects: associations between uncoupling protein 2 polymorphisms and spina bifida. Birth Defects Res [A] 2003;67:158–161.
70 Sever LE: Zinc deficiency in man. Lancet 1973;i:887.
71 McMichael AJ, Dreosti IE, Gibson GT: A prospective study of serial maternal serum zinc levels and pregnancy outcome. Early Hum Dev 1982;7: 59–69.
72 Stoll C, Dott B, Alembik Y, Koehl C: Maternal trace elements, vitamin B_{12}, vitamin A, folic acid, and fetal malformations. Rep Toxicol 1999; 13:53–57.
73 Hambidge M, Hackshaw A, Wald N: Neural tube defects and serum zinc. Br J Obstet Gynaecol 1993;100:746–749.
74 Shoob HD, Sargent RG, Thompson SJ, et al: Dietary methionine is involved in the etiology of neural defect-affected pregnancies in humans. J Nutr 2001; 131:2653–2658.

75 Batshaw M, Brusilow S, Waber L, et al: Treatment of inborn errors of urea synthesis: Activation of alternative pathways of waste nitrogen synthesis and excretion. N Engl J Med 1982;306: 1387–1392.

76 Nicolaides KH, Thorpe-Beeston JG, Noble P: Cordocentesis; in Eden RD, Boehm H (eds): Assessment and Care of the Fetus: Physiological, Clinical and Medicolegal Principles. Norwalk, Appleton & Lange, 1990, p 291.

Yuval Yaron, MD

Prenatal Diagnosis Unit, Genetic Institute, Tel-Aviv Sourasky Medical Center,
6 Weizmann Street, IL–64239 Tel Aviv (Israel)
Tel. +972 3 697 4555, E-Mail yyaron@tasmc.health.gov.il

Blazer S, Zimmer EZ (eds):
The Embryo: Scientific Discovery and Medical Ethics.
Basel, Karger, 2005, pp 259–283

Surgical and Genetic Fetal Therapeutic Interventions

Mark I. Evans[a] Michael R. Harrison[b]

[a]Institute for Genetics and Fetal Medicine, St. Luke's Roosevelt Hospital Center, Columbia University, New York, N.Y., [b]Fetal Treatment Center, and Division of Pediatric Surgery, Department of Surgery, University of California, San Francisco, Calif., USA

For over 30 years, obstetricians have developed a number of approaches to diagnose both structural and functional fetal anomalies [1, 2]. When such abnormalities are severe or lethal, pregnancy termination may provide a reasonable management option for couples in jurisdictions and under cultural norms that permit its availability. With more moderate fetal anomalies, obstetrical care can be altered to optimize outcomes and prevent secondary complications. Sometimes, prenatal correction of the underlying problem has become possible. In general, structural malformations are more logically approached surgically, while metabolic disorders may benefit from pharmacologic or genetic therapies [3].

Over the last two decades, fetal therapy has evolved into four major areas: open surgical approaches, 'closed' endoscopic surgical approaches, pharmacologic therapy, and stem cell/gene therapy. Advances in the field have been characterized by alternating exuberance at dramatic successes, but also periods of intense frustration at technical challenges needing to be overcome to bring new approaches on-line.

Even after nearly four decades since the first transfusions by Lilley, the single most misunderstood issue about fetal therapy continues to be 'why before and not after birth'. There is not one single answer, but rather a series of disorder-specific considerations. If something can be treated safely postnatally, then there is no justification for prenatal intervention. However, for the conditions discussed below, profound and irreparable damage occurs before birth, making fetal intervention the best or sometimes only way to ameliorate the damage. Some procedures have been quite rare. Others are more common, but the expectation is that with improvements and increasing utilization of prenatal diagnosis more women will chose to consider the opportunities of treating fetuses before birth.

Surgical Therapy

In utero 'Closed' Fetal Surgery

The most efficacious percutaneous in utero fetal surgery has been for the evaluation and treatment of obstructive uropathy. Lower urinary tract obstruction (LUTO) is a heterogeneous entity that affects 1:5,000–1:8,000 newborn males. Posterior urethral valves or urethral atresias are the most common causes of LUTO, although other etiologies such as stenosis of the urethral meatus, anterior urethral valves, ectopic insertion of a ureter, and tumors of the bladder have been observed. LUTO can result in massive distention of the bladder with compensatory hypertrophy and hyperplasia of the smooth muscle within the bladder wall, leading to a loss of compliance and elasticity, and poor postnatal function generally requiring surgical reconstruction [2]. Elevated intravesicular pressures prevent urine inflow from the ureters and eventual distortion of the ureterovesicle angles contribute to reflux hydronephrosis. Progressive pyelectasis and calyectasis compress the delicate renal parenchyma within the encasing serosal capsule, leading to functional abnormalities within the medullary and eventually the cortical regions. Focal compressive hypoxia likely contributes to the progressive fibrosis and perturbations in tubular function resulting in urinary hypertonicity which is observed. Obstructive processes can eventually lead to type IV cystic dysplasia and renal insufficiency [4–7].

The affects extend beyond the genitourinary tract. Progressive oligo-anhydramnios leads to compressive deformations as seen in Potter sequence,

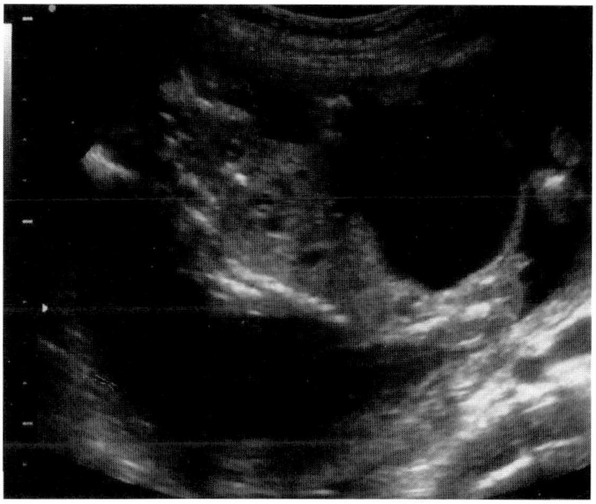

Fig. 1.
Oligohydramnios and dilated bladder in a fetus at 17 weeks with good electrolytes.

including extremity contractures and facial dysmorphology. Absence of normal amniotic fluid volume also interferes with pulmonary growth and development. Constant compressive pressure on the fetal thorax leads to restriction of expansion of the chest through normal physiologic 'breathing movements'. Babies born with LUTO generally die secondary to pulmonary complications and not renal failure.

The prenatal sonographic diagnosis of LUTO includes dilated and thickened walls of the bladder, hydronephrosis, and oligohydramnios (fig. 1). Urethral strictures or atresia, urethral agenesis, megalourethra, ureteral reflux, and cloacal anomalies may be present and have a very similar appearance on ultrasound. The typical 'keyhole sign' of proximal urethral dilation is secondary to urethral obstruction present in PUV or atresia. However, the precise diagnosis can only be made after birth [7].

The prenatal evaluation and management of fetuses with the sonographic findings of LUTO are complex [4–6]. Ruling out other congenital anomalies such as cardiac and neural tube defects is necessary before intervention can be considered.

Karyotyping is essential to confirm a normal male chromosomal status, as cases of LUTO have an increased incidence of aneuploidy. Female fetuses almost always have more complex syndromes of cloacal malformations which do not benefit from in utero shunt therapy. Because of the presence of oligo-/anhydramnios, we commonly obtain karyotypes by transabdominal chorionic villous sampling which gives reliable results within 5 days during which the remainder of the prenatal evaluation is underway. Fluorescence in situ hybridization (FISH) can be used to get rapid status of chromosomes 13, 18, 21, X and Y [8].

Essential to the prenatal workup is the evaluation of underlying renal status in the fetus. Over the past 15 years, a multicomponent approach has developed for the analysis of fetal urine that evaluates proximal tubular and possible glomerular status using sodium, chloride, osmolality, calcium, β_2-microglobulin, albumin, and total protein concentrations [5]. Predictive reliability has been shown to be significantly improved by sequential samplings at 48- to 72-hour intervals [6]. Using such an approach, one can directly correlate the degree of impaired renal function and damage with the extent of urinary hypertonicity and proteinuria. As such, the ability to counsel patients about the renal status of their fetus and the long term prognosis has been dramatically improved.

Vesicoamniotic catheter shunts bypass the urethral obstruction diverting the urine into the amniotic space to allow appropriate drainage of the upper urinary tract and prevention of pulmonary hypoplasia and physical deformations (fig. 2). In fetuses with isolated LUTO, a normal male karyotype, and progressively improving urinary profile that meet threshold parameters (table 1), intervention has been very successful in salvaging fetuses using percutaneous vesicoamniotic shunt therapy.

Subsequent experience in humans has been widely variable and appears to be related to the extent of prenatal evaluation prior to shunt placement, as well as the etiology of obstruction. Freedman et al. [7] have found that Prune Belly infants, without complete urethral obstructions have very good renal outcomes following vesicoamniotic shunt therapy. They have also found significant improvement in survival and renal function in infants with posterior urethral valves treated by shunting; however, many have mild-to-moderate renal insufficiency at birth and several of these have progressed to renal failure, dialysis and transplantation. The worst group of infants appears to be those with urethral atresia. However, there have been survivors with urethral atresia following early shunt intervention. These findings support animal studies, which indicated that early-onset, complete obstructions resulted in more severe renal damage

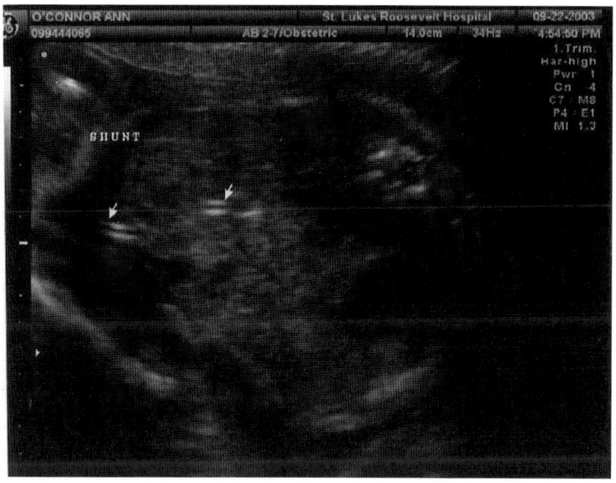

Fig. 2.

Vesicoamniotic shunt with the proximal portion lying within the fetal bladder while the distal portion lies within the amniotic fluid space allowing diversionary draining of urine into the appropriate space.

Table 1.

Upper threshold of urinary values for selecting fetuses that might benefit from prenatal intervention

Sodium	<100 mg/dl
Chloride	<90 mg/dl
Osmolality	<190 mosm/l
Calcium	<8 mg/dl
β_2-Microglobulin	<6 mg/l
Total protein	<40 mg/dl

than later-onset or partial obstructions. Such data emphasize the necessity for early diagnosis, evaluation and intervention in such cases.

More recently, data from our experience over the past 15 years suggest that patients having bladder shunts had a 91% survival, but that long-term renal function was not guaranteed. Just under half had 'normal renal function', and about a quarter had mild impairments. The experience depended highly on the exact etiology of the disorder with posterior urethral value having the best outcomes and urethral atresia the worst. The experience suggests that close pediatric urologic/renal function assessment is essential.

The Paris group found that about 25% of children had serious, long-term renal impairments and about 15% actually developed end-stage renal disease requiring transplant [9].

Although vesicoamniotic shunting has certainly improved survival and renal function in cases of early obstructive uropathy, complications of this procedure remain unacceptably high. We found in the 1980s and 1990s that in 40% of our cases, the shunts became physically displaced into the amniotic or intraperitoneal space, or have become obstructive with loss of drainage function necessitating replacement. On balance, intervention for LUTO has saved fetuses which would otherwise have surely died. Many have normal-to-moderately impaired renal function. A carefully balanced approach in counseling is required for patients to determine what is right for them.

Other Shunts

As early as the late 1970s, shunting was attempted for obstructive hydrocephalus [10]. Attempts in the late 1970s and early 1980s at in utero ventriculoperitoneal shunting were nearly uniformly dismal. However, in retrospect, most operated patients were, in fact, very poor candidates for intervention. Many had multisystem syndromic disorders, including aneuploidy, and hopeless congenital anomalies such as holoprosencephaly.

Ventriculoamniotic shunts were thus abandoned since the early 1980s. With a better understanding of the poor natural history of the anomaly, and better, more accurate diagnostic techniques, we have speculated that there may eventually be limited applications for prenatal neurological shunting in cases of early-onset, isolated, progressive obstructive hydrocephaly.

The other use of percutaneously placed shunts has been for thoracic abnormalities [11, 12]. The macrocystic form of congenital cystic adenomatous malformation can present with a very large intrathoracic mass with a, dominant macrocyst which causes cardiac and mediastinal shift and comes with its potential hemodynamic changes, as well as pulmonary compression and risk of lung hypoplasia. Such dominant cysts can be approached using pleuroamniotic shunts to chronically drain these structures, reducing their volume, and diminishing their space-occupying effects within the thoracic cavity.

Isolated pleural effusions can also accumulate to the point of causing hemodynamic changes and onset of generalized hydrops as well as pulmonary compression which interferes with normal lung development increasing the risk of hypoplasia. Small, unilateral effusions generally do not warrant intervention, but must be followed closely as they have the potential for rapid progression and development of generalized hydrops [12].

As with all fetal interventions, prenatal evaluation prior to intervention is critical for appropriate case selection. Seemingly isolated effusions may be the first sign of a cardiac malformation, aneuploidy, anemia, or an infectious process. Thoracoamniotic shunting is effective in carefully evaluated cases when the risk of pulmonary hypoplasia from large effusions early in gestation is present, or early signs of progressive hydrops (unilateral-bilateral effusion, skin or scalp edema, ascites, pericardial effusion) appear. Fetal anemia, per se, is not an indication for thoracoamniotic effusion shunting, as hydropic changes will usually resolve with timely fetal transfusion therapy. Also, if one waits to intervene until the fetus develops significant ascites, the prognosis even with successful shunt intervention, diminishes considerably [12]. However, several cases with suddenly progressive pleural effusions and onset of generalized hydrops (skin/scalp edema, pericardial effusion, and moderate ascites) have been treated with complete resolution of all hydropic complications and normal postnatal infants.

Open Surgical Approaches

Open fetal surgery has been performed for a limited number of indications for about 20 years [3]. Its application has been limited by the appropriate concern for maternal risk, rigorous selection criteria, and somewhat frustrating results. During this time there has been continuing innovation and development of instruments and techniques, motivated by the clinical necessity to improve the safety of open fetal surgery for both the fetus and the mother.

Congenital Diaphragmatic Hernia (CDH)

The fetal approach to CDH has undergone continuous evolution since the first attempted CDH repair in 1986 and the first success in 1989 [13–16]. Definitive repair of CDH by reduction of viscera from the chest, diaphragmatic patch placement, and abdominal silo construction (to reduce intra-abdominal pressure) had unacceptable mortality, particularly after a clinical trial showed open fetal repair was no better than postnatal repair, when the liver was herniated into the chest [17, 18]. The definitive repair was

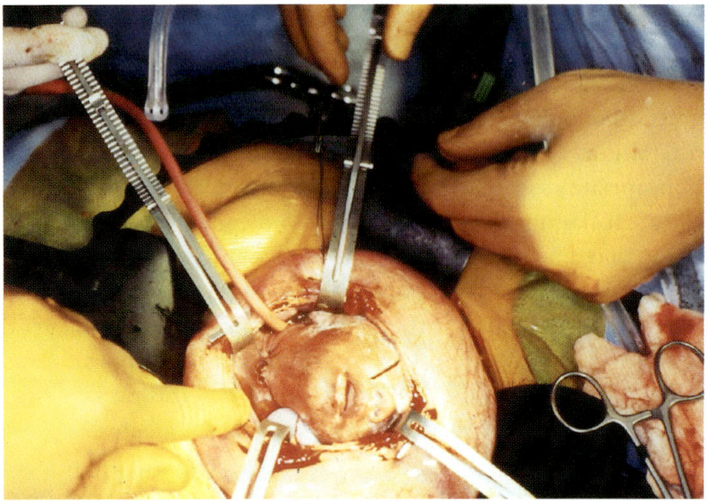

Fig. 3.
Surgical isolation of the fetal trachea prior to placement of hemoclips in a tracheal occlusion procedure for congenital diaphragmatic hernia.

abandoned as an option for CDH; in utero tracheal occlusion took its place [18–25] (fig. 3). Tracheal occlusion leads to an increase in lung size through accumulation of pulmonary secretions, which reduces the herniated viscera from the chest and decreases the risk for lung hypoplasia. The technique of achieving reliable, complete and reversible tracheal occlusion has evolved. Initially, it could only be accomplished by open fetal surgery and fetal neck dissection (taking care to avoid the recurrent laryngeal nerves) and placement of occlusive hemoclips. Next, a fetoscopic technique was developed to accomplish the same neck dissection and tracheal clip (the Fetendo Clip Procedure) [22–25]. While successful, it proved difficult, with a significant learning curve. Attempts to simplify the procedure by developing an appropriate polymer to use as a tracheal plug inserted through the fetal mouth were unsuccessful. Experience quickly showed that unless there was complete occlusion, the pulmonary secretions would leak, thereby defeating the purpose of the plug. Finally, a relatively simple technique was developed in which a fetoscope passed through a single port is advanced into the fetal trachea (fetal bronchoscopy) and a detachable silicone balloon is inflated to occlude the trachea.

CDH has been a classic example of rapid changes in technology clouding any simple attempts to understand the role for fetal surgery. With increasing sophistication of the surgical approach as well as concomitant improvements in neonatal care using extracorporeal membrane oxygenation (ECMO), it was impossible to accurately determine the relative benefits of each approach without a prospective, randomized comparison that held all other details constant. Thus, after much debate, a randomized trial of surgery for CDH versus optimal postnatal care was funded by National Institute of Child Health and Human Development (NICHD) [18]. The principle component of the trial was that patients in the postnatal care (control) arm would receive the same neonatal care by the same center as the surgical arm.

It was originally expected that patients having the surgery would have a survival rate of about 70% as compared to the best data on controls expecting about 35%. The surgically treated patients achieved expected survival. However, the trial was stopped prematurely, when by having the controls cared for at the same tertiary specialty centers as the surgical group, survival in the controls was essentially the same as the surgical group. Such data show conclusively the principle of 'the moving target' and how our use of technology must continually adapt to changing conditions [25].

Congenital Cystic Adenomatoid Malformation (CCAM)

CCAM is a space occupying congenital cystic lesion of the lung which may grow and induce hydrops by causing mediastinal shift and compromise venous return to the heart. When fetuses with CCAM develop hydrops, the fetal mortality approaches 100% [26–28] (fig. 4). Fetal resection of CCAM reverses hydrops and has improved survival dramatically [15]. The fetal operation is performed by exposure of the arm and chest wall on the side of the lesion through the maternal hysterotomy. A large muscle-sparing thoracotomy is performed through the midthorax of the fetus and the lobe containing the CCAM is isolated. The attachments of the lobe to adjacent lung tissue are bluntly divided and the lobar hilum is divided by use of a TIA stapler or a bulk ligature. During the remainder of the pregnancy, the remaining normal lung shows compensatory growth the fill the space left showing mass removal.

Sacrococcygeal Teratoma (SCT)

Fetal SCT arises from the presacral space which may grow to massive proportions and in some fetuses induce high output failure from tumor

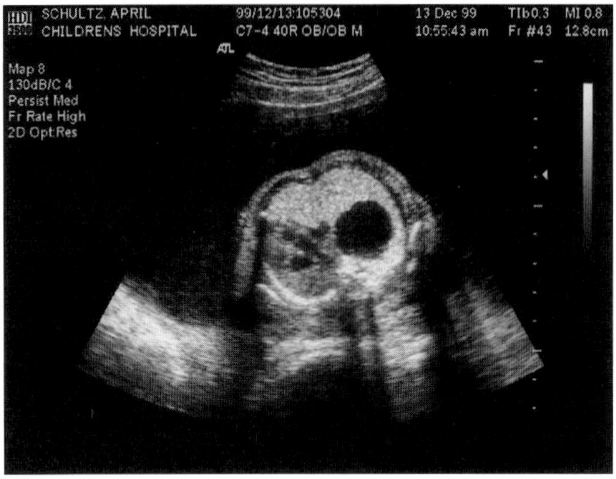

Fig. 4.
Microcystic congenital cystic adenomatous malformation (microcystic) with beginnings of hydrops.

vascular steal. Fetal SCT with high output physiology with associated placentomegaly or hydrops uniformly result in fetal demise [29, 30] (fig. 5). The pathophysiologic rationale for fetal surgery is to ligate the vascular connections to the tumor, remove the vascular 'sinn', and reverse the high output physiology. The fetal operation is performed by exteriorization of the fetal buttocks with attached tumor [29]. Every attempt is made to keep the head, torso, and lower extremities of the fetus in the uterus. Since the tumor can sometimes be larger than the fetus, significant loss of uterine volume occurs, and the uterus may contract increasing the risk for placental abruption, placental dysfunction because of compression, or postoperative preterm labor. Once exteriorized, the anus is identified and the fetal skin incised posterior to the anorectal sphincter complex to avoid injury to the continence mechanism. A tourniquet is then applied to the base of the tumor and brought down gradually as the tumor is finger fractured down to its vascular pedicle. The vascular pedicle is then ligated with suture ligatures or TIA device stapled depending upon the width of the pedicle. The entire fetal procedure can be performed in less than 15 min with minimal blood loss. Because of the increase in afterload following ligation of the low resistance tumor circuit, the fetal hemodynamic status must be monitored by fetal echocardiography during and in the immediate period following the ligation.

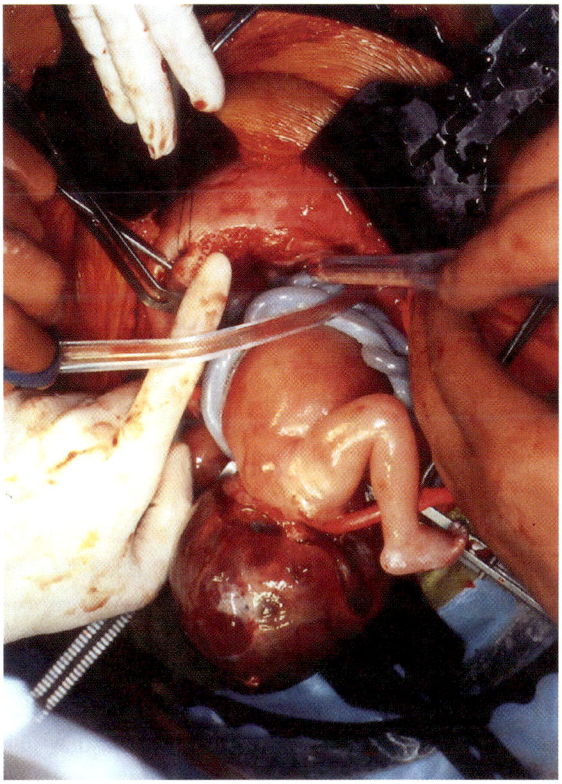

Fig. 5.
Saccrococcygeal teratoma in a fetus.

The EXIT Procedure

The EXIT procedure is a modified cesarean delivery and may be applied to deliver fetuses after fetal surgical procedures such as tracheal ligation, or for fetuses with difficult airway problems such as massive cervical teratomas or cystic hygromas [31, 32]. The most important component of the EXIT procedure is maintenance of uteroplacental perfusion until the fetal airway is secured and ventilation is established. In direct contrast to cesarean section where uterine contraction for hemostasis is encouraged, uterine relaxation is maintained by deep general anesthesia. The fetal manipulations are then performed with maternal support via the placenta. Clips can be removed, chest masses removed, bronchoscopy performed, and stable airway access established in otherwise very difficult circumstances with this approach. Once the fetus is ready for transport to the nursery or adjacent operating suite following these preliminary steps, the cord is clamped and cut and the cesarean delivery completed.

Meningomyelocele

Babies with meningomyelocele have impaired lower motor function and loss of bowel and bladder control. A significant percentage develops obstructive hydrocephalus which requires ventriculoperitoneal shunting [33]. Experience from the 1970s and 1980s showed that babies with meningomyelocele delivered atraumatically by cesarean section had a better level of motor function for the given level of anatomic defect, than those babies delivered through the vaginal canal [34]. Such data suggest that compression and trauma to the cord in the delivery process can have permanent long-term sequelae to motor function. It therefore follows that trauma to the spinal cord in utero, either from banging into the uterine wall, or the toxic effects of the amniotic fluid in the third trimester, per se, could be detrimental to the function of the spinal cord. Furthermore, the traditional dogma that the pathogenesis of meningomyelocele was that an abnormally developed spinal cord, which did not, in turn, engender the proper development of the bony spinal column, may not be the whole story. It is possible that the primary defect is in the bony spinal column, which exposes a presumptively undamaged spinal cord. The cord is then damaged by the toxic affects of amniotic fluid and trauma from the uterine environment and repeated contact with the uterine wall. Thus, the rationale for attempts to cover and protect the spinal cord in utero to minimize the sequelae [35].

Three groups have done most of the work in this area and have attempted to repair meningomyeloceles in utero, both as an open surgical procedure, and endoscopically, with the stated attempt to reduce long-term morbidity and mortality [36–38].

The principal benefit of the surgery is likely secondary, i.e. a significant reduction in the number of babies requiring ventriculoperitoneal shunting for obstructive hydrocephalus [39, 40]. There is still much controversy surrounding the data [33]. A randomized, prospective trial comparing fetal to postnatal neurosurgical closure began in 2003 but will take several years to be completed. A major milestone of this trial has been the agreement among the participating centers not to perform any cases outside the trial, and other centers around the country have agreed not to start programs until the trial is completed.

Prenatal Hematopoietic Stem Cell Transplantation

The engraftment and clonal proliferation of a relatively small number of normal hematopoietic stem cells (HSCs) can sustain normal hematopoiesis for a lifetime. This observation provides the compelling rationale for bone marrow transplantation (BMT) and is now supported by thousands of long-term survivors of BMT who otherwise would have succumbed to lethal hematologic disease [41, 42]. Realization of the full potential of BMT, however, continues to be limited by a critical shortage of immunologically compatible donor cells, the inability to control the recipient or donor immune response, and the requirement for recipient myeloablation to achieve engraftment. The price of human leukocyte antigen (HLA) mismatch remains high: the greater the mismatch, the higher the incidence of graft failure, graft-vs.-host disease (GVHD), and delayed immunologic reconstitution. Current methods of myeloablation have high morbidity and mortality. In combination, these problems remain prohibitive for most patients who might benefit from BMT. A theoretically attractive alternative, which potentially can address many of the limitations of BMT, is in utero transplantation of HSC. This approach is potentially applicable to any congenital hematopoietic disease that can be diagnosed prenatally and can be cured or improved by engraftment of normal HSCs.

Rationale for in utero Transplantation

The rationale for in utero transplantation is to take advantage of the window of opportunity created by normal ontogeny of hematopoietic cell lines. There is a period, prior to population of the bone marrow and prior to thymic processing of self-antigen, when the fetus theoretically should be receptive to engraftment of foreign HSC without rejection and without the need for myeloablation. In the human fetus, the ideal window would appear to be prior to 14 weeks' gestation, before release of differentiated T lymphocytes into the circulation and while the bone marrow is just beginning to develop sites for hematopoiesis [43]. It certainly may extend beyond that in immunodeficiency states, particularly when T cell development is abnormal. During this time, presentation of foreign antigen by thymic dendritic cells theoretically should result in clonal deletion of reactive T cells during the negative selection phase of thymic processing. Recent advances in prenatal diagnosis have made possible the diagnosis of a large number of congenital hematologic diseases during the first trimester. Technical advances in fetal intervention make transplantation feasible by 12–14 weeks' gestation. The ontologic window of opportunity falls well within these diagnostic and technical constraints, making application of this approach a realistic possibility [44–47].

Because of the unique fetal environment, prenatal HSC transplantation could theoretically avoid many of the current limitations of postnatal BMT. There would be no requirement for HLA matching, resulting in expansion of the donor pool. Transplanted cells would not be rejected, and space would be available in the bone marrow, eliminating the need for toxic immunosuppressive and myeloablative drugs. The mother's uterus may ultimately prove to be the ultimate sterile isolation chamber, eliminating the high risk and costly 2–4 months of isolation required after postnatal BMT and prior to immunologic reconstitution. Finally, prenatal transplantation would preempt the clinical manifestations of the disease, avoiding the recurrent infections, multiple transfusions, growth delay, and other complications that cause immeasurable suffering for the patient and often compromise postnatal treatment.

Source of Donor Cells

The source of donor cells may ultimately prove to be critical for the success of engraftment. The most obvious advantage of the use of fetal hematopoietic stem cells is the minimal number of mature T cells in fetal liver-derived populations prior to 14 weeks' gestation. This alleviates any concern about GVHD and avoids the necessity of T cell depletion processes, which can negatively impact potential engraftment [41, 42, 48].

Although there may be important homing, proliferative, and developmental advantages to the use of fetal cells, there are practical and ethical advantages to the use of cord blood or postnatal HSC sources. Legitimate ethical concerns regarding the use of fetal tissue for transplantation must be addressed by the medical and lay community. Fetal tissue obtained by the usual methods at the time of elective abortion has a high degree of microbial contamination [49]. The transplantation of transmissible viral, fungal, or bacterial disease could have disastrous consequences for the recipient fetus or mother. Although the fetal liver is a rich source of HSC, small size limits total cell yield, and current technology does not yet allow undifferentiated expansion of donor cells. In contrast, the use of adult-derived cells would allow a renewable, relatively infection-free, ethically acceptable source of donor cells. Tolerance induction by the in utero transplantation of highly purified adult bone marrow HSC from a living related donor, followed by a single or multiple postnatal 'booster' injections offers an intriguing approach in situations where postnatal BMT is necessary but an HLA-matched donor is not available [50–52].

Diseases Amenable to Prenatal Treatment

Generally speaking, any disease that can be diagnosed early in gestation that is improved by BMT, and for which postnatal treatment is not entirely satisfactory is a target disease. Some diseases, however, are far more likely to benefit from prenatal transplantation than others. The list can be divided into three general categories: hemoglobinopathies, immunodeficiency disorders, and inborn errors of metabolism. Each of the diseases has unique considerations for treatment, and in fact each disease may respond differently (table 2). Issues such as availability of engraftment sites within the bone marrow at time of transplantation, and capacity of a needed enzyme to cross the blood-brain barrier at a particular gestational age need to be considered. Of particular relevance to the prenatal approach, in which experimental levels of engraftment have been relatively low, is the observation that in many of the target diseases, engrafted normal cells would be predicted to have a significant survival advantage over diseased cells. This would have the clinical effect of amplification of the level of engraftment in the peripheral circulation. In addition, even with minimal levels of engraftment, specific tolerance for donor antigen should be induced, allowing additional cells from the same donor to be given to the tolerant recipient after birth.

Hemoglobinopathies

The sickle cell anemia and thalassemia syndromes make up the largest patient groups potentially treatable by prenatal stem cell transplantation

Table 2.

Potential candidates for in utero stem cell fetal therapy: hematopoietic disorders

Disorders affecting lymphocytes
SCID (sex linked)
SCID (adenosine deaminase deficiency)
Ommen syndrome
Agammaglobinemia
Bare lymphocyte syndrome
Disorders affecting granulocytes
Chronic granulomatous disease
Infantile agranulocytosis
Neutrophil membrane GP-180
Lazy leukocyte syndrome
Disorders affecting erythrocytes
Sickle cell disease
α-Thalassemia
β-Thalassemia
Hereditary spherocytosis
Fanconi anemia
Mannosidosis
α-Mannosidosis
β-Thalassemia
Mucolipodoses
Gaucher disease
Metachromatic leukocystrophy
Krabbe disease
Niemann-Pick disease
β-Glucoronidase deficiency
Fabry disease
Adrenal leukodystrophy
Mucopolysaccharidoses
MPS I (Hurler disease)
MPS II (Hunter disease)
MPS IIIB (Sanfilippo B)
MPS IV (Morquio)
MPS VI (Maroteaux-Lamy)

[51–54]. Both groups can be diagnosed within the first trimester. Both have been cured by postnatal BMT, but BMT is not recommended routinely because of its prohibitive morbidity and mortality, and the relative success of modern medical management. In both diseases the success of BMT is indirectly related to the morbidity of the disease, that is, the younger the patient, the fewer transfusions received, and the less organ compromise from iron overload, the better the results. With both diseases the primary questions relevant to prenatal transplantation are: (1) what levels of normal peripheral cell expression are necessary to alleviate clinical disease, and (2) can adequate levels of donor cell engraftment be achieved by in utero HSC transplantation? At present only indirect evidence exists to answer these questions.

In sickle cell disease (SCD) the pathophysiology is directly related to the concentration of hemoglobin S (HbS) within red cells, which results in marked rheologic abnormality, including hyperviscosity, cellular adherence, and sickling, with a result of vaso-occlusion and tissue ischemia. In examining the in vitro relationships between hematocrit (HCT) and viscosity using mixtures of sickle and normal red blood cells (RBCs), Schmalzer et al. [55] observed that the primary determinant of viscosity is the sickle HCT (fraction of RBCs that contain HbS). Adverse effects of HCT on viscosity were seen at a sickle HCT level in the low 20s. Oxygen delivery, as gauged by the maximal point on the HCT versus viscosity curve, was markedly improved by exchanging normal for sickle RBCs (even when the total HCT was held constant). The clinical correlate of this in vitro information presently is chronic exchange transfusion therapy with its inherent discomfort and potential complications. However, prenatal transplantation of normal hematopoietic stem cells was thought of as a solution to this problem. Normal cells were expected to have a developmental advantage over HbS cells such that overall production of Hb-normal RBCs may exceed that of HbS cells. Which could potentially decrease the overall HbS fraction, reducing the risk of hyperviscosity and vaso-occlusive/ischemic complications. However, experimental data have not yet born this out.

The clinical manifestations of thalassemia are secondary to hypoxia related to severe anemia and ineffective erythropoiesis. It is now standard therapy to transfuse patients with thalassemia major chronically from an early age, which suppresses endogenous erythropoiesis and maintains oxygen delivery. When instituted at an early age this effectively prevents the bone marrow expansion and secondary bony changes, as well as the hemodynamic and cardiac manifestations of the disease. The necessary normal hemoglobin (Hb) level required is controversial, but good results have been achieved with maintenance of a Hb of 9 g/dl.

Although these levels of normal Hb are higher than have been achieved experimentally (30% donor Hb is maximal), there would be a significant survival advantage of normal cells in both diseases. In SCD, erythrocytes have a circulating half-life of 10–20 days (normal half-life = 120 days) prior to destruction. In thalassemia, most cells (80%) never leave the bone marrow and also have shortened survival in the periphery. Therefore, engraftment of even a relatively small number of normal stem cells could result in significantly increased levels of peripheral donor cell expression. The problem, however, is creating spaces in the bone marrow for engraftment which is an unsolved dilemma.

Immunodeficiency Diseases

These represent an extremely heterogeneous group of diseases, which differ in their likelihood of cure by their capacity to develop hematopoietic chimerism [41, 42]. Once again, the most likely to benefit from even low levels of donor cell engraftment are those diseases in which a survival advantage exists for normal cells. The best example of this situation is severe combined immunodeficiency syndrome (SCID). Several different molecular causes of SCID have been identified, with approximately two thirds of cases being of X-linked recessive inheritance (X-SCID). The genetic basis of X-SCID has been defined recently [56] as a mutation of the gene encoding the common -Y chain, which is a common component of several members of the cytokine receptor superfamily, including those for interleukin-2 (IL-2), IL-4, IL-7, IL-9, IL-15, and possibly IL-13. Children affected with X-SCID have simultaneous disruption of multiple cytokine systems, resulting in a block in thymic T cell development and diminished T cell response. B cells, although present in normal or even increased numbers, are dysfunctional, either secondary to the lack of T helper cell function or an intrinsic defect in B cell maturation. Another form of SCID is secondary to adenosine deaminase (ADA) deficiency. Clinical experience with HLA-matched sibling bone marrow, fetal liver or thymus transplantation generally has been successful without myeloablative therapy, suggesting that the lymphoid progeny of relatively few engrafted normal HSC have a selective growth advantage in vivo over genetically defective cells [57]. The competitive advantage of normal cell populations in X-SCID is best supported by the discovery of skewed X-inactivation in female carriers [58]. Only T cells containing the normal X chromosome were found to be present in the circulation of recipients. Evidence that ADA production confers a survival advantage derives from the early experience with gene therapy for ADA deficiency SCID. ADA-gene-corrected autologous T cells have persisted for prolonged periods despite discontinuation of the T cell infusions [59]. Transfer of ADA-gene-corrected cells versus uncorrected cells from the same SCID patient into an immunodeficient BNX mouse results in survival of the corrected cells and death of the uncorrected cells, confirming a survival advantage for ADA-producing cells even when there is normal ADA production in the surrounding environment. Unfortunately, other diseases such as chronic granulomatous disease would not be expected to provide a competitive advantage for donor cells. Nevertheless, in all these conditions even a partial engraftment and expression of normal cell phenotype might at least partially ameliorate the clinical manifestations of the disease and should result in donor-specific tolerance for later transplantation. If higher levels of engraftment are needed, further HSC transplants from the same donor could be performed after birth without fear of rejection.

Flake et al. [60] reported the successful treatment of a fetus with X-linked SCIDS in a family in which a previously afflicted child died at 7 months of age. Diagnosis by chorionic villous sampling (CVS) at 12 weeks in the second pregnancy showed another affected male. For this couple, abortion was not an option. After lengthy informed consent, paternal bone marrow was harvested, T cells depleted, and enriched stem cell populations injected intraperitoneally into the fetus beginning about 16 weeks of gestation. Subsequent injections were performed at 17 and 18 weeks. The baby presently shows a split chimerism with all of his T cells being his fathers and the majority of B lymphocytes, monocytes, and natural killer cells being his. He has achieved developmental normal milestones, and immune progress through 8 years of age [60]. Other cases have been recently tried using less T cell-depleted populations resulting in higher T cell concentrations that have ended in fetal demise [61–64].

Inborn Errors of Metabolism

An even more heterogeneous group of diseases, inborn errors of metabolism, can be caused by a deficiency of a specific lysosomal hydrolase, which results in the accumulation of substrates such as mucopolysaccharide, glycogen, or sphingolipid. Depending on the specific enzyme abnormality and the compounds that accumulate, certain patterns of tissue damage and organ failure occur [42]. These include central nervous system (CNS) deterioration, growth failure, dysostosis multiplex and joint abnormalities, hepatosplenomegaly, myocardial or cardiac disease, upper airway obstruction, pulmonary infiltration, corneal clouding, and hearing loss. The potential efficacy of prenatal HSC transplantation for the treatment of these diseases must be considered on an individual disease basis. The purpose of BMT in these diseases is to provide HSC-derived mononuclear cells that can repopulate various organs in the body, including the liver (Kupffer cells), skin (Langerhans' cells), lung (alveolar macrophages), spleen (macrophages), lymph nodes, tonsils, and the brain (microglia). Patients who have been corrected by postnatal BMT, such as Gaucher's disease or Maroteaux-Lamy syndrome (minimal CNS involvement), are certainly reasonable candidates for prenatal treatment. In many cases postnatal BMT has corrected the peripheral manifestations of the disease and has arrested the neurologic deterioration. However, postnatal BMT has not reversed neurologic injury that is present in such disorders as metachromatic leukodystrophy and Hurler's disease [41, 42]. In these cases the neurologic injury may begin well before birth. Postnatal maturation of the blood-brain barrier restricts access to the CNS of transplanted cells or the deficient enzyme. These considerations suggest that prenatal treatment may be beneficial and offer the possibility for a cure. The primary unanswered question is whether donor HSC-derived microglial elements would populate the CNS, providing the necessary metabolic correction inside the blood-brain barrier.

To date, the only definitively successful transplants have been for SCIDS [41, 42]. All others have either failed to take or were afflicted with graft-vs.-host disease. Much more work needs to be done to determine the optimal dosing, timing, and specific protocols for different conditions.

As reviewed recently by Shields et al. [42], as of 2003 39 cases of in utero stem cell transplants have been published. Since the first successful case performed by our group in 1995, only immunodeficiency cases continued to be successful. Of 14 cases of α- and β-thalassemia, none have been successful. Three sickle cell, 3 Rh isoimmunization [7], and storage disease cases have likewise been unsuccessful [42]. Of 12 immunodeficiency cases, 6 have shown at least split chimerism or 'alive and well.' The dosages used, timing, fresh vs. frozen tissue, and methods of evaluation before and after transplantation have been very varied. While no definitive conclusions are possible at this time, it is clear that our lack of understanding of the mechanics or the development of immunocompetency are persuasive. Until we can obtain a better understanding of the process, we will not be able to tailor theories to achieve better outcomes.

Conclusion

There is an increasing number of congenital and genetic abnormalities for which in utero treatment is possible, and in some cases, now relatively routine. Advances in therapies have progressed at different paces for different disorders, but there is great hope and enthusiasm that progress will continue to expand the number of disorders for which therapy can be effective [62].

References

1 Evans MI (ed): Reproductive Risks and Prenatal Diagnosis. Norwalk, Appleton & Lange, 1992.

2 Johnson MP, Flake AW, Quintero RA, Evans MI: Shunt procedures; in Evans MI, Johnson MP, Moghissi KS (eds): Invasive Outpatient Procedures in Reproductive Medicine. New York, Raven Press, 1997.

3 Harrison MR, Evans MI, Adzick NS, Holzgrove W (eds): The Unborn Patient. Philadelphia, Saunders, 2000.

4 Evans MI, Sacks AL, Johnson MP, Robichaux AG III, May M, Moghissi KS: Sequential invasive assessment of fetal renal function, and the in utero treatment of fetal obstructive uropathies. Obstet Gynecol 1991;77:545–550.

5 Wilson RD, Johnson MP: Prenatal ultrasound guided percutaneous shunt for obstruction, uropathy and thoracic disease. Semin Pediatr Surg 2003;12:182–189.

6 Johnson MP, Corsi P, Bradfield, et al: Sequential fetal urine analysis provides greater precision in the evaluation of fetal obstructive uropathy. Am J Obstet Gynecol 1995;173:59–65.

7 Freedman AL, Bukowski TP, Smith CA, Evans MI, Johnson MP, Gonzalez R: Fetal therapy for obstructive uropathy: Specific outcomes diagnosis. J Urol 1996;156: 720–724. Erratum in: J Urol 1996;156: 1786.
8 Feldman B, Aviram-Goldring A, Evans MI: Interphase FISH for prenatal diagnosis of common aneuploidies. Methods Mol Biol 2002;204:219–241.
9 Dommergues M, Mueller F: Experience of 100 obstructive uropathies. Int Fetal Med Surgery Society, 2003, unpubl.
10 Drugan A, Krause B, Canady A, Zador IE, Sacks AJ, Evans MI: The natural history of prenatally diagnosed ventriculomegaly. JAMA 1989;261: 1785–1788.
11 Ahmad FK, Sherman SJ, Hagglund KH, Johnson MP, Krivehcnia EL: Isolated unilateral pleural effusion: The role of sonographic surveillance and in utero therapy. Fetal Diagn Ther 1996;11:383–389.
12 Nicolaides KH, Azar GB: Thoraco-amniotic shunting. Fetal Diagn Ther 1990;5:153–164.
13 Adzick N, Harrison M, Flake A, Glick P, Bottles K: Automatic uterine stapling devices in fetal surgery: Experience in a primate model. Surg Forum 1985;XXXVI:479–481.
14 Jennings RW, Adzick NS, Longaker MT, Lorenz HP, Estes JM, Harrison MR: New techniques in fetal surgery. J Pediatr Surg 1992;27:1329–1333.
15 Jennings RW, Adzick NS, Longaker MT, Lorenz HP, Harrison MR: Radiotelemetric fetal monitoring during and after open fetal operation. Surg Gynecol Obstet 1993;176: 59–64.
16 Harrison MR, Longaker MT, Adzick NS, et al: Successful repair in utero of a fetal diaphragmatic hernia after removal of herniated viscera from the left thorax. N Engl J Med 1990;322:1582–1584.
17 Harrison MR, Adzick NS, Flake AW, et al: Correction of congenital diaphragmatic hernia in utero: VI. Hard-learned lessons. J Pediatr Surg 1993;28:1141–1147; discussion 1417–1418.
18 Harrison MR, Keller RL, Hawgood SB, et al: A randomized trial of endoscopic tracheal occlusion for severe fetal congenital diaphragmatic hernia. N Engl J Med 2003;349:1916–1924.
19 Harrison MR, Sydorak RM, Farrell JA, Kitterman JA, Filly RA, Albanese CT: Fetoscopic temporary tracheal occlusion for congenital diaphragmatic hernia: Prelude to a randomized, controlled trial. J Pediatr Surg 2003;38:1012–1020.
20 Heerema AE, Rabban JT, Sydorak RM, Jarrison MR, Jones KD: Lung pathology in patients with congenital diaphragmatic hernia treated with fetal surgical intervention, including tracheal occlusion. Pediatr Dev Pathol 2003;in press.
21 Sydorak RM, Harrison MR: Congenital diaphragmatic hernia: Advances in prenatal therapy. Clin Perinatol 2003;30:465–579.
22 Danzer E, Sydorak RM, Harrison MR, Albanese CT: Minimal access fetal surgery. Eur J Obstet Gynecol Reprod Biol 2003;108:3–13.
23 Evans MI, Harrison MR, Flake AW, Johnson MP: Fetal therapy. Best Pract Res Clin Obstet Gynaecol 2002;16:671–683.
24 Paek BW, Coakley FV, Lu Y, et al: Congenital diaphragmatic hernia: Prenatal evaluation with MR lung volumetry – preliminary experience. Radiology 2001;220:63–67.
25 Wenstrom KD: Fetal surgery for congenital diaphragmatic hernia. N Engl J Med 2003;349:1887–1888.
26 Adzick NS, Kitano Y: Fetal surgery for lung lesions, congenital diaphragmatic hernia, and saccrococcygeal teratoma. Semin Pediatric Surg 2003;12:154–167.

27 Adzick NS, Harrison MR, Crombleholme TM, Flake AW, Howell LJ: Fetal lung lesions: Management and outcome. Am J Obstet Gynecol 1998; 179:884–889.
28 Crombleholme TM, Coleman B, Hedrick H, et al: Cystic adenomatoid malformation volume ratio predicts outcome in prenatally diagnosed cystic adenomatoid malformation of the lung. J Pediatr Surg 2002;37:331–338.
29 Holterman AX, Filiatrault D, Lallier M, Youssef S: The natural history of sacrococcygeal teratomas diagnosed through routine obstetric sonogram: A single institution experience. J Pediatr Surg 1998; 33:899–903.
30 Paek B, Vaezy S, Fujimoto V, et al: Tissue ablation using high-intensity focused ultrasound in fetal sheep model: Potential for fetal treatment. Am J Obstet Gynecol 2003;189:702–705.
31 Liechty KW, Crombleholme TM, Flake AW, et al: Intrapartum airway management for giant neck masses. The EXIT (ex utero Intrapartum Treatment) procedure. Am J Obstet Gynecol 1997;177:870–874.
32 Hedrick HL: Ex utero intrapartum therapy. Semin Pediatr Surg 2003;13:190–195.
33 Adzick NS, Walsh DS: Myelomeningocele: Prenatal diagnosis, pathophysiology and management. Semin Pediatr Surg 2003; 12:168–174.
34 Lemire RJ: Neural tube defects. JAMA 1988;259:558–562.
35 Meuli M, Meuli-Simmen C, Hutchins GM, et al: In utero surgery rescues neurological function at birth in sheep with spina bifida. Nature Med 1995;1:342–347.
36 Bruner JP, Tulipan N, Paschall RL, et al: Fetal surgery for myelomeningocele and the incidence of shunt-dependent hydrocephalus. JAMA 1999;282: 1819–1825.
37 Sutton LN, Adzick NS, Bilaniuk LT, Johnson MP, Crombleholme TM, Flake AW: Improvement in hindbrain herniation demonstrated by serial fetal magnetic resonance imaging following fetal surgery for myelomeningocele. JAMA 1999;282:1826–1831.
38 Tulipan N, Hernanz-Schulman M, Bruner JP: Reduced hindbrain herniation after intrauterine myelomingocele repair: A report of four cases. Pediatr Neurosurg 1998;29:274–278.
39 Tulipan N, Sutton LN, Bruner JP, Cohen BM, Johnson M, Adzick NS: The effect of intrauterine myelomeningocele repair on the incidence of shunt-dependent hydrocephalus. Pediatr Neurosurg 2003;38: 27–33.
40 Johnson MP, Sutton LN, Rintoul N, et al: Fetal menyongocele repair: Short term outcomes. Am J Obstet Gynecol 2003; 189:482–487.
41 Flake AW: Stem cell and genetic therapies for the fetus. Semin Pediatr Surg 2003; 12:202–208.
42 Shields LE, Lindton B, Andrews RG, Westgren M: Fetal hematopoietic stem cell transplantation: A challenge for the twenty-first century. J Hematother Stem Cell Res 2002;11:617–631.
43 Flake AW, Zanjani ED: In utero hematopoietic stem cell transplantation: Ontogenic opportunities ad biologic barriers. Blood 1999;94:2179–2191.
44 Liechty KW, MacKenzie TC, Shaaban AF, et al: Human messenchymal stem cells engraft and demonstrate site-specific differentiation after in utero transplantation in sheep. Nat Med 2000;6:1282–1286.
45 Zanjani ED, Ascensao JL, Flake AW, Harrison MR, Tavassoli M: The fetus as an optimal donor and recipient of hemopoietic stem cells. Bone Marrow Transplant 1992;10(suppl 1):107–114.

46 Fleischman R, Mintz B: Prevention of genetic anemias in mice by microinjection of normal hematopoietic cells into the fetal placenta. Proc Natl Acad Sci USA 1979;76:5736–5740.
47 Blazer BR, Taylor PA, McElmurry R, et al: Engraftment of severe combined immune deficient mice receiving allogenic bone marrow via in utero or postnatal transfer. Blood 1998;92:3949–3959.
48 Guidos CJ, Danska JS, Fathman CG, Weissman IL: Cell receptor-mediated negative selection of autoreactive T lymphocyte precursors occurs after commitment to the CD4 or CD8 lineages. J Exp Med 1990; 172:835–845.
49 Touraine JL, Raudrant D, Laplace S: Transplantation of hematopoietic cells from the fetal liver to treat patients with congenital disease postnatally or prenatally. Transplant Proc 1997;29:712–713.
50 Flake AW, Zanjani ED: In utero hematopoietic stem cell transplantation: A status report. JAMA 1997;278:932–937.
51 Hayward A, Ambruso D, Battaglia F, et al: Microchimerism and tolerance following intrauterine transplantation and transfusion for alpha-thalassemia-1. Fetal Diagn Ther 1998;13:8–14.
52 Flake AW, Zanjani ED: Treatment of severe combined immunodeficiency syndrome. N Engl J Med 1999;341:291–292.
53 Westgren M, Ringden O, Eik Nes S, et al: Lack of evidence of permanent engraftment after in utero fetal stem cell transplantation in congenital hemoglobinopathies. Transplantation 1996;61:1176–1179.
54 Touraine JL, Raudrant D, Royo C, et al: In-utero transplantation of hematopoietic stem cells in humans. Translant Proc 1991;23:1706–1708.
55 Schmalzer EA, Lee JO, Brown AK, Usami S, Chien S: Viscosity of mixtures of sickle and normal red cells at varying hematocrit levels: Implications for transfusion. Transfusion 1987; 27:228–233.
56 Noguchi M, Yi H, Rosenblatt HM, et al: Interleukin-2 receptor gamma chain mutation results in X-linked severe combined immunodeficiency in humans. Cell 1993;73:147–157.
57 Buckley RH, Schiff SE, Schiff RI, et al: Haploidentical bone marrow stem cell transplantation in human severe combined immunodeficiency. Semin Hematol 1993;30:92–104.
58 Puck JM, Stewart CC, Nissbaum RL: Maximum-likelihood analysis of human T-cell X chromosome inactivation patterns: Normal women versus carriers of X-linked severe combined immunodeficiency. Am J Hum Genet 1992;50:742–748.
59 Slavin S, Naparstek E, Ziegler M, Lewin A. Clinical application of intrauterine bone marrow transplantation for treatment of genetic diseases-feasibility studies. Bone Marrow Transplant 1992;9:189–190.
60 Flake AW, Roncarolo MG, Puck JM, et al: Treatment of X-linked severe combined immunodeficiency by in utero transplantation of paternal bone marrow. N Engl J Med 1996;335: 1806–1810.
61 Blakemore K, Bambach B, Moser H, et al: Engraftment following in utero bone marrow transplantation for globoid cell leukodystrophy. Bone Marrow Transplant 1997;19:399–402.
62 Peranteau WH, Hayashi S, Kim HB, Shaaban AF, Flake AW: In utero hematopoietic cell transplantation: What are the improvement questions? Fetal Diag Ther 2004;19:9–12.

63 Flake AW, Zanjani ED: In utero hematopoietic stem cell transplantation: Ontogenic opportunities and biologic barriers. Blood 1999;94:2179–2191.

64 Porta F, Mazzolari E, Zucca S, Schumacher F, Lanfranchi A, Tettoni K, Notarangelo LD: Prenatal transplant in a fetus affected by Omenn syndrome. Bone Marrow Transplant 2000;25(S):S43.

Mark I. Evans, MD

Institute for Genetics and Fetal Medicine, St. Luke's Roosevelt Hospital Center, Columbia University, 1000 10th Avenue, Suite 11A, New York, NY 10019 (USA)
Tel. +1 212 523 5895, Fax +1 212 523 8372, E-Mail mevans@chpnet.org

Blazer S, Zimmer EZ (eds):
The Embryo: Scientific Discovery and Medical Ethics.
Basel, Karger, 2005, pp 284–290

Evaluating Risks of Drugs in Pregnancy

From Biology to Risk Perception

Gideon Koren

MotherRisk Program, Division of Clinical Pharmacology, The Hospital for Sick Children, Toronto, Ont.; and The Ivey Chair in Molecular Toxicology, The University of Western Ontario, London, Ont., Canada

For centuries it was assumed that medicinal drugs and chemicals do not cross the human placenta, and hence do not pose a risk to the developing fetus. The thalidomide event in the late 1950s utterly changed this view by proving that a small molecule, quite innocuous to the mother suffering from morning sickness, can cause horrendous fetal damage. Naturally, the thalidomide disaster marks the beginning of modern teratology and the increasing recognition that xenobiotics and, indeed, even naturally occurring molecules can have an adverse affect on the developing infant.

However, the thalidomide era has also caused a second wave of reaction, much more insidious, which has a major impact on research and practice: Since the thalidomide disaster medicine is practiced as if every drug is a potential human teratogen. In reality, only a handful of medicinal drugs have been proven to cause fetal damage. This wave has led millions of pregnant women to be orphaned from much-needed medications for pregnancy-related and chronic medical conditions.

For example, the removal of the leading drug for nausea and vomiting of pregnancy Bendectin (doxylamine 10 mg and vitamin B_6 10 mg) from the US market in the early 1980s has led to lack of an FDA-approved drug for morning sickness. This move was temporally accompanied by a 3-fold increase in hospitalization of women in North America for severe morning sickness [1]. Wide epidemiological evidence indicates that Bendectin is safe in pregnancy [2]. Not surprising, the re-introduction of this preparation in Canada (as Diclectin®) was followed by a substantial decrease in hospitalization for morning sickness [3].

Another compelling example for the unwarranted global perception of fetal risk is the use of antidepressants. Modern antidepressants, such as the selective serotonin reuptake inhibitors (SSRIs) have been shown by a large number of studies not to be associated with an increased risk of either morphological or neurobehavioral fetal damage [4].

Yet, many physicians discontinue use of SSRIs in pregnancy 'cold turkey' with resultant morbidity, suicide attempts and hospitalizations [5]. As serious, women still treated by SSRIs tend to receive very low doses with substantial remnant morbidity. Recent research has shown for several antidepressants (e.g. fluoxetine), that in late pregnancy there is almost a doubling of clearance rate [6]. When this phenomenon is added to the very small doses of SSRIs given to this group of pregnant women, they render the dose given to many women homeopathic.

Evaluation of Teratogenic Risk in Pregnancy

Before approval by regulatory agencies, drugs have to undergo animal teratology studies. Typically, two species of rodents (e.g. mice, rats) are exposed before and throughout gestation to a range of drug doses, which should cover up to many folds the planned human exposure. The cumulative experience with this research approach painfully presents its lack of sensitivity and specificity. For example, until very recently, no one has succeeded in producing limb-shortening defects in animals exposed to thalidomide. In contrast, animal studies predicted avidly the huge teratogenic potential of retinoids (e.g. Accutane for acne).

Recently, leflunomide (Arava®) a new antirheumatic drug, inhibiting collagen formation, has been shown to cause substantial teratogenicity in rodents when serum concentrations were similar to those produced during clinical use in humans [7]. Yet, an ongoing study following up accidental human exposure to Arava has not yet shown an increased risk of fetal malformations. It is probable that animals, in this case, are much more sensitive to the teratogenic effect.

The poor predictive value of animal teratology studies underlines the need for rigorous epidemiologic studies in humans. While ethically no one can initiate pharmacotherapy in pregnancy to examine teratogenic potential, more than half of all pregnancies are unplanned, and follow-up of first-trimester human exposure to drugs is the most powerful way to study risk/safety in humans. For example, the Motherisk Program in Toronto counsels every day up to 200 women exposed to drugs, chemicals, radiation and infections during pregnancy and lactation [8]. Prospective follow-up of such exposure yields a powerful opportunity to confirm fetal safety or document fetal risks (www.motherisk.org).

In the laboratory, there are other means, beyond the classical animal teratology, to ascertain fetal exposure and/or risk. Ex vivo perfusion studies with fresh placental cotyledons may serve as a powerful example [9]. Using fresh placenta, one can reconstruct the maternal and fetal circulations. By introducing a drug into the maternal circulation and measuring it in the fetal circulation, one can verify whether the molecule cross the human placenta.

As an example, one may wish to consider the clinical situation when women need anticoagulants to prevent blood clots (e.g. during deep vein thrombosis or prosthetic cardiac valve). Such medications, if they cross the placenta, may increase the risk of bleeding by the fetus or during delivery. Using the placental perfusion model we have recently shown that the drug heparin, a large molecule with a molecular weight of over 20,000, does not cross from the maternal to the fetal circulation, rendering it safe to the fetus. Yet, the introduction into clinical practice of low-molecular-weight heparin has raised the question whether this molecule of 4,000–5,000 molecular weight, is also safe to the fetus. Using the perfusion model we have recently shown that low molecular weight heparin also does not cross the placental barrier, and hence can be safely used in pregnancy.

In contrast, the oral anticoagulant warfarin does cross the human placenta, and has been shown to cause the fetal warfarin syndrome, characterized by bone, cartilage and brain malformations. The implications of these findings are important in treating the mother while protecting the fetus.

Philosophy of Counseling of Teratogenic Risk

In 1985, we established the Motherisk Program with the aim of counseling women, their families and health professionals on the safety/risk of drugs, chemicals, radiation and infection during pregnancy and lactation. In 2003, the Motherisk team included more than 60 faculty, health professionals and students, answering up to 200 inquiries daily and conducting a wide range of research. With many thousands of prospectively collected mother-child pairs, this is the largest international database of its kind. Yet, because specific exposures in pregnancy may occur relatively rarely, we collaborate with similar programs from other parts of Canada and the US, as well as from Europe, Asia, Australia and South America, to collect larger cohorts.

In our outcome research, groups of women exposed to a specific drug are compared to women exposed to non-teratogenic controls (e.g. acetaminophen, dental X-ray). When possible, we are also trying to match a second comparison group consisting of women suffering from the same condition, but who are not taking the drug in question.

In selected drugs and condition, the follow-up of pregnancy outcome extends beyond morphological outcome, and includes neurodevelopmental studies such as IQ, language, and infant behaviors. As examples, we have completed such studies with fluoxetine, antiepileptics, cocaine and binge drinking. The reader may wish to review Motherisk website for complete details (www.motherisk.org).

In addition to research emanated from our clinical consultations, our laboratory has developed analytical methods to estimate fetal exposure by measuring medicinal and abuse drugs in fetal hair and meconium.

The philosophy of Motherisk counseling is based on delivering to the patient the best available evidence-based information regarding her exposure(s), and ensuring that the woman comprehends the information. For that end it is important to deliver the information in an unambiguous manner, using simple, but not simplistic language. Today Western society is very diverse and heterogeneous in terms of religion, beliefs and attitude as it relates to pregnancy. For that reason we never recommend termination/continuation of pregnancy, as women may be 'prolife' or 'pro-choice'. Typically, women ask: 'What do you recommend, Doctor'? The invariable answer is 'This decision must reside with you and your family. We want to ensure that you have accurate scientific information to make an informed decision. We will support you in any decision you make'. In the case of non-teratogenic exposures, the last sentence is commonly followed by the statement 'but it is important for you to know that your exposure to ... does not increase your risk for a malformed child'.

In studies conducted by us during the last 18 years, we have shown that women perceive a high teratogenic risk even when exposed to non-teratogenic agents. We have shown that many women are advised to terminate an otherwise wanted pregnancy when there is no evidence of fetal risk. Evidence-based counseling of these women substantially decreases their fears and prevents many cases of unnecessary terminations of pregnancy [10]. In counseling women exposed to drugs, chemicals, radiation and infections in pregnancy, it is important to synthesize all existing evidence. When human data exist, it generally prevails over animal experience, as it is much more relevant.

To underline the extent of misinformation and misperception commonly rampant among women and their health professionals, it is interesting to consider the situation with drugs on which the message is 'blurred' or 'gray'. The following are examples of three agents originally suspected as being human teratogens, where it is clear now that this is not the case:

While high-dose radiation (e.g. at the intensity created in Hiroshima and Nagasaki) is clearly teratogenic, diagnostic radiation is not [11]. Yet, women accidentally exposed to diagnostic radiation in pregnancy undergo therapeutic abortions substantially more commonly than comparison groups [12].

A similar trend toward pregnancy termination was shown by us for quinolone antibiotics which cause arthropathy in dog pups but are not teratogenic in human pregnancy [13], and among women receiving rubella vaccine in pregnancy; while the rubella virus is very teratogenic, the live attenuated virus used in the vaccination has not been shown by large studies to cause fetal damage in humans [14]. Yet, women inadvertently vaccinated in pregnancy tend to terminate pregnancy significantly more often than control groups, citing teratogenic risk as the reason for such extreme measures.

In summary, unless the medical profession, the pharmaceutical industry and regulatory agencies combine their efforts to identify the field of drugs in pregnancy as a top priority, pregnant women will continue to be orphaned from the advantages of new drug therapy, resulting in continuation of numerous unnecessary pregnancy terminations, suboptimal therapy and poor pregnancy outcome due to untreated maternal conditions.

Acknowledgements

Supported by grants from the Canadian Institutes for Health Research and the Research Leadership in Better Pharmacotherapy during Pregnancy & Lactation, The Hospital for Sick Children's Foundation. The author holds the Ivey Chair in Molecular Toxicology at the University of Western Ontario.

References

1 Neutel CI, Johansen HL: Measuring drug-effectiveness by default: The case of Bendectin. Can J Publ Hlth 1995;86:66–70.

2 McKeigue PM, Lamm SH, Linn S, Kutcher JS: Bendectin and birth defects: A meta-analysis of epidemiologic studies. Teratology 1994;50:27–37.

3 Neutel CI: Variation in rates of hospitalization for excessive vomiting in pregnancy by Bendectin/Diclectin use in Canada; in Koren G, Bishai R (eds): Nausea and Vomiting of Pregnancy. Toronto, Motherisk Program, 2000, pp 54–59.

4 Nulman I, Rovet J, Stewart DE, Wolpin J, Pace Asciak P, Shuhaiba S, Koren G: Child neurodevelopment following exposure to tricyclic antidepressants or fluoxetine throughout fetal life: A prospective controlled study. Am J Psychiatry 2002; 59:1889–1895.

5 Einarson A, Selby P, Koren G: Abrupt discontinuation of psychotropic drugs during pregnancy: Fear of teratogenic risk and impact of counseling. J Psychiatr Neurosc 2001;26:44–48.

6 Heikkinen T, Ekblad U, Palo P, Laine K: Pharmacokinetics of fluoxetine and norfluoxetine in pregnancy and lactation. Clin Pharmacol Ther 2003;73:330–337.

7 Kozer E, Moretti ME, Koren G: Leflunomide: New antirheumatic drug. Effect on pregnancy outcomes. Can Fam Physn 2001;47:721–722.

8 Koren G, Pastuszak A, Ito S: Drugs in pregnancy. N Engl J Med 1998;338: 1128–1137.

9 Boskovic R, Feig DS, Derewlany L, Knie B, Portnoi G, Koren G: Transfer of Insulin Lispro across the human placenta: In vitro perfusion studies. Diabetes Care 2003;26:1390–1394.

10 Koren G: Bias against the null hypothesis in maternal-fetal pharmacology and toxicology. Clin Pharmacol Ther 1997; 62:1–5.

11 Bentur Y: Radiation in pregnancy; in Koren G (ed): Maternal-Fetal Toxicology: A Clinician's Guide, ed 3. New York, Marcel Dekker, 2001, pp 603–651.

12 Cohen-Kerem R, Medina D, Koren G, Nulman I: Diagnostic radiation in pregnancy: Termination of pregnancy due to risk misperception. Birth Def Res [A] 2003;67:392.

13 Loebstein R, Addis A, Ho E, et al: Pregnancy outcome following gestational exposure to fluoroquinolones: A multicenter prospective controlled study. Antimicrob Agents Chemother 1998;42:1336–1339.

14 Bar Oz B, Levichek Z, Koren G: The safety of rubella vaccine in pregnancy. Am J Med Genet, in press.

Gideon Koren, MD, FRCPC

MotherRisk Program, Division of Clinical Pharmacology,
The Hospital for Sick Children, 555 University Avenue, Toronto, ON M5G 1X8 (Canada)
Tel. +1 416 813 5778 / +1 416 813 5781, Fax +1 416 813 7562, E-Mail gkoren@sickkids.ca

Blazer S, Zimmer EZ (eds):
The Embryo: Scientific Discovery and Medical Ethics.
Basel, Karger, 2005, pp 291–308

Fetal Surveillance Tests

Ido Solt[a] Michael Y. Divon[b,c]

[a]Department of Obstetrics and Gynecology, Rambam Medical Center, Haifa, Israel;
[b]The Albert Einstein College of Medicine, Bronx, and [c]Department of Obstetrics and Gynecology, Lenox-Hill Hospital, New York, N.Y., USA

Not long ago, the fetus was considered a passenger, not a separate patient. It was believed that nothing could be done to improve fetal health inside the uterine 'black-box'. Perhaps the first written record we have of a mother and baby surviving a cesarean section comes from Switzerland in 1500 when a sow gelder, Jacob Nufer, performed the operation on his wife. After several days in labor and help from 13 midwives, the woman was unable to deliver her baby. Her desperate husband eventually gained permission from the local authorities to attempt a cesarean. The mother lived and subsequently gave birth normally to 5 children, including twins [1]. Peter Chamberlen presumably invented the obstetric forceps and kept it as a family secret [2]. These interventions were intended to save the parturient life during an obstructed labor, but they also indirectly improved the survival chances of the fetus. The concept of 'the fetus as a patient' has evolved in the twentieth century and now it is fundamental and firmly established in obstetric care.

'Fetal monitoring' in a wide sense means fetal surveillance but, practically, it is an indirect way to measure fetal well-being or the adequacy of fetal oxygenation and, as such, it is an integral part of the concept of 'the fetus as a patient'. The primary goal of fetal monitoring is a healthy newborn with a healthy mother.

Table 1.
Methods of fetal monitoring

Fetal movement assessment
Periodic fetal heart rate (FHR) auscultation (fetoscope)
Continuous electronic FHR monitoring (NST, CST)
Fetal biophysical profile scoring (BPP)
Stimulation techniques: scalp stimulation and vibroacoustic stimulation
Fetal amniotic fluid analysis
Fetal blood evaluation
Fetal pulse oximetry
Doppler velocimetry

There are several methods of antepartum and intrapartum fetal monitoring (table 1). This chapter will focus mainly on the 'continuous electronic fetal heart rate monitoring' (CEFHRM), biophysical profile and Doppler velocimetry which are currently the main clinical assessment techniques.

History of Fetal Heart Rate Monitoring

Direct fetal heart rate (FHR) auscultation with the examining ear placed on the maternal abdomen has been known for a centuries [3], Marsac heard fetal heart beats in the seventeenth century. Mayor [4], a Swiss surgeon, first reported direct FHR auscultation in 1818. Jean Alexandre Le Jumeau and Viscount de Kergaradec first described auscultation of the fetal heart with a Laennec stethoscope or with a wooden fetoscope in 1821 [5]. Le Jumeau, who was not an obstetrician, reported hearing fetal heart beats in 8 pregnant women. Le Jumeau suggested that fetal auscultation could be used to detect pregnancy as well as to identify twin gestation, fetal lie and even fetal health [6]. Le Jumeau was the pupil of Laennec, the founder of medical auscultation. Kennedy, in his monograph from 1833 [7] postulated that 'since newborn hearts beats longer compared to adult hearts when excised, they can better tolerate a hypoxic environment'. Kennedy described the effects of head and cord compression on the fetal heart rate and related a slow return of FHR after a bradycardia to 'fetal sufferance'. This monograph was ahead of its time by including an appendix containing legal notes! Kilian, in 1849, published on 'stethoscopical indications for forceps operation'. He suggested that forceps delivery should be applied without delay when the FHR is less than 100 bpm or more than 180 bpm, when the fetal heart sounds lose their purity of tone or when only one tone could be clearly heard [8]. Kehrer [9], in 1867, described for the first time the association between fetal bradycardia and fetal head compression. Schwartz [10], in 1870, proposed counting the FHR as often as possible between and during the uterine contractions because FHR might change due to fetal 'asphyxic intoxication'. Schatz [11], in 1885, described the mechanism of FHR deceleration due to umbilical cord compression. Ernesto Pestalozza of Pavia described phonocardiography in 1891. In 1893, Winckel [12] suggested criteria for defining fetal distress, among them, FHR under 120 bpm or above 160 bpm. In 1903, Seitz [13] suggested three types of FHR decelerations, two related to enhanced vagal activity and one related to paralysis of all extracardiac nervous activity. He proposed that the changes in the FHR pattern reflect fetal oxygenation. In the same year, in the first edition of Williams Obstetrics [14], J. Whitridge Williams stated: 'The rate of fetal heart is subject to considerable variations which afford us a fairly reliable means of judging as to the wellbeing of the child. As a general rule, its life should be considered in danger when the heartbeats fall below 100 or exceed 160'.

Cremer recorded the first fetal electrocardiogram (ECG) in 1906, only 5 years after the first adult ECG registration by Einthoven in 1901. In 1922, Sach tried to use abdomino-vaginal and abdomino-rectal leads. In 1938, Bell had recorded fetal P waves. In 1958, Hon [15], 'the father of the modern FHR monitor', developed a method for continuous FHR recording. He described three patterns of FHR decelerations: early, variable and late which were related to head compression, cord compression and uteroplacental insufficiency, respectively. In 1963, Hon improved the quality of FHR recordings by introducing a fetal scalp electrode. In 1966, Hammacher [16] indicated that neonates who had FHR late decelerations prior to delivery, had lower Apgar scores after delivery and higher stillbirth rate. Six years later, Ray et al. [17] confirmed the observation of Hammacher in the first prospective blinded trial in the USA. In 1969, Hammacher linked FHR accelerations to fetal wellbeing. Continuous electronic FHR monitoring (CEFHRM) was commercially introduced in 1968; initially it was used for complicated and 'high-risk' pregnancies, but gradually it penetrated into the 'low-risk' pregnancies as well. By 1978, CEFHRM was used in nearly two thirds of deliveries in the USA [18]. By 1998, 84% of laboring women were monitored by CEFHRM [19] and today it is the most prevalent obstetrical monitoring technique, almost universally practiced in the Western world [3, 20].

FHR as an Indirect Measure of Fetal Brain Activity

Continuous recording of the fetal oxygenation would be the ideal method to assess fetal well-being. However, no such technique is presently available. Fetal heart rate monitoring was therefore suggested as an indirect measure of fetal brain oxygenation. Many physiological factors have an impact on the pacemakers of the fetal heart. Most important is the autonomic nervous system (sympathetic and parasympathetic nervous systems). Stimulation of the sympathetic nervous system leads to the release of catecholamines. These hormones increase the fetal cardiac output by increasing the FHR and myocardial contractility. Stimulation of this system occurs in cases of stress while during rest periods the heart rate is controlled by a tonic sympathetic stimulus.

The parasympathetic nervous system is dominated by the vagus nerve, which is the tenth cranial nerve and originates from the medulla oblongata. The vagal fibers supply the heart pacemakers and the sinoatrial and atrioventricular nodes. Vagal stimulation leads to the release of acetylcholine, which decreases the heart rate. There are two main vagal influences on the FHR. The first is a constant tonic stimulus that decreases the normal intrinsic FHR and, the second, an oscillatory stimulus that is responsible for most of the variability in the FHR. The vagal influence increases with gestational age. At 20 weeks' gestation, the average FHR is 155 bpm, at 30 weeks it is 144 bpm and at term it is 140 bpm. Variations of up to 20 bpm above or below the average FHR are regarded as normal. In well-oxygenated fetuses, FHR changes reflect different behavioral states. During active sleep and wakefulness, there are fluctuations in the baseline rate with a clearly visible beat-to-beat variability and heart rate accelerations during fetal movements. During quiet sleep there are only a few or no heart rate accelerations, and the beat-to-beat variability is reduced to some extent.

Hypoxic periods are characterized by an increased activity of both the sympathetic and parasympathetic nervous systems. Initially, the chemoreceptors are activated, leading to α-sympathetic stimulation that constricts the vascular beds of the gastrointestinal tract, liver, spleen, lungs, carcass, kidneys and skin (which are nonessential organs for immediate survival of the fetus) and thus cause hypertension and preferential increase in blood flow to the vital organs, i.e. the brain, heart, adrenals and placenta. At this stage of hypertension, the baroreceptors are activated with afferent link to the brain stem, leading to vagal stimulation and slowing of the heart rate. The decrease in heart rate presents as fetal heart rate deceleration. In cases of severe hypoxia, the fetus becomes acidotic, the brain stem is less responsive, the autonomic reflexes are blunted and there is a direct myocardial depression, which worsens the heart rate deceleration and lead to severe bradycardia.

The various FHR patterns observed in well oxygenated or hypoxic fetuses serve as the basis for the FHR testing.

The Nonstress Test

The nonstress test (NST) is a primary fetal surveillance tool. It is noninvasive, inexpensive, and simple and has no contraindications. Continuous wave Doppler transducers applied to the maternal abdomen record the FHR. The American College of Obstetricians and Gynecologists has defined a normal, i.e. reactive, NST as a tracing with two or more FHR accelerations that peak at 15 bpm or more above baseline, each lasting 15 s or more, and all occurring within 20 min of testing (fig. 1). The absence of two FHR accelerations within 20 min qualifies the tracing as nonreactive; however, in order to conclude that fetal reactivity is absent, at least 40 min of recording are required since most non-reactive tracing are due to fetal sleep. The perinatal mortality within a week of a reactive NST is 2–5/1,000. While a reactive NST is highly predictive of fetal well-being, the opposite is not true as most fetuses with a nonreactive NST are not compromised. Overall, the NST has a specificity of more than 90% and a sensitivity of 50%. The negative predictive value is 90% and the positive predictive value is less than 50%.

Most obstetricians perform a visual interpretation of the FHR tracing. However, the accuracy of this method is questionable and large inter- and intra-observer variations have been noted. The introduction of computerized analysis systems has, therefore, been suggested, but is not widely practiced.

The high false-positive rate of the NST may lead to unnecessary interventions. Most investigators therefore believe that additional testing is needed to confirm the results of the NST.

The Contraction Stress Test

During the late 1960s, as the experience with intrapartum electronic fetal monitoring became more widespread, investigators focused on the contraction

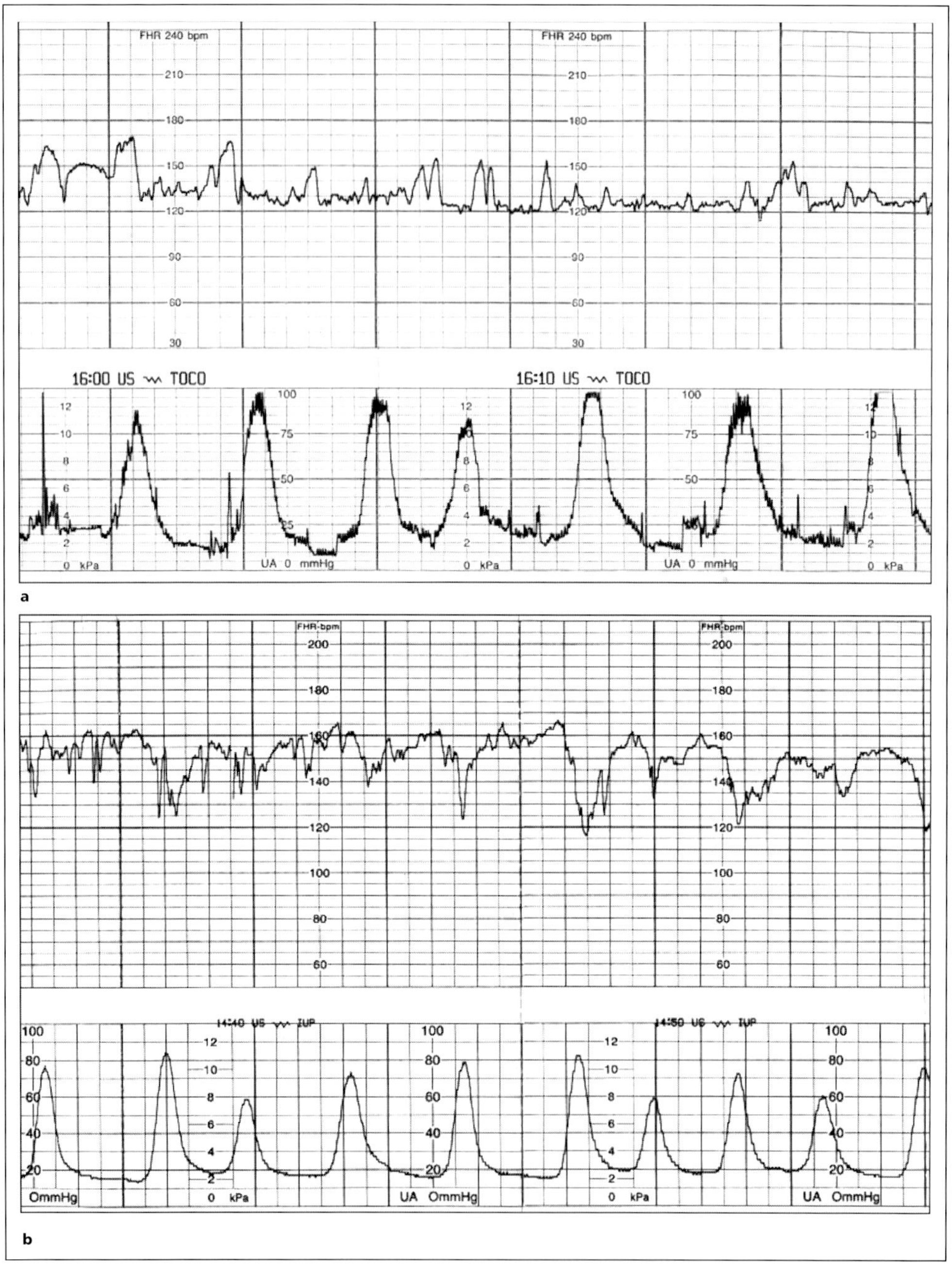
FHR 240 bpm
16:00 US TOCO
16:10 US TOCO
UA 0 mmHg
0 kPa
a
FHR-bpm
14:40 US IUP
14:50 US IUP
UA OmmHg
0 kPa
b

stress test (CST) as an antepartum test of fetal well-being. The hypothesis underlying the CST evolved from animal physiologic observations suggesting that blood flow to the intervillous space is decreased during uterine contractions. The rationale of the CST is to induce uterine contractions in order to uncover cases of uteroplacental insufficiency. Uterine contractions are induced by intravenous administration of oxytocin and the FHR reactivity is assessed. In order to get sufficient data, three 40–60 s contractions should be recorded within 10 min. The CST may induce labor and is therefore contraindicated in cases of a previous classical cesarean section, placenta previa, placental separation and premature rupture of membranes. The test should also be performed cautiously in cases of multiple pregnancy, hydramnios and incompetent cervix.

Fetuses whose oxygenation is suboptimal due to 'placental insufficiency' are likely to display late fetal heart rate decelerations when faced with a further decrease in their oxygenation during uterine contractions. The CST is considered positive when late decelerations occur following 50% or more of uterine contractions. A detailed description of the CST is beyond the scope of this editorial. In general, most authors have demonstrated a favorable perinatal outcome following a negative CST. In 1978, Evertson et al. [21] summarized 14 observational clinical reports that revealed seven fetal deaths among 1,739 high-risk patients within 1 week of a negative CST, for a noncorrected incidence of antenatal fetal death of 4/1,000. In most of these cases fetal demise resulted from 'non-predictable' etiologies such as umbilical cord accidents, severe congenital anomalies or placental abruption. A prospective multi-institutional study by Freeman et al. [22] included 4,626 patients who underwent weekly CST. The study demonstrated a corrected false negative rate of 0.4/1,000.

Later, Freeman et al. [23] combined results from 16 studies and reported a corrected false negative of 1.2/1,000. These figures suggest that the false-negative rate of CST is much lower than the stillbirth rate of 8/1,000 commonly reported in the general obstetrical population. CSTs are commonly performed in high-risk populations, which are by definition expected to have a higher fetal death rate than the general population.

Fig. 1.

Fetal heart rate (FHR) tracings. **a** Normal FHR tracing: The upper panel shows FHR variability and accelerations. The lower panel shows uterine activity. **b** An abnormal FHR tracing: The upper panel shows FHR decelerations. The lower panel shows uterine activity.

Therefore, it is commonly concluded that the use of the CST results in a dramatic decrease in antepartum fetal deaths. However, there are no prospective randomized trials (i.e. tested vs. nontested populations) documenting the presumed benefits of CST in either low-risk or high-risk patient populations.

The false-positive rate for the CST averages about 30%, with a range of 8–57%. This implies that approximately 30% of interventions due to a positive CST were deemed unnecessary following the intervention. In some studies true positives were defined by predicting questionable outcome variables such as thick meconium, 'need for cesarean section for fetal distress' or the presence of fetal growth restriction. Thus, the true false-positive rate of the CST is probably unknown.

As already stated, randomized studies of the CST versus no fetal testing are yet to be performed. However, in a non-randomized study of 1,542 high-risk patients undergoing weekly non stress testing (NST) and 4,626 patients undergoing CST, Freeman et al. [22] have shown that the rate of intervention for an abnormal test is higher for the CST group (4.5 vs. 2.9%, respectively) whereas the NST group had significantly higher incidence of respiratory distress syndrome, intrauterine growth restriction, birth weight <2,500 g and 5 min Apgar score of <7. The false-negative rates for the CST and NST in the prediction of fetal demise were 0.4/1,000 and 3.2/1,000, respectively.

It is generally believed that the CST is superior to the NST in the prevention of fetal death.

Biophysical Profile

In the early 1980s Manning and co-workers [24] introduced the concept of the fetal biophysical profile (BPP). This profile is somewhat similar to the commonly used neonatal Apgar score and consists of combined use of the NST and four biophysical activities observed with ultrasound: (1) fetal heart rate accelerations (NST); (2) fetal breathing movements; (3) fetal body movements; (4) fetal tone, and (5) amniotic fluid volume. Two points are assigned for each normal variable while no points are assigned for each abnormal variable. Thus, the BPP score ranges from zero to ten. The BPP reflect the integrity of the fetal central nervous system. In the original prospective blinded study, Manning and co-workers evaluated 216 high-risk pregnancies and observed no perinatal deaths when all five variables were normal.

Perinatal mortality was 60% when all variables were abnormal. Intermediate score values yielded intermediate perinatal loss rates. Recently, an observational study of 89,184 pregnancies that underwent BPP testing was reported by Dayal et al. [25]. The final BPP results were normal in 86,955 (97.5%) pregnancies (including 84,771 fetuses observed in Manitoba's fetal assessment program and 2,184 fetuses from Columbia Presbyterian's program). The false-negative death rate varied between the two institutions: in the Manitoba population there were 60 fetal deaths among 84,771 fetuses within 1 week of a normal BPP, yielding a false-negative rate of 0.71 per 1,000. In contrast, in the Columbia-Presbyterian study, 5 of 2,184 fetuses died within a week of a normal BPP, yielding a false-negative rate of 2.29 per 1,000. However, when these ratios were compared with the gross perinatal mortality in each center, the ratio of the false-negative rate to the total perinatal mortality rate showed no statistical significance (0.093 and 0.104 for Manitoba and Columbia Presbyterian, respectively) [25].

In 1993, Manning [26] conducted a prospective observational study in order to determine the relationship between the fetal BPP and umbilical venous pH obtained by cordocentesis. Cordocentesis was performed immediately after the BPP. A total of 493-paired observations were made. A biophysical score of zero was associated with significant fetal acidemia (pH <7.20), whereas a normal score (i.e. 8–10) was associated with a normal pH. An equivocal test – a score of 6 – was a poor predictor of an abnormal pH. Other investigators also examined this correlation and concluded that the association of the BPP and umbilical vein pH is strongest at the extremes of the BPP score [27–29].

In a subsequent study, Manning et al. [30] evaluated the association between final BPP score before delivery and the incidence of cerebral palsy (CP). A highly significant inverse exponential relationship was observed in a retrospective study of 26,288 high-risk pregnancies. The authors suggested that antenatal asphyxia is an important and potentially avoidable cause of CP.

In a prospective blinded study, 735 high-risk patients were randomly assigned to either a fetal BPP (375 patients) or a NST (360 patients). Although the sensitivity, specificity, and accuracy were higher with BPP, these differences did not reach statistical significance [31].

In a randomized prospective trial, Platt and co-workers [32] studied a total of 652 patients (1,628 tests were preformed). 279 pregnancies were managed by BPP and 373 were managed by NST. The results of this study suggest that the biophysical profile is more predictive of abnormal outcome than the NST. However, because the groups were too small statistical significance could not be established and the investigators recommended that additional studies be performed.

A modified fetal BPP based on two of the five original variables – the NST and amniotic fluid volume – has been reported [33, 34].

In a prospective observational study of 15,482 high-risk pregnancies, a false-negative rate of 0.8/1,000 and a false-positive rate of 60% were reported [35].

The American College of Obstetrics and Gynecologists has concluded that the modified BPP is an acceptable modality for antepartum fetal surveillance [36].

Alfirevic et al. [37] randomized 145 women with singleton, uncomplicated pregnancies at or beyond 42 weeks of gestation to either BPP comprising of computerized NST, amniotic fluid index and assessment of fetal breathing, tone and gross body movements (n = 72) or the standard NST and a measurement of the amniotic fluid volume as defined by the depth of the largest pocket of amniotic fluid (n = 73). There were significantly more abnormal results in the BPP group. There were no differences in cord blood gases, neonatal outcome or in outcomes related to labor and delivery between the two groups, but a trend towards more obstetric interventions in the BPP group was noted. Another randomized controlled trial compared CST to modified BPP in 5,444 pregnancies. In this population, the frequency of adverse perinatal outcome following a negative modified BPP was no greater than that following a negative CST [38].

Alfirevic and Neilson [39] reviewed the literature concerning BPP and modified BPP in order to determine whether this is an effective and safe test for the assessment of fetal well-being in high-risk pregnancies.

Four randomized controlled studies were included in their analysis. They concluded that biophysical profile testing showed no obvious effect (either beneficial or deleterious) on pregnancy outcome when compared to other fetal testing modalities. However, they have noticed that although many reports of observational studies have been published, less than 3,000 pregnancies have been enrolled into randomized trials. Thus, they concluded that there is insufficient evidence from randomized trials to evaluate the use of BPP as a test of fetal well-being in high-risk pregnancies.

The logic for the clinical use of the BPP is similar to the logic applied for justifying the use of the NST or the CST, i.e. that the use of BPP in high-risk populations is associated with a low antepartum fetal death rate when compared to either the nontested low-risk population or to historical controls. No randomized controlled trials of tested versus nontested are available to substantiate this conclusion.

Doppler Evaluation of the Fetus

Doppler ultrasound is a noninvasive technique used to evaluate blood flow in maternal and fetal vessels. The shift in frequency of the sound wave caused by moving red blood cells enables determination of the blood flow velocity by waveform analysis.

The umbilical artery is the easiest organ to visualize for Doppler studies. The most simple and most common index to be evaluated is the systolic-diastolic ratio (S/D ratio). Normally, there is a forward flow throughout diastole and an S/D of less than 3 is reassuring in the third trimester. In cases of uterine and placental pathology, there is an increase in vascular resistance and decrease in diastolic flow, resulting in an elevated S/D ratio. In severe cases, absence of the diastolic flow or even a reversed diastolic flow may be noted (fig. 2). Randomized controlled trials have shown that abnormal umbilical artery velocity waveforms are valuable in identifying the growth-restricted fetus [40]. A meta-analysis of studies on pregnancies complicated by suspected fetal growth restriction revealed that the use of Doppler evaluation was associated with a significant improvement in prenatal outcome and a reduction of 38% in perinatal mortality [40].

The use of Doppler velocimetry in low risk pregnancies is much less promising. The current data reveal that routine Doppler ultrasound in low-risk or unselected populations does not confer benefit on mother or newborn. The American College of Obstetricians and Gynecologists therefore recommends using Doppler studies in adjunct to other fetal evaluation modalities but not as a screening test for fetal well-being [41].

Pitfalls and Dilemmas in the Interpretation of Continuous Electronic FHR Monitoring

The introduction of continuous electronic FHR monitoring (CEFARM) created a utopian belief that pregnancy and delivery are finally safe and that a perfect outcome could be guaranteed in all cases. There was an

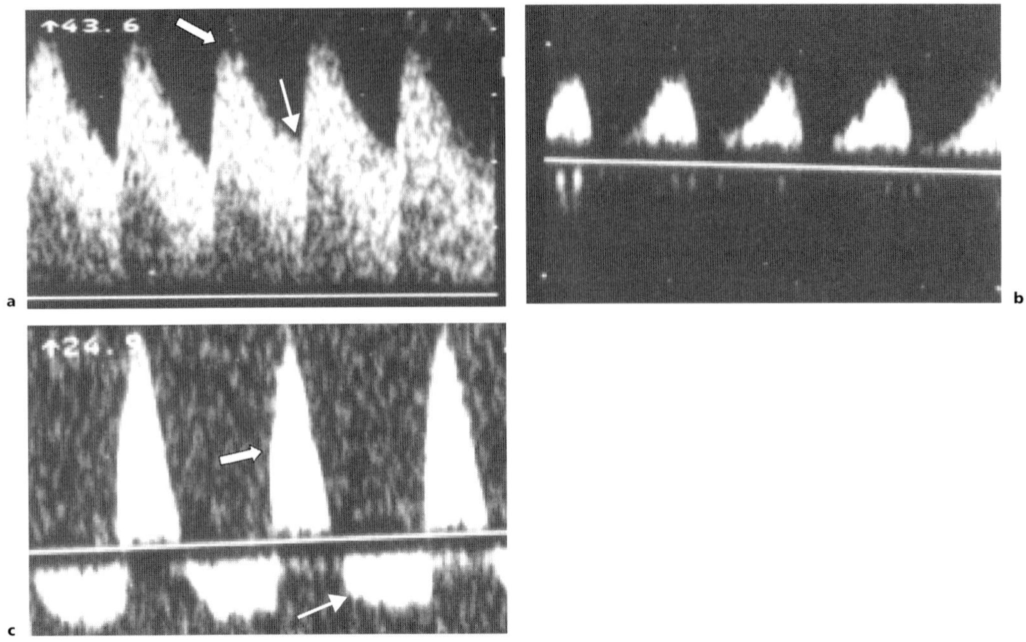

Fig. 2.

Doppler velocimetry in the fetus. **a** Normal flow, the systolic flow is marked by thick arrow. The diastolic flow is marked by a thin arrow. **b** Absent diastolic flow, only the systolic flow is observed. There is no diastolic flow. **c** Reverse diastolic flow, the systolic flow is marked by thick arrow. There is reverse diastolic flow marked by a thin arrow.

expectation that all perinatal damage or death will be prevented. In 1994, Symonds [42] found that about 70% of lawsuits related to neonatal brain damage and neurological disabilities were based on a nonreassuring CEFHRM. An assumption that was never proved is that fetal compromise develops in a gradual, progressive fashion which provides an 'intervention opportunity window' to improve the perinatal outcome. However, it is obvious that not all fetuses 'expire slowly' and that sudden deterioration such as in cases of placental abruption may occur.

Cesarean Section Rate and Neonatal Outcome. In almost all of the randomized controlled trials, CEFHRM was associated with an increase in the cesarean section rate without a significant improvement in neonatal outcome. Metabolic acidosis complicates up to 2% of all deliveries.

However, the rate of cesarean sections due to no reassuring tracing is well over 10%. There is, therefore, an urgent need for improving our ability to detect the hypoxic fetus. Techniques such as fetal ECG and pulse oximetry have been suggested. However, the clinical utility is still unproven.

CEFHRM and Cerebral Palsy. There has been no appreciable decline in the incidence of cerebral palsy (2/1,000) during the last 30 years since CEFHRM was introduced into obstetrical practice. However, there are other factors which influenced the rate of cerebral palsy during this period. The constant gradual improvement in the neonatal intensive care units, the introduction of the surfactant treatment, high-frequency ventilation and other techniques all dramatically improved the survival rates of the preterm and very low-birth-weight infants, which accounts for most of the cerebral palsy cases. The wide use of assisted reproductive technology has resulted in an increased incidence of multiple pregnancy and subsequent prematurity. The increased survival rate of asphyxiated term newborns has also added to the number of cases of cerebral palsy. Thus, the protective effect of CEFHRM might have been obscured by these improvements in survival rates.

Much effort has been devoted to identifying FHR patterns associated with neonatal brain damage. Todd et al. [43] examined the outcome of 2 year-old infants who were delivered electively before 34 weeks with an abnormal NST or Doppler study. Poor cognitive progress was more commonly noted with an abnormal NST compared to an abnormal Doppler. It was suggested that by the time a nonreassuring fetal status is diagnosed by antepartum testing, fetal brain damage has already become irreversible.

Other studies have shown that 75–92% of cerebral palsy cases are not related to perinatal asphyxia and occur during pregnancy or early in labor before CEFHRM has been applied [44, 45]. It seems, therefore, that these cases are not preventable by early obstetric intervention. In 1996, a committee opinion of the American College of Obstetricians and Gynecologists [46] addressed the relationship between perinatal asphyxia and the newborn neurological disability. It was concluded that the following four criteria must be present before a link can be made between perinatal asphyxia and cerebral palsy:

1 Umbilical artery acidemia with pH less than 7.0.
2 Apgar score 0–3 for longer than 5 min.

3 Neonatal neurological sequelae (hypotonia, seizures, coma).
4 Multiorgan system dysfunction.

Does FHR Monitoring Improve Perinatal Outcome?

The fundamental question in fetal monitoring remains whether any of these modalities improves perinatal outcomes.

Thacker and Berkelman [47] reviewed 600 articles to assess the accuracy and efficacy of the NST, CST and recording of fetal movements. Both the CST and the NST generally demonstrated low sensitivity and high rates of false-positivity. Only four randomized controlled trials have addressed these questions and none was of sufficient size to demonstrate whether there is a significant difference in outcome following use of the CST or the NST. A year later, Platt et al. [48] reviewed the impact of fetal testing of more than 200,000 pregnancies; almost 17,000 of these underwent various types of fetal surveillance tests during a 15-year period between 1971 and 1985. They concluded that fetal testing is beneficial since fetal death rate in selected high-risk patients was significantly lower when antepartum testing was utilized.

Mohide et al. [49] used the Oxford database of perinatal trials. The studies that were appropriately designed failed to show that the use of antepartum fetal testing is associated with improved perinatal outcome. Enkin et al. [50], in their 'guide to effective care in pregnancy and childbirth', had declared that antepartum tests are 'forms of care likely to be ineffective or harmful'.

Conclusion

Initially, there were great expectations from CEFHRM. The primary goal of fetal monitoring was, in a broad sense, to improve the short- and long-term perinatal outcome. It was hoped that fetal monitoring will enable an early and accurate diagnosis of fetal distress and will reduce unnecessary obstetric interventions.

In the late 1970s, the lack of randomized controlled trials and a steep rise in the cesarean delivery rate without a concomitant improvement in neonatal outcomes has started the debate about the effectiveness of the routine use of CEFHRM. In 1987, the American College of Obstetricians and Gynecologists recommended that auscultation was an acceptable alternative to CEFHRM in low risk deliveries. The debate continued and provocative statements such as *'Has it been an absurd dream... a kind of game for unoccupied physicists and obstetricians?'* or *'Are we ready to throw it out and go back with confidence to the 175-year-old methodÿof clinical auscultation?'* [51] continued to be heard among obstetricians.

Banta and Thacker [52] discussed the limited evidence-based benefit of CEFHRM compared to the possible additional harm and cost. They conclude that: 'the technical advances required in the demonstration that reliable recording could be done seem to have blinded most observers to the fact that this additional information will not necessarily produce better outcomes. The current daily practice therefore reveals a discrepancy between the evidence-based data, which did not show a significant benefit of CEFHRM, and the widespread use of this technology. However, following 30 years of experience with this technology it seems that it's well-spread use is irreversible at the present time.'

References

1 Douglas RG, Stromme WB: Operative Obstetrics. New York, Appleton-Century-Crofts, 1957, pp 413–430.

2 Da KN: Obstetric Forceps: Its history and Evolution. Mosby, St. Louis, 1929.

3 Gultekin-Zootzmann B: The history of monitoring the human fetus. J Perinat Med 1975;3:135–144.

4 Mayor H: Biblioth Univ. de Geneve, November 9, 1818, quoted by Thomas H: Classical Contributions to Obstetrics and Gynecology. Springfield, Thomas, 1935.

5 Le Jumeau JA (de Kergaradec) (1): Memoire sur l'Auscultation. Applique a l'Etude de la Grossesse, Paris, 1822.

6 Le Jumeau JA (de Kergaradec) (2): Ann Med Physiol 1822;1:344.

7 Kennedy E: Observations of Obstetrical Auscultation, with an Analysis of the Evidence of Pregnancy and an Inquiry into the Proofs of the Life and Death of the Foetus in Utero. Dublin, Hodges & Smith, 1833.

8 Kilian, quoted by Jaggard WW: in Hirst BC (ed): A System of Obstetrics. Philadelphia, Lea Broth, 1888.

9 Kehrer FA, quoted by Fischer WM: in Fischer WM, Halberstadt E, Ruttgers G (eds): Kardiotokographie. Stuttgart, Thieme, 1976.

10 Schwartz S: Arch Gynaekol. 1870;1:361.

11 Schatz F: Arch Gynaekol. 1885;25:159.

12 Winckel F: Lehrbuch der Geburtshilfe. Leipzig, Veit, 1893.

13 Seitz L: Die Fetalen Herztone Unter der Geburt, Munchen, 1903.

14 Cunningham FG, Gant NF, Leveno KJ, Gilstrap LC, Hauth JC, Wenstrom KD: Antepartum assessment; in: Williams Obstetrics, ed 21. New York, McGraw-Hill, 2001, pp 1095–1110.

15 Hon EH: The electronic evaluation of the fetal heart rate (preliminary report). Am J Obstet Gynecol 1958;75:1215–1230.

16 Hammacher K: Früherkennung intrauteriner Gefahrenzustände durch Electrophonocardiographie und Fotographie; in Elert R, Hates KA (eds): Prophylaxe frühkindlicher Hirnschäden. Stuttgart, Thieme, 1966, pp 120–132.

17 Ray M, Freeman RK, Pine S, Hesselgesser R: Clinical experience with the oxytocin challenge test. Am J Obstet Gynecol 1972;114:1–9.

18 Banta HD, Thacker SB: Assessing the cost and benefits of electronic fetal monitoring. Obstet Gynecol Surv 1979;34:627–642.

19 Ventura SJ, Martin JA, Curtin SC, Mathews TJ, Park MM: Births: Final data for 1998. Natl Vital Stat Rep 2000; 48:1–100.

20 Goodlin R: History of fetal monitoring. Am J Obstet Gynecol 1979;133:323–352.

21 Evertson LR, Gauthier RJ, Collea JV: Fetal demise following negative contraction stress tests. Obstet Gynecol 1978;51: 671–673.

22 Freeman RK, Anderson G, Dorchester W: A prospective multi-institutional study of antepartum fetal heart rate monitoring. II. Contraction stress test versus nonstress test for primary surveillance. Am J Obstet Gynecol 1982;143:778–781.

23 Freeman RK, Garite TJ, Nageotte MP: Fetal Heart Rate Monitoring, ed 2. Baltimore, Williams & Wilkins, 1991.

24 Manning FA, Platt LD, Sipos L: Antepartum fetal evaluation: Development of a fetal biophysical profile. Am J Obstet Gynecol 1980;136:787–795.

25 Dayal AK, Manning FA, Berek DJ, Mussalli GM, Avila C, Harman CR, Menticoglou S: Fetal death after normal biophysical profile score: An eighteen-year experience. Am J Obstet Gynecol 1999; 181:1231–1236.

26 Manning FA, Snijders RJ, Harman CR, Nicolaides K, Menticoglou S, Morrison I: Fetal biophysical score. VI. Correlation with antepartum umbilical venous fetal pH. Am J Obstet Gynecol 1993;169: 755–763.

27 Ribbert LMS, Snijders RJ, Nicolaides KH, Visser GH: Relationship of fetal biophysical profile score and blood gas values at cordocentesis in severely growth-retarded fetuses. Am J Obstet Gynecol 1990; 163:569–571.

28 Salvesen DR, Freeman J, Brudenell JM, Nicolaides KH: Prediction of fetal acidemia in pregnancies complicated by maternal diabetes by fetal biophysical profile scoring and fetal heart rate monitoring. Br J Obstet Gynecol 1993;100: 227–233.

29 Yoon BH, Romero R, Roh CR, Kim SH, Ager JW, Syn HC, et al: Relationship between the fetal biophysical profile score, umbilical artery velocimetry, and fetal blood gas status determined by cordocentesis. Am J Obstet Gynecol 1993;169: 1586–1594.

30 Manning FA, Bondji N, Harman CR, Casiro O, Menticoglou S, Morrison I, et al: Fetal assessment by fetal biophysical profile score. VIII. The incidence of cerebral palsy among tested and non-tested perinates. Am J Obstet Gynecol 1998;178: 696–706.

31 Manning FA, Lange IR, Morrison I, Harman CR: Fetal biophysical profile score and the non-stress test: A comparative trial. Obstet Gynecol 1984;64: 326–331.

32 Platt LD, Walla CA, Paul RH, Trujillo ME, Loessor CV, Jacobs ND, et al: A prospective trial of the fetal biophysical profile versus the non-stress test in the management of high-risk pregnancies. Am J Obstet Gynecol 1985;153:624–633.
33 Clark SL, Sabey P, Jolley K: Non stress testing with acoustic stimulation and amniotic fluid volume assessment: 5973 tests without unexpected fetal death. Am J Obstet Gynecol 1989;160:694–697.
34 Nageotte MP, Towers CV, Astra T, Freeman RK: Perinatal outcome with the modified biophysical profile. Am J Obstet Gynecol 1994;170:1672–1676.
35 Miller DA, Rabello YA, Paul RH: The modified biophysical profile: Antepartum testing in the 1990s. Am J Obstet Gynecol 1996;174:812–817.
36 American College of Obstetricians and Gynecologists: Antepartum Fetal Surveillance. ACOG Technical Bulletin 188. Washington, ACOG, 1994.
37 Alfirevic Z, Walkinshaw SA: A randomized controlled trial of simple compared with complex antenatal fetal monitoring after 42 weeks of gestation. Br J Obstet Gynecol 1995;102: 638–643.
38 Nageotte MP, Towers CV, Asrat T, Freeman RK, Dorchester W: The value of a negative antepartum test: Contraction stress test and modified biophysical profile. Obstet Gynecol 1994;84:231–234.
39 Alfirevic Z, Neilson JP: Biophysical profile for fetal assessment in high-risk pregnancies (Cochrane Review). The Cochrane Library, Issue 4. Oxford, Update Software, 1999.
40 Alfirevic Z, Neilson JP: Doppler ultrasonography in high-risk pregnancies: Systematic review with meta-analysis. Am J Obstet Gynecol 1995;172: 1379–1387.
41 American College of Obstetricians and Gynecologists: Intrauterine growth restriction. Practice Bulletin No. 12, 2000.
42 Symonds EM: Fetal monitoring: Medical and legal implications for the practitioner. Curr Opin Obstet Gynecol 1994;6: 430–433.
43 Todd AL, Trudinger BJ, Cole MJ, Cooney GH: Antenatal tests of fetal welfare and development at age 2 years. Am J Obstet Gynecol 1992;167:66–71.
44 Stanley FJ, Blair E: Why have we failed to reduce the frequency of cerebral palsy? Med J Aust 1991;154:623–626.
45 Phelan JP, Ahn MO, Korst L, Martin GI: Is intrapartum fetal brain injury in the term fetus preventable? Am J Obstet Gynecol 1996;174:318.
46 American College of Obstetricians and Gynecologists: Use and abuse of the Apgar score. Committee opinion No. 174, January 1996.
47 Thacker SB, Berkelman RL: Assessing the diagnostic accuracy and efficacy of selected antepartum fetal surveillance techniques. Obstet Gynecol Surv 1986;41:121–141.
48 Platt LD, Paul RH, Phelan J, Walla CA, Broussard P: Fifteen years of experience with antepartum fetal testing. Am J Obstet Gynecol 1987;156:1509–1515.
49 Mohide PT, Keirse MJ: Biophysical assessment of fetal wellbeing; in Chambers I, Enkin M, Keirse MJ (eds): Effective Care Pregnancy and Childbirth, vol I. Pregnancy. New York, Oxford University Press, 1991, pp 477–510.
50 Enkin M, Keirse MJ, Renfrew M, Neilson J: A Guide to Effective Care in Pregnancy and Childbirth, ed 2. New York, Oxford University Press, 1995, pp 410–422.

51 Sureau C: Historical perspectives: Forgotten past, unpredictable future. Baillières Clin Obstet Gynaecol 1996; 10:167–184.

52 Banta DH, Thacker SB: Historical controversy in health technology assessment: The case of electronic fetal monitoring. Obstet Gynecol Surv 2001;56:707–719.

Michael Y. Divon, MD

Department of Obstetrics and Gynecology, Lenox Hill Hospital,
130 E 77th Street, New York, NY 10021 (USA)
Tel. +1 212 434 2160, Fax +1 212 434 2180, E-Mail Mdivon@lenoxhill.net

Blazer S, Zimmer EZ (eds):
The Embryo: Scientific Discovery and Medical Ethics.
Basel, Karger, 2005, pp 309–328

New Horizons in Obstetric and Gynecologic Ultrasound

Ilan E. Timor-Tritsch

Division of Obstetrical and Gynecological Ultrasound, Department of Obstetrics and Gynecology, New York University School of Medicine, New York, N.Y., USA

New technologies, in general, are first regarded by suspicion, by skepticism, overly strong critique, and sometimes treated with overt and aggressive hostility. Ultrasonography is no exception. In the last 36 years ultrasound (US) progressed from the B mode, to grayscale, to transvaginal sonography, to color and power Doppler, and finally to the almost-real-time three-dimensional (3D) and four-dimensional (4D) imaging. All this progress was achieved thanks to the 'explosion' of computer technology, and to the understanding of US physics. However, maybe above all, it is thanks to the endless energy of those, who searched for ways to apply newer and better imaging technologies in clinical medicine.

It all started by an article that appeared in the *Journal of Obstetrics and Gynecology* of the British Commonwealth in 1965 entitled 'Diagnostic imaging on sonar and obstetrics and gynecology' [1]. It was written by Ian Donald who at that time was a professor of midwifery at the University of Glasgow. He wrote, 'We are coming to the stage at which US findings are beginning to be clinical useful as well as scientifically interesting. In solving some problems, we may have created others, but in

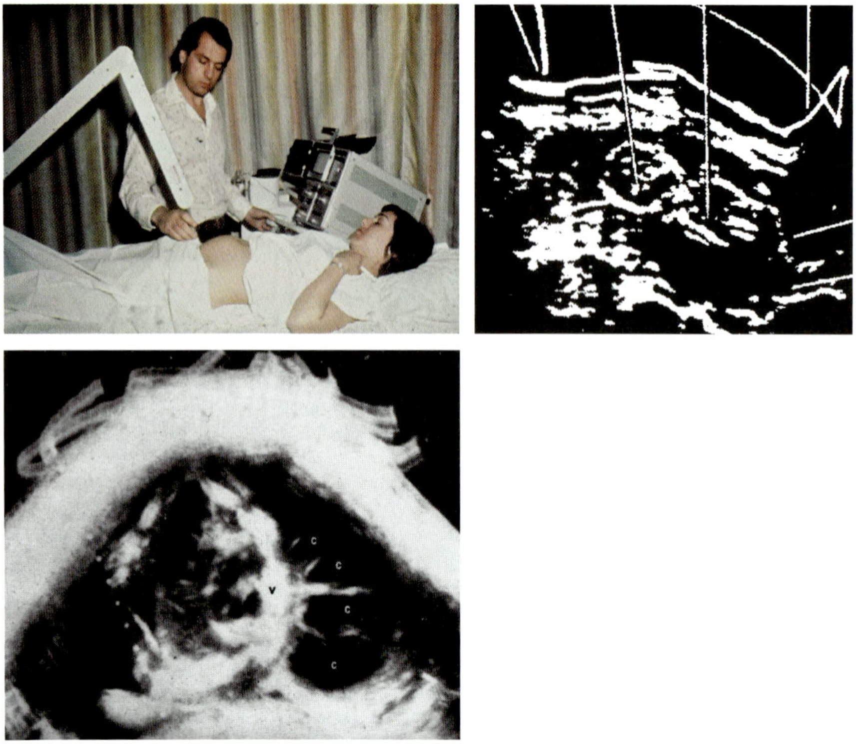

a b c

Fig. 1.

a The static arm B-mode system. **b** The third trimester fetus was depicted using the B-mode technology. **c** Compound scanning using the grayscale technique showing a cystic hygroma.

the hands of more capable than our own new diagnostic horizons may have opened up'.

I was fortunate to be able to watch the development of ultrasonography in the last 30 years. When the first static scanners appeared and the company modified a commercially available oscilloscope adding a scanning arm (fig. 1a) with a single transducer crystal in 1974, they created what appeared to be an amazing static image of the fetus and was able to penetrate the female pelvis outlining the uterus and some obvious pathologies (fig. 1b). A short time after grayscale was added to the system, which improved the resolution and were able to image a structure from almost all angles, displaying shades of gray to better define those structures (fig. 1c).

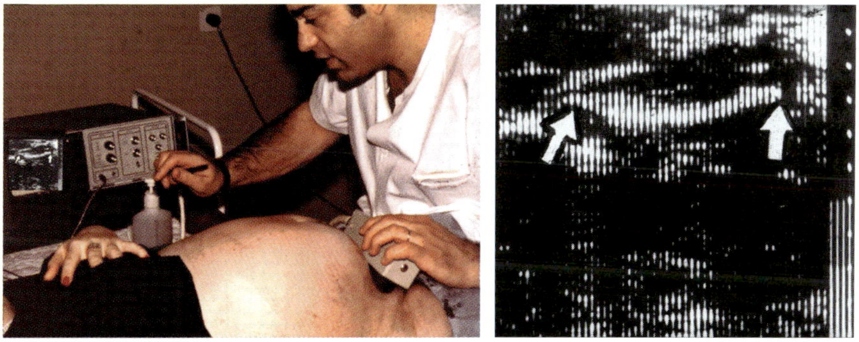

a b

Fig. 2.

a The first 'real-time' US equipment with a linear transducer. **b** A fetal femur depicted with a real-time 64 crystal transducer probe.

In 1975, real-time grayscale US appeared and two or three companies competed to display moving structures using a single row of 64 transducers in a linear transducer head (fig. 2a), generating pictures with eight shades of gray (fig. 2b). At that time this appeared to be an amazing development! My evaluation is that the introduction of the real-time US was indeed the turning point in obstetric and gynecologic diagnostic US. Later, the transducer technology was developed and it was possible to display 64–256 shades of gray representing the continuous improvement of this technology using currilinear linear technology (fig. 3). In 1986, the use of color-coded flow spread and was widely available (fig. 4). Not only could the direction of the flow be displayed but one could perform flow velocity measurements by placing small windows on blood vessels and extract important information to determine blood flow characteristics (fig. 5).

Even though experiments using the US transducer through the vagina started several years earlier the first commercially available high frequency transvaginal US equipment became widely used in 1984–1986. This high-frequency transducer technology at the time used mechanical scan heads made important clinical advances. Using a 5–6.5 MHz transducer placed close to the pelvic organs in gynecological patients or early pregnancy pictures of extremely high resolution became a reality. The extremely accurate description of fetal anatomy became possible.

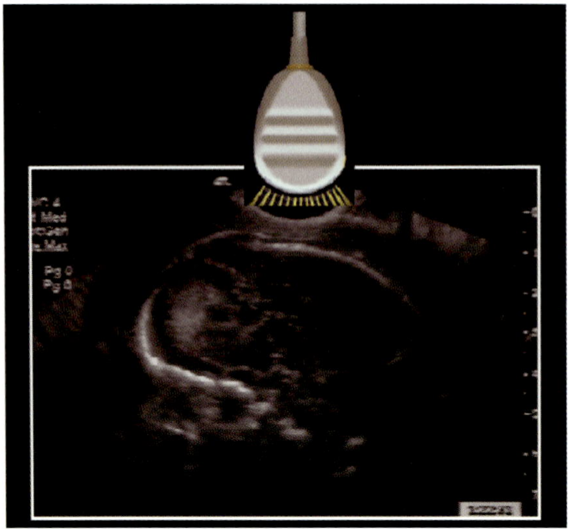

Fig. 3.
Curvilinear US transducer displaying 256 shades of gray and compound scanning combined.

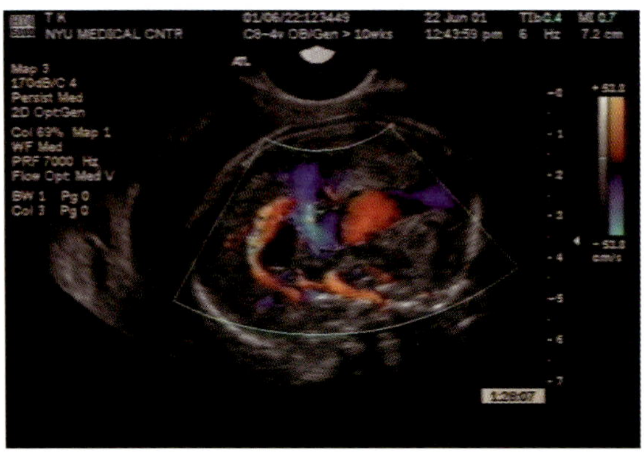

Fig. 4.
Color Doppler images of fetal brain in the median plane.

In 1988, power Doppler US was introduced and in spite of the fact that the direction of the flow cannot be assessed by using this technology, it presented advantages of detecting low velocity blood flow (fig. 6).

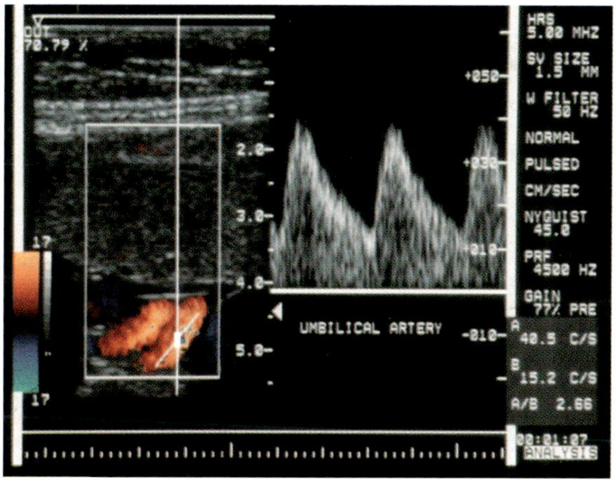

Fig. 5.
Blood flow velocity wave forms enabled by Color Doppler technology.

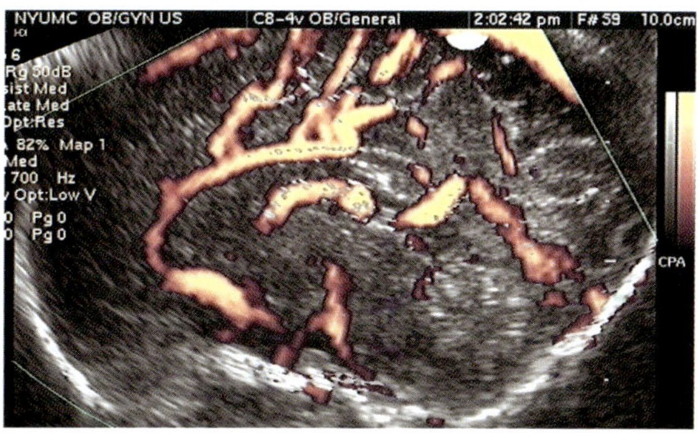

Fig. 6.
Power Doppler depiction of the main blood vessels of the fetal brain in a sagittal plane.

We live in a three-dimensional world. Our vision enables us to estimate distances to remote objects and we are able to assess the form of the object in their true appearance. It was always the goal of imaging specialists to depict organs in three dimensions. The same was the goal of the US manufacturers to enable the production of US technology that would display the fetus (fig. 7) or the female pelvis not only in 2D but also in its

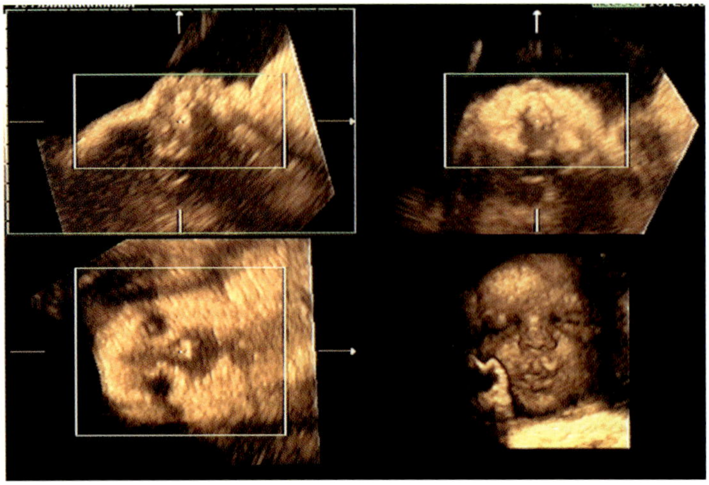

Fig. 7.
Orthogonal US display of the fetal head and the 3D reconstruction of the face.

3D appearance. In 1987, the Japanese Kazunori Baba produced the first 3D pictures of a fetus [2, 3]. At that time computer technology was such that a small room filled with computers could produce one single 3D picture of a fetus in 10–24 h. The fast development of computer technology reached a critical point in the 1990s when 3D US became a reality. From here to the near real-time or 4D US is only a matter of months or several short years (fig. 8). Indeed, at this time 4D US is considered the leading edge of US technology and even though the skeptics are again asking questions about its clinical importance, history teaches us that these in the near future real-time rendering will be achieved. US technology will probably enable a most important step in fetal diagnosis.

The Structural and Genetic Fetal Scan

The development in the structural evaluation of fetuses parallels the development of computer as well as the transducer probe technology. Thirty years ago anomalies were detected at 30 weeks' gestation. Twenty years ago, the same anomalies were detected earlier at 20 weeks. About 10 years ago, we started to detect that same anomalies at 15 weeks. Due to the

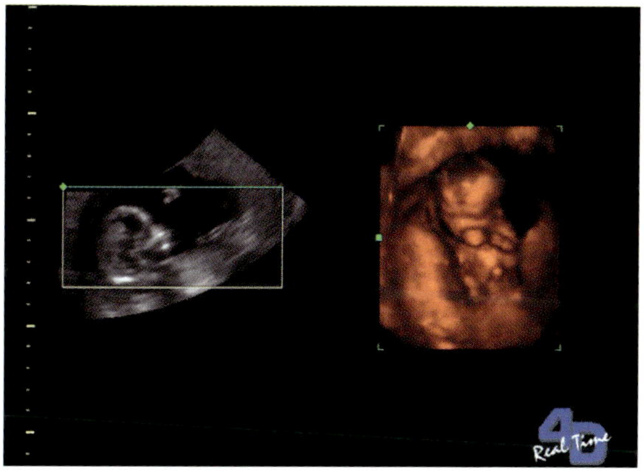

Fig. 8.
The 4D modality displays the 2D as well as the 3D pictures side by side. The 3D image is updated at a high rate to be able to create the impression of a moving fetus.

development of high-resolution transducers, most of them transvaginal, we are able to detect fetal anomalies as early as 11–14 weeks. It is extremely interesting to ask the questions of what limits can we achieve in the future. Of course there are no studies yet to prove that the structure evaluation at 11–14 weeks changes outcome it is, however, expected that it will do so in the future.

The question is why should we perform an early scan at 11–14 weeks. The answer is that it can probably combine nuchal translucency (NT) and nasal bone (NB) screening with a meaningful structural evaluation of the early fetus at the same time. It can potentially reduce the cost of prenatal care providing a one-stop-shopping for prenatal evaluation. It may also reduce the number of patient trips to the doctor. Early diagnosis may lead to early counseling and management plans. We can offer CVS done around 12–14 weeks, and if the need of termination of pregnancy is arising, this can be performed before 14 or 15 weeks making it an easy and less dangerous procedure.

Can anomalies be seen before 13–14 weeks? The answer is very simple and documented in the literature [4]. Some can be seen even before 14 weeks. This is true for a large number of anomalies and because the entire fetus can be put in the focal range of the probe indeed the entire fetal

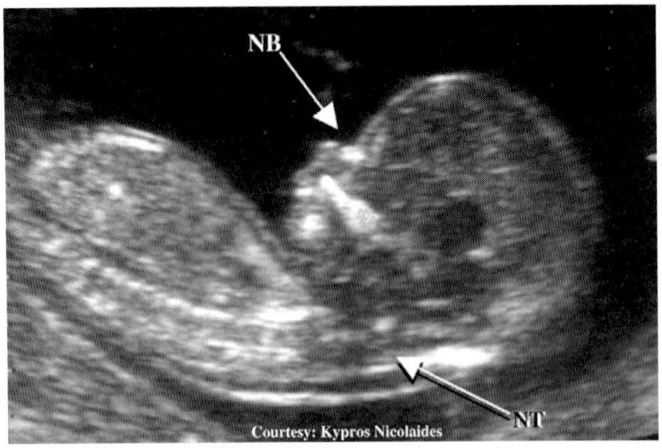

Fig. 9.
Sagittal image of a fetus at about 12 weeks showing the nuchal translucency (NT) and the nasal bone (NB) (courtesy: K. Nicolaides).

body can be evaluated. The same question can be asked for detection of anomalies before 14 weeks. The answer is that one can probably see major anomalies and the advantages cited earlier can be applied to this age as well.

The proliferation of sonographic markers of chromosomal aneuploidies has proliferated in the last 10 years. The NT and the detection of the NB are two extremely important additions to the sonographic detection of anomalies (fig. 9). Kypros Nicolaides at the Fetal Medicine Foundation (FMF) in London was instrumental in testing and introducing these two markers and making them available for mass screening of chromosomal (and other) anomalies [5]. At this time several countries have launched significant and large research projects in duplicating the results of the FMF and it seems that the NT and the NB [6] will be the most important sonographic markers to detect not only chromosomal but other congenital diseases of the fetus. Combining several biochemical tests with the sonographic markers the Fetal Medicine Foundation achieved detection rates close to 90% of chromosomal anomalies.

Ultrasound-Guided Intrauterine Procedures

These procedures are not new. In the early 1980s, intrauterine procedures already started to be performed by image guidance. Termination of

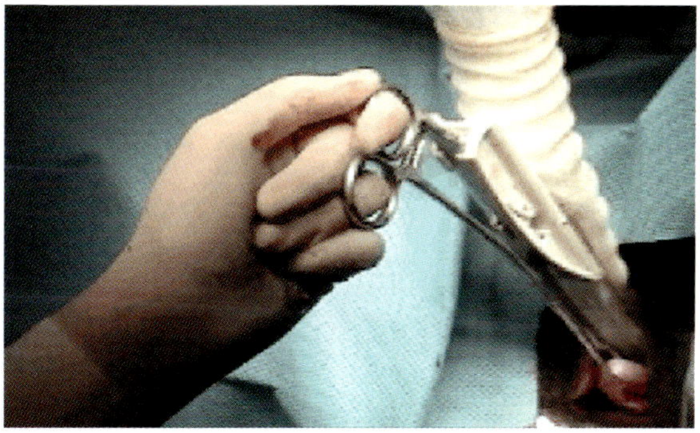

Fig. 10.
Performing intrauterine procedures with real time transvaginal image guidance. The transducer is attached to an adapter which in turn is slid over a special tenaculum.

pregnancies were guided by transabdominal US. The question is what is new in image procedures? The answer again is related to transvaginal US. Using a commercially available transvaginal probe, and attaching to it, an adaptor was developed. A specially designed tenaculum is coupled with the adapter, which then is mated to the transvaginal US probe. A special speculum is also used in which the upper blade is replaced by two lateral blades creating free space to accommodate the transvaginal transducer (fig. 10). When intrauterine procedures are performed a real-time image is provided for the operator who holds the tenaculum in one hand while performing the intrauterine procedure with the other. The aim of this system is to provide additional safety and guide the operator during these procedures.

Image Quality (Resolution)

It is beyond the scope of this chapter to present a description of the gradual improvement in image quality of the different US machines. However, it is important to mention that significant improvements in resolution occur in short periods of time in all US machines. This difference in picture quality can only be really appreciated when one compares images 5–10 years ago to those available today (fig. 11). The constant improvement in resolution is

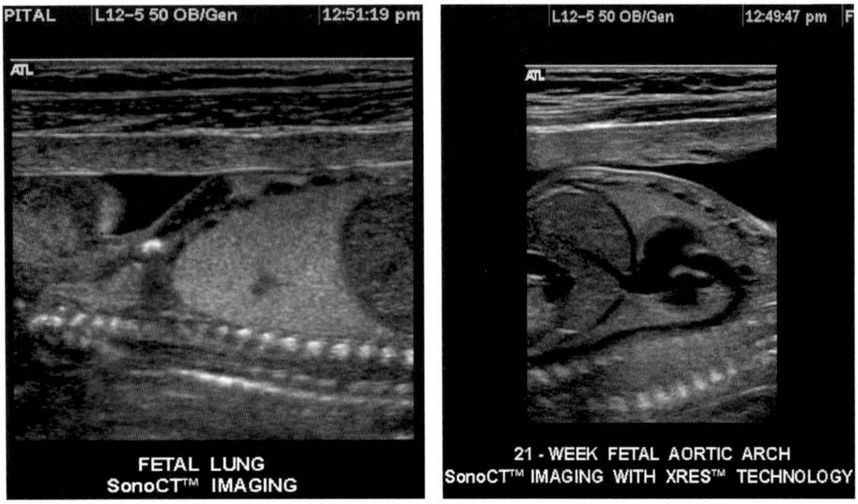

a b

Fig. 11.

Remarkable detail generated by a combination of a high resolution high frequency linear transducer (12–5 MHz) and the Sono CT technology (courtesy: Phillips-ATL).

instrumental in accurately accessing and better determining of therapy at a much earlier point in gestation and finally determining early pregnancy. In gynecology the high resolution images coupled with color Doppler or power Doppler enable better characterization of ovarian pathology as well as the presence or the inflammatory tubal disease. Lately, due to the endless improvements in the US technology the old B mode compound scanning and the high resolution real time technologies were combined creating panoramic pictures (fig. 12). The high quality images in obstetrics and gynecology enable precise needle placement into various organs or organ systems for diagnosis as well as to initiate treatment. The questions is at this point is what really is the limit of resolution? Trying to answer this question a research group in Norway, led by Drs. Sturla Eik-Ness and Harm Gerd Blaas, tries to develop an ultra-high transducer capable of obtaining a 3D volumes with a resolution of 0.2–0.3 mm. One really wonders about the possible tissue details presented by such a high resolution. It is therefore not hard to imagine that pushing back the boundaries the first fetal structural evaluations almost entirely into the late first trimester is not far away.

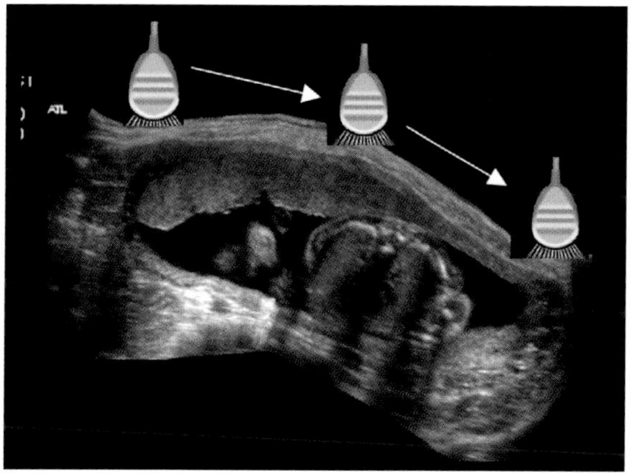

Fig. 12.
The generation of the panoramic US image of an interior placenta by sliding the transducer along the maternal abdomen (courtesy: Phillips-ATL).

Miniaturization of Ultrasound Machines

Producing smaller and smaller US machines is a new trend which started 5–6 years ago. It became a reality when the fast-developing computer technology enabled smaller computer components and faster processing speed. Miniaturization increases portability (fig. 13), therefore a reasonably good US machine can be used at the bedside (fig. 14), in the emergency or operating room (fig. 15), at the battle field and even in space. It certainly decreases the cost and it decreases power needs utilizing batteries. These systems can be small enough to be hand carried, but they also can be coupled to commercially available laptop computers called laptop-based systems or docked to a larger customary US machine. These small scanners present the ultimate in portability. Data can be collected easily, stored on the hard disk, and some of the systems have color and power Doppler, multifocal zones and several other features. The smallest US system is the 'wearable' system (fig. 16) that brings us to the questions of the real limits of shrinking these US machines. Lately the cell phone and the small hand-held computer systems were brought under the same 'cover'. Connecting the small US machines to a phone line may in the future enable the patient to use the system themselves and transmit data to the Medical Center from their homes.

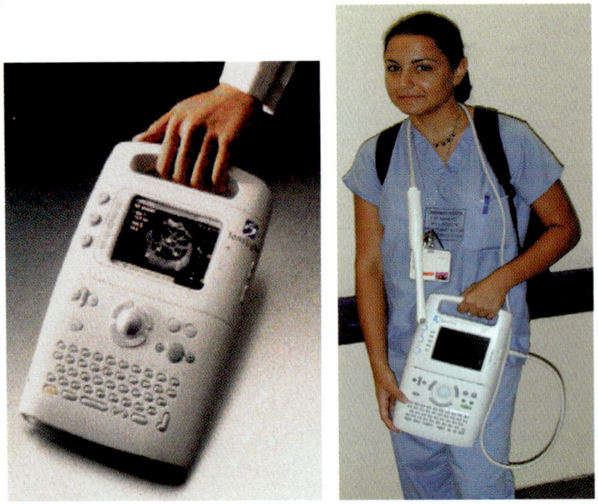

a b

Fig. 13.
a The hand carried small portable US system by Sonosite (courtesy: Sonosite). **b** Residents carry the machine to the emergency room.

Teleultrasound in Obstetrics and Gynecology

At present, teleultrasound is not new any more. The medical data was first transmitted over telephone lines in the United Kingdom. There were two studies validating the use of teleultrasound in patient care by Malone et al. [7, 8] in Boston. At this time, the new addition to using these systems is the Internet. Such a technology is instrumental in education, consultations and teaching at conferences. Teleultrasound is nothing more than transmission of US pictures and voice over (or other) telephone lines and it also provides the convenience of an excellent US service in offices were it is unavailable. It is a relatively inexpensive system which enables the expert to be available for a consult in remote places saving time and resources.

With the development of broadband connection via the Internet or other hardware based connections, the idea of performing US-guided surgery by remote consultation and guidance appeared. In a case of a twin to twin transfusion ligation of the cord of one twin was performed successfully.

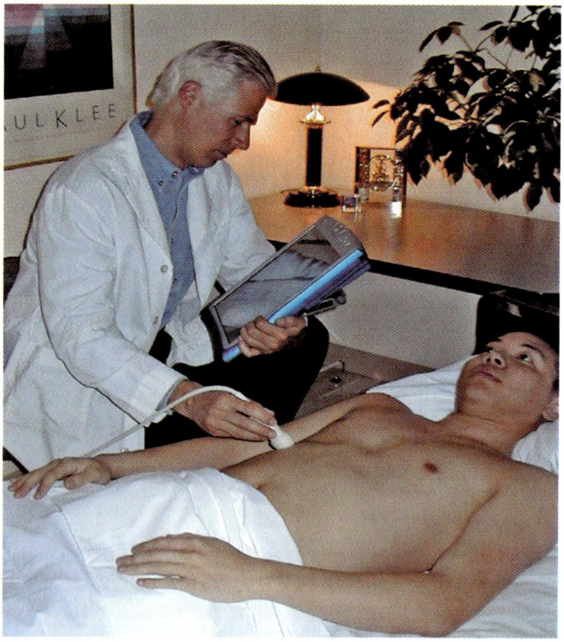

Fig. 14.
The laptop-based system (courtesy: Terason).

The Internet

Internet technology allows us to do old tasks in new ways. But more importantly, we can perform new tasks that were previously impossible. It is known that the Internet is relatively slow to transfer large files; therefore, the future is to increase transmissible volumes by using the broader band lines to transmit more and faster at a lesser expense. However, the use of the Internet provided us with a very interesting and medically relevant interaction. These interactions take place between the provider, the expert, the patient, and the insurance companies (fig. 17). The practitioner can connect to an expert to seek guidance. The patient can seek connection to the doctor wanting to know more about the disease. The same patient can use the Internet and a database, read articles not only about the disease and the treatment but also data on the performance of his or her provider. The situation may become even more complex by the fact that the insurance

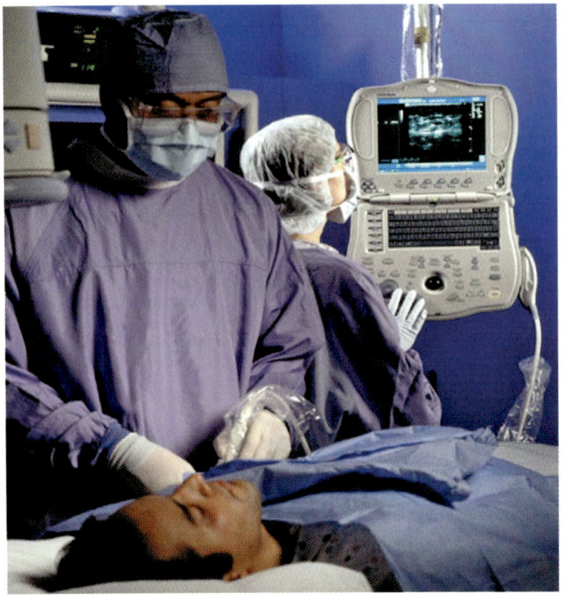

Fig. 15.
The laptop-based hogig-Book in the operating theatre (courtesy: General Electric).

company can keep track of the doctors' practices and at the same time draw information from databases about procedures and about rendering customary medical care to their patients. This situation is changing the reality of practicing medicine (particularly in the USA).

The Internet is based upon digital technology. In the future, digital US data will be transmitted, stored, and available via some future form of the Internet. The fact is that the number of Internet users is increasing constantly. The consequences of patients and insurance companies can scrutinize medical information and information about their caregivers is already in place making all involved quite nervous. We feel that the practice of medicine and of US will never be the same as before.

An additional problem in medicine and in US is that of reporting and of image archiving. Archiving of data using diverse and many reporting systems have to be brought under the same umbrella. This new archiving and reporting system will probably be the DICOM system (digital imaging and communication in medicine). This standard reporting and imaging

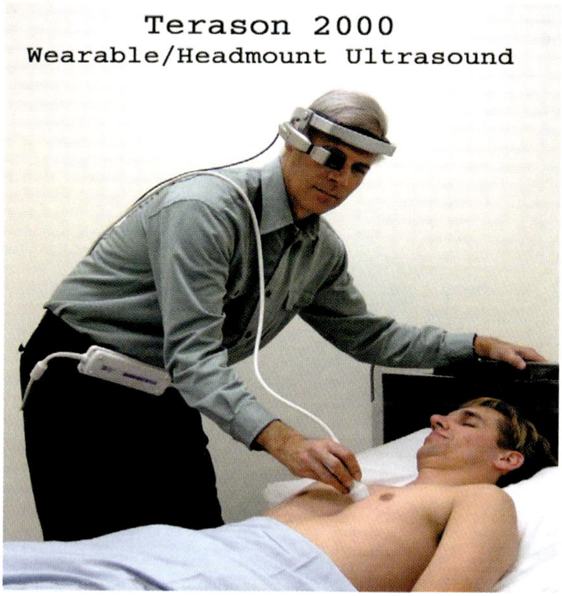

Fig. 16.
The smallest US system of all. The 'wearable' system by Terason.

archiving modality has to be present on every single piece of equipment manufactured after the year 2000.

What does DICOM do for US laboratories? It presents low-cost image archiving. It will make structured reporting uniform. A structured report provides previous reports, procedures, and images. It links the text, measurements, and images. It provides coding and facilitates computer outcome analysis.

3D Ultrasound

3D US is mentioned above; however, since my evaluation is that in the future all US machine will have 3D US available in one form or another, I consider it important to expand on this modality.

3D US is a series of 2D image slices saved into a volume with the possibility to display it with various modalities: multiplanar imaging (fig. 18); surface

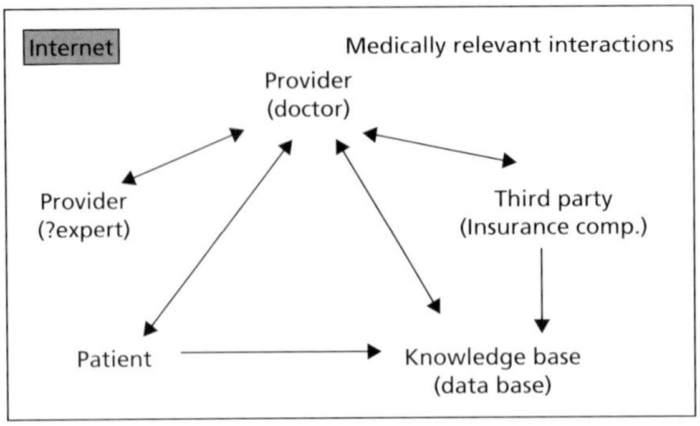

Fig. 17.
Diagram of the relationships between providers, patients, insurance companies and databases (courtesy: Dr. Ivan Zador).

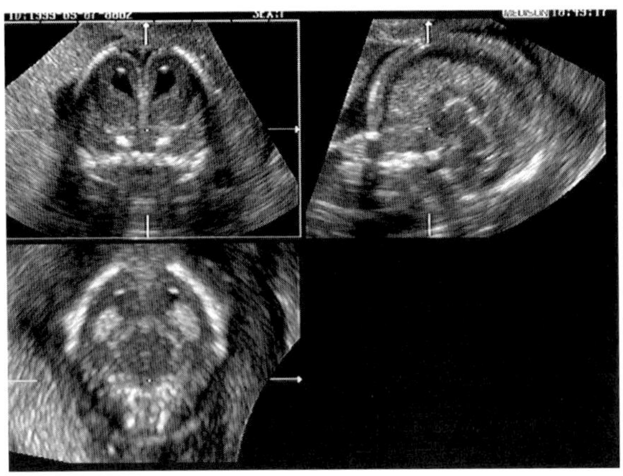

Fig. 18.
Orthogonal planes of the fetal brain at 20 weeks.

rendering (fig. 19) and X-ray mode (fig. 20). The volumes can be displayed, resliced, restudied, saved for future studies, mailed, taught, and used to perform measurements in the saved volume.

One of the important features of 3D US is the speed with which the volume is acquired. Scanning speed is the time required to scan once

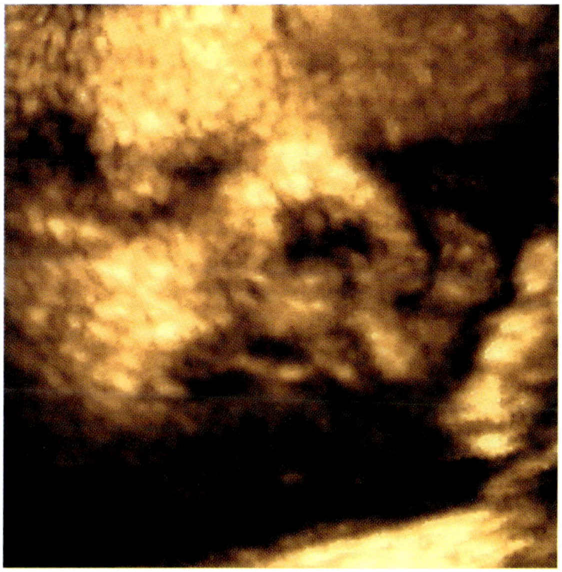

Fig. 19.
3D reconstruction of a fetal face.

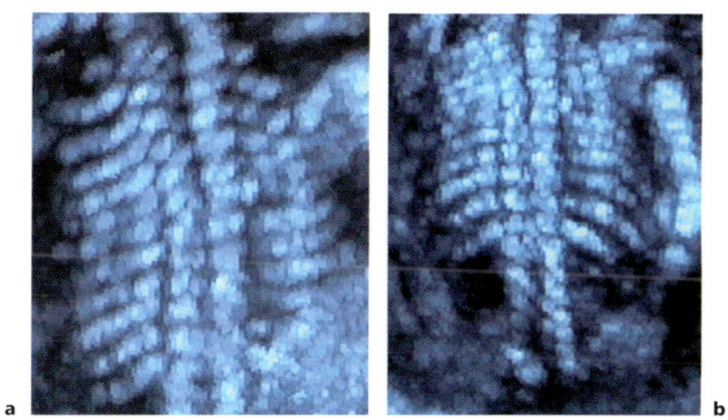

Fig. 20.
Transparency or X-ray mode of the spine and ribs (**a**) the ribs (**b**) the lowest rib is the twelfth rib.

through the volume. Fast scanning speed is considered to be 2–3 s and is good for moving structures. Therefore, it is used in obstetrics. Slower scanning speeds are those of 5–10 s which are employed for acquiring static volumes and used mostly in gynecology. Ultra-fast speed is less than 1s and is used in real-time or near real-time (4D) scanning. Using ultra-fast scanning speeds about 6–24 volumes per second can be displayed on the monitor. The ultra-fast scanning speed enables a near real-time display of motion and is used mostly in obstetrics. True real-time scanning will be developed in the future using two-dimensional array transducers, since the main impediment in displaying volume in real-time is the mechanical transducer. The 2D array transducers will significantly speed up the acquisition of the volumes.

Testimony to the fast developing area of 3D US is the dozens of articles, which appear every month in the different Obstetrics/Gynecology journals.

The future of 3D US is clear: every US machine will eventually have 3D capability. Volume acquisition and later evaluation as well as automated measurements will probably be an important feature. I predict that miniaturization will enable 3D US devices to appear on small US equipment in the near future. Connectivity will enable easy expert input. I predict that in the future expert referrals through the Internet will emerge which in turn change the role of sonographers and sonologists in obstetric and gynecologic US. As far as the future of 4D is concerned, machines will also have 4D capability when this is available fetal physiology and behavior will be reevaluated using the 4D US technology. Intrauterine US-guided procedures may utilize the real time technology to improve outcome.

Training, Education, Accreditation

More sophisticated US equipment needs sonologists and sonographers with better training and a good quality assurance. Educational CD Rom, information via the Internet and conferences of all sorts are vital to enable education.

US training simulators may become important in training sophisticated sonographers and sonologists. The simulators are able to provide grayscale color Doppler mode and volume based US training. Using these simulators

US images can appear on the screen in real-time as the user begins to scan and the images are similar to the images seen when scanning a live patient. Using these simulators, the user can compare his or her performance with those of an expert; therefore, the learning curve can be significantly reduced.

Conclusions

The major milestones in obstetric and gynecologic US were reviewed in order to put those developments and the present status of obstetric and gynecologic US into perspective. US is the right hand of the modern obstetric and gynecologic provider. We are living in exciting times in technical development of computers and therefore of US technology. 3D US opened a new horizon in obstetric and well as gynecologic diagnosis and treatment. The present status of 3D and 4D US may be only the beginning of what technology promises us in the future. Combined with advances in technology and connectivity, the world is shrinking and expertise is becoming available to all those interested in it and to the benefit of our patients. Watch out for new US and other technologies and their clinical utility in the next 5–10 years.

References

1 Donald I: Diagnostic uses of sonar in obstetrics and gynaecology. J ObstetÿGynaecol Br Commwlth 1965; 72:907.

2 Baba K, Okai T, Satoh K: Development of scan head position indicator for ultrasonic fetal three-dimensional reconstruction. Jpn J Med Ultrasonics 1986;13:121–122.

3 Baba K, Satoh K, Sakamoto S, Okai T, Ishii S: Non-invasive three-dimensional imaging system for fetus in utero; in Maeda K (ed): The Fetus as a Patient. Amsterdam, Excerpta Medica, 1987, pp 111–116.

4 Bronshtein M, Zimmer EZ (eds): Transvaginal Sonography of the Normal and Abnormal Fetus. London, Parthenon, 2002.

5 Nicolaides KH, Snijders RJM, Sebire N (eds): The 11–14 Week Scan: The Diagnosis of Fetal Abnormalities. London, Parthenon, 1999.

6 Cicero S, Curcio P, Papageorghiou A, Sonek J, Nicolaides K: Absence of nasal bone in fetuses with trisomy 21 at 11–14 weeks of gestation an observational study. Lancet 2001;358: 1665–1667.

7 Malone FD, Athanassiou A, Craigo SD, Simpson LL, D'Alton ME: Cost issues surrounding the use of computerized telemedicine for obstetric ultrasonography. Ultrasound Obstet Gynecol 1998; 12:120–124.

8 Malone FD, Athanassiou A, Nores J, D'Alton ME: Effect of ISDN bandwidth on image quality for telemedicine transmission of obstetric ultrasonography. Telemed J 1998;4:161–165.

Ilan E. Timor-Tritsch, MD

Division of Obstetrical and Gynecological Ultrasound,
Department of Obstetrics and Gynecology,
New York University School of Medicine,
530 First Avenue, Suite 7V, New York, NY 10016 (USA)
Tel. +1 212 263 0510, Fax +1 212 263 8887, E-Mail Ilan.Timor@med.nyu.edu,
JosepcO2@med.nyu.edu

Blazer S, Zimmer EZ (eds):
The Embryo: Scientific Discovery and Medical Ethics.
Basel, Karger, 2005, pp 329–339

The Status of the Embryo under Israeli Law

Tova Strasberg-Cohen
Supreme Court of Israel, Jerusalem, Israel

Israeli law generally regards the right to life as a supreme right. The recognition of life's sanctity, and its protection by our legal system, have been basic principles of Israel's legislation and adjudication ever since the establishment of the State. Basic Law: Human Dignity and Liberty, which is a part of Israel's emerging constitution, was enacted in 1992. The first clause reads: 'Fundamental human rights in Israel are founded upon recognition of the value of the human being, the sanctity of human life, and the principle that all persons are free; these rights shall be upheld in the spirit of the principles set forth in the Declaration of the Establishment of the State of Israel'.

From the right to life emanates the duty to preserve life. This understanding, which is fundamental to legal and medical ethics, gives rise to complex questions. A few of these have come before Israeli courts. The protection of 'human life' brings up the issue of who is a 'human being'. One facet of that issue is the question whether an embryo is a 'human being'.

Is an Embryo a 'Human Being'?

The boundaries of our definition of a 'human being' are also the boundaries of the application of our law, of our most basic norms, and of the rights and duties which derive therefrom. At what moment does life begin? That is a complex and controversial question. It has received many answers in different legal systems: some regard the moment of insemination as the beginning of life; some position the beginning of life at various stages during pregnancy; and there are several other approaches [for a survey of the various positions on this issue, see ref. 1]. Some modern legal systems consider that giving the embryo rights and protecting those rights is called for starting at the 24th week of pregnancy. This is when the embryo is for the first time able to sustain itself independently [2]. The question is relevant, inter alia, to the protection of pre-birth life during pregnancy, as well as that of pre-embryonic life. It has also been considered in the context of abortion [1, at 24]. Our constitutional approach makes us recoil from turning a human being into an object or an instrument [1, at 29]. Should an embryo, or even a fertilized ovum, be defined as a 'human being', then its genetic manipulation might be regarded as infringing its rights to life, to the wholeness of its body, and to its dignity as a human being.

As Chief Justice Shamgar of the Israeli Supreme Court said, 'The role of law is to protect the human being in its individuality, so that it does not become a mere instrument for the attainment of others' goals' [1, at 29]. If the embryo is not a 'human being', it isn't an 'individual' in the sense mentioned by Chief Justice Shamgar. In this case the consideration of protecting its dignity is relatively minor, and we must look for other justifications for our resistance to its genetic manipulation. This will especially be the case where the parents, whose rights should also be respected, want such manipulation to be performed.

Many statutes use the term 'human being' or 'person' [see, for example: The Nationality Law, 5712–1952, at clause 13; The Adoption of Children Law, 5741–1981, at clause 35; The Defamation Law, 5725–1965, at clause 1; The Law Banning Driving Vehicles on the Beach, 5757–1997, at clause 2; The Anatomy and Pathology Law, 5713–1953, at clause 2]. Yet no statute defines the term. Our Penal Law uses the term frequently but does not define it [Penal Law, 5737–1977]. So does Basic Law: Human Dignity and Liberty, which was meant to accord basic rights to 'human beings' but does not define the term. Clause 2 of the Basic Law states that 'There shall be no violation of the life, body or dignity of any person as such'. Other clauses of this basic law state that one cannot harm or infringe another person's liberty, property and privacy. The Law Banning Genetic Intervention defines 'human cloning' but does not define the term 'human being' [3]. Still, in that Act, the definition of 'human cloning' refers to 'a human being or an embryo' [3, at clause 2]. Therefore, an 'embryo' in this act is a distinct entity from a 'human being'. The regulations of 1980 which permit medical experiments on human beings, subject to certain conditions, do not define a 'human being' either [4]. The lack of a definition of a 'person' or 'human being' in the various statutes might derive from the general difficulty of defining the essence of humanity, or from the difficulty of doing so regarding a particular statute. Still, in cases which come before the courts, these terms must be given a concrete meaning, according to the purpose of the statute under consideration, to our basic law and to the basic principles of our legal system.

Clause 1 of the Capacity and Guardianship Law states that 'Every person shall be capable of having rights and obligations from the completion of his birth until his death' [5]. This act does not state when the completion of the birth process takes place, nor does it define the term 'person'; it sets down the time from when a 'person' is capable of having rights and obligations. It seems that under this act the embryo has no rights [5].[1]

As one court said, 'Where the legislature considered the embryo to have a certain right – it has stated so explicitly…' [6]. So, for example, the Succession Law [5725–1965, at clause 3(b)] explicitly gives a right of inheritance to an embryo born within 300 days after the death of the bestower.

The legislature didn't specify when the 'completion of birth' does occur and at which point a 'person' starts to be capable of having rights and obligations. 'Completion of birth' is usually considered to occur at the moment

[1] See also F.C. (Tel-Aviv) 4570/98 Roe et al. vs. The Attorney General, Dinim (Family Law) Vol. A 45, at paragraph 12 of Judge Geifman's decision. The courts' tendency to regard embryos as lacking legal capacity was also manifested in an obiter dictum by Judge Susskind in Motion (Jerusalem) 249/98 F.C. (Jerusalem) 13751/97 Doe, Represented by his Mother, his Natural Guardian vs. Roe et al., Takdin (district courts) 98(1) 144, 145: 'The court does not pay attention to embryos'.

when the newborn fully emerges from his mother's womb [7]. Recently, a case came up before a Coroner regarding the investigation of the cause of death of an embryo decapitated during birth. The coroner ruled that as, according to law, he is only authorized to investigate the unnatural death of a 'person', he has no jurisdiction to look into the case before him, since the embryo did not fully emerge from his mother's womb and therefore is not a person.[2] The Coroner relied upon the Penal Law [5737–1977, at clause 3089], which states that personhood starts from the time when the embryo emerges completely from his mother's womb. The complexity of defining the moment of personhood is a worldwide phenomenon and is not unique to Israel. Although the general rule amongst the Common Law countries is, as in Israel, the 'Born Alive Rule', it is not always clear at what point is the embryo to be regarded as 'born alive'.

The position of Israeli penal law is that an embryo is not a person. Under the penal law, whoever causes the death of a person shall be charged with murder or manslaughter. This is not the case where an embryo is concerned because an embryo is not considered a 'person'.[3] Criminally, anyone who wrongfully harms an embryo is accused of assaulting the pregnant woman, not the embryo. The mother may have a civil cause of action on her own behalf. Such an assault may give rise to a cause of action for damages accruing to the born child for injuries sustained while he was still an embryo. In the USA, on the other hand, there are states that impose criminal sanctions for the injuring of an embryo.

[2] For the Coroner's powers, see Criminal Procedure Amendment (Investigation of Felonies and Causes of Death) Law, 5718–1958, clauses 19–20, 24–26; See I.C.D. (Inquiry into Causes of Death) 109/98 Hadija Suad et al. vs. Dr. Breitman et al, an unpublished decision of the Tiberias Magistrate Court, at paragraph 12. Decision on file with author.

[3] See Penal Law, 5737–1977, at clause 308; also see the Dr. Dolberg case, at p. 454. This distinction appears already in the English law of the early 17th century. Coke wrote that a woman who intentionally kills an embryo while it is still in her womb, as well as any other person who intentionally kills it while it is still in her womb, shall be convicted of manslaughter, where the embryo was stillborn as a result of their act. Where the embryo was born alive, and only died after being born as a result of the blows or the poison which were given it while it was still in the womb, the perpetrators shall be convicted of murder. This is because the embryo becomes a 'person' only from the time it is born, and murder is defined as the intentional killing of a person. See Coke, 3rd Ins. 50.

The Status of the Embryo Regarding Abortion

Some of the major instances of law's protection of the embryo's right to life are the restrictions it places on intervention in the embryo's life. The most extreme variety of such intervention is the destruction of the embryo through abortion.

Israeli criminal law outlaws abortion, and imposes imprisonment of up to 5 years on those who perform it [Penal Law, 5737–1977, at clause 313]. Nevertheless, this is a much less severe punishment than the maximum punishments set out in our law for those who commit murder or manslaughter. There is a permissive regime for abortion on special grounds, conditioned on the approval of a statutory committee [Penal Law, 5737–1977, at clauses 316–317]. In one case, a mother filed a petition to the statutory committee to grant her leave to have an abortion. The father's objections were rejected by the committee and he therefore appealed to the Supreme Court. The Court decided that the woman's right to control her body overrules the father's right to 'veto' abortion, and that the father has no standing to oppose the mother's application to the committee for permission to abort [8]. One of the judges went on to say that the legislature didn't mean to give the embryo any status at all as regards the decision to abort. The mother did have to justify her petition to the committee as required by the Penal law [8, at 82].

It is indisputable that the protection of the embryo's life is an interest recognized under Israeli law, and that the necessary steps should be taken to ensure that this life shall not be needlessly impaired. Permission to have an abortion may be granted where the pregnant woman gives her informed consent, and abortion is deemed justified, as one of the following conditions holds [Penal Law, 5737–1977, at clause 316]: the woman is under the age of marriage, or above 40 years of age; the pregnancy derives from rape, incest, or an extramarital relationship; the resulting child may be handicapped; or where continuation of the pregnancy will endanger the mother's life or health. A doctor who performs an abortion in order to save a woman's life or prevent irreparable damage from incurring to her isn't liable under the criminal law [Penal Law, 5737–1977, at clause 317(1)]. Similarly, where during medical treatment, abortion becomes indispensable, a doctor who was unaware of the pregnancy isn't liable for performing the abortion [Penal Law, 5737–1977, at clause 317(2)].

Especially problematic is the statutory committee's authority to permit abortion where the embryo suffers from defects or deformities [Penal Law,

5737–1977, at clause 316(3)]. Such a situation gives rise to difficult ethical and moral questions. Which expected defects of the future child justify an abortion? Who shall determine whether any given fault in the embryo justifies such intervention? Shall it be the parents, the mother alone, the treating doctor, the statutory committee, or any other person or body? Where should the boundary between life and the lack thereof pass?

Responsibility in Tort

Under Israeli law, an embryo has, after being born, a right of action in tort for injuries sustained while an embryo. The Civil Wrongs Ordinance includes embryos in its definition of a 'child' [9, at clause 2]. The same Ordinance recognizes that the 'child' of a person who has died as a result of a tortious act is entitled, as the heir, or the dependent of the deceased [9, at clause 78].

Lawsuits in this context are classifiable into three kinds. The first, are suits for compensation arising out of a tortious act committed against the embryo during pregnancy. The courts have held that the embryo being born alive, is a necessary condition for its having a right for compensation and that the damage must still exist after the embryo's birth [10]. The second are suits against medical personnel for acting negligently in treatment during pregnancy or birth. The third and most problematic kind of such actions is called 'wrongful birth' actions. To this group belong cases where due to wrong genetic advice, to non-discovery of deformities in the embryo, and to doctors omitting to inform parents about such deformities, the embryo is born deformed. As a result, the parents were not aware of their risk and so prevented from deciding whether to abort the embryo. Such situations give rise to complex questions, such as: Are the parents, or the embryo, or both, entitled to compensation in such cases for the nonprevention of the defective baby being born? Or is life – any life – always preferred to non-life, so that a person born disabled should not be compensated at all? What criteria should be applied to award compensation? These questions and others were discussed by the Supreme Court in a case involving a newborn with an extremely severe deformity, which wasn't discovered during pregnancy despite its discovery being possible [11]. A woman applied for genetic counseling to find out whether a certain hereditary disease might damage her future offspring. Should this be so, she was determined not to give birth to male children. She received a wrong advice and thus a deformed child was born. The parents claimed that had they received correct genetic counseling, the embryo would not have been conceived. They sued for compensation both as the child's guardians, and on their own behalf as his parents.

In a thorough and perceptive judgment, the court stated that in principle, life – even a flawed life – is preferable to no life. It was unanimously ruled that the parents are entitled to compensation for the damage caused to them and for the expenses involved in bringing up the deformed child. Regarding the child's own right to be compensated, three approaches were expressed. The majority was of the opinion that he does in fact have such a right and the question was how to estimate the damages. Some of the judges considered that as the child's birth defects were of outstanding severity, he would have been better off not having been born. They accordingly decided that the child has a right to be compensated for his deformities and consequently low quality of life, without comparing his situation to that of a healthy person. They considered the rule that compensation is to be determined according to the difference between the injured person's situation before and after the harmful event, not to be applicable. Neither did they compare the newborn's current deformed situation to that it would have been in, had it not been born, since in that case it wouldn't have existed [12]. Another approach was that the child has a right to be compensated for his deformity, comparing his situation to that of a healthy person. One more approach considered that the child is not entitled to any compensation, since any life whatsoever is preferable to non-life.

The Right to Life of Frozen Fertilized Ova

In one of the most complex cases ever adjudicated by the Supreme Court, it faced, inter alia, the question of the status of frozen ova fertilized by an IVF procedure. The case was decided twice: on appeal, by five judges and on a further hearing, by eleven judges [13]. A married couple began an IVF treatment. The couple separated after the ova have been fertilized and frozen. The woman petitioned the Court to receive the frozen fertilized ova, in order to continue the process by implanting them in the womb of a surrogate mother, while the father refused to be a father against his will. The Court considered various legal aspects of the issue, the applicable legislation, the relevant cases, and the basic values of our legal system. One of many legal aspects of the case, which were examined by the Court, was the right to life of the fertilized ova and their status in the couple's dispute.

The Justices, in both hearings, unanimously upheld the supremacy of the right to life in Israeli law and in Israeli society. As to the status of the frozen ova and the point in time which is to be regarded as the beginning of life, it was held on appeal that the ova are not human beings, but merely frozen cells with a potential for life. They do not have an independent status enabling them to demand that the process be completed and life created. The couple whose genetic material was used for fertilization may not make this demand, neither can they do so on behalf of the ova. They may, of course, demand this in their own name as potential parents, when both of them want the process to be completed. A similar approach was put forward by the Supreme Court of Tennessee in the *Davis* decision, where such ova were defined as not being an embryo, but a pre-embryo [14]. A recent decision of the Supreme Court of New Jersey was also based on this approach [15]. On the further hearing of the Israeli case, seven out of eleven judges decided that while the ova are potential for life, such potential is inseparable from life itself. The right to be a parent is a part of the right to life, from which it draws it power.[4] At the end of the day, as a result of further considerations, the majority of the Court decided to hand over the fertilized ova to the woman.

Medical Experiments on Humans and Human Cloning

Medical experiments on human beings, human cloning and the genetic manipulation of reproductive cells have not come before our courts yet. They are relatively new to medicine, as well as to law.

However, Chief Justice Shamgar of our Supreme Court has discussed these issues from a theoretical standpoint, saying that protecting human

[4] One scholar wished to develop this opinion, which was voiced regarding the pre-embryonic stage, into a supposed conclusion that 'the life potential of an embryo is a value which Israeli society regards as worthy of protection, subject to the system of balances the legislature has put in place'. His view is inspired by that of Jewish religious law, which holds that 'the embryo's life must not be curtailed, unless Halakhic considerations such as saving the mother's life make such curtailment permissible' [16].

dignity includes protecting the 'dignity' of fertilized ova, and that this principle should 'be applied as a restriction on the scope of the liberty of biological and medical research' [1, at 42].

Some of these issues were also addressed by the legislature, as follows. Regulations enacted in 1980 incorporated into Israeli law the Helsinki Declaration on Ethical Principles for Medical Research involving Human Subjects [4]. The Helsinki declaration sets down general principles regarding the importance of the protection of the health, rights and welfare of persons which are used for medical research. An 'experiment on human beings' is defined in the Regulations as one which will 'or which is intended to influence the health, body or mental self of a human being, an embryo, or a part thereof, inclusive of the genetic structure' [4, clause 1]. Hence, anywhere in the regulations where experiments on human beings are discussed, one should understand that to mean experiments on either human beings, embryos, or the genetic structure.

The regulations provide that 'an experiment exercised on a human being's genetic structure' and 'an experiment exercised on the fertilization of a woman otherwise than naturally' shall not be done without the approval of the Supreme Helsinki Commission for Medical Experiments on Humans [4, clause 3B]. Thus, we may conclude that the legislator has regarded genetic manipulation as especially intrusive.

The Law Banning Genetic Intervention has been in force for 5 years from its enactment in 1999 [17]. During this period, 'certain kinds of genetic intervention in human beings shall not be performed, so that their moral, legal, social and scientific aspects, and their implications on human dignity, could be examined' [17, clause 1]. This act defines human cloning as 'the creation of an entire human being, genetically and chromosomally exactly identical to another, that other being a person or an embryo, dead or alive' [17, clause 2]. For the period it is in force, the act bans intervention in human cells in order to clone a human being, as well as such intervention in order to create a human being by making use of reproductive cells – human sperm or egg cells – which have been intentionally genetically manipulated in a constant manner [17, clause 3]. Still, the act empowers the Minister of Health to permit by regulations, in pursuance of a recommendation of the advisory committee, certain kinds of genetic intervention which are otherwise banned, should the minister find that such kinds of intervention shall not impair human dignity [17, clause 5(a)].

It should be emphasized that this legislation limits intervention in embryos and reproductive cells, not because it sees them as 'persons' or 'human beings', but because of the need to bring the vast possibilities for genetic engineering of human beings under control.

Finally, I would like to mention another recent statute, the purpose of which is 'to regulate performing genetic tests and giving genetic advice, and to protect the patient's right to privacy regarding genetic information which is identifiably his, all without harming the quality of medical treatment, medical and genetic research, the progress of medicine and the protection of public order' [18]. I shall not discuss this statute in detail, as it does not directly bear on our subject and has not as yet been addressed by the courts.

Conclusion

Technological advances are giving humanity tools for extensive intervention in creation. It seems that this development cannot, and should not, be halted. Still, the possibilities opened up by this development need to be bounded by human, moral, ethical and legal worldviews. Not everything which is technologically possible is also ethically desirable. It appears that the complex problems, some of which I have mentioned, pertain to the very core of the essence of humanity. These problems shall go on perplexing doctors, judges, moralists, philosophers, legal scholars and society in general, both in Israel and abroad. The courts shall be called upon to supply solutions in the cases that will come before them. But legal aspects do not exhaust the essence of these issues. Solving these problems shouldn't be left to one discipline alone. The involvement of every relevant discipline is necessary, so that suitable norms and values could be put in place. On the legal level, legislation is necessary which will be based on the fundamental principles and conceptions of our society which protect the sanctity of life, human dignity and liberty.

References

1 Shamgar M: Fertilization and Birth-Related Issues. Hapraklit 39 (1991) 21.
2 Davis I: On in vitro Fertilization, the status of the embryo and proper birth procedure. Law Med 1995;12:50–51.
3 Law Banning Genetic Intervention (Human Cloning and the Genetic Manipulation of Reproductive Cells), 5759–1999. 'Human Cloning' is defined in clause 2.
4 Public Health Regulations (Medical Experiments in Human Beings), 5740–1980.
5 Englard I: The Capacity and Guardianship Law, 5722–1962, ed 2, 1995; hereinafter: The Capacity Law) 31–32.
6 Cr.C. (Beer-Sheva) 8001/99 The State of Israel vs. Fuad Mussa, Takdin (district courts) 2000(1) 9826, at paragraph 9 of Judge Yaffe-Katz's judgement.
7 Cr.C. (Tel-Aviv) 854/80 The State of Israel vs. Dr. Dolberg, 1987 District Court Decisions, vol B 446 (hereinafter: the Dr. Dolberg case), 454; I. Hadad 'The Status of an Embryo', a paper submitted for the course 'Family Law', the Faculty of Law, Bar-Ilan University, 1979, 5 (unpublished; on file with author).
8 C.A. 413/80 Doe vs. Roe, P.D. 35(3) 57, at 70.
9 Civil Wrongs Ordinance [New Version], 5728–1968, at clause 2.
10 Englard I: The Capacity Law, at 33. Also see C.A. (Nazareth) 39/88 Nesayer vs. Shamir Insurance Company Ltd., Zeltner 568(a).
11 C.A. 518/82 Zeitzov vs. Katz, P.D. 40(2) 85.
12 Tedeschi G: On the Problem of Wrongful Birth Tort Actions. Essays Law 1978;269:287.
13 C.A. 5587/93 Daniel Nahmani vs. Ruthie Nahmani, P.D. 49(1) 485; F.H. 2401/95 Ruthie Nahmani vs. Daniel Nahmani, P.D. 50(4) 661.
14 Davis v. Davis, 842 S.W. 2d 588 (1992).
15 J.B. v. M.B. and C.C., 170 N.J. 9 (2001), at 22.
16 On the Requirement of Informed Consent in Abortion. Mishpatim 29(3) 737, 771, footnote 97.
17 Law Banning Genetic Intervention (Human Cloning and the Genetic Manipulation of Reproductive Cells), 5759–1999.
18 Genetic Information Law, 5761–2000, clause 1 (free translation).

Justice Tova Strasberg-Cohen

Ombudsman of the Judiciary,
Nachum Heftzadi Street 5,
IL–95484 Jerusalem (Israel)
Tel. +972 2 659 5512, Fax +972 2 659 5516, E-Mail zehavaH@justice.gov.il

Blazer S, Zimmer EZ (eds):
The Embryo: Scientific Discovery and Medical Ethics.
Basel, Karger, 2005, pp 340–350

'Wrongful Life' Lawsuits for Faulty Genetic Counselling: Legal, Ethical and Policy Aspects[1]

Amos Shapira

K. Lubowski Chair of Law and Biomedical Ethics, Faculty of Law,
Tel-Aviv University, Tel Aviv, Israel

Consider the following case: Prior to her marriage, a woman consulted with a genetic counselor as to the chances of a certain hereditary defect (Hunter's disease – a rare hereditary disorder which almost exclusively affects males and is characterized by dwarfism, a coarse facies, mental retardation and deafness; prenatal diagnosis is available using chorionic villi sampling and cultured amniotic fluid cells) that exists in her family which could impair her future offspring. If this were to be the case, she was determined not to have any male children.

The genetic consultant, due to his (alleged) negligence in the testing and counseling processes, concluded that no such risk existed, and on the basis of this advice, the woman became pregnant and bore a son. However, the infant was in fact afflicted with the disease, which severely handicapped his physical and psychological development. Consequently, the newborn

[1] This chapter is based on my articles [1–3] mentioned in the reference list.

brought a personal injury suit for 'wrongful life' against the consultant. A 'wrongful life' suit is based on the alleged tort liability of a genetic counselor toward an infant with hereditary defects when the plaintiff asserts that he would not have been born at all if not for the counselor's negligence. This negligence allegedly lies in the failure on the part of the defendant to adequately advise the parents or to properly conduct the relevant testing and thereby prevent the child's conception or birth (where unimpaired life was not possible).

It is my thesis that it would be both feasible and even desirable to endorse a 'wrongful life' compensation action brought by a handicapped newborn against a negligent genetic counselor. Israeli courts rule accordingly. The Israeli Supreme Court accepted such a cause of action. However, for the sake of accuracy let me note that this is not the common position of courts in other countries. For instance, English courts do not recognize a 'wrongful life' cause of action as part of English law of tort. In Germany, up to very recently, courts of law did not accept the 'wrongful life' cause of action. In the United States, decisions have been made in both directions, and in France, there has been a very interesting development recently. Two courts of law recognized the 'wrongful life' cause of action. However, the French parliament interfered, and by legislation now, no case of 'wrongful life' suits may not be brought before a French court.

I shall argue that the genetic counselor owed a duty of due professional care to the impaired newborn who now claims that but for the counselor's negligence he or she would not have been born at all and that the plaintiff's defective life (where healthy life was never an option) constitutes a compensable injury. Moreover, I will maintain that a sufficient causal link may exist between the plaintiff's injury and the defendant's breach of duty of due professional care and that an appropriate measure of damages can be allocated to the disabled newborn. I shall further assert that sanctioning a 'wrongful life' cause of action does not necessarily entail or import abandoning valuable constraints with regard to abortion and euthanasia. Nor does it inevitably lead to an uncontrolled slide down a 'slippery slope' toward the wholesale categorization of a host of impairments as compensable injuries and toward burdening parents with a sweeping responsibility to protect future offspring from illness or suffering by avoiding conception or birth.

Does a genetic counselor owe a duty of due care to a newborn plaintiff when the counselor's alleged professional negligence predates the plaintiff's birth or even conception? The answer, in principle, should be in the affirmative. In exercising professional due care, a genetic counselor enables parents to avoid the conception or the carrying to term of a defective fetus by adequately apprising them of the risks involved. If a genetic counselor fails to adequately perform this duty, he may be regarded as professionally negligent under customary malpractice tort standards. Imposing such a professional duty of care should not be denounced as undue encouragement to avoid conception or to undergo abortion. It is true, of course, that pre-conception professional cautioning as to the chances of bearing an impaired child may induce potential parents to refrain from procreating altogether. But, after all, there is no legal obligation to be fruitful and multiply. Similarly, prospective parents who have taken advantage of the availability of post-conception testing and counseling may subsequently be swayed into terminating the pregnancy. It is conceivable that genetic diagnosis may in fact result in an increase in the incidence rate of elective abortion, as health-care providers will likely act with caution and, accordingly, not shy away from recommending abortion. However, a genetic counselor will meet her professional obligation simply by duly informing potential parents regarding the extent and likelihood of the risks involved, leaving the ultimate decision in their hands. The professional advice provided must be reasonable under the circumstances and must correspond to available contemporary scientific knowledge. Indeed, an unskillful overly 'defensive' counsel not to conceive or to abort could, in itself, be deemed negligent and constitute malpractice.

There is no inherent injustice in holding a genetic counselor liable toward a handicapped newborn for professional misconduct, i.e. behavior that, under the circumstances, falls short of ordinarily required standards of due care. Awareness on the part of professionals that their professional performance is subject to such normative standards of behavior is likely to prompt them to act with skill and caution and thereby reduce the incidence of professional malpractice.

The most perplexing dilemmas relating to 'wrongful life' lawsuits arise in the context of morality and logic. Under the principles of tort law, only a breach of a duty of due cares, which renders a legally recognized injury, will provide the injured party with a cause of action to sue the wrongdoer for compensation. Should the condition of impaired life (in a situation where healthy life was never an option) be regarded as a compensable damage? Even on the assumption that the genetic counselor did act negligently when conducting testing or providing information to the would-be parents, should a newborn be permitted to claim that the defective life forced upon him constitutes a harm for which he deserves to be redressed?

There are those who maintain that endorsement of such a claim is tantamount to a normative affirmation that non-life is preferable to a life afflicted with disease. And, they further assert, such affirmation reflects an expectation of – indeed, a claim to – products of procreation that do not fall short of perfection. Moreover, this endorsement allegedly constitutes a direct challenge to the cherished tenet of the sanctity of life – according to which existence, even defective, is always preferable to non-existence and, furthermore, it is bound to legitimize and promote both abortion and euthanasia.

On the subject of abortion, it is interesting to note that under Israeli law, a gynecologist does not bear criminal responsibility for having interrupted a woman's pregnancy if the procedure was performed at a recognized medical facility with the advance permission of a committee consisting of a medical practitioner specializing in obstetrics and gynecology, another qualified medical practitioner, and a social worker. The committee is authorized (upon obtaining the pregnant woman's informed consent) to allow abortion on each of several specified grounds, including a situation wherein 'the child is likely to have a physical or mental defect'. It would appear that the phraseology adopted by the Israeli legislature reveals an unmistakably lenient policy vis-à-vis abortion for eugenic reasons: A physical or mental defect does not need to be extensive or grievous in order to justify interruption of a pregnancy; an ordinary, perhaps even relatively minor defect seems to be sufficient. Furthermore, the defect need only be 'likely', not certain or probable; the term 'likely' seems to signify a mere reasonable possibility, which falls short of near certainty or high probability. The possible risk of such defects may stem from a variety of causes, such as exposure of the pregnant woman to certain diseases and exposure of the fetus to radiation, medication or other injurious substances taken by the mother, and a known family history of genetic defective traits with a likely hereditary effect.

Legalization of abortion in a given society is generally indicative of that society's value judgments, particularly regarding its recognition of a woman's right to autonomy, dignity, privacy, and bodily integrity. A permissive stand, de jure as well as de facto, on abortion for eugenic reasons actually provides a solid foundation for an impaired newborn's claim that had it not been for the genetic counselor's negligence, his or her parents might have indeed opted for legal abortion. The faulty genetic counseling deprived the parents of realizing their legally-recognized right to abort a defective fetus. Thus, legal recognition of a cause of action for 'wrongful life' corresponds conceptually to legal endorsement of the parental right to refrain from conceiving or giving birth to an impaired child. Moreover, if recognition of eugenic grounds for abortion is the manifestation of a general goal to protect the fetal – and not only the maternal – interest (i.e. if a defective fetus possesses a 'personal' right to be aborted), then denial of that right through faulty prenatal genetic counseling may amount to 'informed consent'-based negligence. In other words, the claim of an impaired infant plaintiff (a former defective fetus) is that had he or she not received negligent advice (by proxy – the parents), he or she would have exercised his or her legal right to choose not to be born into a defective state. Now the infant has no choice but to lead an impaired existence, and for that, he or she seeks to be redressed.

Legal sanctioning of a 'wrongful life' cause of action can also be examined in the context of the 'right to die' debate. One could argue that recognition of impaired life as a compensable harm (when healthy life was never an option) undermines the traditional tenets of the sanctity of human life and blatantly devaluates the social worth of the handicapped. Such an approach may even foster dangerous termination-of-life decisions regarding the elderly and the ailing, ranging from withholding or withdrawing life support to all-out assisted suicide or active euthanasia.

A comprehensive discussion of the intricacies of the death and dying issue – underlying values, policy goals, decision-making mechanisms – falls beyond the ambit of this essay. Suffice it to say that compensating a handicapped newborn for a negligent prenatal genetic diagnosis hardly implies that the disabled life of the infant plaintiff is devoid of all worth; it is precisely because the plaintiff's handicapped life does deserve respect and compassion that he or she ought to be offered pecuniary redress that is geared to ensure a decent, if hampered, existence. Decisions regarding artificial prolongation of the dwindling, agony-filled life of a terminally-ill patient entail a different matrix of values and concerns and raise issues that are quite distinct from those involved in the matter of redressing an impaired infant for faulty prenatal diagnosis when healthy life was never an available alternative. Indeed, administering deliberate and direct action to terminate life is hardly analogous to awarding pecuniary redress for hampered life. In other words, while the concern for the sanctity of life is clearly involved in the comparison of existing (if burdened) life to the termination thereof, it is hardly a self-evident issue in the attempt to measure non-existence against impaired life. A hypothetical preference not to have been born at all over the misery of a handicapped life is one thing; actually opting to terminate a life filled with agony is quite another. Admittedly, there are those who feel that the two are linked both conceptually and consequentially. I do not share such a wholesale, sweeping belief. It might be that permissive stand on the 'right to die' issue could indirectly facilitate endorsement of 'wrongful life' negligent lawsuits; namely, if a certain impairment legally justifies withholding or withdrawing life-sustaining treatment and possibly even direct and deliberate termination of life, then one might surely surmise that such an impairment is to be regarded as a compensable damage for purposes of a tort action for 'wrongful life'. But the logic of this syllogism hardly applies in reverse. That is, willingness to recognize actions for monetary compensation for 'wrongful life' does not necessarily imply a sanctioning of various specimens of mercy killing. A legal system can be lenient toward disabled infants who wish to sue negligent genetic counselors for damages for 'wrongful life', while simultaneously adopting a proscriptive stance on the 'right to die' claim.

Still, can one logically argue that the impaired state into which a child was born (when healthy life was never possible) constitutes a redressable harm?

When a plaintiff asserts a preference for non-existence over hampered life, she is actually claiming that the damage suffered by her is equal to the gap between these two situations. Is a court of law capable of making such an assessment? And which logical yardsticks should be employed?

According to a widely held opinion, favored mostly by philosophers, there is, and can be, no logical foundation to a 'wrongful life' claim. A state of non-existence is devoid of any moral status and legal consequence. It lacks any value and worth, it offers no basis for comparison with any form of existence, and it cannot constitute an object for any claim of right. Therefore, in this view, any attempt to evaluate the meaning of non-life as compared to that of defective life is a logical impossibility. Yet, despite the undeniable force of this argument, two Israeli Supreme Court justices were not averse to comparing non-existence to defective existence. They were prepared to decree that in certain situations (though admittedly rare and extreme), a 'reasonable man' could conclude – even if intuitively – that a person would indeed be better served not to be born at all rather than living with a very serious impairment. According to this view, the cause of action for 'wrongful life' can and should be restricted to only exceptionally severe disabilities. Such a limitation would minimize the alleged affront to the moral value of the sanctity of human life as well as reduce the potential for a flood of 'wrongful life' lawsuits. By the same token, this restriction would lower the cost of liability insurance for genetic counseling and treatment services.

However, this judicial position has a major difficulty: the inherent necessity to distinguish between truly severe handicaps (allowing a cause of action) and less-than-extraordinarily grave defects (not providing a right to sue). How would blindness, for instance, be classified? Or deafness? Or diabetes? Or Down's syndrome? Or being born missing a limb?

An alternative approach, preferred by two other justices of the Israeli Supreme Court, deals with the logical dilemma of comparing non-life with defective life by side-stepping (or even leaping over) it. According to this approach, legal responsibility for 'wrongful life' can be established without measuring non-life against impaired life and without endorsing a 'right not to be born'. Indeed, such a comparison is logically impossible, said the two other justices, and a right to non-existence is inconceivable. Judges are incapable of gauging the meaning of non-life and of evaluating its worth in comparison to hampered life.

These two justices view a physician's 'wrongful life' liability toward a disabled infant as resting on the plaintiff's right to a life free of handicaps. Accordingly, the responsibility of a negligent genetic expert is based neither on the actual generation of life nor on the prevention of non-life, but, rather, on the creation of impaired life. Because a genetic counselor was professionally negligent, he must bear responsibility for the damage that ensued (defective-life), and it is irrelevant, in their view, that a non-defective life was a practical impossibility. Thus, the quantum of damage should be measured by comparing the actual impaired life of a plaintiff to a hypothetical unimpaired life, rather than by comparing defective life to non-existence.

In other words, the reality of the matter is that the handicapped infant exists. She is doomed to impairment, suffering, and to a needy existence due (we assume) to the defendant's professional negligence. It is true that initially, the only alternative to disabled life was not to be born at all. But at the point at which a 'wrongful life' suit is brought, this alternative no longer exists. Indeed, the infant is neither entitled to nor capable of being restored to the pre-injury state of non-existence. However, the impaired plaintiff did acquire a right to appropriate recompense by virtue of the defendant's malpractice. This negligence effected two simultaneous results: the child's actual birth and her inevitably handicapped condition. Though logically these two realities are unequivocally intertwined, a conceptual distinction can still be made. An impaired child brings a suit for his handicapped condition, not for being brought into existence. Non-existence may not in fact constitute a legally protected interest; however, the law can provide an impaired newborn with the right to be compensated by a negligent genetic counselor for the damage inherent to his or her handicapped state as compared to healthy life.

A further issue still to be confronted is whether such a cause of action, although in itself legitimate and even desirable, should nonetheless be rejected lest its endorsement have an undesirable snowball effect and result in unavoidable recognition for purportedly analogous though less or not-at-all deserving claims. For example, what about a newborn who seeks to sue a genetic consultant for alleged negligence in advising the claimant's parents that he would be tall with a fair complexion and blue eyes, when the genetic reality was that the infant could only be, as indeed he is, short with a dark complexion and brown eyes?. And what if a child seeks compensation for 'wrongful life' not from a genetic counselor but from his own parents, claiming that were it not for their parental imprudence, she would not have been born into a life burdened by any number of disadvantages – genetic illness or HIV infection, the stigma of illegitimacy, religious persecution or ethnic prejudice, racial discrimination or socioeconomic deprivation?

A serious 'slippery slope' argument should not be dismissed lightly. A court of law should always be mindful of the potential normative repercussions of its decision in the case-at-hand for future controversies. Still, the rather routine warning against an uncontrollable descent down a dangerous 'slippery slope' is often unduly manipulated and abused in normative discourse. Occasionally, it is nothing more than a false alarm. A 'slippery slope' argument recognizes the inherent acceptability or even desirability of the practice in question but nonetheless calls for its abandonment because of the alleged potential for a snowball effect. But before being convinced by such an argument, one must always consider the alternative to renouncing the practice under debate: to stand firm at the edge of the menacing slope and to effectively avoid, the undesired deterioration. A judge should not ordinarily hesitate to hand down a decision considered justified in the circumstances of the case-at-bar because of mere apprehension that it could be misapplied or improperly extended to future, misleadingly similar cases.

Genetic impairments such as Hunter's disease clearly constitute compensable bodily harm under the customary social conventions manifested in the principles of tort law. Acknowledgement of this fact will not necessarily lead to recognition of being born short with a dark complexion and brown eyes as a redressable harm. A court upholding a 'wrongful life' claim brought by, for example, a Hunter's afflicted child will hardly be compelled by ethics, logic, or social policy to treat in a similar fashion a short, dark-complexioned, brown-eyed newborn plaintiff. Likewise, judicial affirmation of a 'wrongful life' action against a geneticist will not inevitably result in endorsement of 'wrongful life' suits lodged by children against their parents, for, say, failing to initiate necessary and customary pre-natal testing which, had it been performed, would have revealed in time the existence of a genetic defect.

A compensation claim against a genetic counselor for faulty professional conduct is firmly grounded in the traditional legal notion of negligence. There is nothing revolutionary in holding a physician liable toward his or her patient for breach of a professional duty of due care. Imposing upon parents a duty of due care to prevent the conception or birth of a child is a fundamentally different matter. Such a duty would have to be predicated on a completely separate and new concept of a parental responsibility to spare potential offspring a life handicapped by sickness or encumbered by any type of social deprivation. A decision as to whether or not to concede such a parental legal duty to refrain from bringing into life a Tay-Sachs, or HIV-positive, or illegitimate, or religiously-persecuted, or ethnically prejudiced, or racially discriminated, or socioeconomically deprived child would depend on a plethora of sociomoral values and policy considerations. However, many of these considerations are of little relevance to the firmly established and widely recognized general duty of professionals to treat their patients, clients, and customers with reasonable skill and prudence.

In conclusion, if on the basis of its merits, one is inclined to endorse a 'wrongful life' compensation action initiated by a handicapped newborn against a negligent genetic counselor, one need not be deterred by such speculative and highly irrelevant 'slippery slope' apprehensions.

Two final remarks. First, the type of professional conduct that should or should not be considered negligence was not discussed here. What is the appropriate scope of the duty of professional due care owed by a genetic counselor to a newborn in the context of a 'wrongful life' lawsuit? What are the normative yardsticks for measuring the exercise of proper professional skills in genetic diagnosis and therapy? The answer to these questions depends, inter alia, on a public policy decision as to the appropriate range of genetic testing and counseling services offered to the public. Such a decision, in turn, will be affected by a variety of scientific and sociomoral risk-benefit calculations. Difficult societal choices will have to be made in this respect, in light of the continuing progress in mapping and sequencing the human genome, the expansion of available prenatal and preimplantation diagnostic capabilities, and the complex considerations regarding accessibility of genetic testing, counseling, and therapy services and their overall societal implications. In balancing all of these different, sometimes contending concerns, one must be alert to the risk of overly 'defensive' medicine with its negative consequences. Clearly, not in every case is failed therapy, defective testing, flawed diagnosis, or misguided counseling tantamount to professional negligence.

Second, there are those who would prefer a social security solution to providing for the needs of impaired newborns. According to this view, the State should support handicapped children and ensure their welfare as part of a general social policy to support the needy out of the public purse. Proponents of such a public welfare policy are likely to question the suitability of a private lawsuit brought against an allegedly negligent physician as an implement to guarantee the care and services required by disabled infants. They are likely to be skeptical as to whether such an implement has the potential to fulfill the widely hailed policy goals of deterrence, prevention, and efficient and fair spreading of the damage. Furthermore, if the State assumes responsibility for caring for an impaired newborn, it may possibly seek redress (by way of indemnity) for its own expenses from whoever was at fault in creating the need for care and support. A general welfare solution would, of course, require public funding and special enabling legislation. Such a solution would be conditional upon community empathy for and solidarity with the needy and a general commitment to providing them with a fair level of subsistence. It would be contingent upon the existence of a socio-economic ethos and political culture of a welfare state that recognizes the entitlement of its needy to public support. However, the question arises as to whether such socio-political requirements are compatible with current privatization and market economy trends. In any event, my assumption in this presentation was that in the absence of such a pervasive welfare support system, the only possibility open to an impaired newborn seeking proper redress would be to bring a tort law action against a professionally negligent genetic counselor.

References

1 Shapira A: 'Wrongful life' lawsuits for faulty genetic counseling: The impaired newborn as a plaintiff. Tel Aviv University Studies in Law 1997;13:97–114.

2 Shapira A: 'Wrongful life' lawsuits for faulty genetic counseling: Should the impaired newborn be entitled to sue? J Med Ethics 1998;24:369–375.

3 Shapira A: The human right not to be born impaired: Issues of logic value, and policy; in Immenga HC, Möschel W, Reuter D (eds): Festschrift für Ernst Joachim Mestmaecker. Baden-Baden, Nomos, 1996, pp 293–307.

Amos Shapira, MJur, MCL, JSD

Professor, K. Lubowski Chair of Law and Biomedical Ethics,
Faculty of Law, Tel-Aviv University,
PO Box 39040, IL–69978 Tel Aviv (Israel)
Tel. +972 3 640 8105, Fax +972 3 641 6095, E-Mail Shapira1@post.tau.ac.il

Blazer S, Zimmer EZ (eds):
The Embryo: Scientific Discovery and Medical Ethics.
Basel, Karger, 2005, pp 351–370

The Living Fetus – Dilemmas in Treatment at the Edge of Viability

Arthur I. Eidelman

Faculty of Health Sciences, Ben-Gurion University of the Negev, Hebrew University School of Medicine; and Department of Pediatrics, Shaare Zedek Medical Center, Jerusalem, Israel

For over 30 years physicians have been troubled by the dilemma of treating infants who are born at the limits of viability [1, 2]. Both the medical system itself and individual physicians have repeatedly asked if the investment in community resources and the commitment to the individual patient can be justified when the outcome, both as to mortality and morbidity, is seemingly so dismal. One need only peruse the titles of papers published in this last decade to sense the continuing near anguish of those charged with the responsibility for caring for such vulnerable infants:

- 'Medical miracle or pyrrhic victory' [3]
- 'From how small is too small to how much is too much: Ethical issues at the limits of viability' [4]
- Parental rights at the birth of a near-viable infant: conflicting perspectives [5]
- The physician's moral obligations to the pregnant woman, the fetus, and child [6]

- 'Treatment decisions for newborns at the threshold of viability: an ethical dilemma' [7]
- 'Limits of viability: dilemma, decisions, and decision makers' [8]

While this debate and to a degree professional soul searching has raged, the actual limits of viability, conventionally defined by gestational age and birth weight cut offs, have dramatically dropped to earlier and earlier ages (22–23 weeks) and to lower and lower birth weights (less than 500 g) [9]. As such, published recommendations of various governmental agencies and professional organizations that have attempted to draw specific cut offs are, all too often, outdated by the time of publication and, thus, serve little if any value for guiding the clinician facing treatment dilemmas [10, 11]. Even more disconcerting, however, has been the observation that contrary to expectations and experiences of 1970s and 1980s, the improvement in mortality that has occurred in the last decade has not been matched by a comparable improvement in morbidity. This issue was highlighted by Hoekstra [12] who after surveying the experience of a single institution over the last 15 years stated: 'while overall survival improves incrementally with each advancing week of gestation, long-term neurologic improvements are not demonstrated to improve in the same incremental manner'.

This dissociation of mortality rates from morbidity rates is a new phenomenon and has sharpened the debate as to the ethical justification for treating the infants who are born at the limits of viability [13]. Most importantly, one is forced to ask if this observation confirms a basic biologic inevitably or is just a reflection of a lag in our therapeutic and technological prowess; a lag that results in improved survival, but, as yet, does not minimize in comparable way central nervous system damage. Table 1 summarizes the four elements of the therapeutic dilemma that faces physicians when they make their care decisions for infants born at the threshold of viability, and these elements will serve as the basis of the discussion of this chapter. In addition, in an attempt to further sharpen this debate, I will address the issue of treating or not treating the infant at the limits of viability by focusing on three questions:

1 What are the biologic factors that explain the disassociation of mortality and morbidity outcome in infants born less than 26 weeks gestation? Most importantly, is this dissociation a measure of a biologic reality or it is it a result of a lack in knowledge and technological skill?

Table 1.
Dilemma elements

- Increased survival of infant at threshold of viability, i.e. 22–25 weeks' gestational age (10–60%)
- Persistently high morbidity, especially neurodevelopmental (30–50%)
- Profound impact on infant, families, health care system, and society (1% of births = 50% perinatal mortality)
- Inadequate data precludes proper guidance for physicians for counseling families

2 What is the reality of decision making by physicians who are faced with this dilemma and what is the outcome of such decisions? Data will be presented from multi year national studies in addition to physician attitudinal surveys or outcome data from selected institutions.
3 Are there cultural issues and biases that allow or facilitate treatment decisions regarding the borderline viable infant that reflect deep seeded attitudes to the status of newborn infants and not necessarily a reflection of medical outcome statistics?

This chapter will not attempt to extensively summarize the latest mortality and morbidity data but rather will choose to present representative data that will help to clarify the three issues highlighted above.

Survival of the Infant Born at the Threshold of Viability

The decade of the 1990s witnessed a dramatic improvement in the survival of the extremely low birth weight premature infant. Not only in each weight category and week of gestation has there been an improvement in survival, the actual lower limit of viability is now approaching 22 weeks or less. Serial data from the National Institute of Child Health (NICHD) network of 12 perinatal centers summarizes this steady improvement (table 2) [13, 14]. Similarly, serial data over a 15-year period from a single large institution such as the University of Minnesota confirms the dramatic improvement in survival of these high risk newborns (table 3) [12]. Thus, routine resuscitation of infants as young as 23 weeks, if not younger, is becoming normative in many hospitals. In addition, if a 50% survival outcome has

Table 2.
Survival (%) National Institute of Child Health (NICHD) Network

	1987–1988	1993–1994	1999–2000
Gestational age, weeks			
≤23	23	24	30
24	34	56	59
25	54	70	72
Birth weight, g			
501–600	21	30	39
601–700	33	56	59
701–800	53	72	77

Table 3.
Survival (%) in the Children's Hospital, Minnesota

Gestational age weeks	1986–1990	1991–1995	1996–2000
23	40	45	66
24	49	67	81
25	69	87	85
26	78	88	93

conventionally served as the divide between 'routine' and 'experimental' care then this line is clearly crossed at 22–23 weeks in many neonatal intensive care units and thus 'legitimates' maximum intensive care for such infants. The reasons for such increased survival are complex, but can be summarized as combination of aggressive obstetrical and neonatal care; including prophylactic surfactant administration, improved ventilatory techniques and 24-hour in-house medical coverage by an experienced neonatologist (table 4).

Perusal of published survival data, though, should sound a note of caution against extrapolating results from random reports and converting them into a recommendation for a specific case. Single institution data is highly biased by the selection process resulting in the particular case mix of the population treated [15, 16]. Data from the NICHD network emphasize the varied care practices from one unit to another within the network [14]. For example, for infants born with weights between 500 and 750 g there were different rates of usage of antenatal steroids (30–92%), antenatal antibiotics

Table 4.
Reasons for improved survival

- Improved perinatal management of high-risk pregnancy and delivery
- Prenatal steroids
- Postnatal surfactant
- Improved ventilation techniques
- Senior neonatology 24-hour coverage
- More optimal neonatal nutrition

(49–82%), cesarean section (27–69%) and endotracheal intubation (51–96%). As a result, not surprisingly, the mortality data for a given weight group and gestational age varied from institution to institution in the network. For example, for infants born at 24 weeks' gestation the mortality rate for the entire network was 49% with 95% confidence level ranging from 43–55%. Most striking, was the difference in gender outcome. The mortality of a female infant born at 24 weeks who weighed 700 g was 35% while a male infant of same weight and gestational age the mortality was 50%! Thus, extrapolating from mean results of published reports may be inappropriate for decision making in a particular case cared for in a different manner in an altogether different facility and geographic location.

Morbidity of the Infant Born at the Threshold of Viability

It is clear that reports of long-term morbidity of surviving extremely-low-birth-weight and very immature infants reflect the care practices of previous years, practices that may have changed by the time one has to make a difficult treatment decision. Despite this caveat what is striking is the steady improvement in mortality outcome in the past decade and the relatively minimal improvement over this same period in the morbidity outcome for infants born at less than 26 weeks' gestation. Figure 1 graphically depicts this trend. Vohr et al. [17] previously reported on the 18-month outcome of infants (n = 1151) from the 1993–1994 NICHD cohort who were born weighing less than 1,000 g. For the total group, 49% had abnormal neurodevelopment. Table 5 details the breakdown of the type of handicaps that these infants suffered from. Hack et al. [15] reported that

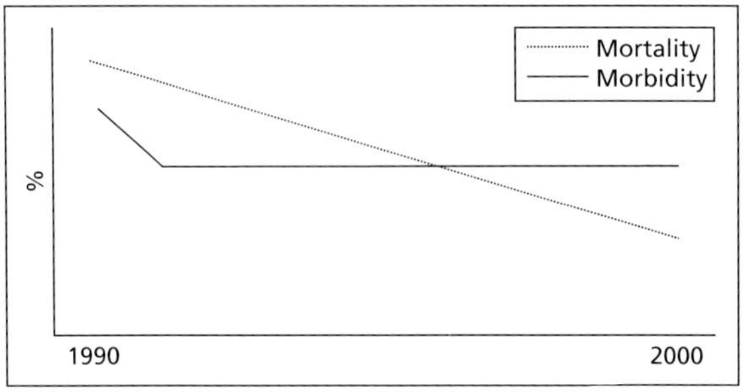

Fig. 1.

Epidemiological trends in the care of the infant at the threshold of viability.

Table 5.

Neurodevelopmental and functional outcome, at 18 months of age, of extreme low birth weight infants in the NICHD Neonatal Research Network, 1993–1994

25% abnormal neurological (17% CP) 37% Bayley MDI <70
29% Bayley PDI <70
9% vision impairment
11% hearing impairment

CP = Cerebral palsy; MDI = Bayley mental developmental index; PDI = Bayley psychomotor developmental index.

48% of the infants born under 750 g (n = 112) in their 1993–1995 cohort had subnormal cognitive development, while Sweet et al. [16] reported that 90% of the infants born with birth weights below 600 g had abnormal neurodevelopment at the 2-year follow-up exam. Wood et al. [18] in a large population study of a 1995 cohort from England and Ireland reported that the moderate-severe disability rate was present in 56% of infants born at 23 weeks, in 53% born at 24 weeks and in 45% in those born at 25 weeks, confirming the minimal improvement in morbidity in this gestational age range. Comparable data was reported by Reichman et al. [19] from the Israel National Database who noted that there was no difference in rate of immediate severe neurological morbidity in surviving infants who were born at either 23, 24 or 25 weeks.

Hoekstra et al. [12] studied 675 infants born at 26 weeks or less at 2 years and noted that 37% had an abnormal neurodevelopmental outcome at the 4-year follow-up. Two striking observations were noted (1) Neurologic outcome of those born after 23 weeks was better than those born at or less than 23 weeks, but, there was no major difference in long-term neurologic morbidity (as opposed to survival) between those born at 24, 25 and 26 weeks. (2) Most importantly, in the infants born at 23–24 and who were followed for 8 years, the percentage with neurodevelopmental abnormalities actually rose as opposed to the findings at the 4-year follow-up (56 vs. 34%).

The Process of Neuromaturation and Development

How can one explain this dissociation between the mortality and morbidity outcome. Traditionally, we have conceptualized that neurological, behavioral and cognitive outcome reflects neurological damage from a combination of cerebral hypoxia, cerebral hypofusion, intracranial hemorrhage, and postnatal nutritional and metabolic derangements and deficiencies. Recently, the effect of transplacental neurotoxic cytokines [20] and postnatal steroids [21] has been added to the list of possible substances that could account for the persistently high nervous system morbidity. Strikingly, even with a documented reduction in incidence of asphyxia, intracranial hemorrhage and postnatal metabolic disorders the incidence of neurologic abnormalities has remained relatively stable [13]. This observation suggests that the mechanism of the neurological morbidity may be, to an extent, the result of the fact that the infant who is born at less than 26 weeks is cut off from specific maternal or placental neurotrophic stimuli at a critical developmental juncture. Thus, given the reality that even the best neonatal intensive care unit and the highest level of conventional medical and nursing is not a substitute for the maternal/placental unit, it is not surprising that in infants born at this gestational age neurodevelopment may be permanently altered or stunted with inevitable negative consequences. In contrast, in infants born after 26 weeks' gestation the basic critical physical organization of the brain has been set and thus such infants can 'tolerate' an extrauterine environment without inevitable central nervous system damage.

Figure 2 depicts graphically the degree of gross physical immaturity of the developing brain for those born at the limits of viability (less than 26 weeks). When one reviews the sequence of normal development summarized in

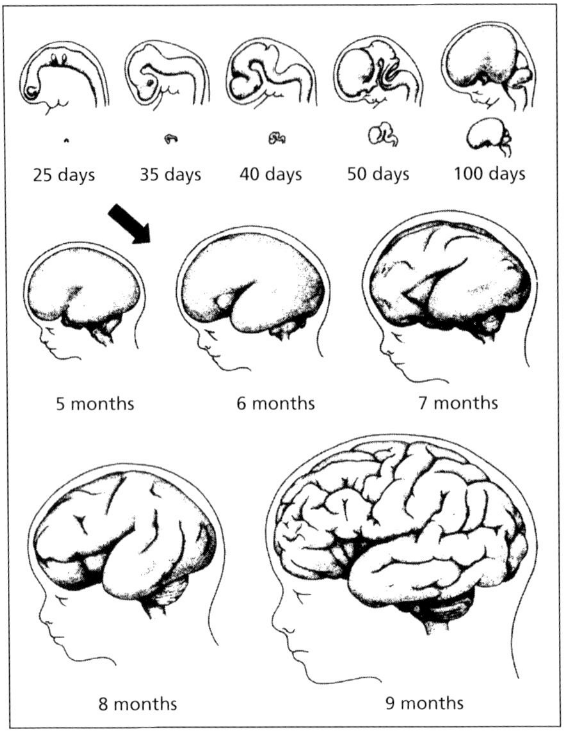

Fig. 2.
Normal gyral development of the human fetal brain (infolding). The arrow indicates the limit of potential viability. From Cowan WM. The development of the brain. Sci Am 1979;241:109, with permission.

table 6, it is clear that the fetus thrust into the extrauterine world at 22–26 weeks will not have completed the process of neural migrtion to the cortical plate, let alone, begin any significant cortical synaptic formation. Much of this development is apparently dependent on the maternal/placental supply of neurotrophic agents that unfortunately such newly born immature infants are deprived of. Thus, there may well be an inevitability of abnormal neurological development, particularly, in those functions that are dependant on a normally functional cortical mantle [22, 23]. Table 7 lists the numerous endogenous growth and neurotrophic factors that the maternal/placental unit provides and are so abruptly deprived from the fetus when it become an

Table 6.

Sequence of central nervous system development

- Neuronal birth: 7–16 weeks
- Neuronal migration: 10–26 weeks
- Dendritic/axonal growth 20 weeks–2 year
- Fetal viability
- Synapse formation: 25 weeks–3 year
- Synaptic pruning: 10 months–14 years

Table 7.

Endogenous neurotrophic and 'growth' factors

• Neurotrophins	NGF, BDNF
• Oligotrophins	CNTF
• Hormones	thyroid, corticosteroid
• Anti-inflammatory cytokines	IL-10
• Angiogenic	EGF
• Growth factors	IGF-1, IL-2
• Neurotransmitters	dopamine, serotonin

NGF = Nerve growth factor; BDNF = brain-derived neurotrophic factor; CNTF = ciliary neurotrophic factor; IL = interleukin; EGF = epidermal growth factor; IGF = insulin-like growth factor.

extremely-low-birth-weight, severely immature neonate. In contrast to the brain, anatomical and histological examination of other organ systems such as the lung, kidney, and liver note only minimal differences between infants born at 24 weeks and those born at term. Most importantly, within a few weeks postnatally, the function of these systems becomes more comparable to infants of similar post natal age, independent of the gestational age at birth. In other words, extrauterine life accelerates maturation. In contrast, not only is the brain of a 24 weeks' gestational age infant strikingly physically different from that of a term infant's, extrauterine life delays the maturation process both as to brain structure and function [24]. This is depicted graphically in figures 3 and 4. Thus, one may conclude that we may 'have hit the wall' and that routine initiation of resuscitation and maximum care may not be appropriate for infants born less than 25–26 weeks' gestation [25].

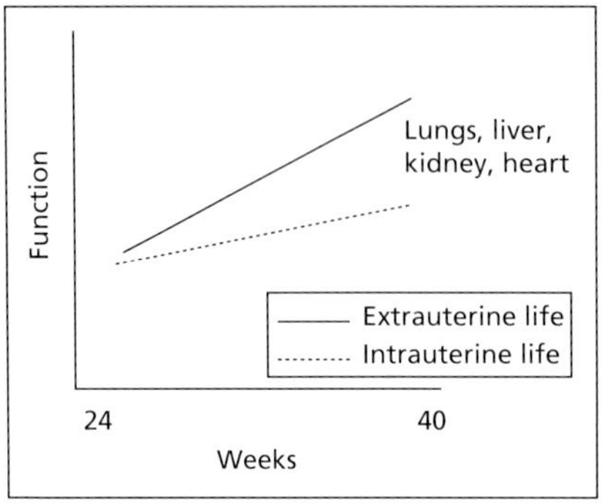

Fig. 3.

Postnatal organ development (lungs, liver, kidney, heart).

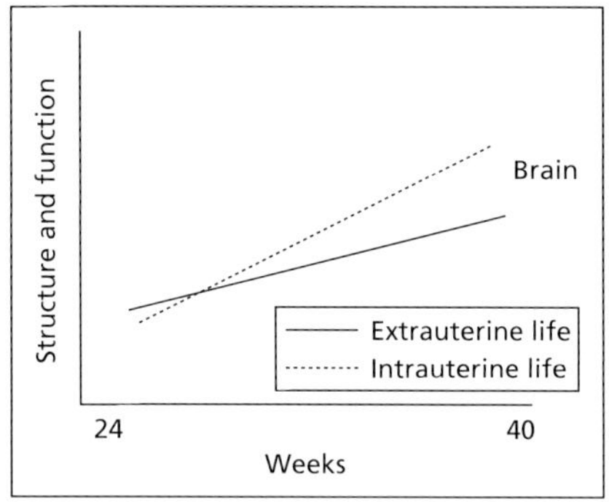

Fig. 4.

Postnatal organ development (brain).

Physician Treatment Practices at the Threshold of Viability

In view of these results and concerns it is most interesting to know what physicians as individuals will recommend regarding treating infants born at the limits of viability.

Published reports outcome of survival from both single institutions and networks do not give us a clear picture as the populations are highly selective and reports do not always include the entire cohort of infants who are born in other hospitals in the same catchment area or who are not resuscitated. Attitudinal studies based on responses to hypothetical case scenarios reflects beliefs and at time wishful thinking of physicians, but may be unrelated to the reality of what is actually happening on the front line. These studies are of interest, however, as they are still a measure of the cultural and religious attitudes of the medical profession in the context of the ethos of a given country. Figure 5 depicts the results of a major study [26] of physicians from a variety of European countries who were posed the question if would they withhold care from extremely low birth weight infants. As the figure shows, save for Italy, between 70 and 90% of the physicians from all other European countries were willing to withhold therapy from very low birth weight infants. Shinwell [27] surveyed Israeli physicians and posed the question 'does one routinely resuscitate infants born at 26 weeks or less. He noted that at 22 weeks 10% of physicians stated that

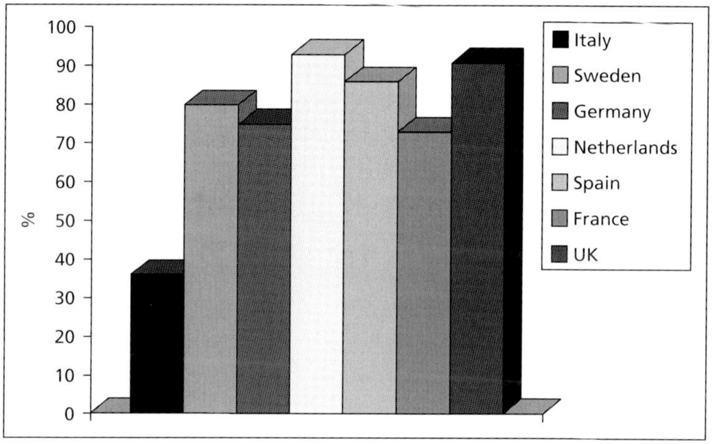

Fig. 5.
Withholding intensive care in very low birth weight infants: european physicians [26].

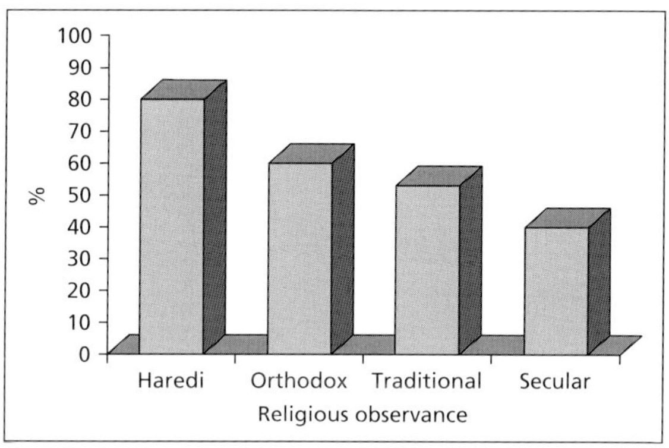

Fig. 6.
Mothers requesting maximal care for extremely low birth weight (<500g) at the Shaare Zedek Medical Center [28].

they would resuscitate, at 23 weeks 20% and 24 weeks 40%, even if the parents objected. Hammerman et al. [28] surveyed the attitude of Israeli mothers and analyzed the results by the degree of religiosity of the parents (fig. 6). Eighty percent of ultra-religious (Haredi) parents would request

Table 8.

Treatment decisions and outcome at threshold of viability: Israel National Very Low Birth Weight Database (1996–2000)

	22 weeks	23 weeks	24 weeks	25 weeks
Livebirths	101	243	423	481
Treated	34 (34%)	165 (68%)	38 (92%)	470 (98%)
Survived	1 (1%)	10 (4%)	86 (20%)	204 (42%)
Severe neonatal morbidity	0 (0%)	6 (60%)	51 (59%)	124 (61%)

resuscitation even for infants born less than 500 g, while at the other end of the religious spectrum; only 40% of the secular mothers would request resuscitation. Such data confirm, once again, the cultural biases of both physicians and families that reflect their own values and not the specific medical status of the infant.

The real test, however, is what is going on in the delivery room and the neonatal intensive care units, not theoretical responses to hypothetical questions of written scenarios. Reichman et al. [19] of the Israel National Very Low Birth Weight Database recently completed such a total population study. The data base encompasses the complete experience of all Israeli hospitals for the period 1996–2000 and analyzes the results of 1,248 deliveries between 22 and 25 weeks' gestational age. These results are summarized in table 8. Of the 101 infants born at 22 weeks, in only 34 was resuscitation and intensive care initiated. All those that did not receive any aggressive care died in the delivery room or shortly after in the neonatal intensive care unit. Of those treated, only one infant survived resulting in a survival rate of those treated of 3% and of those born at this week gestation of 1%. At 23 weeks, of the 243 infants born 68% received intensive care in the delivery room and nursery and in 32% only minimal supportive care was provided. All of the infants who received minimal care died and of those treated only 10 survived to discharge (6% of those treated, 4% of those born). At 24 weeks' gestation the picture changed. Ninety-two percent of the 423 infants born at this gestational age received maximum care. However, only 22% of those treated survived. At 25 weeks 98% of the infants were treated and the survival rate rose to 43%. The neurological and pulmonary morbidity by gestational age was tabulated. Of interest was

Table 9.
Canadian Pediatric and Obstetrics and Gynecology Societies Recommendations 1994 (reconfirmed 2000)

- <22 weeks (<154 days) – compassionate care
- 22 completed weeks (154–160 days) compassionate care; active treatment 'only on request of fully informed parents'
- 23–24 weeks (161–174 days) per parents wishes, flexibility, 'modified by condition of birth'
- 25–26 weeks (175–188 days), resuscitate and treat all except those with fatal anomalies

the observation that with each increase in gestational age the pulmonary morbidity significantly decreased; however, there was no improvement in major neurological morbidity; confirming once again the dissociation between survival and neurological morbidity outcome. These results force one, once again, to question the wisdom of treating aggressively every infant born at this early gestational age (< 26 weeks).

Published Guidelines

Over the past decade, various national and international medical societies have published guidelines for the treatment of infants born at the borderline of viability. In 1991, the Eugenic Protection Act of Japan [29] was amended and the viability limit was reduced from 24 to 22 weeks. Follow-up data of the results of this policy change noted that of the 901 infants born less than 24 weeks since the policy change, 220 (37%) survived and of the survivors 65% had no handicap. This degree of neurological morbidity was deemed acceptable and the authors concluded that this 'viability limit ... is justified' for the Japanese society.

In 1994, the Canadian Paediatric Society and Society of Obstetricians and Gynecologist [30] published detailed guidelines for the 'Management of Woman with Threatened Birth of an Infant of Extremely Low Gestational Age'. Table 9 outlines their recommendations which emphasizes that the absolute cut off for resuscitation is 22 completed weeks of gestation. Between 22 and 23 weeks only compassionate care is recommended, unless fully informed parents request otherwise. Only after completion of a full 24 weeks was resuscitation and maximum care recommended as a routine, save for infants with fatal anomalies.

In 2000, the American Academy of Pediatrics and the American Heart Association [31] published guidelines for resuscitation that stated 'non-initiation of resuscitation in the delivery room is appropriate for infants born less than 23 weeks or with a birth weight less than 400 g'.

In 2002, both the American College of Obstetrics and Gynecology (ACOG) [32] and the American Academy of Pediatrics (AAP) [33] published separate guideline statements on 'Perinatal Care at the Threshold of Viability'.

The thrust of the ACOG guidelines is reflected in the following quote:

> 'Decisions to the extent of resuscitative efforts and subsequent support are complex. The decision to withhold or withdraw ... should be individualized, based on the newborns condition at birth, survival and morbidity data, and parent's preferences.
>
> From a review of the literature it is concluded that there is good and consistent evidence, that infants born below 24 weeks have less than a 50% survival and that 50% of survivors will have disabilities in mental and psychomotor development. Thus, nonresuscitation and non initiation of intensive care is justified at this cut off subject to parental preference'.

The American Academy of Pediatrics summarized its recommendations as follows:

1 Parents should receive appropriate information about survival ... and adverse long-term outcomes.
2 Decisions regarding all aspects of management ... are made jointly by parents and physicians.
3 Parental choice ... is respected within limits of medical feasibility and appropriateness.

What is the appropriate information that should be transmitted? The AAP guidelines quote the Resuscitation Guidelines that [31] 'noninitiation of resuscitation for newborns of less than 23 weeks gestational and/or 400 g is appropriate'. In addition they advise that counseling of parents should include the information that 30–50% of surviving infants born between 23 and 25 weeks or with birth weight less than 750 g will have moderate or severe disability. As a result, given the uncertainty of the prognosis and significant risk of a poor outcome, decision on part of the parents to withhold resuscitation and life support treatment is deemed appropriate. Such a decision presumably will be based on the parental understanding of the realities of the medical situation with all its indefiniteness, the families own cultural, religious, ethnic background and their ethical and personal value system.

One must be honest, however, that advocating that informed parents should have the ultimate responsibility for decision making in the case of infants at the borderline of viability may not be a reality. For one, it is not clear how logistically one can always arrange for an appropriate discussion that will facilitate informed consent, given the medical situation of an unplanned preterm delivery. In addition, it is not clear what the capacity of the families is to fully understand the long-term implications and consequences of the birth of such a high-risk infant. Furthermore, Ballard et al. [34] recently reported that 'there is a strong disposition among neonatologists towards respecting parental wishes. This disposition is stronger when neonatologists are given reason to be concerned about litigation.'

Of interest, the previous statement of the Committee on Fetus and Newborn of the AAP [10], from 1995, entitled 'The Initiation or Withdrawal of Treatment for High Risk Newborn' approached this issue with a somewhat different 'flavor'. That statement (which is not superseded by the 2002 statement) while seemingly emphasizing that 'the rights of parents in decision making be respected' proceeds to state: 'However, physicians should not be forced to undertreat or overtreat an infant if, in their best medical judgment, the treatment is not in compliance with the standard of care for that infant'. Furthermore, its final recommendation states: 'If the viability of the infant is unknown, or if the curative value of the treatment is uncertain, the decision to initiate treatment or continue treatment should be based only on the benefit to the infant that might be derived from such action'. From careful reading of this 1995 statement one can conclude that in the end it is the physician who knows best. This represents what Leuthner [35] has defined as the 'expertise model' for determining what is the best interest of the child. On the other hand, in contrast, the 2002 statements of both ACOG [32] and AAP [33] recommend, in the terminology of Leuthner, a 'negotiated model' of joint decision making, with the parents desires as the critical deciding factor. Which of these two models guarantees that the decisions taken will be in the best interest of the child is not clear.

A Personal Dilemma

There is no doubt that shift from the paternalistic expertise model of deciding what is the best interest of the child to a decision making process which focuses on parental responsibility reflects the reality that it is the family that has to bear the consequences of the birth of such high-risk infants. It is clear that the consequences of the birth and survival of an infant born at the limits of viability may be lifelong, and involve an emotional, financial and logistical burden that some families do not or cannot wish to bear. What should be understood, however, is that a decision based on parental understanding of the consequences of care, of their evaluation of their capacity to meet the future needs of their handicapped child, and the projection into the future as to their own needs and values, more accurately characterizes such a decision as one that is in the 'best interest of the family'. One has to remember that the best interest of the family is not synonymous with best interest of the infant. As such, a more honest and courageous conclusion would be to state that it is possible that the expertise model of decision making, with all its inherent biases, may be a better process for determining what is in the best interest of the infant. No doubt such a medical expert should not impose his or her value system, should have input from the parents as to the desires and capacities, and surely should have access to data on the medical realities in the geographic wherein such a specific infant is being cared. This demands the involved physician to be knowledgeable about the realities of his local resources and potential consultative or referral centers and not to simply quote or extrapolate from experiences of distant centers [36, 37].

Underlying this tension between what can be characterized as the best interest of the child as opposed to what is the best interest of the family is my concern as to what is the basic attitude of society to the newborn, in general, and to the extremely-low-birth-weight immature infant who is born at the limits of viability, in particular. Clinicians who are responsible for the care of such infants, and even more so physicians who care for the mothers of such infants are all too familiar with the common reaction when such an infant dies. 'Don't worry Mrs. Cohen, in a few months you will be pregnant and you will have a healthy newborn'. This seeming consoling statement is essentially saying that the baby who died is replaceable, that the 'tragedy' of its death is no worse than a 'late miscarriage', and that an infants' death is different than a loss of a beloved child.

Table 10.
Mourning practices for the premature infant – not 'bar kayamah' (has not demonstrated viability)

- No blessing (Baruch Dayan Emet)
- No rendering of garment (Kriyah)
- No specific grave – buried, with stillbirth
- No grave marker (Matzevah)
- No 7-day mourning period (Shiva)
- No 30th day memorial and erection of matzevah (Shloshim)
- No annual memorial day (Yartzeit)
- No naming of child

In fact, this reaction and attitude to the death of a newborn, let alone an infant born at the limits of viability, has been institutionalized in most cultures by the unique mourning practices for infants. For example, traditional Jewish ritual law excludes, if not actually proscribes, the family from practicing the mourning rituals that have been standardized for the death of any other member the group. According to Jewish tradition all infants, let alone those born at an extremely early gestational age are defined as having not achieved the status of a '*bar kayamah*', i.e. a viability. That status is not 'earned' for a term baby until it lives 30 days, for a preterm infant it may be months before acquiring the status of a full person. As such, when such an infant dies he is buried, with reverence, along with the remains of stillbirths, miscarriages, and amputated limbs in a common unmarked grave. As listed in table 10, none of the personal or societal rituals that facilitate mourning and concretize the reality that a human being has lived and died take place. Beyond the psychosocial consequences of such a custom, that in the end interferes with the family working through its grief, there is no doubt in my mind that characterizing the infant in such a way defines him as 'other' and inevitably of lesser value. As a result, life and death decisions made by a family or a medical expert that has internalized these values may conclude that the solution to the potential long range problem of this 'nonviable' infant is its death and replacement with a future child. If so, such a decision may not necessarily be in the best interest of the infant! Furthermore, until such time that we acknowledge the existence of these complex value and societal issues and separate them from the objective medical and scientific facts, the dilemma of what to do for these infants will persist [37].

Conclusion and Speculation

In the coming decade we can anticipate a further increase in the survival rate for infants born below 24–25 weeks' gestation and a lowering of the limits of viability to 21–22 weeks or less. However, improvement in morbidity outcome will be dependant on new knowledge and technology that will allow us to simulate the intrauterine environment and its unique neurotrophic features. Until then, physicians, families and society will continue to grapple with the ethical dilemmas of treating infants at the threshold of viability and in evaluating what is truly in the best interests of such infants.

References

1 Duff RS, Campbell AG: Moral and ethical dilemmas in the special care nursery. N Engl J Med 1973;289:890–894.

2 Schechner S: For the 1980s: How small is too small. Clin Perinatol 1980;7:135–143.

3 Harrison H: Medical miracle or Pyrrhic victory. Birth 1992;19:157–158.

4 Peabody JL, Martin GI: From how small is too small to how much is too much: Ethical issues at the limits of neonatal viability. Clin Perinatol 1996;23:473–489.

5 Pinkerton JV, Finnerty JJ, Lombardo PA, Rorty MV, Chapple H, Boyle RJ: Parental rights at the birth of a near-viable infant: Conflicting perspectives. Am J Obstet Gynecol 1997;177:283–288.

6 Fleischman AR, Chervenak FA, McCullough LB: The physician's moral obligations to the pregnant woman, the fetus, and the child. Semin Perinatol 1998;22:184–188.

7 Doroshow RW, Hodgman JE, Pomerance JJ, et al: Treatment decisions for newborns at the threshold of viability: An ethical dilemma. J Perinatol 2000;20:379–383.

8 Campbell DE, Fleischman AR: Limits of viability: Dilemmas, decisions, and decision makers. Am J Perinatol 2001;18: 117–128.

9 Lorenz JM: Survival of the extremely preterm infant in North America in the 1990s. Clin Perinatol 2000;27: 255–262.

10 American Academy of Pediatrics Committee on Fetus and Newborn: The initiation or withdrawal of treatment of high-risk newborns. Pediatrics 1995;96:362–363.

11 American Academy of Pediatrics Committee on Fetus and Newborn. American College of Obstetricians and Gynecologists Committee on Obstetric Practice. Perinatal care at the threshold of viability. Pediatrics 1995;96:974–976.

12 Hoekstra RE, Ferrara TB, Couser RJ, Payne NR, Connett JE: Survival and long-term neurodevelopmental outcome of extremely premature infants born at 23–26 weeks' gestational age at a tertiary center. Pediatrics 2004; 113:e1–6.
13 Fanaroff AA, Hack M, Walsh MC: The NICHD neonatal research network: Changes in practice and outcomes during the first 15 years. Semin Perinatol 2003;27:281–287.
14 Lemons JA, Bauer CR, Oh W, et al: Very low birth weight outcomes of the National Institute of Child Health and Human Development Neonatal Research Network, January 1995 through December 1996. Pediatrics 2001; 107:e1–8.
15 Hack M, Wilson-Costello D, Friedman H, Taylor GH, Schluchter M, Fanaroff AA: Neurodevelopment and predictors of outcomes of children with birth weights of less than 1000 g: 1992–1995. Arch Pediatr Adolesc Med 2000; 154:725–731.
16 Sweet MP, Hodgman JE, Pena I, Barton L, Pavlova Z, Ramanthan R: Two-year outcome of infants weighing 600 grams or less at birth and born 1994 through 1998. Obstet Gynecol 2003;101:18–23.
17 Vohr BR, Wright LL, Duscik AM, et al: Neurodevelopmental and functional outcomes of extremely low birth weight infants in the National Institute of Child Health and Human Development Neonatal Research Network, 1993–1994. Pediatrics 2000;105:1216–1226.
18 Wood NS, Marlow N, Costeloe K, Gibson AT, Wilkinson AR: Neurologic and developmental disbility after extremely preterm birth. EPICure Study Group. N Engl J Med 2000;343: 378–384.
19 Reichman B, Zmora E, Lusky A, Cohen-Manheim I, Levitsky O, Geva-Lerner L: Collaboration with Israel Neonatal Network. Perinatal determinants of active intensive care at the borderline of viability. Womens and Children Health Research Unit, Gertner Institute, Israel Center for Disease Control, Tel Hashomer, 2002.
20 Yoon BH, Jun JK, Romero R, et al: Amniotic fluid inflammatory cytokines (interleukins-6, interleukin-1 beta, and tumor necrosis factor-alpha), neonatal brain white matter lesions and cerebral palsy. Am J Obstet Gynecol 1997; 177:19–26.
21 Shinwell ES, Karplus M, Reich D, et al: Early postnatal dexamethasone treatment and increased incidence of cerebral palsy. Arch Dis Child Fetal Neonatal 2000;83: F177–181.
22 Huppi PS, Schuknecht B, Boesch C, et al: Structural and neurobehavioral delay in postnatal brain development of preterm infants. Pediatr Res 1996;39:895–901.
23 Maalouf EF, Duggan PJ, Rutherford MA, et al: Magnetic resonance imaging of the brain in a cohort of extremely preterm infants. J Pediatr 1999;135:351–357.
24 Peterson BS, Vohr B, Staib LH, et al: Regional brain volumes abnormalities and long-term cognitive outcome in preterm infants. JAMA 2000;284:1939–1947.
25 Sheldon T: Dutch doctors change policy on treating preterm infants. BMJ 2001;322: 1383.
26 Cuttini M, Nadai M, Kaminski M, et al: End-of-life decisions in neonatal intensive care: Physicians' self reported practices in seven European countries EURONIC Study Group. Lancet 2000;355:2112–2118.
27 Shinwell ES. Decision making at the end of very short pregnancies: Input of the neonatologist. Israel J Obstet Gynecol 2001;12: 77–80.

28 Hammerman C, Kornbluth E, Lavie O, Zadka P, Aboulafia Y, Eidelman AI. Decision-making in the critically ill neonate: Cultural background vs individual life experience. J Med Ethics 1997;23: 164–169.
29 Oishi M, Nishida H, Sasaki T: Japanese experience with micropremies weighing less than 600 grams born between 1984 and 1993. Pediatrics 1997;99: e7–11.
30 Fetus and Newborn Committee: Canadian Paediatric Society, Maternal-Fetal Medicine Committee, Society of Obstetricians and Gynecologists of Canada. Management of the woman with threatened birth of an infant of extremely low gestational age. Can Med Assoc J 1994;151:547–553.
31 Niermeyer S, Kattwinkel J, Van Reempts P, et al: International Guidelines for Neonatal Resuscitation: An Excerpt from the Guidelines 2000 for Cardiopulmonary Resuscitation and Emergency Cardiovascular Care: International Consensus on Science. Contributors and Reviewers for the Neonatal Resuscitation Guidelines. Pediatrics 2000; 106:e29.
32 American College of Obstetrics and Gynecology: ACOG Practice Bulletin: Clinical Management Guidelines for Obstetrician-Gynecologists: Number 38, September 2002. Perinatal care at the threshold of viability. Obstet Gynecol 2002;100:617–624.
33 MacDonald H: American Academy of Pediatrics, Committee on Fetus and Newborn. Perinatal care at the threshold of viability. Pediatrics 2002;110:1024–1027.
34 Ballard DW, Li Y, Evans J, Ballard RA, Ubel PA: Fear of litigation may increase resuscitation of infants born near the limits of viability. J Pediatr 2002;140:713–718.
35 Leuthner SB: Decisions regarding resuscitation of the extremely premature infant and models of best interest. J Perinatol 2001; 21:193–198.
36 Lee SK, McMillan DD, Ohlsson A, et al: Variations in practice and outcomes in the Canadian NICU Network: 1996–1997. Pediatrics 2000;106:1070–1079.
37 Eidelman AI: Care of the critically ill newborns: The Israeli experience. J Legal Med 1995;16:247–261.

Arthur I. Eidelman, MD

Department of Pediatrics, Shaare Zedek Medical Center,
PO Box 3235, IL–91031 Jerusalem (Israel)
Tel. +972 2 655 5197, Fax +972 2 655 5297, E-Mail eidel@cc.huji.ac.il

Blazer S, Zimmer EZ (eds):
The Embryo: Scientific Discovery and Medical Ethics.
Basel, Karger, 2005, pp 371–400

At the Edge of Viability: Philosophical, Moral and Ethical Aspects and Proposals

Asa Kasher

Laura Schwarz-Kipp Chair of Professional Ethics and Philosophy of Practice,
Department of Philosophy, Tel-Aviv University, Tel Aviv, Israel

The purpose of the present chapter is to set a conceptual, ethical and moral framework for discussion of medical cases that involve 'tiny babies', at the edge of viability. The first part of the chapter will elucidate the major concepts, such as 'viability' and 'the edge of viability'. The second part of the chapter will outline general grounds for making decisions with respect to neonates at the edge of viability. Principles will be proposed and defended for making decisions concerning such neonates. The third part will discuss several additional problems that are encountered in the area of treatment of neonates at the edge of viability. Solutions will be suggested on grounds of the principles and other insights of the previous parts.

Major Notions: Philosophical Elucidation

Our first step in the development of an appropriate framework for decision-making in medical cases that involve babies at the edge of viability is the preliminary step of a philosophical elucidation of the major concepts that are used or that should be used in such instances of decision making.

At the focus of a typical case of that nature is a 'tiny baby' at the 'edge of viability'.

Decisions are required in matters of life and death of that neonate. Naturally, then, the first notions that need elucidation are those of *viability, the edge of viability,* and *sanctity of human life.* We will now discuss each of them in turn and several other ones as well.

Viability

Literally, the notion of 'viability' is related to the major capabilities of existence and development. Hence, when viability is attributed to a state of a fetus, what is literally asserted is that the fetus is capable of living and growing in the normal way.

However, the notion of 'viability', when applied to a state of a fetus, has gained a different sense. Roughly speaking, it refers to the capability to live outside the mother's womb. When applied to a state of a neonate, 'viability' means, again roughly speaking, the capability to live, with no commitment to the quality of the expected life or development of the neonate.

The notion of 'capability to live' is ambiguous in several respects. First, a question arises as to whether human 'capability to live' means capability to live independently of other human beings, or rather capability to live albeit with help, rendered by other human beings, even if this help is crucial for one's life. As the notion of 'viability' is applied to a fetus or a neonate, it has to be understood as having the latter sense: capability to live, albeit with help, even if it is help crucial for staying alive.

Secondly, a question has to be answered as to whether 'viability' means just capability to live for any period of time, or rather capability to live for a long period of time. Again, as the notion of 'viability' is usually applied to a fetus or a neonate, it is the latter sense that is conveyed: capability to live, for a rather long period of time.

Here it would be natural to ask how long should be a period of time in order to be 'a long period of time'. Should it be a period of years or even decades, or could it be just months or even weeks? Usage of the notion of 'viability' with respect to a fetus or a neonate seems to justify neither of these alternatives. On the one hand, a fetus can be described as having 'viability', even if we do not have grounds for predicting a life expectancy of several years, let alone decades. On the other hand, a neonate can be described as having 'viability', even if we do have grounds for predicting a life expectancy of about a year. Hence, it seems advisable to introduce two different notions of 'viability'. First, there should be a notion of *'ordinary viability'*, which means capability to live, when there are no grounds for predicting life expectancy less than average. Secondly, there should be a parametric notion of *'t-viability'*, where *t* is a certain period of time (weeks, months, years or what have you). The '*t*-viability' notion will be usable when there are grounds for predicting life expectancy in terms of *t*. Accordingly, arguments concerning the fate of a fetus or a neonate that are commonly phrased in terms of 'viability' should be rephrased in terms of 'ordinary viability' and '*t*-viability'. In the sequel, whenever we use the notions of 'viability' or 'the edge of viability', the meaning will be that of 'ordinary viability', unless some notion of '*t*-viability' is used.

Finally, clarification is required of the nature of the 'potential', which is an apparent element of 'viability', given that viability is a capability and every capability is seemingly a potential ability. The question is, now, what is the nature of the potential ability that has to be present for viability to be correctly attributed to a fetus or a neonate. Every claim about a potential is hypothetical: If certain conditions obtain, then a certain attribute appears. For example, a grain of salt is soluble in the sense that *if* it is put in water *then* it dissolves. Similarly, a fetus is viable in the sense that if the condition that it is outside its mother's womb obtains, then the attribute that it stays alive appears. However, when we try to elucidate the notion of the 'potential ability' a fetus has to live, or live, grow and develop, it is not clear what should be the condition or conditions mentioned in the antecedent of the hypothetical presentation of the potential ability. Should there be a single condition, for example, that it is outside the womb? Or should there be a couple of conditions, such as the conditions that it is outside the womb and that it is being provided with external help of one kind or another? Or again, should there be yet another cluster of conditions, such as some conditions that require a process of future development within the womb and then getting outside the womb and being provided with some external help?

It seems that the common usage of 'viability' does not involve conditions of the latter kind as antecedent of the hypothetical presentation of the potential ability. The potential ability is not manifest, when a fetus is inside the womb and therefore cannot at one and the same time appear alive outside the womb. However, not much time is required for the potential ability to materialize, when the condition in the antecedent of the hypothetical presentation obtains, and as a result for the attribute of the consequent of that hypothetical to appear. Thus, a fetus can be viable, but an embryo does not have the potential ability involved in viability, since it has to undergo a long process of growth and development before it becomes a fetus, let alone a fetus that is capable to live outside the womb.

If we combine the observations that have just been made then we get the following elucidation of the notion of 'viability' that would serve us in the sequel. An attribution of 'viability' to a fetus or a neonate is an attribution of a present capability to live outside the womb, for a long period of time, albeit with some crucial external help. The length of the time involved varies. Attribution of 'ordinary viability' means that an average life expectancy is predicted, whereas attribution of some '*t*-viability' means that it is a life expectancy of a period *t* that is predicted.

So far, we have considered attributions of viability as if it is a matter of certainty, as if there is a 'yes' or 'no' answer to the question as to whether a certain neonate, under certain conditions, is viable or not. When we have a highly corroborated theory, on grounds of which it is possible to make highly accurate predictions, our answers to such particular viability questions can reach a level of near certainty. However, as long as this is not the case, practical predictions are of a probabilistic nature, seldom on a level of near certainty. Under such circumstances there seems to be a strong inclination to redefine viability in terms of a certain probabilistic threshold. Let us, then, draw a distinction between the notion of 'absolute viability', which is the notion of 'viability' we have so far discussed, and 'probabilistic viability'. The latter can be defined in terms of the former, using a formula of the following form: A neonate is probabilistically viable if, and only if, the probability of its being absolutely viable is more than 5% (for example).

It is our view that such formulae should be avoided. The probability of a certain neonate being (absolutely) viable, under certain circumstances, is part of the major data about a neonate. Such probabilities will play a practical role, under appropriate circumstances. For example, when resources are scarce, the higher the probability the higher the priority of being treated, ceteris paribus. However, since a definition of '(probabilistic) viability' in terms of a certain probability, say 5%, might lead to a policy of disregarding the fate of neonates whose (absolute) viability is, say, 4% or 3%, it seems advisable to avoid it. Consideration of probabilistic data should accordingly be confined to crafting practices and policies rather than definitions.

The discussion in the sequel is confined to the fate of a viable neonate, though much of what we have to say would apply to a viable fetus as well.

Edge of Viability

Given such notions of 'viability', certain general claims can be made about ordinary viability as well as *t*-viability of a neonate. For example, it can be claimed that under present medical conditions, a healthy neonate is ordinarily viable if it is born after 25 weeks' gestation. General claims of that form can rest on grounds of viability statistics or of embryological theory. Since both data and theory are grounds for different viability claims, the natural question arises as to the *minimal* gestational age of neonates for which it is claimed that if a healthy neonate is of that age or older, then it is viable (in the appropriate sense). Thus, for a given body of knowledge that includes both viability statistics and corroborated theories, the *edge of viability* (in a certain sense) is definable. It is the *minimal* age for which it can be claimed, on grounds of that body of knowledge, that if a neonate is of that gestational age or older, then it is viable (in the same sense).

As we saw earlier, when notions of 'viability' were discussed, attribution of being at the edge of viability is more often than not an ascription of a certain probability rather than a certainty or a near certainty. Again, it seems advisable to resist the temptation to posit a certain threshold probability as constitutive of being at the edge of viability.

Probabilities should be taken into account when actions or policies are pondered, under appropriate circumstances, but this is hardly a reason to use a certain probability for our conceptual analysis of being at the edge of viability.

Strictly speaking, what has so far been defined as 'the edge of viability' is 'the edge of viability, relative to a body of knowledge'. Such a body of knowledge includes not only statistics and theories ('knowledge that'), but also methods of medical treatment intended to save life and enhance viability ('knowledge how'). Evidently, since both our 'knowledge that' and our 'knowledge how' never cease growing, the related edge of viability keeps getting smaller. Claims that the edge of (ordinary) viability is 22 weeks are either already correct or will sooner or later become correct.

Both 'knowledge that' and 'knowledge how' can be specified on two different levels. They can be specified on a local level, of a certain state or even of a certain medical center, but they can also be specified on a global level, which disregards present differences between certain sites, regions or states. An attribution of being at the edge of viability should be clear as to which level is being used in it. A presentation of the present medical conditions of a certain neonate at the edge of viability on one level should also be accompanied by the data with respect to being at the edge of viability on other levels. Ideally, a comprehensive presentation of those medical conditions includes data pertaining to alternative local levels, alternative regional or state levels, and the global level. What data is going to be used, under certain circumstances, depends on the problem tackled under those conditions.

Viability and Edge of Viability

At this point, we would like to point out the nature of these two notions. Attribution of viability or of being at the edge of viability to a certain neonate is a function of three types of knowledge:

Firstly, particular 'knowledge that', which is a specification of the medical conditions of the neonate under consideration.

Secondly, general 'knowledge that', which is statistical knowledge or theoretical knowledge pertaining to neonates under the same or similar conditions.

Thirdly, 'knowledge how', which is the medical and technological means available for treating that neonate.

Thus, attribution of viability or of being at the edge of viability to a certain neonate depends on facts of three kinds and on nothing else. In particular, there is no room for any societal decision as to what viability is or what should be considered as the edge of viability. Clearly, specification of medical conditions, statistical data and scientific theories is outside the confines of a societal deliberations and decision making procedures. Availability of medical and technological means of treatment might seem different, since societal decisions can be made as to whether some means are to be put at the disposal of medical staff for treatment of neonates at the edge of viability or neonates in general. However, such understanding of availability would be misguided. Attribution of viability or being at the edge of viability depends on the facts with respect to the relevant family of methods of treatment, medications, pieces of equipment, etc., in general, and not to any section of it that has been designated by some societal decision of whatever nature. Problems of expenditure give rise to societal deliberations and decisions, but the sharp distinction between matters of fact and matters of societal undertaking of expenses should not be blurred. We will return to matters of cost in the last part of the present chapter.

Person

We move now to a brief elucidation of a notion of 'person', which is of an utterly different nature, as we shall soon see. We are going to elucidate *a* notion of 'person' rather than *the* notion of 'person'. As a matter of fact there is a common usage of the term 'person' neither in daily parlance nor in philosophical literature.

It has often been claimed that the English term 'person' has derived from the Latin term 'persona', which meant a mask as used by an actor in a performance. Hence, to use the term 'person' in some context of utterance is to ascribe a certain role within that context. Thus, for example, in a legal context, to describe someone (a man or a woman) or something (a company or a state) as a '(legal) person' is to ascribe the legal role of having a cluster of legal attributes, such as responsibilities.

Since we are presently interested in moral and ethical considerations, we are going to elucidate a notion of 'person' that is used to ascribe a moral or an ethical role. The difference between a moral context and an ethical one will be explained in the sequel. For the present purpose, suffice it to make three assumptions about these contexts:

Firstly, both of them involve *normative* considerations, namely ones that involve considerations of what *is* the case but also and mainly of what *ought* to be the case. Secondly, both of them involve *principles* and *arrangements* that can justify claims as to what ought to be the case, under certain circumstances. Thirdly, in both of them the role played by a '(moral) person' or an '(ethical) person' is that of a focus of rights and duties that rest on certain normative principles and arrangements.

On the background of these assumptions, it makes sense to ask who is a person, or in other words, what are necessary or sufficient conditions for being a person, in a moral or an ethical context. At a later stage an additional question will arise, namely, what are the necessary *and* sufficient conditions for being a person, in a moral or ethical context. For our present purposes only the former questions will have to be considered.

Philosophical literature provides us with various answers to the former question. Here is one list of personhood elements that was compiled within a certain moral and ethical context, where reproduction issues were under consideration. The list included: minimum intelligence, self-awareness, self-control, a sense of time, a sense of futurity, a sense of the past, a capability of relating to others, concern for others, communication, control of existence, curiosity, change and changeability, balance of rationality and feeling, idiosyncrasy and neo-cortical functioning.

A list often looks arbitrary. Delineation on grounds of a seemingly arbitrary list seems invalid. Our delineation of persons, in a moral or an ethical context, will, therefore, rest on a method of delineation that can be justified as such.

In answering the former question, namely, who is a person, in a moral or an ethical context, we proceed along the following line of argument:

Firstly, we specify some ingredients of moral and ethical contexts.

Secondly, we point out some necessary or sufficient conditions for being able to play a role in a context that has those ingredients.

Thirdly, we draw distinctions between conditions that obtain in a full-fledged manner and those that obtain to a lesser extent. Among the latter we draw a distinction between those that are sufficiently similar to the former ones and those that are not.

Fourthly, on grounds of those distinctions we suggest an approximate answer to the question who is a person, in a moral or an ethical context.

We turn now to a brief presentation of these four steps.

Moral and ethical contexts manifest several distinct features. First of all, they involve values and norms, that is to say, claims or arguments related to what is desirable, from some perspective, or what ought to be the case, from some point of view. Secondly, moral and ethical contexts involve societal arrangements that embody certain values and norms. Thirdly, such arrangements determine certain distributions of rights and duties. Finally, those arrangements bind their participants.

Thus, as a first approximate delineation of persons, in a moral or an ethical context, we have the class of participants in the above-mentioned arrangements, which are ingredients of such contexts.

Accordingly, in the second step of our method, we look for necessary or sufficient conditions for being a participant in those moral or ethical arrangements, which embody values and norms, distribute rights and duties and are binding. A philosophical project of characterizing moral or ethical personhood will have to provide us with a comprehensive description of such necessary or sufficient conditions, but presently we will confine ourselves to a brief presentation of a few examples. A necessary condition for being a party to a binding arrangement, such as a contract, is the cognitive condition of having a temporal self-identity. That is to say, one's view of oneself is that of a temporal being of a nature that enables one to identify one's present stage with some of one's future stages and both as stages of the same being. A necessary condition for being a participant in an arrangement that embodies values is the mental condition of having fixed desires that regulate one's behavior to a significant extent. A necessary condition for being a participant in an arrangement that distributes rights, which are justifications of claims, is the cognitive condition of having the abilities to justify a claim, to identify interests, and to remember states of affairs that give rise to claims and their justifications. Similar examples abound.

Usually, healthy adult human beings seem to have all those necessary abilities. Hence, as a second approximate delineation of persons, in a moral or an ethical context, we have the class of those beings that have all those necessary abilities. This class includes all healthy adult human beings.

However, when we look at some of these abilities, such as the ability to identify certain families of states or the ability to justify certain statements, it becomes clear that a significant distinction should be drawn between different states of ability. On the one hand, we have ability in its most mature form, while on the other hand we have the same ability at an earlier stage of its development, before it becomes mature. Children are our prime examples of human beings who do not have all those necessary abilities, but nevertheless are considered to be parties to the societal arrangements involved in moral and ethical contexts. They are often parties who are different in their distribution of rights and duties, for example, but parties to those arrangements they seem to be all right. Notice, furthermore, that children as well as adults sometimes lack some ability without thereby being put outside the confines of the class of persons, in moral and ethical contexts.

Accordingly, we have now as the third approximate delineation of persons, in moral and ethical contexts, the class of those beings that have all, or almost all, necessary abilities, whether in a mature form or in a well-developed but not yet mature form. This class includes human adults and children, though not all of them.

Finally, we draw a distinction between two developmental stages of ability. To grasp the leading idea underlying the distinction we are going to introduce, consider some ability that involves both a rich genetic endowment as well as a significant process of maturation. Linguistic ability is, indeed, a prime example. Consider, furthermore, the developmental stage of that ability upon birth. The genetic infrastructure of the ability is well developed, to an extent that enables the neonate to start undergoing a process of growth, development and maturation. The distinction we now introduce is between a developmental stage in which we have a well-developed infrastructure of some ability and a developmental stage of that ability in which the infrastructure is not yet well developed.

Now, our philosophical claim is that during a developmental stage in which the infrastructure of an ability is well developed, a significant part of that ability is already extant. Put differently, during such a developmental stage the ability is already extant, though in a significantly non-mature form. Most interesting are the 'edge' states, the first ones during which the infrastructure is already well developed. The most conspicuous example of our distinction is seen when those 'edge' states are compared to the immediately preceding ones. Our empirical assumptions are two: First, that the infrastructures of the above-mentioned necessary abilities reside in the cortex, and secondly, that the cortex is well developed from the 30th week of gestation and on. If a safety zone is added for accommodating individual differences, we reach the 26th week of gestation as the lower edge of the developmental stages during which the necessary abilities are presumably already extant.

We have now reached the fourth and presently final approximate delineation of persons, in a moral or an ethical context. From a conceptual point of view, what we have is the class of persons, in those contexts, delineated as the class of those beings that have all, or almost all, necessary abilities in one of the three following forms:

1 In a mature form.
2 In a well-developed but not yet mature form.
3 In the form of a well-developed infrastructure of the ability.

From an empirical point of view, this means that presumably every adult, child, baby, neonate and fetus during the third trimester of gestation are persons, in a moral or an ethical context.

Sanctity of Human Life

Several conceptions govern prevalent attitudes towards the life of a human being, be it a fetus or an adult, and since they are significantly different from each other, it seems advisable for our present purposes to clarify the gist of each of them.

The most entrenched form of adherence to a conception of the sanctity of life is found in the religious tradition of Jainism, which includes respect to all forms of life and a related strict insistence on non-violence. The sanctity of human life is, then, an interesting consequence of a general principle of sanctity of life.

Another conception of sanctity of life is confined to 'higher' forms of life, including human life as a prime example. One feature that 'higher' forms of life share with each other is sentience. A conception of the sanctity of 'higher' forms of life rests on an ascription of 'intrinsic value' to what manifests high intricacy of structure and functioning. Such forms of life are 'good' as such. Human life is 'good' in the same sense. Moreover, what is intrinsically 'good' should be well protected. Such an attitude of sanctity of human life serves as both a manifestation of the view of the intrinsic value of human life as well as an instrument of protection of human life.

A narrower conception of sanctity of 'higher' form of life applies to those that manifest, for example, both sentience and rationality. Although such conceptions are not proposed and defended as conceptions of the sanctity of human life, since their notion of 'higher' forms of life applies in our era and environment only to human beings, they serve as 'edge' conceptions of the sanctity of human life. All other conception will be, in some sense, narrower than that one.

One such conception is found in the tradition of the Jewish religion. Within such a tradition, any conception of 'sanctity' applies in a primary sense only to the deity. Every attribution of 'sanctity' to human life is, therefore, derivative or even undesirable. However, on the background of some conception of the relationships between the deity and human beings, human life is extremely precious, on the one hand, but is not absolutely protected, on the other hand. According to an ancient Jewish norm, if a Jew is threatened with death, unless one commits idolatry, bloodshed or adultery, then one should be willing to be killed rather than commit such activities. On any other occasion, protection of human life 'overrides everything', every other norm of religious validity. Strictly speaking, this is a conception of the 'preciousness', rather than 'sanctity', of human life, in a somewhat restricted sense.

Finally, we have a 'preciousness' conception of human life that does not rest on any view of the intrinsic value of human life or of a divinely endowed value of human life. This conception rests on the simple observation that being alive is a precondition for being a participant in societal arrangements that embody values and norms and distribute rights and duties. (To be sure, it is not meaningless to speak, for example, about the rights of the deceased, but such figures of speech are not paradigmatic.)

According to this conception, protection of human life is protection of what is a necessary element of any valuable societal arrangement. No wonder that from a democratic point of view, the life of the citizen is of uppermost importance. In a sense, this is a 'necessary precondition' conception of human life. In the sequel, we will argue on grounds of such a conception, which is part and parcel of most of the broader conceptions that prescribe protection of human life.

Dignity

Protection of human life is one dimension of protection of human dignity. Whereas we clearly have a working understanding of human life and its protection, it seems to be advisable to elucidate some notion of human 'dignity' and its protection.

A conception of human dignity involves, first of all, a sharp distinction between human beings and objects. Accordingly, protection of human dignity requires practical adherence to that basic distinction by means of clear and regular manifestations of commitment to practices that do not treat human beings on a par with objects, such as stones, cars, computers and robots. Given such a distinction, a question often arises as to the position of non-human sentient beings. Proponents of human rights may put them together with human beings. Other ones will not put them there. For our present purposes, we will adopt the former way, without drawing from the difference between the two ways any crucial conclusions.

Secondly, every conception of human dignity allows drawing distinctions between different human beings and even expressing them in our practices. We all treat our beloved ones in ways that are very significantly different from ways we treat all the rest. Our states treat citizens and non-citizens quite differently. However, a *moral* conception of human dignity sets a practical threshold of respect to be paid to every human being as such. Moral principles of respecting human dignity apply to every interaction between human beings, not just to interactions between relatives, friends or compatriots. They equally apply to interactions between strangers and even enemies.

Thirdly, a *moral* conception of human dignity puts respect for human autonomy at the center of respect for human beings. To respect a human being is practically, first and foremost, to enable that human being to create, maintain and nurture a form of life in which one manifests one's values and taste, beliefs and desires. No wonder, then, that a democracy, which embodies in its form of regime a moral conception of human dignity, has a constitutional bill of rights that protects the autonomy of every citizen in one's most fundamental spheres of life.

Finally, democratic systems of human rights, which embody conceptions of human dignity, never involve absolute liberties, that is to say, liberties that may be exercised by a human being under all circumstances, without any restriction being imposed on them on any grounds, come what may. Human rights, as we know them from various bills of rights, are always restricted. No citizen has an absolute freedom of movement, for example. One's right of free movement does not apply beyond the gates of one's neighbor's home. Such a restriction is justified, when we have to protect both human privacy and movement. However, restrictions can be imposed on human rights and liberties for various other reasons as well, such as ideological or political ones. A *moral* conception of human dignity restricts those restrictions to ones that are necessary for the protection of a *system* of liberties that enable everyone to equally enjoy one's autonomy in all fundamental spheres of human life.

We have outlined a conception of what has been described as 'human dignity and its protection'. However, what has actually been outlined here is a conception of the dignity of a person (in a moral or an ethical context) and its protection. Accordingly, the four elements that have been mentioned apply not only to an adult human being but also to a fetus during the third trimester of gestation as well.

The Slope of Dignity Protection

Protection of an area can be done at its gates and borders, without anything being done outside its confines. However, effective protection involves protection both of the area itself and some of its adjacent areas. Protection of the area itself will be of a different nature from that of an adjacent area. Whereas attempts to eliminate any hostile activity within the area itself is constitutive of the very idea of protection of the area, attempts to eliminate or at least weaken hostilities in adjacent areas is an auxiliary method, meant to face a potential danger before it turns into an actual one.

The nature of *essential protection* is, then, different from that of *auxiliary protection*, but both kinds are required in a practical system of effective protection.

A major ingredient of auxiliary protection of the dignity of persons, in a moral or an ethical context, is the conception of *the slope of dignity protection*. At the top end of the slope we have a person, whose dignity is protected. The dignity and its protection are fully-fledges. At the bottom end of the slope we have, for example, a grain of sand on a beach, which is not the subject matter of any claim for dignity and its protection. A slope is extended from the bottom end to the top end. The upper something is on the slope, the more dignity it deserves and the more extensive should be its protection. A fertilized egg is above an unfertilized egg, on the slope, but under a blastocyst. A fetus is above an embryo, on that slope, because it is closer in its structure and functioning to a person than an embryo. Protection of the dignity of a fetus is stronger than that of an embryo, in the sense that stronger arguments are required for justifying, say, an abortion of a fetus than an abortion of an embryo.

We will call our duties to protect the life and dignity of a person *primary* ones and the duties to protect the life or dignity of what is on the slope of dignity but not a person *secondary* ones.

Notice that a similar slope of dignity protection is involved in human attitudes towards cadavers, bones and graves. Every culture has its own practices of paying respect to the deceased, but all seem to have an underlying conception of a slope of dignity. At the top end of the slope, one step removed from the living person, we have the corpse of a person who has just died. At the bottom end we have, again, a grain of sand on a beach. A grave is above that grain of sand, on the slope. A cadaver is above a grave, on that slope, because it is closer to the person in the causal chain of states after death.

Mastering practices of paying gradual respect along those slopes of dignity protection is, therefore, a precondition of successful maintenance of any effective practice of paying respect to persons, who are at the top ends of those slopes.

Morality and Ethics

Finally, we have to draw a distinction between moral and ethical contexts. Our distinction does not involve the semantic traditions of using the notions of 'morality' and 'ethics', since during the history of philosophy, theology, law and other adjacent areas, those notions have often been used interchangeably. When you fetch a book on morality or an essay on ethics, they may well discuss the same issues in similar ways, but we should be aware of the fact that they may address rather different, even if related issues.

There are different points of view from which we consider and evaluate human interactions. When we witness an interaction between two human beings, we can depict it in different ways. First of all, it can be depicted as an interaction between two persons. Our descriptions of them will be confined to the fact that each of them is a person. However, under ordinary circumstances, the same interaction is amenable to a variety of richer descriptions. Think of an interaction between a parent and a son, a physician and a patient, a manager and a nurse, to mention just a few examples. Such a description of the same interaction between two persons brings into the picture roles (parent, son, patient), professions (physician, nurse) and organizational affiliation (manager). Now, to bring into the picture a profession, for example, is to bring into it values and norms that regulate activity within that profession. An interaction between a person who is of a certain profession and another person can, then, be analyzed and evaluated from the point of view of those values and norms of the profession. The same holds for roles and organizations.

The distinction one should be aware of is that between such different points of view. On the one hand, we have what we will call the *moral point of view*, which evaluates interactions between person *qua* persons. Principles of human dignity protection reflect the moral point of view. On the other hand, we have what we will call an *ethical point of view*, which evaluates interactions between persons of certain roles, professions or organizational affiliations. A conception of parental duties, a Code of Medical Ethics and Rules of Conduct for a Company Director reflect ethical points of view.

Major Moral and Ethical Principles

On the background of the previous section we move now to a brief proposal and defense of principles for treatment of neonates at the edge of viability. Similar principles hold for fetuses at the edge of viability, but presently they are beyond the scope of this chapter.

Principle of Moral Gradation

> *The moral status of a neonate at the edge of viability depends on whether it is already a person more than it depends on its viability.*

This principle rests on several of the above-mentioned observations. The primary moral status is that of a person. The moral status of what is not a person but rather very similar to a person is a secondary one. Therefore, the first step in a moral evaluation of an attitude towards a neonate is answering the question as to whether it is a person or not. Under ordinary circumstances, the answer to this question depends on the gestational age of the neonate, i.e. whether it has reached its 26th week. A fetus or a neonate of that age is presumably a person. That is to say, if we do not have compelling reasons for assuming it does not have a well-developed cortex, we consider it to be a person and have to treat it accordingly.

If under consideration is a neonate at the edge of viability, which presently means younger than 25 weeks, then its moral status is not primary but secondary. The extent to which we are under a moral duty to protect its life is not that we have when a person is under consideration, even if the difference is a matter of a few weeks. As far as the 20-odd gestational weeks old neonate is under consideration, there are no moral rights that are infringed if its life or dignity is not protected, since only persons have moral rights. However, we do have secondary moral duties with respect to such a neonate, since we encounter it at a very high point on the slope of dignity protection. This is why the principle of moral gradation does not posit personhood as the sole parameter of having a moral status. Viability will play a major role in moral considerations, as we shall see in the sequel.

To be sure, we may also be under a primary moral duty to protect the rights of the mother and the father of such a neonate. We shall see later what are those primary moral duties as well.

Principle of Presumed Medical Duties

> *Presumably, a neonate at the edge of viability ought to be medically treated on a par with a neonate who is a person.*

This principle too rests on observations made during the previous section. Although the *Principle of Moral Gradation* draws a distinction between a neonate who is a person and neonates that are not, whereas the *Principle of Presumed Medical Treatment* puts them on a par with each other, it will soon become clear that the two principles are compatible with each other.

Under ordinary circumstances, a 22- to 25-week-old fetus or neonate is located very high on the slope of dignity protection. First of all, though in some important respects it is different from a 26- to 30-week-old fetus or neonate, in many respects they are quite similar to each other. Moreover, the process of transformation from the earlier stage to the later one is, under ordinary circumstances, natural and relatively short. Hence, the secondary moral duty to respect the dignity of the viable neonate, during the former stage, cannot take a blatant form. In particular it cannot take the form of the difference between taking care, to the best of the medical ability, of the life and health of the neonate, after the edge of viability, and not giving medical attention to the neonate at the edge of viability. The most appropriate form of respect for the dignity of what is very similar to a person would be the form of respect for the dignity of a person. Any other form would involve a steep slope, which is usually ineffectual.

Now, if a viable neonate, too young to be a person, should be treated on a par with a viable neonate who is a person, then a natural problem arises. How can one follow both the *Principle of Presumed Medical Treatment*, which requires it, and the *Principle of Moral Gradation*, which seems to require the opposite? Here is where the first word of the *Principle of Presumed Medical Treatment*, 'presumably', becomes operative.

A presumption reflects a burden of proof. The familiar presumption of innocence reflects a clear distribution of the burden of proof: The prosecution has to prove that the defendant is not innocent, and if it fails in its attempts to do so the defendant does not have to do anything in order to prove one's innocence. In other words, a person should be assumed to be innocent, unless proven otherwise. Similarly, a fetus or a neonate at the edge of viability should be medically treated, in an ordinary way, unless there are compelling reasons for not treating it in an ordinary way or even at all.

Here is where the difference emerges between a viable neonate, too young to be a person, and a viable neonate who is a person. What counts as a compelling reason for the option of no treatment in the former case, may well fail to count as a compelling reason for that option in the latter case. The typical example is that of reasons related to the medical conditions of the neonate under consideration. When it is a person, it has rights, most basically the right to live, even if handicapped. When it is not a person, it does not have rights at all. Hence, the rights or even interests of the parents can give grounds to a compelling reason for the option of no treatment.

Notice that the proposed distinction between a neonate who is a person and a neonate too young to be one is not confined to neonates at the edge of viability. Whenever we consider a fetus or a neonate located relatively high on the slope of dignity protection, the lower it is on the slope, the more are reasons that should be considered compelling for the option of no treatment. Indeed, from a certain point down a similar principle is not going to be justifiable. Discussion of the exact location of that point is beyond the scope of the present chapter.

Principle of Positive Compelling Reasons

> *If the parents of a neonate at the edge of viability wish its life and health to be medically protected, then both morally and ethically the neonate should be administered best possible medical treatment required for protection of life and health and enhancing viability.*

At the edge of viability, chances of healthy survival of a neonate can be low, in which case the question may arise as to whether efforts should be made in order to save its life and protect its health. The *Principle of Positive Compelling Reasons* answers the question affirmatively, on two different grounds, when the parents of the neonate wish the neonate's life and health to be protected.

The wish of the parents is a compelling reason under the circumstances. (Cases of the parents being legally replaced by a custodian, cases of disagreements among the parents as well as similar complicated cases should be treated, but for the present purposes suffice it to treat the most ordinary cases.) First of all, the wish of the parents is highly significant, on grounds of general principles of medical ethics. Providing a viable neonate with the best possible medical treatment in order to save its life, if in danger, and improve its health, when in trouble, is on a par with providing the fetus in uterus the best possible medical treatment, under parallel conditions. In both cases, the duty to provide a neonate or a fetus with such medical treatment is a most natural extension of the duty to provide a person with best possible medical treatment. It is a most natural extension of that duty, because a viable neonate or fetus, even before it develops into a person, is encountered within a developmental process that is bound, if left undisturbed, to cross the threshold of personhood.

Moreover, from the point of view of medical ethics, the wish of the parents is not only significant, but also compelling. During the whole period of a pregnancy, from conception to birth, medical treatment is always provided at the request of the woman, not only to herself, but also to the pre-embryo, embryo or fetus in her womb. Her wish that the two of them be treated is a compelling reason for providing both of them with the best possible medical treatment, even before the fetus becomes a person, even before the fetus becomes viable. The difference between a fetus at the edge of viability and a neonate at the edge of viability is no ground for a radical change in the physician's duty according to medical ethics. In a sense, the difference is technical. When in the womb, the woman's wish that it be treated is, to a significant extent, independent of the wish that she herself be treated. Such an independent wish cannot change its ethical significance when the fetus is removed from the womb into an incubator.

The wish of parents that their viable neonate be given the best possible medical treatment is also morally compelling, even when the neonate is at the edge of viability. Firstly, extending the moral duties of protecting human dignity from persons, including viable neonates of a certain gestational age, to viable neonates several weeks younger, is the best way of protecting human dignity of persons at the border areas of personhood. Secondly, when parents have exercised their rights of procreation in a way that resulted in the existence of a viable neonate, then they ought to be helped in extending the process from the present advanced stage to the later stages, which are naturally most desirable.

So far, we have not discussed ethical and moral problems of resorting to scarce or very expensive extraordinary means of medical treatment, where conflicts may arise between the duty to treat one viable neonate and the duty to treat another neonate or person. So far, we have discussed the right attitude towards a viable neonate as such. Later on, some possible extensions will be discussed briefly.

Principle of Withholding Treatment

a In the absence of compelling reasons for saving the life of a viable neonate, treatment may be withheld from it, provided that:
b Some curable aspects of the neonate's health are treated.
c Pain of the neonate is minimized.
d Its parents are given appropriate palliative treatment.

We assume that under certain conditions there no moral or ethical compelling reasons for protecting the life of a viable neonate. An extreme example would be a neonate whose viability is a matter of several weeks and there is no doubt that it is not going to survive for even several months. Another possible example is a neonate who certainly suffers from the Tay-Sachs disease.

Assuming there are no compelling reasons for life saving treatment, the *Principle of Withholding Treatment* allows medical treatment to be withheld from the neonate, only under certain conditions. Before we briefly defend each of those conditions, we would like to emphasize the passive nature of withholding. Such distinctions between passive and active forms of actions have been shown by philosophers not to be of much moral significance. However, from an ethical point of view, there is a crucial difference between withholding protection of life and killing. Whereas the former attitude can be compatible with medical ethics, for example in the absence of informed consent for treatment, the latter attitude is incompatible with medical ethics, a constitutive element of which is protection of life and health.

The first precondition of withholding, according to the *Principle of Withholding Treatment,* is that withholding treatment that saves life should not take the form of totally neglecting the neonate. Protection of human dignity, whether of persons or viable neonates, cannot involve total neglect, on the part of physicians and others who are in a position to pay respect in a clear and effective way. Medical treatment should go on as if permission to save life and perhaps also to treat some other medical problems has not been given, but permission to treat some present medical treatment has been given. Division of medical problems into those that should be treated and those that should not depends on various aspects of particular circumstances, such as the parent's wishes, but whatever those circumstances are, an apparent total neglect of a neonate should never take place.

The second precondition of withholding is obvious, both morally and ethically. If a neonate suffers, whether it is a person or not, whether it is viable or not, it should be treated in order to eliminate every form of pain or if impossible minimize it to the best of present medical ability. A by-product of a treatment that is intended to alleviate pain is sometimes a reduction of life expectancy. Since under consideration is the case where there are no compelling reasons for saving the life of a neonate, then reduction of life expectancy is consequently permitted, but only if it is a reduction of life expectancy and not setting it at zero. Killing is not a legitimate form of alleviating pain, neither from a moral point of view nor from an ethical one.

The third precondition is also self-evident, even though it is not yet universally followed, for various reasons. A state of withholding a life saving medical treatment from a viable neonate (and even from a nonviable neonate) is presumably a highly significant crisis, from the point of view of each of the parents of the neonate. It is a moral and an ethical duty of the attending medical staff to mitigate the suffering experienced by the mother and the father of the neonate. Ideally, some of the physcians and nurses, psychologists and social workers belonging to the staff will have professional expertise in the required palliative care of the grieving parents.

Principle of Stigma Resistance

> *A public policy of withholding medical treatment of neonates at the edge of viability, when they show certain medical indications and there are no compelling reasons for their medical treatment, should not create or enhance public stigmatization of groups of persons.*

A public policy of withholding medical treatment of a certain group of neonates at the edge of viability can take the form of guidelines to withhold treatment if two conditions obtain. First, there is one or more of several standard indications that the neonate suffers from certain diseases, and secondly, there are no compelling reasons for medical treatment (according to the *principle of positive compelling reasons*).

Such a public policy is problematic, both morally and ethically, when some persons are going to suffer from its implementation. Assume that the policy of withholding treatment applies just to neonates at the edge of viability where there is an indication for CF. There are good reasons to assume that a public policy of eliminating CF carriers from the future population of persons, not by curing them but by not allowing them to survive beyond the edge of viability, will create a stigma or enhance stigmatization of persons who suffer from CF. A person's form of life can be very meaningful, rich in self-fulfillment, achievement and happiness, even if one suffers from CF. A public policy of eliminating CF carriers from future populations not by way of curing them casts a dark shadow on highly meaningful forms of life, which is morally and ethically wrong. Public policy of withholding medical treatment should, therefore, be carefully formulated and implemented, in order to avoid the danger of stigmatization, which is a source of unnecessary suffering.

Principle of Negative Compelling Reasons

When all of the following conditions obtain, with respect to a neonate at the edge of viability, there are compelling reasons for withholding from it medical treatment for saving its life:

a The neonate is bound to suffer, regularly and significantly.

b The chances are nil or very close to it that the neonate grows to become a person who eventually will be able to have a meaningful form of life.

c The parents of the neonate do not wish that its life to be protected, on grounds of both the neonate's predicted fate and their own resulting mental predicament.

Under consideration is a certain neonate, at the edge of viability. Presently, and all the more so in the future, being at the edge of viability means not being a person, on the one hand, but being at an advanced stage of a process that is expected to bring one into becoming a person, on the other hand. Under such circumstances, the neonate does not have a primary moral right to be medically protected, but there are moral and ethical duties that apply to it and require that it be medically protected, unless there are compelling reasons for withholding life saving medical treatment.

In order to see the justification we have for taking conditions (a)–(c) to form a compelling reason for withholding life saving medical treatment from a neonate at the edge of viability, let us consider another situation. Apparently that situation is very different, but under analysis it turns out to be rather illuminating. This is the case of an adult patient, for whom the following conditions obtain:

a He has an incurable disease.

b He is regularly in significant pain.

c He is presently unable to maintain what he considers a meaningful form of life and is also never going to be able to maintain such a form of life.
d He is perfectly competent, fully aware of his medical and personal conditions.

Assume that the patient expressed a clear and firm wish not to be medically treated anymore. Assume that he was asked to explain his wish. His reply was that he knows that he is unable to maintain a meaningful form of life and that he is never going to be able to maintain such a form of life, and therefore he knows that any life-saving medical treatment is going to be worse than worthless. It is not going to provide him with a precondition for maintaining a meaningful form of life but rather with a precondition for maintaining a meaningless living form of regular and significant pain and suffering. When this is the explanation, withholding life saving medical treatment would not only be considered mandatory on grounds of lack of informed consent, but would also seem to be morally and ethically justified on grounds of the compelling reasons the patient has for his wish. A period of regular and significant suffering that does not enable the patient to maintain a meaningful form of life, could still be worth going through. This could happen when there is a reasonable hope that the period of suffering be followed by a period during which the patient is going to be able to maintain a meaningful form of life. In the absence of such hope, on grounds of the best medical evaluation of the patient's condition, extending life is nothing more than extending a precondition for suffering, in which the patient is not interested at all. Since under such conditions, there does not seem to be any moral or ethical reason to enforce life saving treatment on the patient, his wish that such medical treatment be withheld from him is a compelling reason for fulfilling it.

The situation of a neonate, at the edge of viability, for whom conditions (a)–(b) of the *principle of negative compelling reasons* obtain, is on a par with that of that patient, *mutatis mutandis*. Assume a period of regular and significant suffering of a neonate at the edge of viability cannot be responsively depicted as a 'corridor', so to speak, to a period that would eventually enable the emerging person to maintain a meaningful form of life. There is, then, no point in extending the life of the neonate into yet another period of mere pain, unless there are positive compelling reasons for medical treatment, according to the *principle of positive compelling reasons*.

To be sure, there is a major difference between the adult patient of our example and a neonate at the edge of viability. Whereas the former has a view of what he means by maintaining a meaningful form of life, the latter cannot have such a view. Moreover, the view of the neonate's parents as to what is a meaningful form of life pertains just to the two of them and as such has no compelling validity with respect to the neonate's future possible forms of life. In order to overcome the inherently subjective nature of answers to questions with respect to meaningfulness of possible forms of life, condition (b) of the *principle of negative compelling reasons* is carefully phrased. It is couched in terms of 'a meaningful form of life' in general, and not in terms of 'a meaningful form of life' according to the views of the neonate's parents. Consequently, in order to show that condition (b) obtains, it is not enough to show that a certain form of life that is commonly held to be meaningful could not be maintained under the circumstances medically predicted for the neonate. What should be shown is that any form of life that can be reasonably be held to be meaningful could not be maintained under those circumstances.

Condition (c) of the *principle of negative compelling reasons* also requires some clarification. In the absence of a wish on the part of the neonate's parents that it be medically treated, there are no positive compelling reasons for treatment and the gate is open for negative reasons and possibly negative compelling reasons for not applying to the neonate any life saving treatment. The same condition requires that parents have two reasons for not having a wish to protect the neonate. The two conditions are required rather than just one of them, because for a principle that allows withholding life saving treatment from a viable neonate to be compatible with moral and ethical principles of protecting human life and dignity, it should be confined to extreme cases.

The condition requires that the attitude of the parents be shaped not only by self-centered considerations, but also by considerations related to the predicted fate of the neonate. Given the proximity of the state of being a neonate at the edge of viability to that of being a person, it would be morally unacceptable to opt for withholding life saving treatment on parental self-centered grounds only. A parental attitude is immoral when it does not rest on considerations of the fate of the neonate, fetus or baby under consideration. Parents are morally expected to be the party most devoted and responsible to the fate of an offspring, at least as long as it is not an independent person.

The condition requires that the attitude of the parents be shaped not only by considerations related to the predicted fate of the neonate, but also by considerations that pertain to the predicament of the parents themselves.

If they have the stamina to carry the burden of supporting a suffering baby, who does not have any prospects of becoming a person who can maintain a meaningful form of life, then they are going to be admired and praised. However, their condition cannot then count as an ingredient of a negative compelling reason.

Now, that we have seen the *principle of positive compelling reasons* as well as the *principle of negative compelling reasons*, the natural question arises as to whether the two principles exhaust all possible or even prevalent conditions under which neonates at the edge of viability are encountered. The answer is clearly in the negative, mainly because those are principles of compelling reasons for treatment and withholding of treatment. Quite often, reasons we have for action are sufficient even if they are not compelling. When under consideration is a neonate at the edge of viability, for whom there are neither positive compelling reasons for medical treatment nor negative compelling reasons for withholding life saving treatment, both principles should serve as sources of guidelines for morally and ethically proper decision making. Roughly speaking, the distance, so to speak, between the conditions under consideration and those of the pole of positive compelling reasons, on the one hand, and those of negative compelling reasons, on the other hand, should be evaluated. Action should be taken on grounds of the emergent balance of distances.

In case of a remaining doubt or hesitation, one should prefer the attitude of the positive pole to that of the negative one. One defense of this preference rests on comparison of errors and their effects. If one commits an error and treats a neonate that should not have been treated, the results are possibly an unnecessary pain and a reversible general condition. However, if one commits an error and does not treat a neonate that should have been treated, the result is probably death, which is an irreversible general condition. When in such a doubt, then, opting for treatment rather than for withholding is the right preference.

Matters of Application

In the concluding part of the present chapter, we would like to address a few problems that have been encountered in practice or in the literature. We will mention problems related to different aspects of the whole area of medical treatment of neonates at the edge of viability.

Problem 1: Matters of Consistency

The set of principles outlined in part II of the present chapter results in a delineation of a class of medical conditions that allow withholding life saving treatment of a neonate at the edge of viability, if there are no compelling reasons for treatment. Strictly speaking, this is a class of medical conditions under which the death of the neonates is brought about. Another set of principles is applied, in the same institutional contexts, to requests for abortion during, for example, the first weeks of pregnancy. This set of principles also results in a delineation of a class of medical conditions that allow causing death of an embryo, upon maternal request. We have, then, two classes of medical conditions under which an embryo or a neonate will die, as a result of the medical treatment involved.

What is the reasonable relationship between those two classes of medical conditions? The natural answer is that the class of medical conditions pertaining to neonates at the edge of viability should be much narrower than the class of medical conditions pertaining to aborted embryos, as far as the medical conditions of neonates are detectable at a the early stages of gestation. The moral reason is obvious: The upper something is on the slope of dignity protection, the more dignity it deserves and the more extensive should be its protection. A medical condition that justifies an early abortion of an embryo can fail to justify withholding medical treatment from a neonate at the edge of viability, let alone from a neonate who is a person.

Consistency is required of any cluster of guidelines concerning medical practices with respect to gametes, pre-embryos, embryos, fetuses, neonates at the edge of viability, neonates beyond the edge of viability, and neonates who are persons. Since what is detectable at a later stage is sometimes detectable at an earlier stage but sometimes is not, consistency cannot be gained by following a principle of constant reduction of the above-mentioned classes of medical conditions. The principle governing those classes should introduce sensitivity to the moral difference between the earliest stage of gestation, during which a medical condition is presently detectable, and later ones.

Problem 2: Matters of Cost

So far, we have hardly mentioned expenditure considerations, when treatment of neonates at the edge of viability has been discussed. It is our view that moral and ethical deliberations should always involve two steps: First, discussions of the basic problems and conflicts, principles and attitudes, disregarding restrictions imposed on certain contexts of treatment for financial reason. Secondly, discussions of the different ways of implementing the consequences reached in the previous step, taking into account the given financial restrictions.

To grasp the reason for our view that deliberations should take such a two step form, consider the simple case of a physician who has to administer some medication to a sick person, within the framework of some health care service. The seemingly simple and ordinary interaction of prescribing certain pills may, actually, take one of two forms that are morally and ethically different from each other. One way of doing it would involve a list of pills the physician is allowed to prescribe to the patient. The physician would prescribe for the patient the best pills on the list. For financial reasons, the list does not include all available pills. It is quite possible that what is the best pill the physician could have prescribed to the patient under the circumstances is not on the list. Presumably, the physician knows about such pills, but neither prescribes them nor informs the patient about their availability elsewhere. In a variant of this procedure, if the physician knows that better pills are available elsewhere, this fact is brought to the attention of the patient.

Another procedure involves a clear distinction between the medical and the financial aspects of the interaction. The physician informs the patient about several possible pills, in the order of their medical value, under the circumstances. The best pill is mentioned, even if it much more expensive than the other ones. The patient gets from the physician a clear description of available treatments, whether within the framework of the service or only elsewhere. Having such a description at one's disposal, the patient is in a position to make, with the help of the service, a decision as to which pill he or she is going to use. One possibility would be using the best available pill, the purchase of which involving an additional payment. Another possibility would be using another effective pill that is not the best one, but the purchase of which involves no additional payment.

The merits of the later procedure are clear. Considerations of different kinds are kept separately from each other. The patient's trust in the physician's prescriptions can be maintained, as long as it is mutually agreed that financial considerations do not have a hidden effect on the professional quality of the physician's behavior.

When the treatment of neonates at the edge of viability is to be planned the same general considerations should be applied. The map of possible treatments should be described, using the standards involved in informed consent. Financial considerations should, then, be superimposed on the medical ones. When the distinction between medical considerations and expenditure considerations is not blurred, the decision made, with respect to issues of life and death, is expected to be of higher moral and ethical qualities.

A crucial consequence of this argument pertains to the very specification of the edge of viability. It follows from our previous argument that it is unjustified, both morally and ethically, to withhold treatment of neonates at the edge of viability as a matter of policy on grounds of financial considerations. Information to the effect that a neonate is at the edge of viability should always be given to its parents. Their wish to protect the neonate's life and health is a compelling reason for treating the neonate, according to the *principle of positive compelling reasons.* Deliberations of the financial aspects of the treatment should be carried out after the medical information has been given to the parents who are then been given some time for pondering their wishes. Meanwhile medical treatment of the neonate continues. After a while, which may be required to be rather short, the parents make up their mind. It is only at this stage that financial considerations should enter the picture resulting in a distribution of the ensuing expenses. Ideally, on grounds of governmental or other public support and health insurance policies all neonates at the edge of viability are treated, unless the *principle of negative compelling reasons* applies. Notice that that principle does not make any reference to financial considerations.

Problem 3: Matters of 'Trespassing'

Assume that it is commonly held that neonates are at the edge of viability when their gestational age is more than 23 weeks, in the absolute sense of their having an ordinary life expectancy, if appropriately treated. Assume, furthermore, that during an operation related to the medical conditions of a pregnant woman, a physician finds oneself with a neonate whose gestational age is, say, 21 weeks. What treatment if any should such a neonate get? What is the right policy of medical treatment of neonates under the edge of viability?

One possible policy would forbid any attempt on the part of the medical staff to save the life of a neonate under the edge of viability, on grounds of futility. Let us draw a distinction between the two elements of the policy: the guideline and the purported justification of it. For the policy to be acceptable, the latter element should well justify the former one. The policy that forbids treatment on grounds of futility is unacceptable. Specification of the edge of viability is related to medical ability in general. Under our assumptions, it is known how to protect the life and health of a neonate of at least 23 weeks' gestational age *in general*, but it is not known how to do it for neonates of 21 weeks' gestational age *in general*. This does not mean that given a certain 21-week neonate, any attempt to save its life is bound to fail. If there is a chance to save a neonate under the edge of viability, disregarding it is morally and ethically improper, according to the conception of the slope of human dignity protection.

Another possible policy would have the same guideline but another purported justification. It would forbid any attempt on the part of the medical staff to save the life of a neonate under the edge of viability, on grounds of incompetence. If you do not have the professional competence for carrying out a certain action, do not attempt to do it. This line of justification sounds stronger than the previous one, but this policy is also unacceptable. Life saving treatment of a neonate under the edge of viability cannot presently be performed with full professional competence. However, it may well be the case that the extent to which such a treatment can be predicted to be effective is not smaller than the extent to which a treatment carried out in the context of a proper 'grace experiment' can be predicted to be effective.

Accordingly, medical treatment of a neonate under the edge of viability may take place if it is possible to carry it out as a proper 'grace experiment'.

A policy that allows treatment of neonates under the edge of viability, on grounds of proper 'grace experimentation', seems acceptable, but it raises a new problem. What should be done in case the experiment is successful in the sense of the neonate's life having been saves, but is unsuccessful in the sense that the saved neonate is handicapped to an extent previously unknown? This is a difficult issue, in need of much clarification and analysis. Here, suffices it to suggest that principles applying to experimentation in general and to 'grace experimentation' in particular should be applied, in advance, to such cases as well.

Suggested Reading

Anand KJS, McGrath PJ: Pain in Neonates. Amsterdam, Elsevier, 1993.

Doran K: What Is a Person: The Concept and the Implications for Ethics. Lewiston, Edwin Mellen Press, 1989.

Dworkin R: Life's Dominion. New York, Alfred A. Knopf, 1993.

Fletcher J: Humanhood: Essays in Biomedical Ethics. Buffalo, Prometheus Books, 1979.

Jankov RP, Asztalos EV, Skidmore MB: Favourable neurological outcomes following delivery room cardiopulmonary resuscitation of infants < or = 750 g at birth. J Paediatr Child Hlth 2000;36: 19–22.

Kuhse H, Singer P: Should the Baby Live? The Problem of Handicapped Infants. London, Oxford University Press, 1985.

McHaffie H: Holding On? Amsterdam, Elsevier, 1994.

Miller vs. Hospital Corporation of America, 01–0079 Supreme Court of the State of Texas, 2001.

Mishell DR (ed): Yearbook of Obstetrics, Gynecology, and Women's Health. St Louis, Mosby, 2002.

Planned Parenthood of Southeastern Pennsylvania vs. Casey, 505 US 833 (1992).

Roe vs. Wade, 410 US 113 (1973).

Silverman WA: Proximate moral anguish. Paediatr Perinat Epidemiol 2000;14:293–294.

Strudee D, Olah K, Declan K (eds): The Yearbook of Obstetrics and Gynaecology, vol 9. London, Royal College of Obstetrics and Gynaecology Press, 2001.

Tooley M: Abortion and Infanticide. New York, Clarendon Press, 1983.

Warren MA: Moral Status: Obligations to Persons and Other Living Things. London, Oxford University Press, 1998.

Asa Kasher, MSc, PhD

Department of Philosophy, Tel-Aviv University,
PO Box 39040, IL–69978 Tel Aviv (Israel)
Tel. +972 3 640 9425, Fax +972 3 640 7953, E-Mail asakasher@hotmail.com

Subject Index